MAIMONIDES

ON THE
BOOK OF EXODUS

Rambam on Sefer Shemoth
Edited and Annotated by

Rabbi Alec Goldstein

KODESH PRESS

מרכז מורשת
הרמב״ם Maimonides
Heritage Center

Maimonides on the Book of Exodus:
Rambam on Sefer Shemoth

© Alec Goldstein, 2019

ISBN: 978-1-947857-32-2

Paperback Edition

Distributed Exclusively by

Kodesh Press L.L.C.
New York, NY
www.kodeshpress.com
kodeshpress@gmail.com

מרכז מורשת
הרמב"ם Maimonides
Heritage Center

This Book is Proudly Dedicated
In Honor of Our Dear Fathers

Joshua and Morris Setton
By
Mia and Lee Cohen & Family
And
Gloria and Joseph Setton & Family

The Maimonides Heritage Center is proud to collaborate with Kodesh Press and Rabbi Alec Goldstein in the publication of Rambam on Sefer Shemoth. The study of Rambam's approach to Parshanuth Hamiqra, the exegesis of the Torah, is a field that has not yet been fully explored. The publication of this Sefer is an indispensable tool in studying how Rambam interpreted the biblical text and the Rabbinic comments he selected in clarifying the Torah's message.

I take this opportunity to congratulate my colleague and friend Rabbi Alec Goldstein on the publication of this book. It is an important contribution to the study of Rambam. I want to especially thank Mia and Lee Cohen and Gloria and Joseph Setton on sponsoring the publication of this book. They honor, not only those who they have dedicated this work to, namely their fathers Joshua Setton and Morris Setton but they honor their entire families.

Yamin Levy, Rabbi
Founder, Maimonides Heritage Center
2019 / 5780

Table of Contents

Introduction

Rabbi Moses son of Maimon, known in Hebrew as Rambam and English as Maimonides (1135-1204), is one of the great luminaries of Judaism whose contributions can hardly be overstated. His legal magnum opus, *Mishneh Torah*, is perhaps the most important codification of Jewish law, while his philosophical work *Guide for the Perplexed* (Hebrew, *Moreh Nevukhim*) is the most systematic attempt to reconcile biblical and Greek thought. Besides these works, he has bequeathed to us the *Sefer ha-Mitzvot* ("Book of Commandments"), which is an enumeration of all 613 biblical laws; *Perush Mishnayot* ("Commentary on the Mishnah"), which remains one of the most important commentaries on this early rabbinic work; and he additionally authored a volume of responsa, medical writings, and a handful of epistles. There are also further additional works which have been attributed to Maimonides, though their authenticity is a matter of scholarly debate.

Since he produced such a wide variety of works, one may easily quip that if Maimonides wanted to write a commentary on the Torah, he would have done so. However, even though he never authored a verse-by-verse commentary, he quotes biblical passages throughout all of his writings. With the welcome and renewed interest in learning Tanakh, it seems that there would be an interest in collecting the places where he quotes biblical verses and arranging them accordingly.

This project starts with the book of Exodus (*Shemot*), which blends narrative and law. This gives the reader an opportunity to see how Maimonides interpreted both philosophical and legal passages of the Bible. I have drawn primarily from *Mishneh Torah*, *Sefer ha-Mitzvot*, *Peirush ha-Mishnayot*, and *Moreh Nevukhim*, as well as some of his letters. I have also delved into the commentary of his son, Rabbi Abraham Maimonides, who did bequeath to us a commentary on Exodus; however I have not quoted every time Rabbi Abraham relayed an idea in the name of his father.

Maimonides devoted the bulk of his writings to *halakhah*, philosophy, and proper character refinement. As such, it does not appear that he devoted much space to emphasizing the plain meaning (the *peshat*) of the verses. However, one should not be mistaken into believing Maimonides did not have a notion of *peshat*. For example, in the second *Shoresh* ("Principle") of the *Sefer ha-Mitzvot*, Maimonides criticizes his predecessors for confusing the *derash* of the verse with the *peshat*, and he quotes the well-known talmudic adage *ein ha-mikra yotzei miydei peshuto*, "a verse does not depart from its plain meaning" (in Frankel ed., page *nun dalet*).

Similarly, in *Sefer ha-Mitzvot*, Neg. 4, Maimonides differentiates between the homiletic and simple meaning. He is dealing with the verse *lo ta'asun itti elohei khesef v'elohei zahav lo ta'asu lakhem*, "you shall not make with Me gods of silver or gods of gold, you shall not make them for yourselves" (Exod. 20:20). He quotes from the *Mekhilta*: "one might say, 'I will make them for decoration as other people do in their lands.' Therefore the Torah says, 'you shall not make them *for yourselves* [i.e., even for ornamental purposes, idols are forbidden].'" Then Maimonides alludes to an alternate interpretation from the Talmud. Since the word *elohim* can also mean "judges," the verse homiletically means that you should not promote people who are *elohei khesef*, meaning people who have attained their status through bribery (*Sanhedrin* 7b). However, Maimonides says that the *pashteih di-kra*, the "plain meaning of the verse," is like the *Mekhilta* and not like the passage in *Sanhedrin*.

Therefore it is clear that Maimonides had a sense of *peshat*, even if such was not his primary concern, unlike the pursuers of *peshat* like Rashi, Rashbam, Radak, and others. *Peshat* does not mean "literal," since Midrashim are in fact often more literal (i.e., hyperliteral) than *pashtanim* (see, e.g., on Exod. 2:14). Rather, while a comprehensive analysis of *peshat* is beyond our ken, my operating definition of *peshat* is how the original audience would have understood the text. I do not believe that this was Maimonides' primary concern.

If not primarily *peshat*, then what was Maimonides' point in quoting biblical verses? It appears to me that there are three basic times he quotes verses. First, he does so to teach a *halakhah*. The Bible is filled with laws, and then the Rabbis added additional legislation. One of Maimonides' goals was to differentiate biblical laws from rabbinic ones. Therefore, when quoting a law as biblical, he brings a verse as a prooftext.

As an aside, it should be noted that Maimonides does not always quote the Talmud's prooftext, but sometimes supplies his own. These deviations are pointed out by the commentaries, and the general consensus is that Maimonides quotes the simplest possible verse to make the point, even if the Talmud used a different source (see *Leḥem Mishneh* to *Melakhim* 1:2, quoted at Exod. 17:15-16 for an example).

Second, Maimonides quotes a verse to prove a philosophical point. In Medieval philosophy, there were two basic sources of truth: reason and revelation. Reason refers to Greek philosophy, usually Aristotle or Plato. These were truths that could be arrived at by analysis, and their validity was proven by reason alone. But there was another source of truth: revelation. The received text is unassailably true and therefore could be used as a proof in its own right. The Medieval philosopher would, ideally, try to bring a proof both from Greek ratiocination and from the revealed text to make a point, because that way there would be no contradiction. This was the method not just of Jewish philosophers like Maimonides and Joseph Albo, but also of Thomas Aquinas.

This method, however satisfying, posed something of a challenge. While the Bible is a great repository of philosophical ideas, the Bible itself is not a work of philosophy. A passage from Aristotle can be much more linear and expository than a biblical passage. As such, it seems that when a philosopher used a biblical verse, he sometimes used it out of context. For example, Maimonides says that the phrase "I AM THAT I AM" (Exod. 3:13-14) refers to God's absolute existence; Philo of Alexandria and Saadiah have made similar comments. However, this interpretation strains the context. The situation is that the Jews are oppressed and crying out to God. On the surface, it appears at that juncture they have no need for a philosophy lesson of God's absolute existence. Therefore it is no surprise that Nahmanides rejected this comment in favor of Rashi's interpretation that the phrase teaches about an unbreakable bond between God and the Jewish people. Nonetheless, there have been those—like the *Kuzari* and Sforno—who attempt to bridge the gap between the philosophers and the exegetes. Sforno interprets the phrase to mean, "I am an independent existence, not subject to influences by other phenomena or even caused by them. Seeing that this is so, it follows that I love existing, and beings that exist. As a corollary to this love of Mine for existence, it follows that I deeply resent anything or anyone who tries to terminate such an existing being from continuing to do so." Maybe the oppressed Jews really did take solace in God's absoluteness after all!

The third interest of Maimonides was character refinement (which differs from philosophy in the abstract sense). For example, the Rabbis understand the verse "And you shall serve the Lord your God" (Exod. 23:25) to refer to both prayer and Torah study. Maimonides uses this as a source for the biblical obligation for prayer; he uses the selfsame verse to support his thesis that even in mundane activities like working, eating, or marital relations, the individual should be focused on serving God, rather than on the baser pleasure these acts provide. He will frequently find allusions to character refinement in the biblical text.

In many cases, these comments—whether halakhic, philosophical, or ethical—are not *peshat* as embraced by Rashbam, Radak, or others. How then shall we square Maimonides' method with that of the *pashtanim*? Perhaps the answer is that since the Torah is open to different layers of interpretation, the levels of *peshat*, *halakhah*, and philosophy do not contradict each other at all; they only represent different facets of Torah.

While Maimonides makes comments in multiple directions, I have tried to not be guilty of overreading or engaging in the game of "What would Maimonides say about so-and-so?" (though I did engage in such thinking in at least one place, at Exod. 4:6 and whether or not Moses' *tzara'at* was punitive). At times I have taken Maimonides' own words and applied them thematically to a verse he does not quote, but I clearly label when doing so, in order to not mislead the reader. This interpretive restraint is, I believe, more respectful, defensible, and less speculative. We do not know for sure what Maimonides would have said about anything unless he already told us so.

I have utilized the same interpretive restraint in the position of Maimonides' critics; rather I have presented the opinions—even contradictory ones—as fairly and charitably as I could. My assumption is that if Maimonides were here to defend himself from the criticisms of Nahmanides or others, he would be able to acquit himself masterfully; the same is true for Rashi, Nahmanides, and others. Therefore I have tried to be charitable where possible and focus on exactly why the two sides argue. When a linear commentator like Rashi or Nahmanides is quoted, the reader should assume that those comments are from the verse being analyzed; if I draw from comments elsewhere, that will be noted.

I do not believe that this project is unearthing some secret, latent biblical commentary. Indeed sometimes the opposite is true: the entries are sometimes stilted when read back-to-back, since Maimonides will quote the same verse for a technical legal matter and then for an abstract philosophical concept. Such is the nature of a work of this character. Nonetheless, certain themes emerge. For example Maimonides uses many passages to prove the existence and eternality of God; these passages are used by others to prove the eternality of the *relationship* between God and the Jewish people; see, e.g., Exod. 3:13-14 and 15:18.

Another theme I found very instructive is the debate between Maimonides and Nahmanides about the purpose of the tabernacle. According to Maimonides, ever the rationalist, the purpose of the tabernacle is so that the Jews have a place to bring offerings and a place to make the pilgrimage to Jerusalem three times a year; according to Nahmanides, who was versed in mysticism, the tabernacle's purpose is so that God could dwell among the Israelites; this is the *Shekhinah* (see at Exod. 25:8). The verses admit both interpretations. Maimonides accepts the idea of *Shekhinah* as either created light (which might refer to intellectual perception) or continuous guidance (i.e., Divine providence). The *Shekhinah* for Maimonides is not a mystical concept; but more importantly it is barely a relational concept at all. In these and other places Maimonides seems to downplay the relational—or what we might today call covenantal—aspect between God and man. I will however leave for the reader to decide if I have fairly presented the sources, and interpreted them faithfully.

I have made use of additional material besides the words of Maimonides, and those can be broken down into several categories:

(1) Maimonides' potential sources, or at least sources he probably had access to: these include biblical and rabbinic sources, as well as Greek sources. It also includes Rabbi Simon

Kayyara's *Halakhot Gedolot* (*Behag*), written in the eighth century, which Maimonides devoted much time to refuting, both methodologically and substantively. I have not, however, attempted to cite Maimonides' sources in all cases

(2) Sources that Maimonides did not have access to and that did not have access to him: it is important to keep in mind that in the Medieval world information travelled slowly, so even if two books were written a century apart, the latter might not have had the former. I quote these sources for parallels, with the understanding that there probably was no influence in either direction. These sources include Rashi, *Kuzari*, *Tosafot*, and other Rishonim. On the subject of Rashi, there is some scholarly discussion that at the end of Maimonides' life he was introduced to those writings; even if this is true, it did not change the overarching philosophy of Maimonides. Similarly, *Tosafot* does on rare occasion quote Maimonides, but the Tosafists' methodology developed independently from Maimonides.

(3) Sources that quote Maimonides and criticize and/or defend him: these include Ra'avad, Nahmanides, *Mizraḥi*, *Kesef Mishneh*, Sforno, and Shadal (Samuel David Luzzatto), among others. These are sources that consider Maimonides' writings and either accept, reject, or modify them based on competing arguments. Nahmanides' contribution is extremely consequential here, because he frequently arbitrates between Rashi and Maimonides, sometimes favoring one, sometimes the other, and sometimes neither. As one example, see *Guide* 3:45 and Nahmanides' response, quoted at 20:22; there Rashi quotes a Midrash that the altar should not be made from hewn stones because "It is not right that the tool that shortens man's life should be lifted up upon that which gives length of life." Maimonides quotes this as a nice homiletic explanation, but says the real explanation is, "the heathen used to build their altars with hewn stones, and we ought not to imitate them." However, Nahmanides masterfully crafts a disproof of Maimonides and then sides with Rashi.

(4) Twentieth-century Jewish sources such Rabbi Joseph B. Soloveitchik, Rabbi J. David Bleich, Nehama Leibowitz, and Rabbi Netanel Wiederblank. These sources penetrate to the depth of the debate between Maimonides and his disputants. See for example, how Rabbi Bleich explained the debate about if it is a commandment to believe in God (Exod. 20:2), and Rabbi Soloveitchik's explanation of when prayer rises to the level of a biblical commandment (Exod. 23:25).

(5) Additional sources various and sundry that can enhance our understanding, including biblical dictionaries, halakhic authorities, modern Bible commentaries, works of general philosophy, and even works of fiction.

By quoting Maimonides' predecessors, contemporaries, critics, and expounders, I hope to show precisely where Maimonides differed from other interpreters.

I have tried to be exhaustive in terms of Maimonides' comments, while understanding that it is impossible to quote every quotation and allusion in his vast corpus of writings. Additionally, Maimonides frequently makes substantially the same point at least three times: once in the *Perush ha-Mishnayot*, once in the *Sefer ha-Mitzvot*, and once in the *Mishneh Torah*. In many cases, I was comfortable quoting the source just once, and adding a reference to the other places, so the serious researcher can furrow further. At times, I have quoted multiple sources when each adds something the other omits. Similarly, there are many passing references in the *Guide*, especially in the lexical sections, where Maimonides will quote concrete meanings of words before transitioning to abstract meanings and how those words apply to God; if Maimonides quoted a verse to prove a concrete meaning of the word, at times I omitted it.

As for the secondary literature, it would take a hundred lifetimes to sift through all the relevant literature, and so I have not made an attempt at comprehensiveness in that regard.

16

I have been studying Maimonides for most of my adult life. When a rabbi in Israel, seeing I was philosophically inclined, recommended I study *Sefer ha-Madda*, I completed its study before the end of the academic year. Several years later I had completed a study of the entire *Mishneh Torah*, complete with notes and chapter summaries. I also studied *Guide for the Perplexed* in depth as part of a curriculum of Jewish philosophy. There is an old joke in yeshivas that men know where a verse is in the Gemara (Talmud), while women know where it is in Tanakh (Bible). I elaborated that I knew neither but knew where Maimonides quoted it!

Despite my own study, there were several sources that were invaluable in finding where Maimonides quoted sources. First, in two places the *Mishneh Torah* is available online, complete with biblical references, and those are the Chabad website (with a fully translated *Mishneh Torah*), and the website mechon-mamre.org. Second, the *Guide* has been indexed at least three times, in the Friedlander, Pines, and Kapach editions. Third, others before me have—in Hebrew— collected where Maimonides quotes verses, and those are *Rambam al ha-Torah: Leket Divrei ha-Rambam le-Ḥamishei Ḥumshei Torah u-Mafte'aḥ*, by Rabbi Shraga Feivel Cohen, *Sefer Rambam al ha-Torah* by Natan Menachem Mendel, *Moreh Nevukhim la-Rambam al ha-Torah* by David Makover, and Rabbi Meir David ben-Shem's *Torat ha-Rambam*. The latter is by far most comprehensive and has been the most useful of the works. Yet even this work had omissions that I have supplied from elsewhere. Furthermore, some of the newest printings of the *Mikraot Gedolot* include passages from Maimonides' *Sefer ha-Mitzvot*. And despite all these resources, there no doubt are omissions in the present work.

What makes the present work unique, in my opinion, is not just that it quotes Maimonides' treatment of a verse, but it also shows his sources, his critics, and his defenders, to bring the reader into the world of Torah discussion and the Jewish legal and philosophical methods. These interpretations come to life when differing opinions are presented side by side. I hope that this present work is more of a contribution than a curiosity.

A note about translations: translations from the Bible are based on the King James Version and the New Revised Standard Version, as well as other translations, but I have updated them freely. For *Sefer ha-Mitzvot* and *Mishneh Torah*, I have at times relied on the Chabad translations but freely revised them. Translations of the *Guide* are from Friedlander, which is in the public domain, but again are slightly updated. Translations from the *Perush ha-Mishnayot* are my own unless otherwise noted. I have abbreviated *Sefer ha-Mitzvot* as *ShM*, and *Perush ha-Mishnayot* as *PhM*. Due to the multiple sources quoted, it is possible that translations are not consistent throughout the work, though I have tried to standardize them.

I have many people to be grateful for who assisted me with this project. Rabbi J. David Bleich and Rabbi Ari Kahn fielded many questions. Rabbi Gil Student, in addition to also answering questions, posted an earlier iteration of this work in weekly form on his wonderful blog *Torah Musings*. Rabbi Bezalel Naor frequently emailed me additional resources, including his own sterling writings. Thank you as well to my rabbis in Israel and America who taught me, and—more importantly—encouraged me to learn on my own.

Thank you to the editors and proofreaders who worked vigorously and thoughtfully to enhance this project: Mitchell First, Daniel A. Klein, Michele Scheer, and Rabbi Johnny Solomon. Any errors in the final product, whether substantive or typographical, are entirely my own responsibility.

I extend my deepest gratitude to Rabbi Yamin Levy and the Maimonides Heritage Center for believing in this project. Thank you for your support and encouragement. It is a pleasure to be collaborating with you in this endeavor. I most heartily thank Mia and Lee Cohen and family, and Gloria and Joseph Setton and family, who graciously are sponsoring this project in honor of their dear fathers, Joshua and Morris Setton. May their generosity merit them to continue to influence and enhance Torah learning throughout *kelal Yisrael*. *Yasher koach* and *hazaq u-barukh!*

Thank you especially to my darling, loving, and extremely patient wife Caroline. You motivate me in every way and your encouragement to complete this task has made this project possible. I love being married to you and I love that we have a great opportunity of going through life together. I thank God also for the newest edition to our family, Emilia Raiya.

Any comments, additions, corrections, or questions that are constructively extended will be warmly received.

Alec Goldstein
New York
December 2019
Kislev 5780

PARASHAT SHEMOT

Exodus 1

INTRODUCTION: Our father Jacob taught all of his children, and he designated Levi and appointed him as head of the academy to teach the ways of God and to observe the commandments of Abraham.[1] And he commanded his children to not take leave from the Levites, so their learning would not be forgotten. This concept [of monotheism] continued to grow strong among the children of Jacob and their followers, so in the world there was a nation who knew God. When the Jews prolonged their time in Egypt, they regressed to learn from their [the Egyptians'] ways and practiced idolatry and the like,[2] except for the tribe of Levi, who stood firm to the commandments of the patriarchs. And the tribe of Levi never practiced idolatry (*Ḥagigah* 6b, based on Exod. 32:26). Soon the principle which Abraham had implanted would have been uprooted, and the descendants of Jacob would have returned to the folly of the nations and their crookedness. However because of God's love for us (cf. Deut. 7:8), and because He vouchsafed the oath to our father Abraham, He appointed Moses, our teacher and greatest of all our prophets, and sent him [to redeem Israel]. When Moses our teacher prophesied, and God chose Israel as an inheritance, He crowned them with commandments and made known to them the way of His service, and the punishment for idolatry and for those who follow after it in error (*Avodah Zarah* 1:3).

1:10. Come, let us deal shrewdly [*nithakkemah*] with them, or they will increase and, in the event of war, join our enemies and fight against us and escape from the land. — The term *ḥokhmah* ("wisdom") in Hebrew is used for four different things:

---

1. "In all the days of our ancestors, the academy never departed from them" (*Yoma* 28b). Jacob gave the Levites as a tithe (*Genesis Rabbah* 70:7, *Pirkei de-Rabbi Eliezer* 37).
2. "When Israel was in Egypt they were practicing idolatry and would not let it go" (*Exodus Rabbah* 16:2).

(1) It denotes the knowledge of those truths which lead to the knowledge of God: e.g., "But where shall wisdom be found?" (Job 28:12), "If you seek her like silver" (Prov. 2:4). The word occurs frequently in this sense.

(2) The expression *hokhmah* denotes also knowledge of any workmanship, e.g., "Whoever is wise-hearted of you shall come and make everything that the Lord has commanded." (Exod. 35:10), "And all the women that were wise-hearted did spin" (Exod. 35:25).

(3) It is also used of the acquisition of moral principles, e.g. "And teach his princes wisdom" (Ps. 105:22), "With the ancient is wisdom" (Job 12:12), for it is chiefly the disposition for acquiring moral principles that is developed by old age alone.

(4) It implies, lastly, the notion of cunning and subtlety, e.g., "Come, let us deal wisely with them" (Exod. 1:10)....[3]

It is possible that the Hebrew *hokhmah* expresses the idea of cunning and planning, which may serve in one case as a means of acquiring intellectual perfection, or good moral principles; but may in another case produce skill in workmanship, or even be employed in establishing bad opinions and principles. The attribute *hakham* ["wise"] is therefore given [not only] to a person that possesses great intellectual faculties, or good moral principles, or skill in art, but also to persons cunning in evil deeds and principles. According to this explanation, a person that has a true knowledge of the whole Law is called "wise" in a double sense: he is wise because the Law instructs him in the highest truths, and second, because it teaches him good morals (*Guide* 3:54).

Maimonides' definition of *hokhmah* in this verse might find antecedent in Aristotle, who writes, "There is a faculty which

---

3. Rashi explains the word *mirmah*, commonly translated "deceit," to mean *hokhmah* (Gen. 27:35).

we call cleverness—the power of carrying out the means to any proposed end, and so achieving it. If then the end be noble, the power merits praise; but if the end be base, the power is the power of the villain. So we apply the term 'clever' both to the prudent man and the villain" (*Ethics* 1144a).

Maimonides does not offer an explanation of how Pharaoh would deal shrewdly with them. Nahmanides writes, "Pharaoh and his wise counsellors did not see fit to slay them by the sword. For it would have been a gross treachery to smite without reason a people that had come into the land by command of a former king.... Rather, Pharaoh said he would do it wisely so that the Israelites would not feel that it was done in enmity against them. It is for this reason that he placed a levy upon them, as it was customary that strangers in a country contribute a levy to the king.... Afterwards he secretly commanded the midwives to kill the male children upon the birthstool so that even the mothers should not know it. Following that, 'he charged all his people: Every son that is born, you, yourselves, shall cast into the river' (Exod. 1:22)."

For how this verse relates to Maimonides' opinion of Pharaoh's loss of free will, see at Exod. 4:21.

1:14. And they made their lives bitter with hard bondage, in mortar, and in brick, and in all manner of labor in the field: all their service, wherein they made them serve, was with rigor. — [From the Haggadah:] This bitter herb that we eat—what is its reason (cf. Exod. 12:8)? Because the Egyptians embittered the lives of our forefathers in Egypt, as it says, "And they made their lives bitter with hard bondage, in mortar, and in brick, and in all manner of labor in the field: all their service, wherein they made them serve, was with rigor" (Exod. 1:14) (*Nusaḥ ha-Haggadah*; quoted also at Exod. 12:8; see also *Ḥametz u-Matzah* 7:5, based on m. *Pesaḥim* 10:5).

Exodus 2

2:4. His sister stood [*va-tetatzav*] at a distance, to see what would happen to him. — Although the two roots *natzav* and *yatzav* are distinct, yet their meaning is, as you know, identical in all their various forms. The verb has several meanings: in some instances it signifies "to stand" or "to place oneself," as in, "And his sister stood [*va-tetatzav*] afar off" (Exod. 2:4), "The kings of the earth set themselves [*yityatzevu*]" (Ps. 2:2), "They came out and stood [*nitzavim*]" (Num. 16: 27). In other instances it denotes continuance and permanence, as, "Your word is established [*nitzav*] in Heaven" (Ps. 119:89), i.e., it remains forever (*Guide* 1:15).

> Ibn Ezra, against Maimonides, says וַתֵּתַצַּב is a foreign word (short commentary). The *Bekhor Shor* says that this word looks like a *hif'il* (causative), "others set her there." The word וַתֵּתַצַּב is also understood as a reflexive, "she set herself" (*Ha'amek Davar*).

2:10. When the child grew up, she brought him to Pharaoh's daughter, and she took him as her son. She named him Moses, "because," she said, "I drew him out of the water [*meshitihu*]." — [The Hebrew root] *m-sh-h* means "pulling" [*meshikhah*] and "dragging" [*gereirah*] (*PhM Shabbat* 22:6).

> The Mishnah is discussing what activities are permitted and forbidden on the Sabbath that could be considered types of forbidden medical treatment. Maimonides is commenting on the word מתמשין, and he uses the present verse as an example. However the printed Talmud has ממשמשין, "touch" (*Shabbat* 147a).[4] Rashbam, like Maimonides, says *m-sh-h* means *meshikhah*.

---

4. Soncino translates this as "massage." Danby translates it "rub."

2:11-12. One day, after Moses had grown up, he went out to his people and saw their forced labor. He saw an Egyptian beating a Hebrew, one of his kinsfolk. He looked this way and that, and seeing no one he killed the Egyptian and hid him in the sand. — A gentile who strikes an Israelite incurs capital punishment, as it says, "And he looked this way and that [...] and killed the Egyptian" (*Hovel u-Mazzik* 5:3, based on *Sanhedrin* 58b. Rashi quotes this Talmudic teaching in his biblical commentary; see however *Melakhim* 10:6 and *Kesef Mishnah* there).

2:13. When he went out the next day, he saw two Hebrews fighting; and he said to the wicked man [*la-rasha*], "Why do you strike your fellow Hebrew?" — It is even forbidden to raise one's hand against one's colleague, and whoever raises his hand against his fellow, even if he does not strike him, is wicked [*rasha*] (*Hovel u-Mazzik* 5:2).

This ruling is based on Resh Lakish's reading, which assumes that Moses spoke to the person before he struck his adversary, because the Hebrew uses *takkeh* ("you shall strike") rather than *hikkita* ("you struck") (see *Sanhedrin* 58b).

In his *ShM*, Maimonides applies the same teaching in a peculiar way. He starts by saying that when lashes are administered, there is an injunction to not inflict more lashes than the criminal can tolerate (based on *Makkot* 22a). He continues, "And from this prohibition comes a [separate] prohibition of striking any Jew. If we are warned not to strike a sinner [more than his punishment], how much more so anybody else. And the Sages even prohibited threatening to strike someone else, even without striking him. They said, 'He who lifts his hand against his neighbor to strike him is called wicked, as it says, "And he said to the wicked man: Why do you strike your fellow Hebrew"''" (*ShM*, Neg. 300).

2:14. He answered, "Who made you a ruler and judge over us? Do you desire [*omer*] to kill me as you killed the Egyptian?" Then Moses was afraid and thought [*va-yomar*]... — [Maimonides addresses the multiple meanings of *amar*] ... the words "speaking" [*dibbur*] and "saying" [*amirah*] are synonymous terms, denoting:

(1) "Speech," e.g., "Moses shall speak [*yedabber*]" (Exod. 19:19), "And Pharaoh said [*va-yomer*]" (Exod. 5:5);

(2) "Thought" as formed in the mind without being expressed in words; e.g., "And I thought [*ve-amarti*] in my heart" (Eccl. 2:15), "And I thought [*ve-dibbarti*] in my heart" (ibid.), "And your heart will imagine [*yedabber*]" (Prov. 23:33), "Concerning You my heart thought [*amar*]" (Ps. 27:8), "And Esau thought [*va-yomer*] in his heart" (Gen. 27:41); examples of this kind are numerous;

(3) "Will," e.g., "And he said [*va-yomer*] to slay David" (2 Sam. 21:16), that is to say, he wished or he intended to slay him; "Do you desire [*omer*] to kill me" (Exod. 2:14)....

I need not explain that in Hebrew *amar* and *dibber* have the same meaning, as is proved by the passage, "For it has heard all the words [*imrei*] of the Lord which He spoke [*dibber*] to us" (Josh. 24:27) (*Guide* 1:65).

Maimonides argues that *amirah* and *dibbur* are synonyms, and that they both have multiple meanings: speech, thought, and will. Rashi says that *dibbur* is language of rebuke (*lashon kasheh*), while *amar* is the language of comfort (*lashon taḥanunim*) (see, e.g., Rashi on Num. 12:1). Maimonides does not appear to accept this distinction.

On the current verse, Maimonides says *ha-lehargeni attah omer* means, "Do you desire to kill me?" Rashi, based on a Midrash, assumes a hyperliteral understanding of *ha-lehargeni attah omer*, meaning that Moses killed him by uttering the Tetragrammaton, i.e., by "speech." Nahmanides in different places in his commentary quotes different understandings of *amar*, though he entertains the meaning "thought" on the current verse (see his comments on the current verse and on Gen. 1:3 and 18:17).

2:17. And the shepherd came and drove them away, but Moses arose and came to their defense and watered their flock. — Included in the phrase "men of valor" (Exod. 18:21) means that they should have a courageous heart to save a victim from his oppressor, as it says on the matter, "but Moses arose and came to their defense" (Exod. 2:17) (see further *Hil. Sanhedrin* 2:7, quoted at Exod. 18:21).

FURTHER: [This passage comes from a longer discussion of prophecy. Maimonides states that there are different levels of prophecy. The first level inspires someone to do something "good and grand." The second level is when one feels "as if something came upon him." People in these two categories are not actually prophets, but are called so because they are "almost prophets." Maimonides argues that even from a young age, Moses had this first level of prophecy.] — The first degree of prophecy consists in the Divine assistance which is given to a person, and induces and encourages him to do something good and grand, e.g., to deliver a congregation of good men from the hands of evildoers; to save one noble person, or to bring happiness to a large number of people; he finds in himself the cause that moves and urges him to this deed. This degree of divine influence is called "the spirit of the Lord," and of the person who is under that influence we say that the spirit of the Lord came upon him, clothed him, or rested upon him, or the Lord was with him, and the like. All the judges of Israel possessed this degree, for the following general statement is made concerning them, "The Lord raised up judges for them; and the Lord was with the judge, and He saved them" (Judg. 2:18). Also all the noble chiefs of Israel belonged to this class. The same is distinctly stated concerning some of the judges and the kings: "The spirit of the Lord came upon Jephthah" (Judg. 11:29); of Samson it is said, "The spirit of the Lord came upon him" (Judg. 14:19); "And the spirit of the Lord came upon Saul when he heard those words" (1 Sam. 11:6). When Amasa was moved by the Holy Spirit to assist David, "A spirit clothed Amasa, who was chief of the captains, and he said, 'We are yours, David...'" (1 Chron. 12:18).

This faculty was always possessed by Moses from the time he had attained the age of manhood: it moved him to slay the Egyptian, and to prevent evil from the two men that quarreled. It was so strong that, after he had fled from Egypt out of fear, and arrived in Midian, a trembling stranger, he could not restrain himself from interfering when he saw wrong being done; he could not bear it: "And Moses arose and came to their defense" (Exod. 2:17) (*Guide* 2:45).

2:21. Moses agreed to stay with the man, and he gave Moses his daughter Zipporah in marriage. — see at Exod. 4:19.

2:24. God heard their groaning, and God remembered his covenant with Abraham, Isaac, and Jacob. — For Maimonides' understanding of the phrase "God heard," see at Exod. 22:21-23.

2:25. God looked upon [*va-yar'*] the Israelites, and God took notice of them. — [Maimonides is commenting on the fact that Onkelos translates *va-yar'* in this verse as *u-glei kadam*, "it was revealed" before God] ... as regards the verb "to see" [*ra'ah*], his [Onkelos's] renderings vary in a remarkable manner, and I was unable to discern his principle or method. In some instances he translates literally, "and God saw." In others he paraphrases "it was revealed before the Lord."

The use of the phrase "and God saw" [*haza*] by Onkelos is sufficient evidence that the term *haza* in Aramaic is homonymous, and that it denotes mental perception as well as the sensation of sight. This being the case, I am surprised that, in some instances avoiding the literal rendering, he substituted for it: "And it was revealed before the Lord." When I, however, examined the various readings in the version of Onkelos, which I either saw myself or heard from others during the time of my studies, I found that the term "to see" when connected with wrong, injury, or violence, was paraphrased, "It was manifest before the Lord."

There is no doubt that the term *haza* in Aramaic denotes complete apprehension and reception of the object in the state in which it has been perceived. When Onkelos, therefore, found the verb "to see" connected with the object "wrong," he did not render it literally, but paraphrased it, "It was revealed before the Lord." Now, I noticed that in all instances of the Torah where "seeing" is ascribed to God, he translated it literally, except those instances which I will mention to you: "For my affliction was revealed before the Lord" (Gen. 29:32); "For all that Laban does to you is revealed before Me" (Gen. 31:12). Although the first person in the sentence refers to the angel [and not to God], Onkelos does not ascribe to him that perception which implies complete comprehension of the object, because the object is "iniquity": "The oppression of the children of Israel was known to the Lord" (Exod. 2:25): "The oppression of My people was surely known to me" (Exod. 3:7), "The affliction is known to Me" (Exod. 3:9), "Their oppression is known to Me" (Exod. 4:31) (*Guide* 1:48).

Exodus 3

3:2. And an angel of the LORD appeared to him... — Even Moses our teacher received his first prophecy through an angel: "And an angel of the Lord appeared to him in the flame of fire." It is therefore clear that the belief in the existence of angels precedes the belief in prophecy, and the latter precedes belief in the Law (*Guide* 3:45).[5]

> Earlier, Maimonides writes, "Some prophets see angels in the form of man, e.g., "And behold three men stood by him" (Gen. 18:2); others perceive an angel as a fearful and terrible being, e.g., "And his countenance was as the countenance of an angel of God, very terrible" (Judg. 13:6); others see them as fire, e.g., "And an angel of the Lord appeared to him in a flame of fire."

... in a flame of fire [*be-labbat eish*] out of a bush; he looked, and the bush was blazing, yet it was not consumed. — The Hebrew *lev* [heart] is a homonymous noun, signifying that organ which is the source of life to all beings possessing a heart, e.g., "And thrust them through the heart of Absalom" (1 Sam. 18:14). This organ being in the middle of the body, the word has been figuratively applied to express "the middle part of a thing," e.g., "unto the midst [*lev*] of heaven" (Deut. 4:11); "the midst [*labbat*] of fire" (Exod. 3:2) (*Guide* 1:39).

> Maimonides says that in addition to the two meanings above, *lev* can mean "thought" (e.g., 2 Kings 5:26), "counsel" (e.g., 1 Chron. 12:38), "will" (e.g., Jer. 3:15), and "understanding" (Eccl. 10:2). He concludes, "It must, in each passage, be

---

5. See *Maimonides Between Philosophy and Halakhah: Rabbi Joseph B. Soloveitchik's Lectures on the Guide of the Perplexed* by Lawrence J. Kaplan, pp. 162-163, where Rabbi Soloveitchik is critical of Maimonides' view of angels.

explained in accordance with the context." Ibn Ezra, like Maimonides, understands *lev* as *emtza*, "center" (long comm. to Exod. 15:8). However Rashi, on the phrase "heart of the sea" (Exod. 15:8), assumes the word "heart" refers to the sea's attribute of strength, rather than its center.

3:6. He said further, "I am the God of your father, the God of Abraham, the God of Isaac, and the God of Jacob." And Moses hid his face, for he was afraid to look upon [*me-habbit*] God. — This verb [*hibbit*], when applied to God [as the object], is employed in this figurative sense; e.g., "to look upon [*me-habbit*] God" (*Guide* 1:4).

FURTHER: … we must understand the words, "And Moses hid his face, for he was afraid to look upon God," though retaining also the literal meaning of the passage, that Moses was afraid to gaze at the light which appeared to his eye; but it must on no account be assumed that the Being which is exalted far above every imperfection can be perceived by the eye. This act of Moses was highly commended by God, who bestowed on him a well deserved portion of His goodness, as it is said, "And the similitude of the LORD shall he behold" (Num. 12:8). This, say our Sages (*Berakhot* 7a), was the reward for having previously hidden his face, lest he should gaze at the Eternal (*Guide* 1:5).

Maimonides' understanding of "looking at God" remains unclear to me. "Looking at God" cannot be literal, because God has no body and therefore cannot be seen. And the figurative sense of verbs for "to see" (i.e., *ra'ah*, *ḥazah*, and *hibbit*) means "to understand," but God is too great to be understood. (See also at Exod. 6:18.)

3:7. And God said, "I have surely seen the affliction My people that are in Egypt, and I have heard their cry because of their

33

oppressors for I have known their sorrows." — See at Exod. 2:25. Furthermore, Joseph Albo writes, "... though Israel had sinned and were not deserving at that time of such great deliverance, nevertheless God saved them of His own accord as if He was affected by their trouble and misery, as we read, 'I have surely seen the affliction of My people that are in Egypt...'" (*Ikkarim* 2:14). This is an example of Maimonides-style "as-if theology" being applied to a biblical passage.

3:9. The cry of the Israelites has now come to Me... — See at Exod. 2:25.

... I have also seen how the Egyptians oppress [*laḥatz*] them. — [Maimonides is explaining the meaning of *mi-doḥak* (M. *Ma'aser Sheni* 2:6)] And they said *mi-doḥak* (*Maaser Sheni* 2:6), meaning "great need" [*tzorekh gadol*]. The translation [of Onkelos] for *laḥatz* is "distress" [*duḥka*] (*PhM Maaser Sheni* 2:6; Menahem ben Saruk also translates *laḥatz* as *matzok*).

3:12. And he said, "Surely I will be with you... — The prophets must have had these two forces, courage and intuition, highly developed, and these were still more strengthened when they were under the influence of the Active Intellect. Their courage was so great that, e.g., Moses, with only a staff in his hand, dared to address a great king in his desire to deliver a nation from his service. He was not frightened or terrified, because he had been told, "I will be with you" (*Guide* 2:38).

... and this shall be a sign for you... — Consider how the action of Divine Providence is described in reference to every incident in the lives of the Patriarchs, to their occupations, and even to their passions, and how God promised to direct His attention to them.

Thus God said to Abraham, "I am your shield" (Gen. 15:1); to Isaac, "I will be with you, and I will bless you" (Gen. 26:3); to Jacob, "I am with you, and will keep you" (Gen. 28:15); to [Moses] the chief of the prophets, "Surely I will be with you, and this shall be a sign for you" (Exod. 3:12); to Joshua, "As I was with Moses, so I shall be with you" (Josh. 1:5). It is clear that in all these cases the action of Providence has been proportional to man's perfection (*Guide* 3:18).

... and this shall be the sign for you that it is I who sent you; when you have brought the people out of Egypt... — ... all Israel were witnesses to [the appointment of] Moses, our teacher, at the [revelation] at Mount Sinai, and it was unnecessary for him to perform any further wonders for them. And this is what the Holy One, blessed be He, said at the beginning of his [Moses'] prophey when He gave him the signs [and wonders] to perform in Egypt, saying, "And they will listen to your voice" (Exod. 3:18).

Moses, our teacher, knew that one who believes [in another person] because of signs has apprehension in his heart; he has doubts and suspicions. Therefore, he sought to be released from the mission, saying, "They will not believe me" (Exod. 4:1), until the Holy One, blessed be He, informed him that these wonders [were intended only as a temporary measure] until they left Egypt. After they would leave, they would stand on this mountain [i.e., the mountain referenced at Exod. 19:9] and all doubts which they had about him would be removed. [God told him:] Here, I will give you a sign so that they will know that I truly sent you from the outset, and thus, no doubts will remain in their hearts. This is what is meant by "This will be your sign that I sent you: When you take the people out of Egypt, you will serve God on this mountain" (*Yesodei ha-Torah* 8:1-2; see further at Exod. 19:9).

... you shall worship God on this mountain." — see at Exod. 14:3.

3:13-14. And Moses said to God, "If I come to the Israelites and say to them, 'The God of your ancestors has sent me to you,' and they ask me, 'What is his name?' what shall I say to them?" God said to Moses, "I AM THAT I AM.'" He said further, "Thus you shall say to the Israelites, 'I AM has sent me to you.'" — ... Moses [said], "And they shall ask me, 'What is His name?' what shall I say unto them" (Exod. 3:13). How far was this question, anticipated by Moses, appropriate, and how far was he justified in seeking to be prepared with the answer? ...[6] When God appeared to our teacher Moses, and commanded him to address the people and to bring them the message, Moses replied that he might first be asked to prove the existence of God in the Universe, and that only after doing so he would be able to announce to them that God had sent him. For all men, with few exceptions, were ignorant of the existence of God; their highest thoughts did not extend beyond the heavenly sphere, its forms or its influences.[7] They could not yet emancipate themselves from sensation, and had not yet attained to any intellectual perfection. Then God taught Moses how to teach them, and how to establish among them the belief in the existence of Himself, namely, by saying *Ehyeh asher Ehyeh*[8] (Exod. 3:14), a name derived from the verb *hayah* in the sense of "existing," for the verb *hayah* denotes "to be," and in Hebrew no difference is made between the verbs "to be" and "to exist."

---

6. Text from ellipsis is placed at Exod. 4:1.

7. Nahmanides objects to this interpretation, writing, "In my opinion, the elders of Israel never doubted the existence of the Creator, as the Rabbi [Maimonides] said." Rather, according to Nahmanides, the question is what attribute of God Moses should refer to when saying he was sent by God.

8. Maimonides says that *Ehyeh* is one of the seven names of God that cannot be erased (*Yesodei ha-Torah* 6:2). The Talmud says the full name *Ehyeh asher Ehyeh* cannot be erased (*Shevuot* 35a, based on Deut. 12:3), but says nothing about the name *Ehyeh*. The *Kesef Mishnah* surmises the inconsistency is because Maimonides had a variant text of the Talmud.

The principal point in this phrase is that the same word which denotes "existence" is repeated as an attribute. The word *asher* ["that"] corresponds to the Arabic *illadi* and *illati*, and is an incomplete noun that must be completed by another noun: it may be considered as the subject of the predicate which follows. The first noun which is to be described is *ehyeh*: the second, by which the first is described, is likewise *ehyeh*, the identical word, as if to show that the object which is to be described and the attribute by which it is described are in this case necessarily identical. This is, therefore, the expression of the idea that God exists, but not in the ordinary sense of the term: or, in other words, He is "the existing Being which is the existing Being," that is to say, the Being whose existence is absolute. The proof which he was to give consisted in demonstrating that there is a Being of absolute existence, that has never been and never will be without existence. This I will clearly prove.

God thus showed Moses the proofs by which His existence would be firmly established among the wise men of His people. Therefore the explanation of the name is followed by the words, "Go, gather the elders of Israel" (Exod. 3:16), and by the assurance that the elders would understand what God had shown to him, and would accept it, as is stated in the words, "And they will hearken to your voice." Then Moses replied as follows: "They will accept the doctrine that God exists convinced by these intelligible proofs. But," said Moses, "by what means shall I be able to show that this existing God *has sent me*?" Thereupon God gave him the sign. We have thus shown that the question, "What is His name" means "Who is that Being, which according to your belief *has sent you*?"

The sentence, "What is His name?" (instead of "Who is He?") has here been used as a tribute of praise and homage, as though it had been said, "Nobody can be ignorant of Your essence and of Your real existence"; if, nevertheless, I ask, "What is Your name?" I mean, "What idea is to be expressed by the name?" (Moses considered it

37

inappropriate to say to God that any person was ignorant of God's existence, and therefore described the Israelites as ignorant of God's name, not as ignorant of Him who was called by that name.) (*Guide* 1:63).

There are two main strands of interpreting the phrase I AM THAT I AM. For Philo (*Moses* 1.74ff), Maimonides (*Guide* 1:63), Joseph Albo (*Ikkarim* 2:27), and Rabbi Joseph Soloveitchik ("Confrontation"), this is a statement of God's absoluteness, either about His essence or His eternality.

However, according to the Talmud (*Berakhot* 9b), Rashi, and Nahmanides, the phrase I AM THAT I AM is a relational phrase; in effect, God is saying, "I am the One that will be with you and the Jewish people always." For them, the phrase does not teach anything about God's essence (as Maimonides and others claim), and in a time of distress it seems the Jewish people did not need a lesson in philosophy, but emotional assurance and inspiration that God would be receptive to their cries, act for their sake, and bring about their redemption.

Yet it might be possible to resolve the two sides. The *Kuzari* writes, "The name *Ehyeh*... is to prevent the human mind from pondering over the incomprehensible but real entity. When Moses asked, 'And they shall say to me: What is His name?' the answer was: Why should they ask concerning things they are unable to grasp? ... 'Say to them *Ehyeh*,' which means 'I am that I am,' the existing one, existing for you whenever you seek Me" (*Kuzari* 4:3). The *Kuzari* concedes it is a statement about God's essence, though he posits that God's essence is not something to be examined too closely; hence the name is almost a diversion. In a similar vein, Sforno writes, "I am an independent existence, not subject to influences by other phenomena or even caused by them. Seeing that this is so, it follows that I love existing, and beings that exist. As a corollary to this love of Mine for existence, it follows that I deeply resent anything or anyone who tries to terminate such an existing being from continuing to do so." Sforno's commentary seems to contain both sides of the debate—that of Maimonides and that of Rashi—and argues that one argument flows naturally from the other.

3:15. God also said to Moses, "Thus you shall say to the Israelites, 'The LORD, the God of your ancestors, the God of Abraham, the God of Isaac, and the God of Jacob, has sent me to you': This is my name for ever, and this my title for all generations. — The Patriarchs... attained this degree of perfection; they approached God in such a manner that with them the name of God became known in the world. Thus we read in Scripture: "The God of Abraham, the God of Isaac, and the God of Jacob.... This is My name forever" (Exod. 3:15). Their mind was so identified with the knowledge of God, that He made a lasting covenant with each of them (*Guide* 3:51).

One must ask: what is the difference in revelation between the Patriarchs and Moses? Of course, for Maimonides, the prophecy of Moses was categorically different than any other prophecy. But is there also a difference in function? That too is answered in the affirmative. The Patriarchs were able to establish the name of God in the world, but Moses was tasked with something even harder: he was sent not just to pave the path for monotheism, but to actually introduce and impose belief to the Israelites, who would question everything about Moses' mission, from his initial dispatch onwards, and trouble him for most of his prophetic career (see *Guide* 1:63, quoted at Exod. 4:1).

3:16. Go and assemble the elders of Israel, and say to them, "The Lord, the God of your ancestors, the God of Abraham, of Isaac, and of Jacob, has appeared to me, saying: I have surely taken notice [*pakod pakadti*] of you and to what has been done to you in Egypt. — [Maimonides is discussing the fact that on Rosh Hashanah, we recite blessings in the themes of *Malkhiyyot* (Kingship), *Zikhronot* (Remembrance), and *Shofarot* (Trumpets). He discusses which verses can be included in the blessing of *Zikhronot*:] Verses using *p-k-d* cannot be used for *Zikhronot*, such as "I have surely taken notice [*pakod pakadti*] of you" (*Shofar* 3:9).

> Maimonides' ruling is based on BT *Rosh Hashanah* 32a; however that source quotes Gen. 21:1, not Exod. 3:16. In many instances, the verbs *z-k-r* and *p-k-d* can be used interchangeably; however Nahmanides points out at least one difference between these words; see his commentary to Exod. 20:5.

Further: God... showed Moses the proofs by which His existence would be firmly established among the wise men of His people (*Guide* 1:63, quoted at length on Exod. 3:13-14).

3:18. They will listen to your voice; and you and the elders of Israel shall go to the king of Egypt and say to him, "The Lord, the God of the Hebrews, has met with us; let us now go a three days' journey into the wilderness, so that we may sacrifice to the Lord our God." — See *Guide* 1:63, quoted at 4:1.

Exodus 4

4:1. Then Moses answered, "But suppose they do not believe me or listen to me, but say, 'The Lord did not appear to you.' — Moses, our teacher, knew that one who believes [in another person] because of signs has apprehension in his heart; he has doubts and suspicions. Therefore, he sought to be released from the mission, saying, "They will not believe me" (Exod. 4:1), until the Holy One, blessed be He, informed him that these wonders [were intended only as a temporary measure] until they left Egypt (*Yesodei ha-Torah* 8:2; see further at Exod. 19:9).

FURTHER: Any prophet who arises and tells us that God has sent him does not have to [prove himself by] performing wonders like those performed by Moses, our teacher [referenced in Exodus 4], or like the wonders of Elijah or Elisha, which altered the natural order. Rather, the sign of [the truth of his prophecy] will be the fulfillment of his prediction of future events, as, "How shall we recognize that a prophecy was not spoken by God?" (Deut. 18:21).

Therefore, if a person whose [progress] in the service of God makes him worthy of prophecy arises [and claims to be a prophet]— if he does not intend to add to or diminish [the Torah], but to serve God through the commandments of the Torah, we do not tell him, "Split the sea for us, revive the dead, or the like, and then we will believe in you." Instead, we tell him, "If you are a prophet, tell us what will happen in the future." He makes his statements, and we wait to see whether [his "prophecy"] comes to fruition or not. Should even a minute particular of his "prophecy" not materialize, he is surely a false prophet. If his entire prophecy materializes, we should consider him a true [prophet] (*Yesodei ha-Torah* 10:1).

There is a question that must be asked about Maimonides' perspective on signs. In *Yesodei ha-Torah* 8:2, he writes, "Moses, our teacher, knew that one who believes [in another person] because of signs has apprehension in his heart; he has doubts and suspicions," and he reiterates in *Yesodei ha-Torah* 10:1 that we do not require a prophet to perform signs and miracles in order to be believed. However Maimonides elsewhere writes, "But, said Moses, by what means shall I be able to show that this existing God has sent me? Thereupon God gave him the sign" (*Guide* 1:63; quoted next). This problem can be resolved by saying that according to Maimonides, a sign is sufficient for preliminary reliance ("belief") but does not impart certainty ("knowledge").

FURTHER: Moses was correct in declaring, "But, behold, they will not believe me, for they will say, 'The Lord has not appeared unto you'" (Exod. 4:1), for any man claiming the authority of a prophet must expect to meet with such an objection so long as he has not given a proof of his mission.

Again, if the question, as appears at first sight, referred only to the name, as a mere utterance of the lips, the following dilemma would present itself: either the Israelites knew the name [of God], or they had never heard it. If the name was known to them, they would perceive in it no argument in favor of the mission of Moses, his knowledge and their knowledge of the divine name being the same. If, on the other hand, they had never heard it mentioned, and if the knowledge of it was to prove the mission of Moses, what evidence would they have that this was really the name of God? Moreover, after God had made known that name to Moses, and had told him, "Go and gather the elders of Israel" (Exod. 3:16), "and they shall hearken to your voice" (Exod. 3:18), he replied, "Behold, they will not believe me nor hearken unto my voice" (Exod. 4:1), although God had told him, "And they will hearken to your voice." Whereupon God answered, "What is that in your hand?" and he said, "A rod" (Exod. 4:2).

In order to obviate this dilemma, you must understand what I am about to tell you. You know how widespread the opinions of the Sabeans were in those days. All men, except a few individuals, were idolaters, that is to say, they believed in spirits, in man's power to direct the influences of the heavenly bodies, and in the effect of talismans. Anyone who in those days laid claim to authority, based it either, like Abraham, on the fact that, by reasoning and by proof, he had been convinced of the existence of a Being who rules the whole Universe, or that some spiritual power was conferred upon him by a star, by an angel, or by a similar agency; but no one could establish his claim on prophecy, that is to say, on the fact that God had spoken to him, or had entrusted a mission to him. Before the days of Moses, no such assertion had ever been made.

You must not be misled by the statements that God spoke to the Patriarchs, or that He had appeared to them. For you do not find any mention of a prophecy which appealed to others, or which directed them. Abraham, Isaac, or Jacob, or any other person before them did not tell the people, "God said unto me, you shall do this thing, or you shall not do that thing" or "God has sent me to you." Far from it! For God spoke to them about nothing but of what especially concerned them, i.e., He communicated to them things relating to their perfection, directed them in what they should do, and foretold them what the condition of their descendants would be: nothing beyond this. They guided their fellow men by means of argument and instruction, as is implied, according to the interpretation generally received among us, in the words "and the souls that they had gotten in Haran" (Gen. 12:5) (*Guide* 1:63).

Nehama Leibowitz points out a seeming contradiction between God saying "They will listen to your voice" (Exod. 3:18) and Moses saying "perhaps they will not believe me or listen to me" (Exod. 4:1). Rashi and some midrashim believe that Moses acted improperly. Other commentaries, including Ibn Ezra, Maimonides, and Nahmanides "try to show there is no contradiction between the Almighty's statement and Moses' reply." She continues that Maimonides "makes a distinction between the authenticity of God and that of His emissary. The people would believe in God, in the message of ehyeh asher ehyeh, but not in Moses."[9]

FURTHER: ... although they were corrupt as all this [i.e., they neglected circumcision and committed incest (see at Exod. 12:48)], God rebuked Moses for saying, "What if they do not believe me?" (Exod. 4:1).[10] And He retorted: They are believers, children of believers (cf. Amos 7:14); believers as Scripture reports, "and the people... believed" (Exod. 14:31); sons of believers, "because he believed, He reckoned it to his merit" (Gen. 15:6). But you will end up not believing; it is told in Scripture, "Because you did not believe Me enough to affirm My sanctity" (Num. 20:12). In fact, he [Moses] was punished at once, as the Rabbis understood, "He who suspects the innocent suffers physically. What is the proof? Moses" (*Epistle on Martyrdom*, ch. 2).[11]

---

9. Nehama Leibowitz, *New Studies in Shemot (Exodus)* I, "Did Moses Speak Unbefittingly," pp. 75-82.

10. Abraham Halkin writes, "This is another illustration of the method of taking an apt phrase out of its context" (*Crisis and Leadership: Epistles of Maimonides*, p. 36). See at Exod. 3:13-14. Obviously, Maimonides' purpose in writing an encouraging letter might differ from his general analysis in a more dispassionate context.

11. Abraham Halkin and David Hartman, *Crisis and Leadership: Epistles of Maimonides*, pp. 17-18.

4:2. The Lord said to him, "What is that in your hand?" He said, "A rod." — See *Guide* 1:63, quoted at Exod. 3:13-14.

4:4. Then the Lord said to Moses, "Reach out your hand, and seize it by the tail"—so he reached out his hand and grasped it, and it became a staff in his hand. — ... miracles in the naturally impossible class will not last at all, nor will they tarry or remain with their features. For, if they persisted, they would open the way to suspicion. If the rod remained a serpent, the uncertainty would be entertained that it had been originally a serpent, so that the miracle is achieved by its return to a rod, "And it became a rod in his hand" (Exod. 4:4). If, in the incident of the followers of Korah, the ground had burst asunder, and stayed open for good, the miracle would be challenged. In fact, the miracle was completed when the ground returned to its former condition: "The earth closed over them" (Num. 16:33); so also "And at daybreak the sea returned to its normal state" (Exod. 14:27). Because of this fact, I refuse to accept the duration of an unnatural situation....[12]

Maimonides is saying that the return to the natural order is an even greater component than the original miraculous transformation. See also Rashi on Exod. 4:7.

4:6. And the Lord said to him furthermore, "Place now your hand in your bosom." And he put his hand in his bosom; and when he took it out, behold it was leprous [white] as snow. — [The Sages said:] "Anyone who carries on a dispute transgresses a prohibition, as it is written, 'Do not be like Korah and his congregation,'" (*Sanhedrin* 110a, quoting Num. 17:5), [which] is also a type of hermeneutics.... Our Sages explained that God notified that anyone in future generations who disagrees with [the

---

12. Abraham Halkin and David Hartman, *Crisis and Leadership: Epistles of Maimonides*, p. 232.

status of] the priests and claims it for himself will not meet the same fate as Korah and will not be punished by being swallowed up (Num. 16:32). His punishment will instead be, "As God said to him through [literally, 'by the hand of'] Moses," i.e., *tzara'at* [which is white], as God, may He be exalted, told Moses, "Place now your hand in your bosom [... and when he took it out, behold it was white as snow]," and as is explained regarding Uzziah (2 Chron. 26:16-21; *Tanḥuma*, "Tzav" 15) (*ShM*, Neg. 45; similarly at *ShM*, *Shoresh* 8).[13]

The Hebrew word *tzara'at* is generally (and loosely) translated as "leprosy," based on the divinely imposed skin disease, described at Leviticus 13 and elsewhere. Rashi sees *tzara'at* as a punishment for Moses maligning the Jewish people by questioning whether they will believe God had sent him.

Does Maimonides, like Rashi, interpret this *tzara'at* is a form of punishment? Maimonides merely writes Moses' *tzara'at* is a sign that when future people agitate against the priesthood, they will be punished. However, there is another Midrash, quoted by Rashi (Exod. 4:14), that Moses was destined for the priesthood but lost it during his hesitations. Perhaps Maimonides would say that Moses' protestations about his own worthiness for the mission was a form of agitation about the priesthood for which he was punished. This might carry more weight when one asks why the lesson about the priesthood needed to be taught at this moment.

More likely, Maimonides does not see any punishment here, since elsewhere he writes, "The word *tzara'at* is a

13. See at Exod. 4:14, where it is explained that according to Rabbi Simeon b. Yohai, Moses lost the priesthood because of his recalcitrance. The Midrash, quoted above, says that the punishment for complaining about priesthood is *tzara'at*, and it would be worth investigating if Maimonides believes that Moses was punished with *tzara'at* for the same reason, or if the two interpretations are unrelated.

general word that includes many meanings which are not related, for whitening of the skin is called *tzara'at*, some hair falling out of the head or beard is called *tzara'at*, and the change of color in clothing or a house is called *tzara'at*" (*Tumat Tzara'at* 16:10). Furthermore, Saadiah on this verse understands *tzara'at* merely as "white," without an implication of disease, and R. Abraham (Maimonides' son) quotes that interpretation approvingly.

Dr. Isadore Twersky classifies this as a type of "explanatory statement" that "contain[s] a juridical definition or semantic clarification which has clear repercussions for the mechanics and dynamics of classification" (*Introduction to the Code of Maimonides (Mishneh Torah)*, p. 282).

4:11. Then the Lord said to him, "Who gives speech [mouth] to mortals? Who makes them mute or deaf, seeing or blind? Is it not I, the Lord?" — [We] condemn lowness of speech, and justly so, for speech is likewise peculiar to man and a boon which God granted to him that he may be distinguished from the rest of living creatures. Thus God says, "Who gave a mouth to man?" (Exod. 4:11); and the prophet declares, "The Lord God has given me a learned tongue" (Isa. 1:4). This gift, therefore, which God gave us in order to enable us to perfect ourselves, to learn and to teach, must not be employed in doing that which is for us most degrading and perfectly disgraceful; we must not imitate the songs and tales of ignorant and lascivious people. It may be suitable to them, but is not fit for those who are told, "And you shall be to me a kingdom of priests and a holy nation" (Exod. 19:6). Those who employ the faculty of thinking and speaking in the service of that sense which is no honor to us, who think more than necessary of drink and love, or even sing of these things: they employ and use the divine gift in acts of rebellion against the Giver, and in the transgression of His commandments. To them the following words may be applied: "And I multiplied her silver and gold, which they prepared for Baal" (Hos. 2:10) (*Guide* 3:8).

FURTHER: [The following is from Maimonides' Epistle on Martyrdom, in which he is criticizing a contemporary of his, and considers quoting him, but is afraid of being too verbose.] — [Speech is] the gift that God, blessed be He, bestowed on mankind... "Who gives speech to mortals? ... Is it not I, the LORD?" A man should be more sparing with his speech than of his money, and should not speak much yet do little. Indeed the Sage [i.e., King Solomon] has condemned verbosity with little content in his declaration, "Just as dreams come with much brooding, so does foolish utterance come with much speech" (Eccl. 5:2). You know of course what Job's friends said as he talked on and on: "Is a multitude of words unanswerable? Must a loquacious person be right" (Job 11:2). "Job does not speak with knowledge; his words lack understanding" (Job 34:35) (*Epistle on Martyrdom*).[14]

There are many ways that "man" has been defined. For example, Rene Descartes defined man as a "thinking thing." However, Jewish tradition has historically classified created beings into four categories: *domem* (inanimate objects), *tzome'ah* (plants), *hai* (animals), and *medabber* (humans). The word *medabber* used for "mankind," is the same root as the word for "speech." Maimonides is consistent with this classification, since he views the ability to speak as a gift given uniquely to man.

FURTHER: [In this passage, Maimonides first said that speech is a quality which is created from nothing, a point which he has already made in *Guide* 3:8 and in the *Epistle on Martyrdom*. In *Guide* 3:10,

14. Abraham Halkin and David Hartman, *Crisis and Leadership: Epistles of Maimonides*, p. 15.

Maimonides starts the section by discussing whether properties and their opposites are both said to exist. For example are lightness and darkness both said to exist, or does only lightness exist and darkness is merely the absence of light. He then quotes this passage:] … here the creation took place from nothing. Only in this sense can non-existence be said to be produced by a certain action of an agent. In the same way we must explain the following passage: "Who has made man's mouth? or who makes the dumb, or the deaf, or the seeing" (Exod. 4:11). The passage can also be explained as follows: Who has made man able to speak? or can create him without the capacity of speaking, i.e., create a substance that is incapable of acquiring this property? for he who produces a substance that cannot acquire a certain property may be called the producer of that privation (*Guide* 3:10).

Maimonides is driven by a question that is both exegetical and philosophical: how can one say that the verb "place" (*simah*) can apply to muteness, which is the absence of a quality; how can an absence be created *ab initio*? On the philosophical side, the question of privation goes back at least to Aristotle (*Metaphysics*, Book Delta, XXII "Privation").

In the present verse, what does it mean to "create muteness"? Nahmanides quotes Maimonides' interpretation without qualification. Chavel, in his translation of Nahmanides, writes, "The difficulty presents itself: Since the absence of a property is nothing positive and dumbness is the lack of the property of speech, how can one speak of 'the making' of dumbness when it is nonexistent? See Rambam's Moreh Nebuchim III, 10, where the author discusses this problem. The answer, quoted here by Ramban, that it refers back to 'the man,' suggesting, 'Who can create a man without the capacity of speech?' is mentioned there by Rambam."

Rashi, based on the *Tanḥuma*, may have been motivated by a similar concern that "muteness" cannot be "created."

Rashi's interpretation resolves this philosophical difficulty, taking a different approach: "Who made Pharaoh dumb, that he did not exert any effort [to issue his] command to kill you? And [who made] his servants deaf, so that they did not hear his commandment concerning you? And who made the executioners blind, that they did not see when you fled from the [executioner's] platform and escaped?" (Rashi based on *Tanḥuma*, Shemot 10).[15]

4:14. Then the anger of the LORD was kindled against Moses and he said, "What of your brother Aaron the Levite? I know that he can speak fluently; even now he is coming out to meet you, and when he sees you his heart will be glad. — [Maimonides does not quote this verse but the following comment can be applied to the phrase "the anger of the LORD was kindled":] He [God] performs acts similar to those which, when performed by us, originate in certain psychical dispositions, in jealousy, desire for retaliation, revenge, or anger: they are in accordance with the guilt of those who are to be punished, and not the result of any emotion: for He is above all defect! (*Guide* 1:54).

Maimonides is addressing the famous question of what it means for God to get angry, if according to the Aristotelian model, God doesn't have emotions. Maimonides concludes that God behaves in a way that if the same action is performed by a person, it would be performed out of anger.

This is only a partial answer, because it does not directly address the question of what action God took as a result of His "anger" in this case. We will present two possible answers. First, The Talmud states: "R. Joshua b. Korha said: Wherever it says *ḥaron af* [fierce anger] in the Torah there is

15. This analysis is based in part of the notes to Nahmanides' commentary in the *Torat Ḥayyim* edition.

50

an imprint [roshem, a lasting impression] but here (i.e., Exod. 4:14), there is no imprint. R. Simeon b. Yohai said: There is an imprint in this instance too, for it is said, 'Is there not Aaron your brother the Levite? (Exod. 4:14). Now surely he was a priest [kohen]? Rather, this is what He meant: I had said that you would be a priest and he a Levite; now however, he will be a priest and you a Levite" (Zevaḥim 102a; Rashi in his commentary on this current verse quotes this talmudic passage. In his commentary on the Talmud, Rashi points out that roshem means different forms of punishment or curse.). According to this approach, the result of God's anger is Moses' loss of the priesthood.

A second answer is that Moses was punished as being aral sefatayim (Exod. 6:12). R. Abraham suggests that this was Moses' punishment, which would be in keeping with the theological value of "measure for measure." In Exod. 4:10, Moses demurs from his mission, saying he is not eloquent (lo ish devarim anokhi… kevad peh u-khvad lashon anokhi). In the next two verses God reassures Moses that speech is a divine gift and that God will be with Moses throughout the process. Moses still asks to be excused. At that point, God becomes angry. According to R. Abraham, the anger is manifest in a punishment that Moses' compromised ability to speak is further impaired, as he becomes aral sefatayim.

Nahmanides sees the anger manifest in God's not removing the speech impediment: "The correct interpretation appears to me to be that God said to Moses, 'Who gives speech to mortals? Who makes them mute or deaf… ? Is it not I, the Lord' (Exod. 4:11). 'Who does all this? I could heal you. But now since you did not want to be healed, nor have you prayed to me about it, go and I will be with your mouth (Exod. 4:12), and I will cause you success in My mission.' It is also possible that there is a hint in the verse, 'the anger of the Lord was kindled against Moses' (Exod. 4:14), that He did not want to heal him, and that He sent him against his will" (on Exod. 4:14).

Thus there are two ways to understand God's anger in this verse: (1) Moses' loss of the priesthood (R. Simeon b. Yohai), (2) the speech impediment, either being imposed (R. Abraham) or not being removed (Nahmanides). This approach is taken by Onkelos, Rashi (*le-rav u-le-sar*, "a master and a minister"), R. Saadiah, and Rashbam (*sar ve-shofet*, "minister and judge"). See however Ibn Ezra (long) and Sforno.

4:19. The LORD said to Moses in Midian, "Go back to Egypt... — One who vows not to benefit from his neighbor can only have the vow absolved in his [neighbor's] presence. The Sages learned this from what is written, "Go back to Egypt" (Exod. 4:19). He [God] said, "In Midian you made your vow; now go and annul your vow in Midian," as is says, "And Moses was content [*va-yo'el*] to dwell with the man" (Exod. 2:21) (*PhM Nedarim* 9:4).[16]

4:21. And the LORD said to Moses, 'When you go back to Egypt, see that you perform before Pharaoh all the wonders that I have put in your power; but I will harden his heart, so that he will not let the people go. — It is possible that a person will commit a great sin or many sins until judgment is rendered before the true Judge, which will be punishment against this sinner for these sins that he did voluntarily and deliberately., which prevent him from repenting and do not allow him the possibility to repent from his wickedness until he dies and is destroyed in his sin [i.e., he dies in a state of sinfulness without repentance].

---

16. Based on *Nedarim* 65a, understanding *shevuah* and *alah* as synonyms. Maimonides codifies this law in *Shevuot* 6:7 and *Nedarim* 4:5, but without quoting the verse. Shadal sees a difference between *alah* and *shevuah* (see his comments at Gen. 24:41).

This is implied by what the Holy One, blessed is He, said to Isaiah, "Make the heart of this people fat" (Isa. 6:10). And it says, "They mocked the messengers of God, scorned His words, scoffed at His prophets until the anger of God mounted up against His people until there was no remedy" (2 Chron. 36:16). This means that they sinned willingly and continued to err until repentance—the "remedy" [*marpei*]—was prevented from them.

Therefore, it is written in the Torah, "And I will harden Pharaoh's heart" (Exod. 14:4). Because he sinned willingly [*me-atzmo*] and inflicted evil on the Israelites who dwelled in his land, as it says, "Come, let us deal wisely with them" (Exod. 1:10), the judgment was given to withhold repentance from him until punishment was inflicted upon him. Therefore the Holy One, Blessed is He, hardened his heart.

And why did [God] send Moses, saying "send [them] and repent" when the Holy One, Blessed is He, had already stated that he [Pharaoh] would not let them go, as it says, "I know that you and your servants [still do not fear God]" (Exod. 9:30)? [The answer is:] "For this reason I have established you to inform the inhabitants of the earth" (Exod. 9:16) — when the Holy One, Blessed is He, withholds repentance from a sinner, he cannot repent but instead dies in his state of wickedness as he began....

In sum, God did not decree that Pharaoh act wickedly towards Israel, nor Sihon to sin in his land (Deut. 2:30), nor on the Canaanites to commit abominations (Josh. 11:20), nor on the Israelites to worship idols (2 Kings 18:37). Rather, they all sinned willingly [*me-atzman*], and they all become liable to have repentance withheld from them (*Teshuvah* 6:3; Maimonides makes a substantively similar point in *Shemonah Perakim*, ch. 8).

Ra'avad harshly disagrees, writing, "These are lengthy words that are tasteless, and for the life of me, I almost say they are childish. If God were to say to those who strayed 'Why did you stray; I did not designate you?' they would respond, 'Upon whom was Your decree made, on those that did not stray? If so, Your decree was not fulfilled" (Wiederblank trans.).

Rabbi Netanel Wiederblank writes that Maimonides "might respond that certain events are predictable on a macro level even while individual actors retain freedom... For example, government statisticians (or cooks in cafeterias) can very accurately predict certain general behavioral patterns that free actors will follow. Indeed, analysis of big data has allowed statisticians to make remarkable predictions about future behavior without any violation of free will. And if humans are capable of such predictions, certainly God can make such forecasts" (*Illuminating Jewish Thought*, vol. 2, pp. 258-259).

How could God deny Pharaoh the possibility of repentance, when freedom of the will is one of the cornerstones of religious theology? Maimonides writes that Pharaoh's heart was hardened only after Pharaoh himself began to sin earlier, when he said, "Come, let us deal shrewdly with them" (Exod. 1:10). When Pharaoh and his advisors exercised his own free will to oppress the Jews, he inculcated evil behavior in himself, which inhibited his own ability to repent. Maimonides writes, "they willingly sinned, multiplying their iniquity until it was obliged to hold back their repentance, [which is referred to as] the 'remedy.'" A few other opinions worthy of comparison:

- **Rashi:** "Pharaoh acted wickedly and defied Me, and it was revealed before Me that there is no goodwill among the heathens to repent with a full heart. It is better that his heart should be hardened so that I may multiply My signs against him, so that you will recognize My strength. And this is the trait of the Holy One, Blessed be He: He brings punishments on the nations of the world so that Israel should hear and be awed, as it says, 'I have cut off nations, their towers are desolate... I have said: You shall surely fear revere Me and receive correction' (Zeph. 3:6-7). Nonetheless, regarding the first five plagues, it does not say 'God hardened Pharaoh's heart,' but 'Pharaoh's heart was hardened'" (on Exod. 7:3).

- **Saadiah:** "Pharaoh needed a bolstering of the spirit in order not to die from the plagues [that befell the Egyptians], but remain alive until the rest of the punishment had been completely visited upon him" (*Emunot ve-De'ot* 4:6).

- **Sforno:** "God hardened Pharaoh's heart" so that "Pharaoh was strengthened to endure the plagues and not, out of fear of the plagues, send out the Israelites" so that God should make His strength manifest (Sforno on 7:3; see also on the present verse).

Nahmanides appears to quote both Rashi and Maimonides and claim they are both correct: "there are two explanations, and both of them are true. One [i.e., Maimonides] is that Pharaoh in his wickedness had unjustifiably perpetrated such great evils against Israel that justice required that the ways of repentance be withheld from him.... The second explanation [Rashi] is that half of the plagues came upon him because of his transgressions, for in connection with them it is only said, 'And Pharaoh's heart was hardened' (Exod. 7: 13, 22, 8:15), 'And Pharaoh hardened his heart' (Exod. 8:23, 9:7). Thus Pharaoh refused to let the children of Israel go for the glory of God. But when the plagues began bearing down upon him and he because weary to suffer them, his heart softened and be considered sending them out on account of the onslaught of the plagues, not in order to do the will of his Creator." (on Exod. 7:3).

According to Maimonides, God begins to harden Pharaoh's heart here (at Exod. 4:21), as it says, "I will harden his heart, so that he will not let the people go," based on Pharaoh's sin of "dealing shrewdly" at Exod. 1:10. According to Rashi, God does not harden Pharaoh's heart until the sixth plague. However, according to Rashi (as read by Nahmanides), who says that Pharaoh voluntarily hardened his own heart during the first five plagues, the current verse presents a difficulty. Nahmanides offers the resolution that the current verse is a prophecy about what will happen after the first five plagues. Thus Maimonides' reading is smoother on the current verse. However, the merit to Rashi's reading is that God did not harden Pharaoh's heart until the sixth plague. Furthermore, it appears that Nahmanides understands Rashi as saying the opposite of Maimonides: God hardened Pharaoh's heart so that he would be strong enough to withstand the plagues so that God could "multiply My signs and wonders in the land of Egypt" (Exod. 7:3), which is also the opinion of Saadiah, Ibn Ezra (short commentary; cf. long commentary), Sforno and Shadal. Thus Maimonides appears to be a minority opinion in arguing that God hardening Pharaoh's heart is a punishment to remove Pharaoh's ability to repent (see also Rabbi Netanel Wiederblank, *Illuminating Jewish Thought*, vol. 2, Unit 5, passim).

4:24. On the way, at a place where they spent the night, the LORD met him and tried to kill him. — Come and see how strict is the obligation of circumcision, since our teacher Moses was not granted a temporary reprieve even though they were travelling (*Milah* 3:9; based on Rabbi Joshua b. Korḥah in *Nedarim* 3:10).

4:25. ... and she cast it at his feet. — [Maimonides understands the word *naga* as having both literal and metaphorical meanings. He uses the word *va-tigga*, "and she cast," as a literal usage of the root *naga*; see *Guide* 1:18, quoted in part at Exod. 14:10 and Exod. 24:1-2.]

4:31. And the people believed and heard that God had remembered the children of Israel for He had seen their affliction... — For Maimonides' understanding of the phrase "God heard," see at Exod. 22:21-23.

... and they bowed down and prostrated [*va-yikdu va-yishtaḥavu*]. — [Maimonides does not quote this verse, but he draws a distinction between *kidah*, "bowing down," and *hishtaḥavayah*, "prostration":] What is meant by *hishtaḥavayah* [prostration]? ... [He] sits on the ground and falls on his face towards the ground and he entreats with all sorts of supplications that he desires. "Kneeling" [*keri'ah*] wherever it is mentioned means [falling on one's] knees. *Kidah* means [falling on one's] face. *Hishtaḥavayah* [prostration] is extending his arms and legs until he is flat with his face on the ground (*Tefillah* 5:13; based on *Megillah* 22b; see *Tur, Oraḥ Ḥayyim* 131).

Exodus 5

5:2. And Pharaoh said, "Who is the LORD, that I should listen to His voice and let Israel go? I do not know the LORD, and I will not let Israel go." — See at Exod. 9:27.

5:4. And the king of Egypt said to them, "Why do you, Moses and Aaron, take the people away [*tafri'u*] from their works? Return to your work. — Maimonides does not quote this verse, but see his comments quoted at Exod. 32:25 on the meaning of *para* (פר"ע).

5:12. So the people scattered throughout the land of Egypt, to gather stubble for straw. — This verse ends with the words *le-koshesh kash la-teven* ("the gather stubble for straw"), which Onkelos translates as *le-gavava gillei le-tivna*. The Mishnah uses the phrase *ve-ha-megabbev be-yavash*, "and one who collects dry herbs" (*Shevi'it* 9:6),[17] where *megabbev* is the same root as *le-gavava*. Maimonides writes that in this Mishnah, *megabbev* means "gather" (*PhM Shevi'it* 9:6). The Kapach translation uses the word *osef* (אס"ף), which means "gather." Hence the Hebrew *le-koshesh* corresponds to Targumic Aramaic/Mishnaic Hebrew in the root *g-b-b*, which in turn corresponds to *osif*.[18]

---

17. Jastrow suggests that *megabbev* is used for collecting dry plants, while *melakket* is used for green plants (p. 203).
18. Elsewhere in his *Commentary*, Maimonides says *gevavah* is straw mixed with manure (*PhM Kelim* 17:1), or just manure (*PhM Shabbat* 3:1).

PARASHAT VA'ERA

Exodus 6

6:3. I appeared to Abraham, Isaac, and Jacob as God Almighty [*El Shaddai*]... — "Shaddai" ... is derived from *dai*, "enough," e.g., "for the stuff they had was sufficient [*dayyam*]" (Exod. 36:7) [and] the *shin* is equal to *asher*, "which," as in *she-kevar*, "which already" (Eccl. 2:16). The name "Shaddai" therefore signifies "He who is sufficient," that is to say, He does not require any other being for effecting the existence of what He created, or its conservation. His existence is sufficient for that (*Guide* 1:63).

> Compare the statement of the Midrash about the sacred name *Shaddai*: "R. Nathan said in R. Aha's name: I am El Shaddai. It is I was said to My world *dai* [enough]! And had I not said *dai!* to My world, the heaven would still be spreading and the earth would have gone on expanding to this very day" (*Genesis Rabbah* 46:3).

... but by my name "The LORD" I did not make myself known to them. — Tetragrammaton, the *Shem ha-meforash* (the *nomen proprium* of God)... is not an appellative: it does not denote any attribute of God, nor does it imply anything except His existence. Absolute existence includes the idea of eternity, i.e., the necessity of existence (*Guide* 1:63).

> Isaac Husik explains further, that according to Maimonides, "All the names of God except the tetragrammaton designate his activities in the world. Jhvh alone is the real name of God, which belongs to him alone and is not derived from anything else." (*A History of Mediaeval Jewish Philosophy*, p. 265).

FURTHER: ... That his [Moses'] prophecy was distinguished from that of all his predecessors is proved by the passage, "And I appeared to Abraham... but by My name, the Lord, I was not known unto them" (Exod. 6:3). We thus learn that his prophetic perception was different from that of the Patriarchs, and excelled it; *a fortiori* it must have excelled that of other prophets before Moses (*Guide* 2:35).

6:7. I will take you as My people, and I will be your God. You shall know that I am the Lord your God, who has freed you from the burdens of the Egyptians. — God commanded us to abstain from work on the Sabbath, and to rest, for two purposes; namely, (1) That we might confirm the true theory, that of the Creation, which at once and clearly leads to the theory of the existence of God. (2) That we might remember how kind God has been in freeing us "from the burden of the Egyptians" (cf. Exod 6:7). The Sabbath is therefore a double blessing: it gives us correct notions, and also promotes the well-being of our bodies (*Guide* 2:31; see further at Exod. 20:11).

6:9. Moses told this to the Israelites; but they would not listen [*shame'u*] to Moses, because of their broken spirit and their cruel slavery. — Maimonides says that in this verse, *shame'u*, from the Hebrew שמ"ע, means "obey" (*Guide* 1:45). See further at Exod. 22:21-23.

6:12. But Moses spoke to the LORD, "The Israelites have not listened to me; how then shall Pharaoh listen to me, poor speaker that I am?" — Regarding Moses' reluctance, see Maimonides' comments on Exod. 4:14. On another note, this verse uses the phrase *aral sefatayim*, literally, "uncircumcised lips." However, Maimonides uses it to mean "inarticulate" (see *Tefillah* 1:1, quoted at Exod. 23:15).

6:13. Thus the LORD spoke to Moses and Aaron, and gave them orders regarding the children of Israel and Pharaoh, king of

Egypt, charging them to free the Israelites from the land of Egypt.
— The Oral Tradition relates that God told Moses and Aaron to
accept this mission even though the people would curse them and
stone them (*Hil. Sanhedrin* 25:2; based on *Sifrei*, Beha'alotekha 91).

Maimonides uses this source to teach that all leaders should
be humble and calm. Even though Moses and Aaron knew
they would be cursed and stoned, they accepted their mission
with dignity, and this is the paradigm for all future judges.

Rashi points out that the simple meaning of this verse is
that God instructed Moses and Aaron to speak to Pharaoh
regarding Israel. However the Midrash infers that the brothers
would receive hostile treatment from both Pharaoh as well
as the Israelites, perhaps based on the parallel phrases *el
bnei Yisrael ve-el Par'oh melekh Mitzrayim*, "to the children
of Israel and to Pharaoh, king of Egypt."

**6:18. And the sons of Kohath: Amram, and Izhar, and Hebron,
and Uzziel...** — [Maimonides gives a history of when the
commandments were given:] ... in Egypt, Amram was commanded
with additional commandments, until Moses came and by his hand
the Torah was completed (*Melakhim* 9:1).

The source for this statement is opaque. The *Meshekh
Ḥokhmah* argues it is from the verse "I am the God of your
father, the God of Abraham, the God of Isaac, and the God of
Jacob" (Exod. 3:6). This implication is that just as Abraham,
Isaac, and Jacob had separate new commandments, so too
did Amram, since it says, "God of *your father*" — Amram.

A second answer is from the *Yad Eitan*, quoted in the *Sefer
Likkutim* of the Frankel edition, who writes, "In the *Mekhilta*
(Yitro), it is stated that they were given commandments in
Egypt beyond the Noahide laws. And it makes sense that

these were given through Amram, who was the greatest scholar of his generation."

And what were these commandments? Rabbi Israel Eliezer Rubin analyzed this question, and presents several possibilities[19]:

- First, the *Tzafnat Pa'ane'aḥ* suggests Amram instituted the laws of marriage. Rabbi Rubin rejects this answer, since Isaac and Rebekah had a formal marriage, and Joseph also had a marriage contract.

- Second, he quotes from the *Yad Eitan* that Amram learned the law of remarrying one's ex-wife, since Amram re-married Jochebed; this too Rabbi Rubin rejects, since Abraham married Keturah, whom the Sages identify as Hagar.

- Third, according to the *Torat ha-Melekh*, Amram learned the prohibition of abortion, which is why the midwives refused Pharaoh's decree (Exod. 1:16). Rabbi Rubin rejects this opinion, since the verse clearly refers to killing the babies after they were born.

Having exhausted these possibilities, Rabbi Rubin argues that Amram was given the commandment of procreation, and he marshals the opinion of Tosafot that non-Jews (and similarly Jews before Sinai) do not have the commandment to procreate (*Sanhedrin* 59b, *s.v. ve-ha*).

19. *Amram Nitztavveh be-Mitzvot Yeteirot* (http://www.haoros.com/Archive/index.asp?kovetz=912&cat=8&haoro=2)

Exodus 7

7:3. But I will harden Pharaoh's heart, and I will multiply My signs and wonders in the land of Egypt. — See at Exod. 4:21.

7:12. Each one threw down his staff, and they became snakes; but Aaron's staff swallowed up theirs. — … they tried to counter the miracles of Moses with their magic.[20]

> This line, if it is authentically written by Maimonides, raises the question of whether Maimonides believed that the Egyptian sorcerers actually practiced magic, since Maimonides generally rejects such an idea (as opposed to Nahmanides, who admits the possibility but rules that use of the black arts is forbidden).
>
> A separate observation is the verse Maimonides chose to quote in relation to this verse. Aaron's staff swallowing the sorcerers' staves is indicative that Moses and Aaron would triumph over the Egyptians. Miracles are authentic, magic is illusory, and the genuine will prevail over the counterfeit.

7:21. And the fish in the river died. The river stank so that the Egyptians could not drink its water, and there was blood throughout the whole land of Egypt. — [Maimonides is commenting on the Mishnah which states, "Ten miracles were performed for our ancestors in Egypt and ten at the [Red] Sea" (*Avot* 5:4).] — The ten miracles wrought for our ancestors in Egypt refer to saving them from the ten plagues. For each of the plagues was directed against the Egyptians alone, without affecting the Jews. This is without a doubt a miracle. The Torah explicitly states that every plague affected the Egyptians alone, with the exception of lice, in which instance this

---

20. "The Essay on Resurrection," Halkin & Hartman, p. 229.

was not mentioned explicitly. But it is a well known matter that the Jews were not punished. Instead, there were [lice] among them, but they were not bothered by them. This was explained by our Sages.[21]

Concerning the other plagues, however, [the Torah] explicitly states that they did not affect the Jews. With regard to blood, it is written, "And the Egyptians could not drink water from the river" (Exod. 7:21), implying that the affliction affected them alone. With regard to the frogs it is written, "And they shall enter *your* homes, *your* bedrooms, *your* beds, *your* nation, and *your* servants" (Exod. 7:28-29). With regard to the swarms [of beasts], it is written, "And I will make a sign on that day concerning the Land of Goshen" (Exod. 8:18).

With regard to the cattle plague, it is written, "And the herds of the Israelites, not one died" (Exod. 9:6). With regard to the boils, it is written, "For the boils were upon the wizards and upon all the Egyptians" (Exod. 9:11). And it is written with regard to the hail, "Only in the Land of Goshen, where the Israelites were, there was no hail" (Exod. 9:26). With regard to the locusts, it is written, "They will fill *your* homes, the homes of *your* servants, and the homes of all the Egyptians" (Exod. 10:6). And it is written with regard to the darkness, "And for the Israelites, there was light in their dwellings" (Exod. 10:23) (*PhM Avot* 5:4; Touger trans.).

Maimonides writes that the Israelites were not subject to any of the punishments of the plagues. However a different interpretation, quoted by Rashi, based on the *Mekhilta*, says that four fifths of the Israelites died in the plague of darkness which lasted three days, and only one fifth survived (on Exod. 13:18; the Midrash is punning on the word *ḥamushim*, which literally means "prepared, armed," but shares the same letters as *ḥamesh*, "five"). It seems likely that Maimonides did not accept this *Mekhilta* as literal.

---

21. Kapach and Touger note that this source is not known today.

7:28-29. The river shall swarm with frogs; they shall come up into your palace, into your bedchamber and your bed, and into the houses of your officials and of your people, and into your ovens and your kneading bowls. The frogs shall come up on you and on your people and on all your officials. — See at Exod. 7:21.

Exodus 8

8:10. And they gathered them together in heaps [*ḥomarim ḥomarim*], and the land stank. — Maimonides makes passing reference to this verse at *PhM Uktzin* 2:5-6.

8:18. But on that day I will set apart the land of Goshen, where my people live, so that no swarms of flies shall be there... — Maimonides (quoted at Exod. 7:21) says that none of the plagues affected the Israelites; this is the meaning of "I will set apart the land of Goshen." God set it apart to not be afflicted with plagues. Nahmanides quotes two answers: first he says that the previous plagues were not migratory, so there was no reason to distinguish between Egypt and Goshen. Second, he states that even if a Jew was in Egypt proper (and not Goshen), the plague only affected the Egyptians but left the Jews unharmed. Although Nahmanides on this verse does not quote Maimonides by name, he reached the same conclusion.

... that you may know that I am the Lord in the midst of the earth. — [Maimonides writes that the Sabeans included their religious beliefs in a book on agriculture. He notes that this is not coincidental, but intentional.] They [these inclusions] were intended as criticism and attack on the evident miracles by which all people learned that there exists a God who is judge over all people, e.g., "That you may know that the earth is the LORD's" (Exod. 9:29); "That I am the Lord in the midst of the earth" (Exod. 8:18) (*Guide* 3:29).

> There is a long-standing tension between science and religion. Maimonides' point is well-taken; one would not expect a book on agriculture or science to include theological teachings as well. However, according to Maimonides, the Sabeans did so specifically to undermine knowledge of God's

presence in the world. Once science develops a theory of how a specific process occurs, that allegedly removes the necessity for God in understanding the world. This can lead to a slippery slope of writing God entirely out of the natural world, which is precisely what the Sabeans sought to do.

8:22. And Moses said, "It is not right to do so; for we shall sacrifice the abomination of the Egyptians to the LORD our God: see, shall we sacrifice the abomination of the Egyptians before their eyes, and will they not stone us? — Scripture tells us, according to the version of Onkelos, that the Egyptians worshipped Aries, and therefore abstained from killing sheep, and held shepherds in contempt, e.g., "Behold we shall sacrifice the abomination of the Egyptians" (Exod. 8:22); "For every shepherd is an abomination to the Egyptians" (Gen. 46:34). Some sects among the Sabeans worshipped demons, and imagined that these assumed the form of goats, and called them therefore "goats" [se'irim]. This worship was widespread, e.g., "And they shall no more offer their sacrifices unto demons, after whom they have gone whoring..." (Lev. 17:7). For this reason those sects abstained from eating goats' flesh. Most idolaters objected to killing cattle, holding this species of animals in great estimation. Therefore the people of Hodu [India] up to this day do not slaughter cattle even in those countries where other animals are slaughtered.

In order to eradicate these false principles, the Law commands us to offer sacrifices only of these three kinds: "You shall bring your offering of the cattle—of the herd and of the flock" (Lev. 1:2). Thus the very act which is considered by the heathen as the greatest crime, is the means of approaching God, and obtaining His pardon for our sins. In this manner, evil principles, the diseases of the human soul, are cured by other principles which are diametrically opposite.

This is also the reason why we were commanded to kill a lamb on Passover, and to sprinkle the blood thereof outside on the gates. We had to free ourselves of evil doctrines and to proclaim the opposite, namely, that the very act which was then considered as being the cause of death would be the cause of deliverance from death, e.g., "And the Lord will pass over the door, and will not let the destroyer to enter your houses to strike you" (Exod. 12:23). Thus they were rewarded for performing openly a service every part of which was objected to by the idolaters (*Guide* 3:46; see also *Me'ilah* 8:8 and *Guide* 3:32).

> Onkelos does not explicitly state that the *to'evah*-animal refers to a sheep, something Maimonides imputes to him. The word *be'ira* is a generic word meaning "livestock" or "cattle." However, Maimonides likely observed that this is one of only two verses where Onkelos translates *to'evah* as *be'ira*. Furthermore, in both cases, the *to'evah* being referred to is in the context of Egypt: "You shall say, 'Your servants have been keepers of livestock from our youth even until now, both we and our ancestors'—in order that you may settle in the land of Goshen, because all shepherds are abhorrent to the Egyptians" (Gen. 46:34); and "And Moses said, It is not right so to do; for we shall sacrifice the abomination of the Egyptians to the LORD our God: see, shall we sacrifice the abomination of the Egyptians before their eyes, and will they not stone us?" (Exod. 8:22).
>
> Many sources, but not all, quote that the Egyptians worshipped sheep. This tradition is quoted by Rashi, as well as Ibn Ezra (long commentary), as opposed to Rashbam, who says the Egyptians considered it a filthy creature.

Exodus 9

9:3. The hand of the LORD will strike with a deadly pestilence your livestock in the field: the horses, the donkeys, the camels, the herds, and the flocks. — [Maimonides addresses the phrase "hand of the Lord" and similar anthropomorphism.] ... what is the meaning of what it says in the Torah: "below His feet" (Exod. 24:10), "written by the finger of God" (Exod. 31:18), "God's hand" (Exod. 9:3), "God's eyes" (Gen. 38:7, Deut. 11:12), "God's ears" (Num. 11:1), and expressions similar to these? All of these are according to man's ability to comprehend, since he can only understand by using [images] of material beings, and the Torah speaks in a human language (e.g. *Berakhot* 31b),[22] and they are metaphorical, as in "I will whet my lightning sword" (Deut. 32:41). Does He have a sword, and does He kill with a sword? This is just an allegory! A proof to this is when one prophet says that he saw the Holy One, blessed is He, "his vesture was white as snow" (Dan. 7:9), and another saw Him "[coming] in dyed garments from Bozrah" (Isa. 63:1). Moses himself, our teacher, saw Him at the [Red] Sea like a warrior waging battle, and at Sinai like a prayer-leader shrouded [in a prayer shawl]. This is to say that He has no likeness or form; rather it is just prophetic vision and images. And man cannot understand or grasp the depth of this truth. And this is what Scripture, "Can you by searching, find God? Can you find the limits of the Almighty?" (Job 11:7) (*Yesodei ha-Torah* 1:9; see also *Guide* 1:26 and 1:46).

Here it is worth noting other explanations why the Torah describes God in human terms:

---

22. Touger's translation notes that the original meaning of *dibrah Torah ki-lshon bnei Adam* referred to doubled words, and was not originally used as a justification for corporeal imagery in the Bible.

- **Philo of Alexandria:** "... a severe master is a beneficial thing for untractable and foolish servants; for they, fearing his inflictions and his threats, are chastened by fear, in spite of themselves" (*Unchangeable* 64),

- **Judah Halevi:** Do not reject the literal meaning of such verses as "And he [Moses] beheld the likeness of God" (Num. 12:8), "They saw the God of Israel" (Exod. 24:10).... because in the opinion of some interpreters the reverence of God is implanted in the human mind, as it is written, "that His reverence be upon you" (Exod. 20:17) (*Kuzari* 4:3).

- **Joseph Albo:** "The purpose of the prophets is to lead all mankind to worship God and to love Him. But the masses of the people cannot be made to humble themselves for service except from fear of punishment. Therefore it was necessary for the prophets to speak in a language understood by the generality of the people.... The other expressions of corporeal affections must be understood in the same way, as a mode of bringing to the human understanding the nature of the act which emanates from Him [*nimshakh mimmennu*], in a manner consonant with human habits of perception.... as a human person writes with a finger, finger is attributed to God; as strength in man comes from the right hand, right hand is ascribed to Him; as human acts are done with hands and fingers, hands and fingers are attributed to God; and as the acceptation of words in man is attributed to the hearing of ears, the Bible says, 'Let your ears be attentive.... They are used in order to bring the matter before human understanding, but not to indicate that it is so in reality" (see *Ikkarim* 2:14).

9:6. And on the next day the Lᴏʀᴅ did so; all the livestock of the Egyptians died, but of the livestock of the Israelites not one died. — See Exod. 7:21.

9:11. The magicians could not stand before Moses because of the boils, for the boils afflicted the magicians as well as all the Egyptians. — See Exod. 7:21.

9:13. And the Lord said to Moses, "Arise early in the morning and stand before Pharaoh and you shall say to him, 'So says the Lord God of the Hebrews: Let My people go that they may serve Me.'" — See on v. 30.

9:16. And in very deed for this cause have I raised you up, for to show in you My power; and that My name may be declared throughout all the earth. — Now, when God willed to give Israel the Torah, and to promulgate His commandments and prohibitions in the entire world through the chief of his prophets [Moses]—as it is written, "that My fame may resound throughout the world"—He produced the miracles that are recorded in the Torah, to authenticate with them the messages of the prophets and the creation of the world (*Essay on Resurrection*. p. 229; see also at Exod. 4:21).

9:23. Then Moses stretched out his staff towards heaven, and the Lord sent thunder and hail, and fire went along upon the ground [*va-tihalakh esh artzah*]. And the Lord rained hail on the land of Egypt. — [Maimonides gives three definitions of the verb *holekh*, "go," and says the current usage corresponds to the second definition:]

• The term *halakh* is likewise one of the words which denote movements performed by living beings, as in "And Jacob went on his way" (Gen. 32:1), and in many other instances.

- The verb "to go" was next employed in describing movements of objects less solid than the bodies of living beings, e.g., "And the waters were going on [*halokh*] decreasing" (Gen. 8:5); "And the fire went along upon the ground."
- Then it is employed to express the spreading and manifestation of something incorporeal, e.g., "The voice thereof shall go like a serpent" (Jer. 46:22) (*Guide* 1:24)

9:24. So there was hail, and fire mingled with the hail, very grievous, such as there was none like it in all the land of Egypt since it became a nation. — See Exod. 10:14.

9:26. Only in the land of Goshen, where the Israelites were, there was no hail. — See Exod. 7:21.

9:27. Then Pharaoh summoned Moses and Aaron, and said to them, 'This time I have sinned; the LORD is in the righteous, and I and my people are in the wrong. — [Maimonides is commenting on the following Mishnah: A Galilean heretic said, "I take issue with you, you Pharisees, for in a bill of divorce you write the name of the ruling king alongside the name of Moses." The Pharisees responded, "We take issue with you, you Galilean heretic, for you write the name of the ruler alongside the Name [of God] on the same page, and furthermore you write the name of the ruler above [i.e., first] and the Name below, as it says, 'And Pharaoh said, "Who is the LORD, that I should listen to His voice and let Israel go?"' (Exod. 5:2)." However after he was stricken, what did he say? "... the Lord is righteous, and I and my people are in the wrong" (*Yadayim* 5:8).] The heretic says, "You are disgracing the name of Moses our teacher when you write his name on your contracts alongside the name of the regnant." That is to say that we write the dates of contracts [by referring] to a certain king, and we write the document in accordance with the religion of Moses and Israel. The Sages responded to them, "This is not a disgrace to [Moses'] name, peace be upon him, and this is not a sign of respect to the king, since we write the name of God beside Pharaoh in the Torah. Moreover, we write the name of Pharaoh first, as the verse says, 'And Pharaoh said, "Who is the LORD [that I should listen to His voice and let Israel go?]"' (Exod. 5:2)." And once this verse was mentioned, it did not seem proper to end any of the tractates with heresy against God, but [they wanted to end it] with faithfulness, therefore it says, "However after he was stricken, what did he say? '… the LORD is righteous, and I and my people are in the wrong'" (*PhM Yadayim* 5:8).

9:29. Moses said to him, 'As soon as I have gone out of the city, I will stretch out my hands to the LORD; the thunder will cease, and there will be no more hail, so that you may know that the earth is the LORD's. — See on Exod. 8:18.

… the earth is the LORD's. — [This phrase means:] His providence extends to the earth in accordance with its nature, in the same manner as it controls the heavens in accordance with their nature (*Guide* 3:54).

9:30. But as for you and your servants, I know that you will not yet fear the Lord your God. — See on Exod. 4:21 and Exod. 9:13.

PARASHAT BO

Exodus 10-11

10:1. Then the LORD said to Moses: Enter [*bo*] to Pharaoh... —
Maimonides does not quote the present verse, but at *Guide* 1:22 he
discusses the multiple meanings of *bo*, which he says can mean both
"come" or "enter." Onkelos on the present verse translates *bo* as *ul*,
"enter." See further at Exod. 19:9.

**... for I have hardened his heart and the heart of his officials, in
order that I may show these signs of Mine among them...."** — For
the idea of loss of free will, see Exod. 4:21.

**10:2. And so that you may tell in the ears of your children, and of
your children's children, how I have dealt severely with Egypt,
and My signs which I have done among them; that you may
know that I am the LORD.** — You know how much the Law insists
that we shall always remember the plagues that have befallen the
Egyptians, e.g., "... that you will remember the day that you came
forth from Egypt all the days of your life" (Deut. 16:3), "And that
you may tell in the ears of your sons and your son's sons, what things
I have wrought in Egypt..." (Exod. 10:2). Such a law was necessary
in order to perpetuate the memory of the departure from Egypt;
because such events verify prophecy and the doctrine of reward
and punishment. The benefit of every commandment that serves to
keep certain miracles in remembrance, or to perpetuate true faith, is
therefore obvious (*Guide* 3:39).

**10:6. They shall fill your houses, and the houses of all your
officials and of all the Egyptians—something that neither your
parents nor your grandparents have seen, from the day they
came on earth to this day." Then he turned and went out from
Pharaoh.** — See Exod. 7:21.

10:13. ... and the Lord brought an east wind [*ruaḥ*]... —
Maimonides uses this as an example where the word *ruaḥ* means
"wind." Other definitions are "air," "breath," "that which remains after
death," "divine inspiration," and "intention, will" (see *Guide* 1:40).

**10:14. The locusts came upon all the land of Egypt and settled
on the whole country of Egypt, such a dense swarm of locusts as
had never been before, nor ever shall be again... —** "... upon all the
land of Egypt" — and not Israel. See Maimonides' comments quoted
at Exod. 7:21.

**... such a dense swarm of locusts as had never been before, nor
ever shall be again. —** ... miracles may occur in the realm of the
naturally impossible—like the change of the rod into a serpent
(Exod. 4:3), or the sinking of the earth in the story of the followers of
Korah (Numbers 16), or the splitting of the Red Sea (Exodus 15)—
and they may occur in the realm of the naturally possible—like the
onset of the locust, hail, and the pestilence in Egypt. It is the way of
these latter happenings to occur at certain times and certain places....
However, these possible occurrences become miracles by one of
three conditions or by all of them:

- One: that the possible incident comes when the prophet says it
  will....
- Two: that that possible happening is singular and exceptional
  beyond anything imaginable of its kind. The locust is described,
  "such a dense swarm of locusts as had never been before, nor
  ever shall be again" (Exod. 10:14). Of the hail it is written:
  "Such as had not fallen on the entire land of Egypt since it had
  become a nation" (Exod. 9:24). Of the pestilence it is stated,
  "But of the livestock of the Israelites not a beast died" (Exod.
  9:6). The particularity of that possible happening, whether

in a class referred to, or some specific place, or some species mentally conceived, is the singularity and the exclusiveness of that possible event.

- Three: the duration and the persistence of that possible event [longer than would be possibly naturally], like the blessings and maledictions [of Leviticus 26 and Deuteronomy 28] (*Ma'amar Teḥiat ha-Meitim*).

10:19. And the Lord turned a mighty strong west wind, and it took away the locusts, and cast them into the Red Sea; there remained not one locust in all the coasts of Egypt. — [Maimonides is addressing the phrase "And the Lord turned a mighty strong west wind":] the motion of air is, as a rule, ascribed to God (*Guide* 2:30).

10:23. People could not see one another, and for three days they could not move from where they were; but all the Israelites had light where they lived. — See Exod. 7:21.

11:8. And all of these slaves of yours will come down to me and will bow down to me, saying, "Leave, you, and this entire nation that is at your feet." ... — Maimonides uses this as an example of where the word *regel* means a literal foot, and not some other abstraction (*Guide* 1:28).

Exodus 12

12:2. This month shall be for you the beginning of months: it shall be the first month of the year to you. — ... God, may He be exalted, commanded us to sanctify months and to calculate years.[23] This is the commandment of sanctifying the moon. The source of this commandment is what God, may He be exalted, said, "This month shall be for you the beginning of months...." In explaining this commandment, the Sages said, "this testimony should be given to you [Hebrew, *lakhem*, 'to you,' plural, meaning Moses and Aaron]." This means that this commandment is not given to each and every individual like the Sabbath, where each individual counts six days and rests on the seventh. Otherwise, each individual seeing the new moon would observe a new month, or would employ a biblically-sanctioned method of intercalation to mark the new month, or he would notice that the spring is not falling when it should and would add a leap month. Rather, this commandment was given specifically to the high court, and only in the land of Israel.[24]

[It also says:] "And you shall keep this statute day to day [*mi-yamim yamimah*]" (Exod. 13:10). The Sages said, "This teaches that one may only intercalate the year close to the holiday [of Passover]." And they said, "How do we know that we may only intercalate the year during the day and one may only sanctify the new moon during the day? From the verse 'day to day [*mi-yamim yamimah*]'" (*Mekhilta de-Rashbi*).

God, may He be exalted, also said, "for months of the years [*le-hodshei ha-shanah*]" (Exod. 12:2). Regarding this verse, the Sages said, "You shall calculate [the years] in terms of months, but you shall not calculate in terms of days" (*Megillah* 5a), which teaches that

---

23. Nahmanides, in his gloss on the *Sefer ha-Mitzvot*, quotes opinions that "sanctifying the months" and "calculating the years" are two separate commandments.

24. Rashi on Gen. 1:1 says that this was a communal commandment.

the addition can only be in terms of a full month. And it is said, "a month of days [*ḥodesh yamim*]" (Num. 11:21). Regarding this verse, the Sages said, "You shall calculate months on the basis of days, and you shall not calculate on the basis of hours" (*Megillah* 5a). And it is stated, "You shall observe the month of the spring" (Deut. 16:1), which teaches that we must observe the seasons in calculating the years, which means they shall be solar years (*ShM*, Pos. 153; see also *Kiddush ha-Ḥodesh* 5:1).

FURTHER: The months of the year are solar months, as it says, "the burnt offering of the month when throughout the months [of the year]" (Num. 28:14), and "This month shall be for you the beginning of months" (Exod. 12:2), about which the Sages said, "The Holy One, Blessed is He, showed Moses in a vision of prophecy an image of the moon and to him 'like this' — see and sanctify [it]." And the years are calculated as solar years, as it says, "You shall observe the month of the spring" (Deut. 16:1) (*Kiddush ha-Ḥodesh* 1:1).

> Hebrew *ka-zeh*, "this," corresponding to *ha-ḥodesh ha-zeh*, "this month," where the word "this" is interpreted to mean God showed Moses a sign and pointed to this image (*Mekhilta*); see *Gur Aryeh* on Rashi to the present verse. Similarly, the phrase *ba-avur zeh* (Exod. 13:8), which is understood by the *Mekhilta* to mean that one can only fulfill the commandment of *ve-higgadta le-vinkha* when (this) matzah and *maror* are on the table. In modern philosophy, this is called "ostensive definition," or definition by pointing. The speaker defines something by pointing to an example, in this case the example of an image related to a calendar.

12:3. Speak ye unto all the congregation of Israel, saying: In the tenth day of this month they shall take to them every man a lamb,

according to the house of their fathers, a lamb for a house. — The reason of the particular laws concerning the Passover lamb is clear. It was eaten roasted by fire (Exod. 12:8-9), in one house, and without breaking the bones thereof (Exod. 12:46). In the same way as the Israelites were commanded to eat unleavened bread, because they could prepare it hastily, so they were commanded, for the sake of haste, to roast the lamb (Exod. 12:9), because there was not sufficient time to boil it, or to prepare other food; even the delay caused by breaking the bones and to extract their marrow was prohibited: the one principle is laid down for all these rules, "You shall eat it in haste" (Exod. 12:11). But when haste is necessary the bones cannot be broken, nor parts of it sent from house to house; for the company could not wait with their meal till he returned. Such things would lead to laxity and delay, while the object of these rules was to make a show of the hurry and haste, in order that none should be too late to leave Egypt with the main body of the people, and be thus exposed to the attacks and the evil [designs of the enemy]. These temporary commandments were then made permanent, in order that we may remember what was done in those days: "And you shall keep this ordinance in his season from year to year" (Exod. 13:10). Each Passover lamb was only eaten by those who had previously agreed to consume it together, in order that people should be anxious to procure it, and should not rely on friends, relations, or on chance, without themselves taking any trouble about it before Passover (*Guide* 3:46).

Maimonides asks why the Passover offering must be roasted, and he answers that this was for the sake of making haste in leaving Egypt (*Guide* 3:46). Rashbam, who predated Maimonides, uses this rationale to explain why the animal must be cooked whole—*derekh mehirut*, "for the sake of quickness." Alternatively, Hizkuni explains the reason in order that the Egyptians would be able to see that their deity was being eaten by the Jews. However, Maimonides, earlier in the chapter in the *Guide*, suggests the reason for the Passover offering was to slaughter the Egyptian deity (quoted at Exod. 8:22). Thus Maimonides has a spiritual rationale (à la Hizkuni) and a practical answer (à la Rashbam). Perhaps Maimonides intended that the sheep was chosen because it was the Egyptian deity, but the obligation to roast it whole is based on a practical concern.

... a lamb [*seh*]... — [the word] *seh* means a sheep or a goat that is alive (*Bikkurim* 12:8).[25]

While this may seem like a minor statement, Maimonides is presenting two requirements of the Passover offering. First, since *seh* means an animal that is alive at the time of designation (a point made in the Talmud, *Yoma* 49b); the Passover cohort must be established before the animal is sacrificed (see next verse). Second, *seh* includes a sheep (*keves*) or goat (*eiz*), so no other animals can be used as a Passover offering. See also Maimonides' introduction to *Seder Kodshim*. His source is the following Midrash: Included in the word *seh* is *gedi* (young goat) and *teleh* (young lamb), as it says, "the sheep [*seih khevasim*] and goat [*seih izzim*]" (Deut. 14:4) (*Mekhilta de-Pisḥa* 4, quoted by Rashi at Exod. 12:5). Furthermore, the word seh contrasts with other types of animals. For example, Lev. 22:28 uses *seh* in contrast to "cow." Exod. 22:9 reads, "a donkey, or an ox, or a *seh*, or any beast of the field," suggesting that *seh* does not mean donkey or ox (also Judg. 6:4).

However, the *Lehem Mishnah* argues that in general the word *seh* can apply even to an animal that has been slaughtered, and it is only because of a *gezeirah shavah* that

---

25. Tosafot say that as a practical matter, most Passover offerings were lambs (*Pesaḥim* 3b, s.v. *me-eliah*).

in this case *seh* must refer to an animal that is alive (*Avodat Yom ha-Kippurim* 5:13, s.v. *nikhnas*; see there).

12:4. And if the household be too small for a lamb, then he and his neighbor next to his house shall take one according to the number of souls; every man according to his [ability to] eat shall be counted for the lamb. — The Passover offering should only be slaughtered for those who are designated for it, as it says, "shall be counted for the lamb" (Exod. 12:4), which teaches that they were designated for it while it [the offering] was still alive (*Pesaḥim* 61a, 89a). Those who are designated for a Passover offering are called "members of the group...." If an individual who slaughters a Passover offering only for himself, it is valid, as long as he capable of eating the whole thing.[26] However, we try, ideally,[27] to not have him slaughter for one individual, as it says, "*they* shall do it" (Exod. 12:47; Num. 9:12). The Passover offering is only slaughtered for those who are fit to eat. If one of the members of the group is young or elderly or infirm—if that person is able to eat an olive's measure, he may be considered among the people for whom the Passover offering is slaughtered. If not, he cannot be considered part of the group, as it says, "every man according to his [ability to] eat [*le-fi okhlo*]" (Exod. 12:4), which means he must be able to partake [of it]. Even if the group has a hundred members, but not one of them can eat an olive's measure, we may not slaughter for them (*Korban Pesaḥ* 2:1-3; see similarly *PhM Pesaḥim* 5:3; see also *Pesaḥim* 8:7 (91a)).

Rashi on this verse writes: "'And if the household will be too little for the lamb' — If they will be too few for a single lamb,

---

26. In the Mishnah, R. Yehudah does not permit a Passover offering to be brought on the behalf of one individual, but R. Yosi permits it (*Pesaḥim* 8:7; see also *Pesaḥim* 91a). In *PhM*, Maimonides says that the law follows R. Yosi, while in the *Mishneh Torah* he takes a more cautious attitude.
27. The *Kesef Mishnah* asks about this circuitous formulation: ומשתדלין שלא ישחט לכתחלה, "we try... ideally," especially because one should be able to follow R. Yosi's opinion even *ab initio*; see there.

so that they would not be able to eat all of it and it come to be left over, then 'he and his neighbor' [eat them together]. This is the plain meaning. However, there is also a midrash on [the verse]—to teach that after people have been designated for it, they are able to reduce their size, and to withdraw from it, and be appointed to another lamb [instead]. However, if they came to withdraw from it and reduce their size, they should do so while it is still a *seh*, i.e., when the lamb is still alive, but not after it has been slaughtered." Thus Rashi gives the simple meaning (*peshat*) of the verse, as well as a legal principle (halakhic midrash). Maimonides, however, only quotes the halakhic midrash on this verse.

12:5-6. Your lamb shall be without blemish, a male of the first year: you shall take it out from the sheep, or from the goats. And it shall be unto you a charge until the fourteenth day of the same month: and the whole assembly of the congregation of Israel shall slaughter it in the afternoon. — We are commanded to slaughter the Passover offering on the fourteenth day of Nisan, as God, may He be exalted, said, "and the whole assembly of the congregation of Israel shall slaughter it in the afternoon." And one who violates this commandment and intentionally does not offer it in its proper time is worthy of *karet* (*ShM*, Pos. 55).

FURTHER: It is a positive commandment the slaughter the Passover offering on the fourteenth of the month of Nisan after noon.[28] And we may only slaughter from lambs and goats alone,[29] which are

---

28. Rashi writes, "from six hours [after sunrise = halakhic noon] and onward is called *bein ha-arbayim*" (Exod. 12:6). Both Maimonides and Rashi are based on *Mekhilta de-Pisha* 5.
29. See Ibn Ezra on Exod. 12:5 (long commentary), who quotes an opinion that only the first Passover required sheep and goats, but later observances of Passover could be fulfilled even with bullocks. However, Ibn Ezra roundly rejects that opinion, and it is not accepted as normative practice.

male of one year. And both men and women are obligated in this commandment (*Korban Pesaḥ* 1:1).

FURTHER: We have a general principle that a person's agent is like himself (e.g. *Berakhot* 5:5). And we learn this from what it says, "and the whole assembly of the congregation of Israel shall slaughter it," which means that it is permissible for one person to slaughter all of the Passover offerings, because he is the agent of the congregation (*PhM Kiddushin* 2:1; Rashi quotes this teaching at the present verse. The Talmud entertains several possible scriptural sources for this principle; see *Kiddushin* 41a).

FURTHER: The Passover offering is slaughtered in three groups, as it says, "and the whole assembly of the congregation of Israel shall slaughter it." [Three distinct terms are used:] *kahal* [assembly], *edah* [congregation], and Israel (*Korban Pesaḥ* 1:9: Based on m. *Pesaḥim* 5:5; Rashi quotes this teaching on the present verse).

12:7. And they shall take of the blood, and strike it on the two side posts [*mezuzot*] and on the upper door post [*ha-mashkof*] of the houses, wherein they shall eat it. — The *shakof* is the highest part of the doorframe, which the Scripture calls *mashkof* (*PhM Oholot* 9:10; see also *PhM Oholot* 10:7).

Maimonides appears to take the same interpretation as Rashi, who writes, "This is the highest part [of the doorframe], which the door strikes against when it is closed; a *lintel* in Old French."

According to Maimonides, the commandment to affix parchment to the doorposts is derived from the verse, "And you shall inscribe them on your doorposts of your house, and on your gates" (Deut. 6:9, 11:20; *ShM*, Pos. 15). I.e., the commandment to hang a *mezuzah* does not originate with the present verse.

Elsewhere he adds, "An individual is obligated to be exceedingly cautious concerning the *mezuzah*, because it is an obligation on everyone at all times. And whenever he enters and departs he will encounter the unity of the name of the Holy One, blessed is He, and he will remember his love, and he will be aroused from his slumber and his fixation about the vanities of the age, and he will know that there is nothing that endures forever and all eternity but for the eternal Rock, and immediately he will return to his senses [*le-da'ato*] and walk in the ways of the righteous. And the Sages said that whoever has *tefillin* on his head and his arm, and *tzitzit* on his garment and a *mezuzah* on his doorway, it is assured to him that he will not come to sin, because there are many reminders, which are the angels that save him from sinning, as it says, "The angel of God camps around those who fear Him, and protects them" (Ps. 34:8; *Mezuzah* 6:13).

12:8. And they shall eat the flesh on that night, roasted with fire, and unleavened bread; and with bitter herbs they shall eat it. — It is a positive commandment that we are commanded to eat the lamb of the Passover offering on the night of the fifteenth, with its other conditions that are mentioned—that it be roasted,[30] that it be eaten in one house[hold], and that it be eaten with unleavened bread and bitter herbs, as God, may He be exalted, said, "And they shall eat the flesh on that night, roasted with fire, and unleavened bread; and with bitter herbs they shall eat it."

And perhaps a difficulty will arise and we will ask why eating the Passover offering, the bitter herbs, and the unleavened bread should be counted as one commandment, and not as three separate commandments—eating the Passover offering, eating the bitter

---

30. See Hizkuni on the present verse, who writes that it must be roasted in order that "its smell will waft in the noses of the Egyptians, and they will know that you are eating their deity." This will relate to Exod. 12:12 (see there).

herbs, and eating the unleavened bread. I should answer him that indeed eating the unleavened bread is a commandment in its own right, as we will explain (see *ShM*, Pos. 158, based on Exod. 12:18).

Likewise, it is true that eating the Passover offering is a commandment in its own right. However, [eating] the bitter herbs is secondary to the commandment of the Passover offering, and is not counted as a [biblical] commandment in its own right. And the proof of this matter is that we eat the meat of the Passover offering regardless of whether we have bitter herbs, but bitter herbs may only be eaten with the Passover offering, to fulfill what He, may He be exalted, said, "with bitter herbs they shall eat it." And if he ate the bitter herbs without meat [of the Passover offering], he has not accomplished anything, and we do not say that he has fulfilled [even] one commandment of eating the bitter herbs.

The language of the *Mekhilta* is, "'roast with fire, and unleavened bread; and with bitter herbs'—the verse teaches that the commandment of the Passover offering is roasted [meat] with unleavened bread and bitter herbs," which means that the commandment is the inclusion of all of them. And there it says, "From where do you know that if someone lacks unleavened bread and bitter herbs, he has still fulfilled the obligation to eat the Passover offering? As it says, *yokhluhu* [he shall eat *it*]," which means the meat [even] alone.

One might think that just as one who lacks unleavened bread and bitter herbs can fulfill his commandment to eat the Passover offering, so too if he does not have a Passover offering, he may fulfill his commandment of unleavened bread and bitter herbs. One might think that since the Paschal offering is a positive commandment, and the matzah and bitter herbs are positive commandments, once you learn that if he lacks matzah and bitter herbs, he may fulfill his obligation by [just] eating the Passover offering, similarly if he lacks the Passover offering, he may fulfill his obligation by just eating matzah and bitter herbs. Therefore we come to learn—*yokhluhu* ["they shall eat *it*" = the Passover offering].

And there it also states, "'they shall eat it' — from here the Sages said that the Passover offering should be eaten even if one is already sated, but matzah and bitter herbs may not be eaten if one is sated." This is because the primary commandment is to eat the meat, as it says, "and they shall eat the flesh on this night" (Exod. 12:8), and the bitter herbs are secondary to the Passover offering and its obligations, as will be clear from these passages to he who understands them.

And the clear proof of this principle is what the Talmud rules, "Today, [eating] bitter herbs is only a rabbinic obligation" (*Pesaḥim* 120a). This is because from the Torah, there is no separate obligation to eat it; rather it is only eaten with the Passover offering. And this is a clear proof that it is a secondary obligation after the [primary] commandment [of eating the Passover offering], not that eating [the bitter herb] is an independent commandment (*ShM*, Pos. 56; similarly at *Korban Pesaḥ* 8:1-2; see also *PhM Pesaḥim* 2:6 and Nahmanides on the present verse).

FURTHER: If he ate an olive's measure [of the Passover offering] while it was still day, he transgressed a positive commandment, as it says, "And they shall eat the flesh on that night"—at night and not during the day (*Korban Pesaḥ* 8:5, based on *Pesaḥim* 41b. See also Nahmanides, *Shikhḥat he-Asin* 12).

FURTHER: [From the Haggadah:] This bitter herb that we eat—what is its reason (cf. Exod. 12:8)? Because the Egyptians embittered the lives of our forefathers in Egypt, as it says, "And they made their lives bitter with hard bondage, in mortar, and in brick, and in all manner of labor in the field: all their service, wherein they made them serve, was with rigor" (Exod. 1:14) (*Nusaḥ ha-Haggadah*; quoted also at Exod. 1:14; See also *Ḥametz u-Matzah* 7:5, based on m. *Pesaḥim* 10:5).

This is the standard rabbinic interpretation for why Jews eat bitter herbs on the night of Passover. However, Maimonides does not appear to quote this reason in any of his writings except in his transcription of the Haggadah. While it is not clear if Maimonides had any reason for omitting the standard reason given in the Mishnah, it is worth pointing out that other commentaries gave alternate explanations for this commandment. Ibn Ezra writes that since Egypt was always humid, natives had the practice of dipping their food in bitter herbs as a remedy (long and short commentaries). Hizkuni writes that the Passover offering was a symbolic slaying of the Egyptian deity, and eating the lamb with bitter herbs was a way to show contempt for the Egyptian belief system (also at Exod. 12:10, s.v. *ba-eish*).

FURTHER: Passover teaches us to remember the miracles which God wrought in Egypt, and to perpetuate their memory; the Feast of Tabernacles reminds us of the miracles God wrought in the wilderness. The moral lessons derived from these feasts is this: man ought to remember his evil days in his days of prosperity. He will thereby be induced to thank God repeatedly, to lead a modest and humble life. We eat, therefore, unleavened bread and bitter herbs on Passover in memory of what happened unto us (*Guide* 3:43).

12:9. Do not eat it raw [*na*]... — "Raw" [*na*], which the Torah warns about refers to meat which was initially exposed to fire and became slightly roasted, but which was not yet fit for human consumption.[31] However, if he eats of it while it is still raw, he is does not receive lashes, but he did squander the opportunity to perform a

31. Rashi on the present verse writes, "that which is not entirely roasted is called *na* in the Arabic language." Ibn Ezra also points to the relationship between Hebrew and Arabic to understand *na* as "raw" (long and short commentaries). See also *Pesaḥim* 41a, where it is suggested *na* means "half cooked."

positive commandment, as it is written, "roasted with fire" (Exod. 12:9), which means that if it is not roasted in the fire, it is prohibited (*Korban Pesaḥ* 8:6; elsewhere (*PhM Pe'ah* 8:3), Maimonides says the word *ḥai* is a synonym for *na*, and that both mean "raw.")

... nor boiled at all in water... — This prohibition of "cooking," which the Torah prohibited, refers to cooking in water or other liquids, or fruit juice. The phrase *bashel mevushal*[32] is expansive to include any type of cooking [in liquid] (*Korban Pesaḥ* 8:7; see also *PhM Pesaḥim* 2:8).

> Maimonides ruling is based on *Pesaḥim* 41a; so also Rashi on the present verse. Hizkuni points out that *bashel* can indeed refer to "roasting," not just "cooking in water, i.e., boiling" using 2 Chron. 35:13 as a prooftext (see Hizkuni on Exod. 12:11).

Do not eat it raw nor boiled at all in water, but roasted with fire; its head with its legs, and with its entrails. — Regarding the Passover offering it is stated, "Do not eat it *na* nor boiled in water," and we will count this prohibition as one commandment. We will not count "Do not eat it *na*" as one commandment and "Do not eat it cooked [in water]" as a separate commandment, since the verse did not specify each matter as a separate prohibition, and it did not state, "Do not eat of it *na* and not cooked." Rather, this one prohibition comes and include two separate but related activities (*ShM*, Principle 9).

FURTHER: It is a negative commandment that we are warned against eating the Passover offering either cooked [in water] or undercooked. [It can be eaten] only roasted by fire, as He, may He be exalted, said, "Do not eat it raw or boiled at all in water..." (*ShM*, Neg. 125).

---

32. A double language of "cooking."

FURTHER: [Generally, if someone violates a negative prohibition, the default punishment is lashes. However, in some cases, a negative prohibition does not receive lashes, and one of those cases is prohibition of a "general nature" (לאו שבכללות); see *Hilkhot Sanhedrin* 18:1-3:] What is a prohibition of a general nature? This is a prohibition that includes many different matters, like "do not eat blood" (Lev. 19:26). Similarly, if a negative commandment is stated, "Do not do such an action," since it did not specify which action was intended, he does not receive lashes for violating any of them unless the Torah divides them into separate prohibitions or it is stated in the oral tradition that they are so divided. How so? As it states, "Eat not of it *na* or cooked [in water]," so he if he partakes of it *na* or cooked [i.e., part of it is *na* and part of it has been cooked in water], he does not receive two sets of lashes, only one (*Hilkhot Sanhedrin* 18:3; also *PhM Makkot* 3:1; see also *Korban Pesaḥ* 8:4).

... but roasted with fire... — One may not roast the Passover offering on a stone or metal vessel, as it says, "roasted with fire," and not roasted on anything else (*Korban Pesaḥ* 8:9; see also 8:10).

12:10. You shall let nothing of it remain until morning... — It is a negative commandment that we are warned against allowing any amount of the meat of the Passover offering to remain until the next day, that is to say, the fifteenth[33] [of Nisan]. And this is what He said, "You shall let nothing of it remain until morning." And we have already explained that this is a negative commandment. We have already explained (Pos. 91) that this prohibition is a negative commandment connected to a positive commandment, which stated, "and that which remains of it to morning you shall burn with fire." And in the *Mekhilta* [*de-Rashbi*], "the verse, 'and that which remains of it' comes to connect a positive commandment to a negative

---

33. Other versions say the "sixteenth."

commandment." Therefore one who violates this prohibition does not receive lashes (*ShM*, Neg. 117).

FURTHER: It is prohibited to allow any sacral meat to remain after the time that it should be eaten, as it says about the *korban todah*, "you shall not leave any of it over until the morning" (Lev. 22:30), and this law applies to all offerings. And one who leaves it over does not receive lashes, since the verse connected it to a positive commandment, as it says, "that which remains of it to morning you shall burn with fire" (*Pesulei ha-Mukdashin* 18:9; based on *Pesaḥim* 84a and *Ḥullin* 83a).

FURTHER: A person should try to make sure that no meat of the Passover offering remains until morning, as it says, "You shall let nothing of it remain until morning" (Exod. 12:10). And similarly regarding the Second Passover, it says, "You shall leave nothing over until morning" (Num. 9:12). And if he lets it remain, whether during the First or Second Passover, he violates a negative commandment. However he does not receive lashes, since it is a negative commandment connected to a positive commandment, as it says, "and that which remains of it to morning you shall burn with fire" (*Korban Pesaḥ* 10:11).

FURTHER: And He said, "You shall let nothing of it remain until morning" (Exod. 12:10), and this is a prohibition whose violation is not by the commission of an act (*PhM Makkot* 3:3).

> As noted above, the punishment for many negative prohibitions is lashes. However, there are many exceptions to this rule. For example, if a negative act can be corrected by a positive act (*lav ha-nittak le-aseh*), then the person does not receive lashes, but is required to perform that positive

action. Another exception is if a prohibition is violated passively (*lav she-ein bo ma'aseh*), then lashes will not be administered. Maimonides gives two explanations for why someone who violates "You shall let nothing of it remain until morning" does not receive corporal punishment. In his *PhM*, he suggests the reason is that it is a passive prohibition. However, in the *Mishneh Torah*, he twice says the reason is because the negative prohibition can be remedied by a positive act of burning the remains of the Passover offering.

... and that which remains of it to morning you shall burn with fire. — It is prohibited on a festival day to burn holy offerings that require burning on account of impurity or degradation, since God only allowed us [to use fire] for things that are eaten [on the festival day]. And it is stated, "and that which remains of it to morning you shall burn with fire," and [the Sages] stated that this verse comes to teach that this burning should take place on the second morning, which means the day after the festival day it should be incinerated, but not on the festival day itself (*PhM Shabbat* 2:1).

Maimonides' ruling is based on BT *Shabbat* 24b, BT *Pesaḥim* 83b, BT *Temurah* 4b; see also *PhM Pesaḥim* 7:10, where according to that Mishnah, if 16 Nisan falls on the Sabbath, then the burning is delayed until 17 Nisan. In the *Mishneh Torah*, Maimonides derives the same general prohibition against burning offerings on festivals from Lev. 7:19 (see *Shevitat Yom Tov* 3:8).

Rashi on the present verse writes, "What does [the phrase] 'to morning' come to teach? To give one morning to another morning, since 'morning' means from sunrise, and this verse comes to make it earlier—even from dawn. And this is the simple meaning. However, there is another implication: it teaches that [the remains of the Passover offering] are not incinerated on the festival day, but on the day following, and so we derive, 'and that which remains of it to [the first] morning' shall remain and be burned on the second morning." Rashi says the first explanation is the simple meaning (*peshat*), and the second explanation is a derived meaning (*midrash*). Maimonides quotes only the second explanation.

12:11. And thus shall you eat it; with your loins girded, your shoes on your feet, and your staff in your hand; and you shall eat it in haste; it is the LORD's Passover. — Maimonides says this is all so that they could leave Egypt hastily. See *Guide* 3:46, quoted at Exod. 12:3. Rashi also says that *hippazon* is "language of panic and haste [*lashon bahalah u-mehirut*]." Sforno adds that this is a demonstration of the faith the Jews had in God at that moment.

FURTHER: In each generation, a person must show himself[34] as having personally left the bondage of Egypt, as it says, "And he took us out from there" (Deut. 6:23). And regarding this, the Holy One, blessed is He, commanded us in the Torah, "Remember that you were slaves" (Deut. 5:15), which means as if you, yourself, were a slave and went forth to freedom and were redeemed (*Ḥametz u-Matzah* 7:6; see also Ibn Ezra [long]).

Rabbenu Manoah on this passage in Maimonides elaborates: "And by this remembrance, the fear of God will always be before him, when he sees the Providence of God towards

---

34. The standard printings of the Mishnah have *lir'ot*, "to see oneself" (m. *Pesaḥim* 10:5), but Maimonides appears to have the language *le-harot*, "to show oneself" (see *Maggid Mishneh*). Maimonides uses the same word *le-harot*, "to show," regarding Purim and Hanukkah as well (*Megillah* 2:12 and *Ḥanukkah* 3:3). See my "Philosophical Implications of *Pirsumei Nissa*" *Torah Musings* December 29, 2016 (end of appendix). It is worth noting that the Kaufmann Codex of the Mishnah omits this phrase entirely.

Israel, and he will never turn his heart from Him, may He be blessed. And if he lives in a time of great oppression, he will trust in God the Hope of Israel who will save him in a time of distress. And just as the redemption from Egypt was a cause to improve their future, so too all the troubles of this exile are the cause for Israel to have an eternal redemption."

FURTHER: See *Guide* 3:46, quoted at v. 3.

12:12. And I will pass through [*ve-avarti*] the whole land of Egypt on that night... — Maimonides explains there are five meanings of *avar* (עבר), literally, "pass over" or "pass through," and he says the third meaning applies to the present verse:

1. ... the motion of a body in space, and is chiefly applied to living creatures moving at some distance in a straight line, e.g., "And He passed over [*avar*] them" (Gen. 33:3).
2. ... [it] is applied to the passage of sound through air, as "And they caused a sound to pass [*va-ya'aviru*] in the camp" (Exod. 36:6).
3. Figuratively it denoted the appearance of the Light and the Divine Presence (*Shekhinah*) which the prophets perceived in their prophetic visions, as it is said, "And behold a smoking furnace, and a burning lamp that passed [*avar*] between those pieces" (Gen. 15:17). This took place in a prophetic vision, for the narrative commences, "And a deep sleep fell upon Abram." The verb has this latter meaning in Exod. 12:12, "And I shall pass [*ve-avarti*] through the land of Egypt" (denoting "I shall reveal myself," etc.), and in all similar places.
4. The verb is next employed to express that a person has gone too far, and transgressed the usual limit, in the performance of some act, as, "And as a man overcome [*avaro*] by wine" (Jer. 23:9).
5. It is also used figuratively to denote: to abandon one aim, and turn to a different aim and object, e.g., "He shot an arrow causing it to miss [*le-ha'aviro*] the aim" (1 Sam. 20:36) (*Guide* 1:21; see also Exod. 13:12).

Rashi writes, "Like a king who passes from one place to the next, and with one [act of] passing and in one moment they are all smitten." This appears to be Maimonides' first definition of *avar*, but Maimonides insists that this definition can never apply to God, writing, "God, being incorporeal, cannot be said to move, and consequently the verb 'to pass' cannot with propriety be applied to Him in its primary signification" (see the end of *Guide* 1:21). There appears to be a major debate between these two on the proper understanding of this verse, specifically this word *ve-avarti*.

12:14. And this day shall be unto you for a memorial, and you shall celebrate it as a festival to the Lord; throughout your generations you shall keep it as an eternal statute. — God said, "and you shall celebrate [*ve-ḥaggotem*] it as a festival to the Lord" (Exod. 12:14, Lev. 23:41), which means one should bring a peace offering, which is called a *ḥagigah* (*PhM Ḥagigah* 1:2; in the *Mishneh Torah*, Maimonides says the obligation to bring the *ḥagigah* originates from Deut. 16:15, not from the present verse).

12:15. Seven days you shall eat unleavened bread... — It is a positive commandment from the Torah to eat matzah on the night of the fifteenth of Nisan, as it says, "in the evening you shall eat unleavened bread" (Exod. 12:18).... On the other days of the festival, eating matzah is discretionary. If he desires, he may eat matzah. If he desires, he may eat rice, millet, roasted seeds, or fruit (*Ḥametz u-Matzah* 6:1).

The phrase "you shall eat unleavened bread" is understood in the negative: "you shall not eat any leavened bread" on Passover. The affirmative obligation to eat matzah only applies to the first night; for on, consuming matzah is discretionary.

FURTHER: ... if the eating of unleavened bread on Passover were only commanded for one day, we would not have noticed it, and its object would not have been manifest. For it frequently happens that we take the same kind of food for two or three days. But by continuing for a whole period [of seven days] to eat unleavened bread, its object becomes clear and evident (*Guide* 3:43).

...surely [akh] — And it is said, "on the first day you shall remove leaven from your houses" (12:15), so we know that that refers to the fourteenth, and it was proper to perform the destroying [burning] of leaven on the fourteenth, were it not for saying, "surely [*akh*] on the first day" (Exod. 12:15), since the word *akh* ("surely") comes to as an exclusion. It is as if He qualified[35] and said, "That which I said, 'on the first day' is not from the beginning of the day, but from part of the day" [i.e., only part of 14 Nisan] (*PhM Pesaḥim* 1:4).

> Maimonides is employing the hermeneutical principle that the words *akh* and *rak* allude to limitations (e.g., *Rosh Hashanah* 17b, *Sanhedrin* 49a). In this case the word *akh* means that the verse does not refer to the entire day of 14 Nisan, but only the latter part of the day.

... on the first day you shall remove leaven from your houses... — We are commanded to remove the leaven from our houses on the fourteenth of Nisan, and this is the commandment of destroying leaven [lit. "sourdough"], as God, may He be exalted, said, "surely on the first day you shall remove leaven from your houses." And the Sages called this the commandment of destroying (*bi'ur*), meaning "destroying the leaven." And the Jerusalem Talmud, tractate *Sanhedrin* (5:3), teaches, "[for possessing] leaven, one violates a positive and a negative commandment. The positive commandment

---

35. Hebrew *mi'et*, "limited, excluded."

of destroying (*bi'ur*), as it says, 'you shall remove leaven from your houses,' and the negative commandment of 'leaven [*se'or*] shall not be found in your homes' (Exod. 12:19)" (*ShM*, Pos. 156).

FURTHER: It is a positive commandment from the Torah to remove the leaven before the time when it becomes prohibited to eat it, as it says, "on the first day you shall remove leaven from your houses." And through the oral tradition it is learned that this word "first" refers to the fourteenth [of Nisan]. And a proof of this matter is what is written in the Torah, "You shall not slaughter the blood of My sacrifice with leaven" (Exod. 34:25), which means that you shall not slaughter the Passover offering while leaven is still present [in your domiciles]. And the Passover offering should be slaughtered on the fourteenth [of Nisan] after noontime. And what is this removal (*hashbattah*) that is mentioned in the Torah? It is that we nullify the leaven mentally [lit., "in his heart"] and consider it like the dust of the earth and to mentally conclude that there is no leaven at all in his domain, and that all of the leaven in his domain is like dust and like a thing that has no purpose at all (*Ḥametz u-Matzah* 2:1-2; based on *Pesaḥim* 6b).

> Maimonides appears to believe there are two components to the biblical commandment to rid one's property of leaven. In *ShM*, he interprets the commandment of *bi'ur ḥametz* as physically removing the leaven from their homes. However, in the *Mishneh Torah*, Maimonides says that the biblical commandment of *bi'ur ḥametz* is to mentally nullify the leaven in one's possession. Rabbi Joseph Karo, in the *Kesef Mishnah*, argues that according to Maimonides the Torah requires both physical destruction and mental nullification (*bi'ur* and *bittul*).

... for whoever eats leaven [*se'or*]... — This is *se'or* itself which is kneaded in the dough in order to make leaven (*PhM Eduyot* 4:1; Hebrew *se'or* is usually translated as "sourdough." See *ShM*, Neg. 200 where Maimonides says the punishment is the same for consuming either *hametz* or *se'or*. R. Saadiah (Exod. 13:7) makes the same comment).

... from the first day to the seventh day—that soul shall be cut off from Israel. — Whoever eats an olive's measure of leaven on Passover from the night of the fifteenth until the end of the twenty-first day of Nisan receives *karet*, and if he eats it accidentally he must bring a *korban hattat kavu'ah* (M. *Kereitot* 1:1). This applies to one who eats leaven or one who grinds it into a liquid and drinks it (*Hametz u-Matzah* 1:1, based on *Hullin* 120a; see also Exod. 13:3).

... that soul shall be cut off [*ve-nikhretah ha-nefesh ha-hi*] from Israel... — [Maimonides addresses the meaning of eternal reward in relation to *karet*]: The goodness that is hidden for the righteous is the life of the world to come, and this is life which has no death, and goodness that has no evil. And this is what is written in the Torah, "... so that it will be well with you and you will lengthen [your] days" (Deut. 22:7). And from the oral tradition we learn "so that it will be well with you [*le-ma'an yitav lakh*, lit., 'so it will be *good* for you']" refers to a world that is entirely good, and "you will lengthen [your] days" refers to a world that is infinitely long, and that is the world to come (*Kiddushin* 39b). The reward of the righteous is that they will merit this pleasantness and this goodness.

And the punishment of the wicked is that they will not merit this life; rather they will be cut off [*yikkaretu*] and they will perish. And whoever does not merit this life is like someone who is dead and will not live forever, but will be cut off on account of his wickedness and will be destroyed like an animal. And this is the *karet* mentioned in the Torah, as it says, "That soul will surely be cut off; its sin is upon it" (Num. 15:31). From the oral tradition, we learn that *hikkaret* means being cut off from this world, and *tikkaret* means being cut off from the world to come (e.g., Rabbi Akiva at *Sanhedrin* 64b among other places). This means that the soul, once it has separated from the body in this world, does not merit the world to come. Instead it is also cut off from the world to come (*Teshuvah* 8:1; see also *Teshuvah* 8:5, *ShM* Root 14, *PhM Sanhedrin* 10:1).

The word *karet* (originally *hikkaret*) has sparked a lot of interpretations, including

- death at the hands of Heaven, whose days are cut short and he dies before his time, and childless (Rashi on Lev. 17:9 and on BT *Shabbat* 25a; Ibn Ezra and Shadal on Gen. 17:14);
- death before the age of fifty (BT *Mo'ed Katan* 28a);
- death between the ages of fifty and sixty (Rava in BT *Mo'ed Katan* 28a);
- destruction of the soul (Maimonides based on R. Akiva; this is the rejected opinion in Ibn Ezra)
- "that soul shall be cut off," not that human body or that man, but that soul and mind. Cut off from what? From its generation; for the whole generation is incorrupt. Therefore the wicked man is removed from incorruption to corruption" (Philo, *Questions and Answers on Genesis* 3.52);
- being banished from the Jewish people or treated as a foreigner so that he would have to exile himself among the Gentiles (Clericus as quoted by Shadal on Gen. 17:14).[36]

---

36. See Jacob Milgrom, *Leviticus 1-17*, p. 457. See also Tosafot on *Yevamot* 2a, s.v. *eishet* in the name of the Riva.

Nahmanides (Lev. 18:29) differentiates between three types of karet (see also his *Sha'ar ha-Gemul* §8):

1. *ve-nikhreta ha-ish ha-hu* (Exod. 30:33, 38; Lev. 17:4, 9)
2. *ve-nikhretu ha-nefashot ha-osot* (Gen. 17:14, Exod. 12:19, Lev. 18:29)
3. *hikkaret tikkaret ha-nefesh ha-hi avonah bah* (Num. 15:31). This is the verse Maimonides uses to explain that the punishment for *karet* is loss of this world and the next world. However Nahmanides points out that this verse is referring only to idolatry and *megaddef*, not other sins for which one is deserving of *karet*. Whereas Maimonides applies this rabbinic dictum to the default meaning of *karet*, Nahmanides says it applies only to the isolated cases of idolatry and *megaddef*.

FURTHER: The eating of leavened bread on Passover (Exod. 12:15) and breaking the fast on the Day of Atonement (Lev. 23:29) are likewise punished with excision [*karet*]: first on account of the great discomfort which the laws causes in these cases; second on account of the principles of faith which the laws of Passover and of the Day of Atonement inculcate: they confirm fundamental principles of the Law, namely, the belief in the wonderful departure [of Israel] from Egypt... (*Guide* 3:41).

12:16. And on the first day there shall be a holy convocation...
— It is a positive commandment that we are commanded to rest on the first day of Passover, and He, may He be exalted, said, "And on the first day there shall be a holy convocation." And know by way of introduction that whenever it is stated in the Torah *mikra kodesh* ["holy convocation"], [the Sages] explain it with the term *kadshehu*

[sanctify it] (*Rosh Hashanah* 32a).[37] And the meaning of *kadshehu* is that we should do no labor unless it is to prepare food, as the Scripture explains (Exod. 12:16) (*ShM*, Pos. 159).

... and on the seventh day will be a holy convocation for you... — It is a positive commandment that we are commanded to abstain from work on the seventh day of Passover (*ShM*, Pos. 160).

... no labor shall be done on them... — It is a negative commandment that we are prohibited from doing work on the first day of Passover (*ShM*, Neg. 323).

FURTHER: Whoever rests from constructive labor [*melakhah*] on one of these days [i.e., festivals] fulfills a positive commandment, as it says, *shabbaton* (e.g., Lev. 23:24), which means "rest" [*shevut*]. And whoever performs one of these constructive labors that is not for the sake of eating, such as building, destroying, weaving, or the like, on any of these days squanders a positive commandment, and violates a negative commandment, as it says, "You shall not perform any constructive labor" (Lev. 23:7), "no labor shall be done on them" (Exod. 12:16). And if a person does [labor] with witnesses and warning, he receives lashes from the Torah (*Shevitat Yom Tov* 1:2).

... except for what shall be eaten for any soul... — This is true for other festival days as well [and not just Passover] (*ShM*, Neg. 328).

FURTHER: On the following six days, Scripture prohibited work. They are: the first and seventh day of Passover; the first and eighth day of the festival of Sukkot; the day of the festival of Shavuot; and the first day of the seventh month (i.e., Rosh Hashanah). These days

---

37. Hebrew *mikra* from *kara*, meaning "call, proclaim," so *mikra kodesh* means one should "call it holy," hence our obligation to verbally declare it holy. See my *A Theology of Holiness*, pp. 126-130.

are called *yomim tovim* (festivals). And [the obligation to] rest on all of them is equal with respect to any laborious work, except for work that is for the purpose of eating, as it says, "except for what shall be eaten for any soul" (*Shevitat Yom Tov* 1:1).

FURTHER: Washing and anointing are included [in the category of] eating and drinking, so one may perform these activities on a festival day, as it says, "except for what shall be eaten for any soul" — for all the needs of the body. Therefore we may heat up water on a festival and wash our faces, hands, and feet in it. However, it is forbidden to wash one's entire body, because of the [rabbinic] prohibition against going to a bathhouse (*Shevitat Yom Tov* 1:16; see also *PhM Betzah* 2:4).

... that may be done only for you. — We are not permitted to bake or cook on a festival for the purpose of feeding Gentiles or dogs, as it says, "that may be done only for you" — *for you*, and not for Gentiles; *for you*, and not for dogs (*Shevitat Yom Tov* 1:13, based on *Betzah* 20b, 21b; see also *PhM Ḥallah* 1:8).

FURTHER: Preparing [the two loaves] does not override [the prohibitions of] the festival day, and needless to say, it does not override the Sabbath. Instead, we should bake them on the day before the festival, as it says, "that may be done only for you" — *for you*, and not for the Almighty (*Temidin u-Musafin* 8:8).

12:17. And you shall observe the [feast of] unleavened bread, for on that very day I brought your armies forth from the land of Egypt; and you shall observe this day for all generations as an eternal ordinance. — [The Hebrew phrase וּשְׁמַרְתֶּם אֶת הַמַּצּוֹת is understood rabbinically in its literal sense, "and you shall guard the unleavened bread":] That is to say that we are warned about the unleavened bread and we should guard it from any possibility of becoming leaven. Therefore the Sages said that a person must be careful regarding grain—that no water comes [into contact with] it after it has been harvested, in order that it will not contain any leaven (*Ḥametz u-Matzah* 5:9).[38]

FURTHER: [The reason] one does not fulfill his obligation with thanksgiving loaves and Nazirite's cakes is that they were made for himself, that is to say, to bring them with the offering which he is obligated to bring, as we have been commanded. Yet even though these are *bona fide* matzah, since it says, "and you shall guard the unleavened bread," the tradition requires unleavened bread that was watched for the sake of matzah, which excludes whatever was not watched for the sake of matzah but for the sake of an offering (*PhM Pesaḥim* 2:5; see also *Ḥametz u-Matzah* 6:9, based on *Pesaḥim* 38b).

12:18. In the first [month] on the fourteenth of the month in the evening you shall eat unleavened bread until the twenty-first day of the month in the evening. — It is a positive commandment from the Torah to eat matzah on the night of the fifteenth of Nisan, as it says, "in the evening you shall eat unleavened bread." [This applies] to every place and every time. And this [obligation] of eating [matzah] is not dependent on the Passover offering (see Exod. 12:8); rather it is a separate commandment, and this obligation lasts all night long. On the other days of the festival, eating matzah is discretionary. If he desires, he may eat matzah. If he desires, he may eat rice, millet, roasted seeds, or fruit. However on the night of the fifteenth alone there is an obligation [to eat matzah]. And one who eats an olive's measure has fulfilled his obligation (*Ḥametz u-Matzah* 6:1; see also *ShM*, Pos. 158).

---

38. In some MS's, this passage is spread over *halakhot* 8 and 9. The *Maggid Mishneh* notes that in terms of "guarding," Maimonides does not differentiate between matzah for Seder night and matzah for the other days of Passover.

FURTHER: Eating matzah on the night of Passover is a positive commandment, as God said, "in the evening you shall eat unleavened bread." And it is also said, "You shall eat no leavened bread with it [the Passover offering]; seven days you shall eat unleavened bread with it" (Deut. 16:3). Any grains whose dough ferments can be used to fulfill the obligation of [eating] matzah. And only these five species can ferment. However, other species like rice, millet, or *jari* [sorghum], their dough spoils [*nitkalkel*] if it is left out but does not ferment (*PhM Pesaḥim* 2:5).

12:19. Seven days no yeast shall be found in your houses... — [According to rabbinic interpretation, the prohibitions "no yeast shall be found in your houses" (Exod. 12:19) and "no leaven shall be seen among you" (Exod. 13:7) under the term *bal yeira'eh bal yimmatzei*— shall be neither seen nor found:] — We are warned against seeing leaven in all your borders for seven days. The source is what God said, "no yeast shall be seen in all of your borders" (Exod. 13:7). These [*ḥametz* = leaven, and *se'or* = yeast/sourdough] are not two separate matters; rather they are one matter. And in the explanation of this, the Sages said, "The verse begins with *ḥametz* and ends with *se'or*. That is to say that there is no difference between *ḥametz* itself and something that causes fermentation [*se'or*]. And one who transgressed and allowed leaven to remain on his property does not receive lashes unless he purchased leaven on Passover and acquired it, for that would be an action. And the language of the Tosefta: "One who allows leaven to remain [on his property] and one who allows *kilayim* to grow in his vineyard does not receive lashes" (*ShM*, Neg. 200 quoting T. *Makkot* 4:5. In *Ḥametz u-Matzah* 1:3, Maimonides explains that one is only liable for lashes if he purchases or actively makes leaven, because otherwise the prohibition would be passive).

FURTHER: We are prohibited to have leaven found on our property, even if it is not visible, and even if it is a deposit. And this is what

God said, "Seven days no yeast shall be found in your houses." And as mentioned above (Neg. 200), that one receives lashes for violating this prohibition only when there is an action performed, in accordance with the principles explained in tractate *Shevuot* (21a). And the Sages have explained in many places that one violates "it shall not be seen" and "it may not be found."[39]

And at the beginning of tractate *Pesaḥim* (4-14), these two commandments are discussed, where it is explained, "no [yeast] shall be seen in all of your borders" (Exod. 13:7) and "no yeast shall be found in your houses" (Exod. 12:19). There it is taught that each prohibition teaches something that the other one does not, and someone who keeps leaven violates both "it shall not be seen" and "it may not be found" [even if it is seen to the eye, even if it is hidden] (*ShM*, Neg. 201; see further *Ḥametz u-Matzah* 2:4, and *Kesef Mishneh* to *Ḥametz u-Matzah* 1:3).

FURTHER: It is written in the Torah, "No leaven shall be seen among you" (Exod. 13:7). [One might think] if it were buried or lent to a Gentile, one would not be in violation, [therefore] we learn, "no yeast shall be found in your houses" — even if it is buried or lent away. Perhaps he will only commit a violation if the leaven was in his house, but if it was far away from his house, in a field, or in a different city, he would not be in violation; therefore we learn "in all of your borders" (Exod. 13:7) — anywhere in your possession. Perhaps he will be obligated to destroy leaven belonging to a Gentile or that is consecrated; therefore we learn, "[no leaven] shall be seen among *you*" (Exod.13:7) — you may not see what belongs to you, but you are permitted to see what belongs to others or what has been consecrated (*Ḥametz u-Matzah* 4:1).

Nahmanides takes issue with this and says that a Jew is not liable if his leaven is deposited with a Gentile (On Exod.

---

39. Meaning these are two separate prohibitions.

12:19). However the *Shulḥan Arukh*, following Maimonides, writes, "If a Jew entrusts his leaven to a neighboring Jew or a Gentile, even if [the latter] took upon responsibility, nonetheless the one who entrusts is in violation (*Oraḥ Ḥayyim* 440:4).

FURTHER: God said, "Seven days no yeast shall be found in your houses." We learn from here that the obligation to destroy the leaven is certainly before the seven-day holiday, in order that there be seven days from beginning to end during which time leaven shall not be found (*PhM Pesaḥim* 1:4).

... for whoever eats of leaven, that soul shall be cut off from the congregation of Israel... — For a discussion of the meaning of *karet*, see at Exod. 12:15.

... whether stranger or a native of the land [*ba-ger u-va-ezraḥ ha-aretz*]. — The preposition *ba-* in this passage [of *ba-amal Yisrael*, lit., "*in* the misery of Israel" (Judg. 10:16)] has the force of the preposition *min* [from, of]; and *ba-amal* is identical with *me-amal*.[40] Grammarians give many instances of this use of the preposition *ba-*: "And that which remains of [*ba-*] the flesh and of [*ba-*] the bread" (Lev. 8:32); "If there remains but few of [*ba-*] the years" (Lev. 25:52); "Of [*ba-*] the strangers and of [*ba-*] those born in the land" (Exod. 12:19) (*Guide* 1:41; Saadiah and Ibn Ezra (long) make the same point on *lo yokhal bo*, "shall not eat it," which they say means *mimmennu* "*from* it.").

12:20. You shall not eat anything that is leavened... — We are forbidden to eat foods that have a mixture of leaven, even if they are not bread. [This includes] *muryas*, *kutaḥ*, and beer, and anything similar. And this is what God said, "You shall not eat anything that is

---

40. A contraction of *min ha-amal*.

leavened." And the language of the *Mekhilta* is, "'You shall not eat anything that is leavened' — to include *kutaḥ* from Babylonia, beer from Medea, and beer from Edom. (*ShM*, Neg. 198; see also *Ḥametz u-Matzah* 1:6).

FURTHER: [In most cases of prohibited food becoming mixed with permitted food, the prohibited food can be nullified if the mixture is large enough. However, no such leniency exists for leaven on Passover:] Do not be surprised about leaven not being nullified on Passover, since the Torah prohibited "*anything* that is leavened," therefore the Sages were strict with this matter (*Ma'akhalot Asurot* 15:12; see also *halakhah* 9).

Normally a mixture of two unalike substances is easier to allow than a mixture of two like substances. Based on this fact, the *Kefesh Mishnah* (Rabbi Joseph Karo) asks why the normal rules of *bittul* would not apply, even when two unalike substances are involved. He concludes, "it made sense to him [Maimonides] that they were strict because it says, 'anything that is leavened.'"

... in all your habitations you shall eat unleavened bread. — Priests may fulfill [their obligation to eat matzah using grain that was given as] *ḥallah*[41] or *terumah*,[42] even though this is not matzah that can be eaten by anyone. Similarly matzah [made from] the second tithe[43] [can be used if he is] in Jerusalem. However, one does not fulfill his obligation with first-fruit[44] even if he is in Jerusalem, since these cannot be eaten in all habitations (cf. present verse). And it is

---

41. The obligation to give a dough offering to the priest, pursuant to Num. 15:20.
42. The grain offering mentioned in Num. 18:24.
43. The tithe eaten within the walls of Jerusalem as mentioned in Deut. 14:22-27.
44. The bringing of first fruits mentioned in Deut. 26:1-11.

possible to redeem[45] the second tithe and eat it anywhere [thereby fulfilling the verse "in all your habitations"]. And it is written, "in all your habitations you shall eat unleavened bread," which means matzah that theoretically could be eaten in any habitation can be used to fulfill the obligation of matzah (*Ḥametz u-Matzah* 6:8; based on BT *Pesaḥim* 36a-b).

12:22. And you shall take a bundle of hyssop and dip it in the blood that is in the basin, and touch the lintel and to the two doorposts with the blood that is in the basin. And no man among you shall go out from the doorway of his out until morning. — Regarding the Egyptian Passover, it says "and you shall take a bundle of hyssop." Therefore we require a "bundle" [*agudah*], which is not less than three stalks (*PhM Parah* 11:9).

Further: I do not know… why a bundle of hyssop was commanded for the sprinkling of the blood of the Passover lamb. I cannot find any principle upon which to found an explanation why these particular things have been chosen (*Guide* 3:47).

> It is possible that the hyssop represented purity, as in "Cleanse me with hyssop, and I will be clean" (Ps. 51:7), as well as the purification from *tzara'at* (Leviticus 14).

… hyssop [*ezov*]… — *ezov* is *altzatar* that is used by people when eating (*PhM Negaim* 14:6).

> Shadal understands *altzatar* is origan (a relative of oregano); Kapach protests and says it is thyme. Alternatively, my friend Rabbi Yair Shahak tells me *altzatar* almost certainly is za'atar (which was my intuition as well).

---

45. The second tithe usually needs to be eaten within the walls of Jerusalem, but the owner has the option of redeeming the second tithe with silver, so the produce becomes completely desanctified, and the silver must be brought to Jerusalem and used to purchase new produce.

12:23. For the Lord will pass through[46] to strike down the Egyptians and will see the blood on the lintel and on the two doorposts, and the Lord will pass over the door and he will not let the destroyer to enter your houses to strike you. — Scripture tells us, according to the version of Onkelos, that the Egyptians worshipped Aries, and therefore abstained from killing sheep, and held shepherds in contempt, e.g., "Behold we shall sacrifice the abomination of the Egyptians" (Exod. 8:22); "For every shepherd is an abomination to the Egyptians" (Gen. 46:34). Some sects among the Sabeans worshipped demons, and imagined that these assumed the form of goats, and called them therefore "goats" [se'irim]. This worship was widespread, e.g., "And they shall no more offer their sacrifices unto demons, after whom they have gone whoring..." (Lev. 17:7). For this reason those sects abstained from eating goats' flesh. Most idolaters objected to killing cattle, holding this species of animals in great estimation. Therefore the people of Hodu [India] up to this day do not slaughter cattle even in those countries where other animals are slaughtered.

In order to eradicate these false principles, the Law commands us to offer sacrifices only of these three kinds: "You shall bring your offering of the cattle—of the herd and of the flock" (Lev. 1:2). Thus the very act which is considered by the heathen as the greatest crime, is the means of approaching God, and obtaining His pardon for our sins. In this manner, evil principles, the diseases of the human soul, are cured by other principles which are diametrically opposite.

This is also the reason why we were commanded to kill a lamb on Passover, and to sprinkle the blood thereof outside on the gates. We had to free ourselves of evil doctrines and to proclaim the opposite, namely, that the very act which was then considered as being the cause of death would be the cause of deliverance from death, e.g., "And the Lord will pass over the door, and will not let the destroyer

---

46. Hebrew, *avar*; see *Guide* 1:21 quoted at Exod. 12:12.

to enter your houses to strike you" (Exod. 12:23). Thus they were rewarded for performing openly a service every part of which was objected to by the idolaters (*Guide* 3:46).

12:25. And it will be when you enter [*tavo'u*] into the land which the Lord gives you as He has said, and you shall keep this service. — See *Guide* 1:22 (quoted below at Exod. 19:9), where Maimonides differentiates between several meanings of *bo*. On the present verse, Maimonides says *bo* means "enter" (not "come"), basing himself on Onkelos, who translates *tavo'u* as *tei'alun*.

12:26-27. And it shall come to pass when your children will say to you, "What is this service to you." And you shall say, "This is the sacrifice of the LORD's Passover, who passed over the houses of the children of Israel in Egypt when he struck down the Egyptians, but our houses He saved," and the people bowed down and worshipped. — What is the reason for this Passover offering? Because the Omnipresent One, may He be blessed, passed over the houses of our forefathers in Egypt, as it says, "And you shall say, 'This is the sacrifice of the Lord's Passover...'" (*Ḥametz u-Matzah* 7:5; see also 8:4).

"This is the sacrifice of the LORD's Passover." — It is forbidden to have an improper intention [when performing sacred service....] Therefore, if an offering was slaughtered as a different offering, or took a grain offering for a different purpose, then whether he did so intentionally or accidentally, he is obligated to finish the remainder of the services with the proper intentions.... [Maimonides explains why this general principle does not apply to some specific offerings, including the Passover:] And with regard to the Passover offering, it is stated, "And you shall offer the Passover to the Lord your God"

(Deut. 16:1), which means that the entire service must be performed as a Passover offering. And it is stated, "And you shall say, 'This is the sacrifice of the LORD's Passover,'" so it must be slaughtered as a Passover offering. And if he had in mind a different purpose, or for a different owner, it is invalid (*Pesulei ha-Mukdashin* 15:3; see also 15:11, *PhM Pesaḥim* 5:2, and *PhM Zevaḥim* 1:1).

There are two similar verses that are in operation simultaneously: "And you shall say, 'This is the sacrifice of the LORD's Passover'" (Exod. 12:27) as well as "And you shall offer the Passover to the LORD your God" (Deut. 16:1). There are two derivatives that are learned from these verses. First, the Passover offering must be brought qua a Passover offering; in other words, for most offerings, if the officiant had the wrong intention at the beginning but corrected it later, then the offering is still valid. However, the Passover offering must be brought qua Passover offering from beginning to end.

Second, only people who had previously grouped together could eat the Passover offering, and the Passover offering had to be slaughtered with that group in mind. If the officiant had the wrong group in mind, then the offering is invalid.

According to the Babylonian Talmud, "And you shall offer the Passover to the Lord your God" teaches that it must be offered as a Passover offering, while "And you shall say, 'This is the sacrifice of the Lord's Passover'" teaches that it must be offered in the owners' names (BT *Zevaḥim* 7b). However, the Jerusalem Talmud presents the matter differently: "From where do we know that the Passover offering must be brought for its own sake [i.e., as a Passover offering, and not as a different offering]? As it says, "And you shall say, 'This is the sacrifice of [the Lord's] Passover'" (JT *Pesaḥim* 5:2).

Maimonides quotes both versions in different places (one in *PhM Pesaḥim* 5:2 and one in *PhM Zevaḥim* 1:1), as has been pointed out by Kapach in his notes to Maimonides' *PhM*. He also observes that in the *Mishneh Torah*, Maimonides does not specify which law is derived from which verse.

12:39. And they baked unleavened cakes of dough that they had brought out of Egypt, for it had not leavened; for they had been driven out of Egypt and could not delay, nor had they prepared any food for themselves. — This matzah that we eat—what is its reason? Since our forefathers did not have time for the dough to rise before the supreme King of kings, the Holy One, blessed is He, appeared before them and redeemed them immediately, as it says, "And they baked unleavened cakes of dough that they had brought out of Egypt, for it had not leavened; for they had been driven out of Egypt and could not delay, nor had they prepared any food for themselves" (*Nusaḥ ha-Haggadah*; see also *Ḥametz u-Matzah* 7:5).

12:43. And the Lord said to Moses and Aaron: this is the statute of the Passover, no stranger may eat of it. — We are forbidden from giving [meat] from the Passover offering to a Jew who has apostatized, as He, may He be exalted, said, "no stranger [*ben neikhar*] may eat of it." And [Onkelos] translates this, "any child of Israel who has apostatized." And the language of the *Mekhilta* (*de-Rashbi*, BT *Zevaḥim* 22b): "'Any *ben neikhar*' — this refers to a Jew who has converted and practices idolatry" (*ShM*, Neg. 128).

Rashi understands the verse more broadly than Maimonides. While Maimonides understands it as referring to an apostate (following Onkelos), Rashi believes the verse applies to both a Gentile and an apostate Jew.

116

FURTHER: One who gives an olive's measure [of meat] from the Passover offering, whether from the First Passover or the Second Passover, to an apostate who practices idolatry, or a resident alien, or a [Gentile] worker, violates a negative commandment. However, he does not receive lashes, but he does receive [rabbinic] lashes for insubordination. And the *ben neikhar* mentioned in the Torah refers to someone who worships a foreign [*neikhar*] deity (*Korban Pesaḥ* 9:7).

> Maimonides' takes an expansive reading of the verse, which states that a "stranger" may not "eat" [*yokhal*] from the Passover offering, but Maimonides writes that we may not "feed" [*ma'akhil*] the Passover offering to a "stranger." The Noahide Code, applicable to Gentiles, does not include a prohibition of eating from the Paschal offering. For this reason, Maimonides does not say it is prohibited for a Gentile to eat of this offering, but that it is prohibited for a Jew to feed it to a Gentile.

12:44. And any slave that a man purchased with money, you shall circumcise him and then he may eat of it. — Just the circumcision of one's son (v. 48) and his servants prevents him from slaughtering the Passover offering, it also prevents him from being allowed to eat of it, as it says, "you shall circumcise him and then he may eat of it" (*Korban Pesaḥ* 9:9).

> See BT *Yevamot* 71a. The verse Maimonides quotes refers only to slaves, not to sons. Mahari Korkus writes, "Our Rabbi was not precise in quoting the *baraita* since there is no difference" whether he attributed it to v. 44 or v. 48. Alternatively, Maimonides might be basing himself on *Mekhilta de-Rashbi*, "Pisḥa" 15.

FURTHER: Regarding a minor, the circumcision of his [i.e., the minor's] male servants and [ritual] immersion of his maidservants does not prevent him joining in a group to eat the Passover offering, as it says *ve-khol eved ish* ["and any servant of a *man*" rather than just "any servant"] — to exclude a minor (*Korban Pesaḥ* 5:6).

12:45. No foreigner or hired worker may eat of it. — We are forbidden to allow a resident alien to eat from the Passover offering,[47] as it says, "No foreigner or hired worker may eat of it" (*ShM*, Neg. 126; see also *PhM Yevamot* 8:1).

FURTHER: We may not allow a Gentile, even a resident alien or hired worker, to eat from it, as it says, "no foreigner or hired worker may eat of it" (*Korban Pesaḥ* 9:7; see also at v. 43).

12:46. In one house shall it be eaten; you shall not carry any of the meat outside of the house... — We are forbidden from taking any part of the meat out of the place where we have assembled to eat it. This is what God, may He be exalted, said, "you shall not carry any of the meat outside of the house." And the language of the *Mekhilta*, "'outside' — outside of the place where it is eaten." And once it is carried outside, one is prohibited to eat it, and it is like *tereifah*.[48] And the Sages said, "If someone carries meat outside from one group to another, even though he violates a negative commandment, it is still pure, and one who eats it [also] violates a negative commandment" (*Pesaḥim* 85a). And there they said, "One who carries the meat of the Passover offering from one group to another does not become liable until he puts it down, [based on the common word] *hotza'ah* ("carrying out") regarding the Sabbath (Exod. 16:29). And if he puts it down, he becomes liable for lashes (*ShM*, Neg. 123; see also *Korban Pesaḥ* 9:1-3 and *PhM Pesaḥim* 7:12).

... and you shall not break any of its bones. — We are forbidden from breaking any of the bones of the Passover offering. This is what

47. Lit., "from feeding the Passover offering to a resident alien."
48. Literally, "torn," but in legal texts refers to any meat prohibited to eat.

He said, "and you shall not break any of its bones." And someone who broke one of the bones is liable to receive lashes. And in explaining it, the Sages said, "One who breaks a bone of the Passover offering when [the congregation is ritually pure] is liable to receive lashes" (*ShM*, Neg. 121; see also *Korban Pesaḥ* 10:1-2 and *PhM Makkot* 3:3). See *Guide* 3:46, quoted at Exod. 12:3, where Maimonides argues that the bones could not be broken because of the haste in which the Jews left Egypt.

12:47. The entire congregation of Israel shall observe it. — On this verse as the source that ideally the Passover offering should be offered on behalf of a group, not an individual, see on Exod. 12:4.

12:48. And when a stranger shall sojourn with you, and will keep the Passover to the Lᴏʀᴅ, let all his males be circumcised, and then let him come near and keep it... — Just as his own circumcision prevents him from observing the Passover, so too the circumcision of his minor sons and the circumcision of his servants, whether minors or adults, prevents him, as it says, "let all his males [be circumcised], and then let him come near and keep it." And if he slaughtered [it] before circumcising them, the Passover offering is invalid. And similarly the [ritual] immersion of his maidservants for the sake of servitude prevents him [from observing the Passover]. And this matter we learn from the oral tradition: the immersion of maidservants is like the circumcision of manservants (*Korban Pesaḥ* 5:5).

... and he shall be as one that is born in the land; for no uncircumcised male shall eat of it. — Someone uncircumcised is forbidden from eating the Passover offering, as He, may He be exalted, said, "no uncircumcised male shall eat of it." And someone who ate of it while uncircumcised is liable to receive lashes (*ShM*, Neg. 127; see also *PhM Pesaḥim* 5:3 and *PhM Yevamot* 8:1).

FURTHER: By three acts the Jews entered into the covenant [with God]: circumcision, [ritual] immersion, and sacrifice. Circumcision was [practiced] in Egypt, as it says, "no uncircumcised male shall eat of it." Moses circumcised them all, since in Egypt they had all neglected the rite of circumcision, except for the tribe of Levi, of whom it is said, "they upheld your covenant" (Deut. 33:9) (*Issurei Biah* 13:1-2).

FURTHER: If someone uncircumcised eats an olive's measure of meat of the Passover offering, he is liable to receive lashes, as it says, "no uncircumcised male shall eat of it [*bo*]." And *bo* ("of it") means he may not eat of it [the Passover offering], but he may eat matzah and bitter herbs. Similarly, we may not allow a foreigner or hired worker (cf. v. 45) to eat of it (*Korban Pesaḥ* 9:8).

FURTHER: The reason of the prohibition that the uncircumcised should not eat of it (Exod. 12:48) is explained by our Sages as follows: The Israelites neglected circumcision during their long stay in Egypt,[49] in order to make themselves appear like the Egyptians.[50] When God gave them the commandment of the Passover, and ordered that no one should kill the Passover lamb unless he, his sons, and all the male persons in his household were circumcised, that only "then he could come near and keep it" (Exod. 12:48), all performed this commandment, and the number of the circumcised being large the

---

49. Except for the Levites; see next source.
50. Nahmanides also says the Jews in Egypt did not practice circumcision, based on Ezek. 20:8 (on Exod. 12:42). Kapach observes that here Maimonides adds an additional reason as to why an uncircumcised male may not eat from sacrifices. Earlier in the chapter, Maimonides says that state of uncircumcision is inherently detestable. Here Maimonides adds that stigma is because the Egyptians did not practice this rite. Kapach also explains that the Jews did not neglect circumcision on account of negligence or due to the oppression of slavery, but because they wanted to appear like Egyptians, referencing the following Midrash: "When Joseph died, they neglected the obligation of circumcision, saying, 'Let us be like the Egyptians'" (*Exodus Rabbah* 1:8).

blood of the Passover and that of the circumcision flowed together. The prophet Ezekiel, referring to this event, says, "When I saw you sprinkled with thine own blood I said unto you, 'Live because of your [two kinds of] blood'" (Ezek. 16:6), i.e., because of the blood of the Passover and that of the circumcision (*Guide* 3:46).

The interpretation of Ezek. 16:6 is based on *Pirkei de-Rabbi Eliezer* 29. Rashi on that verse writes, "by the blood and the Passover and the blood of circumcision, they were redeemed" (Ezek. 16:6, so also Targum; he quotes it again on the present verse). Others interpret this verse as referring to childbirth (Radak).

FURTHER: [Maimonides offers the following rationale for the commandment of circumcision, though does not quote the current verse in that context:] As regards circumcision, I think that one of its objects is to limit sexual intercourse, and to weaken the organ of generation as far as possible, and thus cause man to be moderate. Some people believe that circumcision is to remove a defect in man's formation; but everyone can easily reply: How can products of nature be deficient so as to require external completion, especially as the use of the fore-skin to that organ is evident. This commandment has not been enjoined as a complement to a deficient physical creation, but as a means for perfecting man's moral shortcomings. The bodily injury caused to that organ is exactly that which is desired; it does not interrupt any vital function, nor does it destroy the power of generation. Circumcision simply counteracts excessive lust; for there is no doubt that circumcision weakens the power of sexual excitement, and sometimes lessens the natural enjoyment: the organ necessarily becomes weak when it loses blood and is deprived of its covering from the beginning. Our Sages (*Bereishit Rabbah* 80) say distinctly: It is hard for a woman, with whom an uncircumcised had

121

sexual intercourse, to separate from him. This is, as I believe, the best reason for the commandment concerning circumcision. And who was the first to perform this commandment? Abraham, our father! of whom it is well known how he feared sin; it is described by our Sages in reference to the words, "Behold, now I know that you are a fair woman to look upon" (Gen. 12:11).

There is, however, another important object in this commandment. It gives to all members of the same faith, i.e., to all believers in the Unity of God, a common bodily sign, so that it is impossible for any one that is a stranger, to say that he belongs to them. For sometimes people say so for the purpose of obtaining some advantage, or in order to make some attack upon the Jews. No one, however, should circumcise himself or his son for any other reason but pure faith; for circumcision is not like an incision on the leg, or a burning in the arm, but a very difficult operation. It is also a fact that there is much mutual love and assistance among people that are united by the same sign when they consider it as [the symbol of] a covenant. Circumcision is likewise the [symbol of the] covenant which Abraham made in connection with the belief in God's Unity. So also every one that is circumcised enters the covenant of Abraham to believe in the unity of God, in accordance with the words of the Law, "To be a God to you, and to your seed after your" (Gen. 17:7). This purpose of the circumcision is as important as the first, and perhaps more important.

This law can only be kept and perpetuated in its perfection, if circumcision is performed when the child is very young, and this for three good reasons. First, if the operation were postponed till the boy had grown up, he would perhaps not submit to it. Second, the young child has not much pain, because the skin is tender, and the imagination weak: for grown-up persons are in dread and fear of things which they imagine as coming, some time before these actually occur. Third, when a child is very young, the parents do not think much of him: because the image of the child, that leads the parents to love him, has not yet taken a firm root in their minds. That image becomes stronger by the continual sight; it grows with the development of the child, and later on the image begins again to decrease and to vanish. The parents' love for a new-born child is not so great as it is when the child is one year old; and when one year old, it is less loved by them than when six years old. The feeling and love of the father for the child would have led him to neglect the law if he were allowed to wait two or three years, while shortly after birth the image is very weak in the mind of the parent, especially of the father who is responsible for the execution of this commandment (*Guide* 3:49).

FURTHER: It is well known from the account of our Rabbis that before the Israelites left Egypt, they corrupted their ways and violated the covenant of circumcision, so that none of them save the tribe of Levi was circumcised. Only when the Passover commandment was promulgated, in connection with which God instructed Moses, "No uncircumcised shall eat of it" (Exod. 12:43), he ordered them to perform the rite. Our rabbis described the performance: Moses did the cutting, Joshua the ripping, and Aaron the sucking. The foreskins were collected in heaps. The blood of circumcision got mixed with the blood of the Paschal lamb, and this made them deserving of the redemption. This is the implication of God's narration through Ezekiel, "When I passed by you and saw you wallowing in your blood, I said to you, 'Live by your blood,' Yea I said to you, 'live by your blood'" (Ezek. 16:6). Our rabbis added that they became degenerate with incest, deriving it from the verse, "O mortal, once there were two women, daughters of one mother" (Ezek. 23:2) (*Epistle on Martyrdom*, ch. 2).

Maimonides maintains that the Jews in Egypt practiced idolatry, save the Levites (*Avodah Zarah* 1:3, based on Exod. 32:26 and Ḥagigah 6b).

Exodus 13

13:1-2. And the Lord spoke to Moses, saying: Sanctify to Me every firstborn, whatever opens the womb of the children of Israel, of man and of beast, is Mine. — God, may He be exalted, listed three types of firstborn in one verse, as it says, "whatever opens the womb [of the children of Israel, of man and of beast, is Mine]" of any flesh that you offer to the Lord of either man or beast shall belong to you, but you shall surely redeem the firstborn human and the firstborn of an non-kosher animal (Num. 18:15) (*PhM Ḥallah* 4:9).

Rabbi Samson Raphael Hirsch observes that sanctifying firstborn humans, kosher animals, and donkeys represents the sanctification of "Man, his food, and his possessions" (on Exod. 13:13).

FURTHER: We are commanded to sanctify firstborn [animals], that is to say, to set them aside and separate them for whatever is necessary to do with them. And this is what God, may He be exalted, said, "Sanctify to Me every firstborn, whatever opens the womb, of man and of beast, is Mine." And it is explicitly mentioned in the Torah that this [word] "beast" (Deut. 15:19) refers only to cattle, sheep, and donkeys. And this commandment is repeated regarding kosher animals, and this is the commandment that we are speaking about now, "Your animal that is born among your cattle and your sheep you shall sanctify to the Lord your God" (Deut. 15:19). The law is that the firstborn of every kosher animal must be brought to the priests, who will offer its fat and its blood and will eat the rest of the meat.... It is already explained at the end of tractate *Ḥallah* that this commandment only applies in the land of Israel.[51] In the language of

---

51. Nahmanides writes, "They should sanctify them immediately, because it is to be a commandment that was practiced in the wilderness."

the *Sifrei*, "One might think that we bring firstborn from outside the land [of Israel] to the land—therefore the Torah says, 'And you shall eat before the Lord your God... the tithe of your grain, wine, and oil and the firstborn of your cattle and your sheep...' (Deut. 14:23). [Only] from a place where you bring the [second] grain tithe shall you bring firstborn. But from outside of Israel, from where you do not bring the [second] grain tithe, you do not bring your firstborn." It has been explained that this commandment only applies in the land [of Israel], but only in regards to it being sacrificed. Nonetheless, even though a firstborn in the Diaspora is not sacrificed, it remains holy [and cannot] be eaten until it develops a blemish. And there is no difference whether the Temple is standing or is in ruins, like in our era, just like regarding the [second] grain tithe. And the Levites are not obligated in this commandment[52] (*ShM*, Pos. 79; see also *ShM*, Pos. 80, the commandment to sanctify the first born human males, quoted at Exod. 22:28).

FURTHER: It is a positive commandment to separate all firstborn male issues, whether human, kosher animals, or donkeys. This applies whether the animals are healthy or *tereifot*, as it says, "Sanctify to Me every firstborn, whatever opens the womb of the children of Israel, of man and beast...." And all of it is given to the priests.[53] Firstborn humans and firstborn donkeys are redeemed, and their redemption is given to the priests. A kosher firstborn animal is slaughtered in the Temple [*azarah*] like other lesser holy offerings. And their blood is sprinkled, and its organs are incinerated, as we have explained in *Ma'aseh ha-Korbanot*.[54] And the rest of the meat

---

52. Elsewhere Maimonides writes that the Levites are obligated to sanctify the firstborn (*Bekhorot* 1:7). Therefore Kapach suggests this might belong to the end of the next commandments, *ShM*, Pos. 80.

53. M. Ḥallah 4:9. R. Ovadiah writes, "he redeems it with a sheep [*seh*] and it [the donkey] has no more sanctity."

54. *Ma'aseh ha-Korbanot* 5:17. Mahari Korkus here points out that Maimonides here uses the word "sprinkle" (*zarak*) rather than "pour"

is eaten by the priests, as it says, "You shall surely redeem firstborn non-kosher animals, but firstborn of a cow... you shall not redeem; they are holy.... And their meat shall be for you" (Num. 18:15-18) (*Bekhorot* 1:1-2).

FURTHER: If [a Jew] receives an animal from a gentile to care for it, and the offspring are to be owned jointly, or if a gentile received an animal from a Jew under this arrangement, the animals are exempt from [the mandates] of firstborn, as it says, "whatever opens the womb of [the children of] Israel,"[55] [meaning] it must belong to a Jew the entire time (*Bekhorot* 4:3).

Maimonides rules like the Sages against R. Yehudah (BT *Bekhorot* 2b-3a). The Talmud quotes the biblical phrase *kol bekhor*, a phrase which appears at both Exod. 13:2 and Num. 3:13. Rashi understands it as a reference to Num. 3:13 (3a, s.v. *kol bekhor*; see also 2a, s.v. *she-ne'emar*), as does Tosafot (3a, s.v. *ve-Rabbi Yehudah savar*). However, Maimonides seems to impute the talmudic passage to Exod. 13:2.

The *Leḥem Mishnah* writes, "The words of our Rabbi are imprecise [*megumgam*], since he did not bring the proof of *kol bekhor*." In other words, the *Leḥem Mishnah* also assumes the Talmud is quoting from Num. 3:13, not Exod. 13:2. One final point: The present passage addresses a kosher animal; for a parallel case regarding a donkey, see *Bikkurim* 12:15.

FURTHER: In reference to the law concerning the firstborn of man and cattle it is distinctly said, "And it came to pass, when Pharaoh would

(*shafakh*), though the latter is the technical word used in the verse (Num. 18:17); he points out that in *Ma'aseh ha-Korbanot*, Maimonides' language is consistent with the verse. He argues *shefikhah bikhlal zerikah*, "'pouring' is in the category of 'sprinkling.'"

55. The verse reads בבני ישראל while the printed versions of Maimonides read בישראל. However, Num. 3:13 uses בישראל.

hardly let us go, that the Lord slew all the first-born in the land of Egypt... therefore I sacrifice to the Lord..." (Exod. 13:15). But it can easily be explained why only cattle, sheep, and asses are mentioned in this law; these are kept as domestic animals, and are found in most places, especially in the land of Israel, where the Israelites were shepherds, they, their fathers, and forefathers: e.g., "Your servants are shepherds, both we and also our fathers" (Gen. 47:3).

Horses and camels, however, are not wanted by shepherds, and are not found in all places; thus in the spoil of Midian (Numbers 31) no other animals are mentioned but oxen, sheep, and asses. But asses alone are indispensable to all people, especially to those who are engaged in the field or in the forest. Thus Jacob says, "I have oxen and donkeys" (Gen. 32:6). Camels and horses are not possessed by many people, but only by a few, and are only found in a few places. The law that the firstborn of a donkey was to have its neck broken [in case it is not redeemed] (Exod. 13:13; see there), will only ensure the redemption of the donkey. It has, therefore, been said (M. *Bekhorot* 1:7) that the act of redeeming the donkey is to be preferred to that of breaking its neck (*Guide* 3:39).

13:3. And Moses said to the people, "Remember this day that you went forth from Egypt from the house of bondage, for with a mighty hand the Lord brought you forth from it... — See Exod. 13:8, where *ShM*, Pos. 157 and *Ḥametz u-Matzah* 7:1 are quoted. It must be noted that Maimonides understands this verse to teach the annual commandment of recounting the Exodus. However Rashi understands this verse to each "we must remember the Exodus from Egypt every day."

Maimonides also records a commandment to remember the Exodus from Egypt in both the day and night (*Keri'at Shema* 1:3, to be quoted at Deut. 16:3). This question dovetails into the question of why we recite Hallel on Passover night, and especially why we do it without a blessing. Rabbi Soloveitchik answered that Hallel during the day (and with a foreblessing) is an independent mitzvah, while the Hallel of Seder night is part of *sippur yetziat Mitzrayim*, "relating the exodus from Egypt." For other resolutions, see Rav Yaacov Francus, "Hallel on the Night of Pesach" (VBM: https://etzion.org.il/en/hallel-night-pesach#_ftnref13).

... and no leaven shall be eaten." — We are prohibited to eat leaven on Passover, and God said, "no leaven shall be eaten." And the verse clarifies that the punishment is *karet* (see Exod. 12:15), as it says, "whoever eats leavened bread... that soul shall be cut off from Israel" if it was intentional. And if it was accidental, he must bring a *ḥattat* offering (*ShM*, Neg. 197).

FURTHER: One may not benefit in any way from leaven on Passover, "no leaven shall be eaten" (Exod. 13:3), which means it is not permitted [to benefit in a manner that leads to] eating.[56] And one who allows leaven to remain on his property on Passover, even if he does not eat it, violates two prohibitions, as it says, "no leaven shall be seen within your borders" (Exod. 13:7), and it is [further] stated, "leaven shall not be found in your houses" (Exod. 12:19). And the prohibition of *ḥametz* [leaven] and the prohibition of *se'or* [leavening agent] that causes leavening is equivalent. One does not receive lashes on account of "shall not be seen" or "shall not be found" unless he purchases leavened goods on Passover or he ferments it, in order that it be an action. However, if there was leaven with him from before Passover, and when Passover came he did not destroy it but allowed it to remain on his property—even though he has violated two prohibitions, he does not receive biblical lashes, since he has not committed an act. However he gets [rabbinic] lashes for insubordination (*Ḥametz u-Matzah* 1:2-3).

___
56. "The default type of benefit is by eating" — Rabbenu Manoah.

FURTHER: One who eats leaven itself on Passover, even in the smallest amounts, [violates] a Torah prohibition, as it says, "no leaven shall be eaten." Nonetheless, he does not receive *karet* [for intentional eating] or bring an offering [for unintentional eating] unless he consumes an olive's measure. Someone who consumes less than an olive's measure receives [rabbinically imposed] lashes for insubordination (*Ḥametz u-Matzah* 1:7).

FURTHER: [There is a standard distinction between how the Jews in Egypt kept the first Passover (*Pesaḥ Mitzrayim*) and all subsequent observances of Passover (*Pesaḥ le-Dorot*; see M. *Pesaḥim* 9:5):] On the *Pesaḥ Mitzrayim*, they were only prohibited from eating leaven for one day, as it says, "no leaven shall be eaten. Today that you go forth" (Exod. 13:3-4). It is like saying: no leaven shall be eaten today that you are going forth.[57] And there it says "one night," which means on that night leaven was forbidden (*PhM Pesaḥim* 9:5).

Based on the opinion of R. Yosi ha-Gelili (BT *Pesaḥim* 96b). It seems that this verse teaches the annual prohibition of eating leaven on Passover for seven days, and it also teaches that in the "Egyptian Passover" the prohibition for eating leaven was one day only.

13:5. ... and you shall keep this service in this month. — [Maimonides is commenting on the Mishnah which states that the Passover offering must come from non-sacral animals (i.e., animals that are not reserved or sanctified for another purpose):] This law that the Passover offering may only come from non-sacral offerings we learn from the *Pesaḥ Mitzrayim*, which was without a doubt not [yet] sacred, since that time was not yet a time of sanctification, since there had been no commandment that preceded it. And that which is

---

57. Maimonides here quotes these two verses as if it is a continuous phrase.

said, "… and you shall keep this service in this month" means that all of the services shall be like this. Just as the Passover offering in Egypt only came from non-sacral animals, so too the Passover for [future] generations can only come from non-sacred animals (*PhM Menaḥot* 7:6; based on BT *Menaḥot* 82a-b).

13:7. Unleavened bread shall be eaten for seven days, and no leaven shall be seen with you and no yeast shall be seen with you in all of your borders. — See Exod. 12:19.

13:8. And you shall tell your son on this day, saying: on account of this which the Lord did for me when I went forth from Egypt. — We are commanded to relate the Exodus from Egypt on the night of the fifteenth of Nisan at the beginning of the night with all the expressiveness of the language of the story-teller. And whoever extends the story and adds details in telling what God did for us and what the Egyptians did to us with oppression and violence, and how God took vengeance on them, and in thanking God, may He be exalted, for what He bestowed for His kindnesses—all the better!

This is as the Sages said [in the Haggadah], "Whoever extends the discussion of the Exodus from Egypt is praiseworthy." Scripture teaches this commandment, as He, may he be exalted, said, "And you shall tell your son on this day...." The explanation of the verse: "'And you shall tell your son on this day': Perhaps from the first day [of Nisan]. Rather we come to learn 'on this day.' But could 'on this day' not mean while it is still daytime? Rather we come to learn 'on account of this' (see Exod. 12:2). I cannot only say it when matzah and bitter herbs are set before you" (*Mekhilta*). This means that at the beginning of the night you are obligated to relate [the Exodus].

And the language of the *Mekhilta*: "Since it is stated, 'when your son will ask' (Exod. 13:14), perhaps [this means] that if he asks, you will tell him, and if not, you do not tell him. Rather we come to learn 'And you shall tell your son," even if he does not ask you.

[Further] I only know this applies if he has a child, but if he is alone, or among other adults, from where [is there an obligation to relate the Exodus]? We come to learn, 'And Moses said to the people, "Remember this day that you went forth from Egypt"' (Exod. 13:3). This means that God commanded us to remember the Exodus just as He said, 'Remember the Sabbath day to sanctify it' (Exod. 20:8)." And you already know the language of the Sages: Even if we were all wise, all people of understanding, knowing the entire Torah, it would still be a commandment for us to relate the Exodus from Egypt, and whoever tells of the Exodus from Egypt is considered praiseworthy (*ShM*, Pos. 157).

FURTHER: It is a commandment to inform one's son, even if he did not ask (*Mekhilta de-Rashbi*), as it says, "And you shall tell your son." And his father should teach the son according to his [level of] intelligence.[58] How so? If he is young or foolish, he should say, "My son, we were all slaves like this bondmaid or like this slave, in Egypt, and on this night the Holy One, blessed is He, redeemed us and brought us to freedom." And if the son is older and wise, he tells him what occurred to us in Egypt and the miracles that were performed for us through Moses. All is according to the son's knowledge (*Ḥametz u-Matzah* 7:2).

Mitchell First has researched how commentaries understand the word *ve-higgadta*: explain (Shadal), demonstrate by action (Rabbi S.R. Hirsch), study (Rabbi Soloveitchik), elaborate (Radak). He points out that according to Maimonides, *ve-higgadta* means *le-hodi'a*, "to inform" (*Roots and Rituals*, pp. 223-225).

---

58. Maimonides uses a similar phrase as the Mishnah, *da'at ha-ben* (M. *Pesaḥim* 10:4). However, the scriptural derivations are original and not present in the Mishnah; see there and *PhM*. Based on this phrase, the Rema rules that the Haggadah should be recited in a language the people understand (*Oraḥ Ḥayyim* 473:6).

13:9. And it shall be a sign for you on your hand... — We are commanded to wrap hand *tefillin*, as He said, "And you shall bind them as a sign on your hand" (Deut. 6:8). And this [commandment] is repeated four times (Exod. 13:9, Exod. 13:16, Deut. 6:8, Deut. 11:18) (*ShM*, Pos. 13).

... and a remembrance between your eyes so that the teaching of the Lord shall be in your mouth, for with a mighty hand the Lord brought you out of Egypt. — We are commanded to wrap the head *tefillin*, as He, may He be exalted, said, "they shall be as frontlets between your eyes" (Deut. 6:8). This commandment is repeated in the Torah four times (Exod. 13:9, Exod. 13:16, Deut. 6:8, Deut. 11:18) (*ShM*, Pos. 12).

> According to Rashbam, the simple meaning of "between your eyes" is that we should always be conscious of the Exodus from Egypt (in other words, for Rashbam, these verses do not teach the mitzvah of *tefillin*). However, Ibn Ezra suggests that this reading, which is also adopted by the Karaites, is metaphorical (based on the book of Proverbs, which is by definition metaphorical). Rather, Ibn Ezra insists, this phrase teaches the commandment of *tefillin shel rosh*. See also *Gur Aryeh*, who uses the phrase "you shall not make a bald spot between your eyes" (Deut. 14:1) to prove that we "must place them in a place of hair," i.e., above the forehead (see on Lev. 21:5; see also Nahmanides on Exod. 13:16). Maimonides is consistent with Ibn Ezra, Nahmanides, and *Gur Aryeh* that the phrase teaches *tefillin shel rosh*.
>
> Hizkuni adds, "The hand *tefillin* refers to [that God took us out with] a mighty hand, and the head *tefillin* is a remembrance of the signs and wonders that God performed before our eyes" (v. 16).

FURTHER: [Maimonides explains why he counts the two different tefillin as two separate commandments:] And the proof that the head *tefillin* and hand *tefillin* are two separate commandments is based on the end of *Menaḥot* (44a). And the Sages were perplexed that the suggestion that if one has only head *tefillin* or hand *tefillin*, he should not wear it unless he has both of them available at once. And the made the statement, "Should one who has not two *mitzvot* not have one mitzvah?"[59] This means that if someone does not have the possibility of performing two *mitzvot*, should he not perform one? Certainly not! Rather, he should perform the mitzvah that is before him, and he should wrap whichever one is available. We see it is clear to you from this that they are called two commandments: head *tefillin* and hand *tefillin*. Women are exempt from these two commandments, as God, may He be exalted, said, regarding the reason for *tefillin*, "so that the teaching of the Lord shall be in your mouth," and women are exempt from Torah study. And this is the explanation of the *Mekhilta* (*ShM*, Pos. 13).

> The *Behag* understood that the two *tefillin* comprise one commandment. However, R. Manaoh quotes that the Rif counted them as two separate commandments (*Tefillin* 4:4). Nonetheless, based on Maimonides' understanding of the Talmud (*Menaḥot* 36a), despite the *tefillin* being two commandments, they only require one *berakhah*.

FURTHER: These four passages: *Kaddesh li* (Exod. 13:1-10), *Ve-hayah ki yevi'akha* (Exod. 13:11-16), *Shema* (Deut. 6:4-9), and *Ve-hayah im shamo'a* (Deut. 11:13-21)—should be written separately and covered in leather. These are called *tefillin* (phylacteries). They are placed on the head and tied on the arm... (*Tefillin* 1:1; based on *Menaḥot* 34b; see also *Mekhilta de-Pisḥa* 17).

---

59. There the Talmud is referring to a case where he definitely has both the head and hand *tefillin*, not Maimonides' case of someone who has either one or the other.

FURTHER: As the sacrificial service is not the primary object [of the commandments about sacrifice], while supplications, prayers, and similar kinds of worship are nearer to the primary object, and indispensable for obtaining it, a great difference was made in the Law between these two kinds of service... We were not commanded to sacrifice in every place, and in every time, or to build a temple in every place, or to permit any one who desires to become priest and to sacrifice. On the contrary, all this was prohibited to us... But prayer and supplication can be offered everywhere and by every person. The same is the case with the commandment of *tzitzit* (Num. 15:38), *mezuzah* (Deut. 6:9, 11:20), *tefillin* (Exod. 13:9, 16), and similar kinds of divine service (*Guide* 3:32)

13:10. And you shall keep this ordinance in its season from year to year.[60] — The time for putting on *tefillin* is in the day and not at night, as it says, "from day to day." The "ordinance" [in this verse] is the commandment of *tefillin*. And similarly Sabbaths and festivals are not times for *tefillin*, as it says, "And it shall be a sign for you" (Exod. 13:9), but the Sabbaths and festivals are already a sign.... (see BT *Eruvin* 96a, *Menaḥot* 36a-b). And whoever puts on *tefillin* beginning after sunset violates a biblical prohibition, as it says, "And you shall keep this ordinance..." (*Tefillin* 4:10-11, following R. Yohanan in *Menaḥot* 36b).

FURTHER: These temporary commandments [regarding the Passover] were then made permanent, in order that we may remember what was done in those days: "And you shall keep this ordinance in its season from year to year" (*Guide* 3:46; this passage is quoted at length at Exod. 12:3).

---

60. Hebrew *mi-yamim yamimah*, which literally means "from day to day," but it colloquially means "from year to year" (Rashi, R. Saadiah). Compare: "Tomorrow, and tomorrow, and tomorrow / Creeps in this petty pace from day to day, to the last syllable of recorded time..." (*Macbeth*, Act 5, scene 5).

The word *ḥukkah*, here translated as "ordinance" refers to the rite of the Passover offering (R. Akiva, Rashbam); this point should be clear from context. Maimonides takes this understanding in *Guide* 3:46. However, as a legal matter, he accepts the halakhic midrash that *ḥukkah* here refers to the obligation of *tefillin* (R. Yosi ha-Gelili, BT *Menaḥot* 36b).

FURTHER: It is a positive commandment from the Torah for the court to calculate and to determine if whether or not the moon will be seen. And they must examine the witnesses before the new moon is declared. And they must dispatch [emissaries] to notify the rest of the nation about which day will be new month, so that they will know on which day the festivals [will fall], as it says, "which you shall proclaim them as holy convocations" (Lev. 23:2); and it is stated, "And you shall keep this ordinance in its season" (*Kiddush ha-Ḥodesh* 1:7; see *Rosh Hashanah* 21b, and *ShM*, Pos. 153, quoted at Exod. 12:2).

The *Leḥem Mishnah* writes that the court's ability to intercalate the months is based on Exod. 12:2, not the present verse. However the *Peirush* [a commentary on this passage] has a different explanation: "It is written, 'which you shall proclaim them [*otam*].' Do not read otam but *attem* [you]." (The words *otam* and *attem* have the same consonantal structure.)

13:12. And you shall set apart to the Lord all that opens the womb...
— Maimonides gives five definitions of *avar*, literally, "to pass, to pass over" (*Guide* 1:21, quoted at Exod. 12:12), but does not quote the present verse. Rashi, Saadiah, and Nahmanides all give a meaning of *ve-ha'avarta* as *hafrashah*, "separation," but Maimonides does not supply that meaning. It is not immediately clear what meaning of *avar* Maimonides would provide in this context.

Further: [Maimonides is commenting on the Mishnah which states that there is a firstborn for the sake of inheritance and firstborn for the sake of priesthood (M. *Bekhorot* 8:1):] The firstborn for inheritance is the first issue that is born to a man from a Jewish woman, and it does not matter if she had already given birth [from another man] or not, as God said, "first of his strength" (Deut. 21:17). The firstborn for the priesthood is the first issue of a woman, and there is no difference if the father already had issue before him or not, as it says "that opens the womb" (Exod. 13:12, 13:15, 34:19, Num. 3:12, 18:15) (*PhM Bekhorot* 8:1).

The "firstborn for the priesthood" means that the firstborn male issue requires *pidyon ha-ben*, since those males were originally destined to be the priests.

13:13. And the firstborn of every donkey you shall redeem with a sheep, and if you do not redeem it you shall break its neck... — We are commanded to redeem a firstborn donkey only with a sheep and not redeem it with anything else. And this sheep must be given to the priest. And this is what God, may He be exalted, said, "And the firstborn of every donkey you shall redeem with a sheep." ... And the Levites are also exempt from this commandment (*ShM*, Pos. 81).

FURTHER: We are commanded to break the neck of the donkey if we do not want to redeem it, as He, may He be exalted, said, "and if you do not redeem it you shall break its neck." ... And you could ask me and say, "Why did you count 'redeeming' and 'breaking the neck' as two separate commandments? Why not count it as one commandment, with 'breaking the neck' as part of this commandment, as explained in the seventh principle?" Surely this would be true, had the Sages not made a statement that teaches they are two commandments. And here is what they said: "the commandment of redemption takes precedence over the commandment of breaking its neck, and the commandment of *yibbum* takes precedence over the commandment of *halitzah*."[61] Just as a *yevamah* may receive either *yibbum* or *halitzah*, and *yibbum* it a mitzvah and *halitzah* is a commandment, each in its own right, similarly, as has been stated, a donkey may either be redeemed or have its neck broken, and each is an independent commandment ... (*ShM*, Pos. 82; see also *Bikkurim* 12:1 and *PhM Hallah* 4:9).

> The Ra'avad (*Bikkurim* 12:1) takes objection to counting these as two separate commandments, writing, "even though the Sages wrote 'the commandment of redeeming precedes the commandment of breaking its neck,' you should not think that this is a commandment. Rather it is a transgression and it is called an act of destruction and it destroys the property of the priest."

FURTHER: One who does not wish to redeem it should break its neck with a hatchet from behind, as it says, "and if you do not redeem it you shall break its neck." And we do not kill it with a staff, a reed, an axe, or a saw—only with a hatchet. And we may not place it in a room and lock the door behind it until it dies, as it says, "and you shall break its neck" (*Bikkurim* 12:7).

FURTHER: After its neck has been broken it is forbidden to derive benefit from it, according to all opinions. And this verb [*ve-arafto*] comes from the word *oref* [neck, back of the neck], because we are not permitted to ritually slaughter it [i.e., from the front of the neck] or to strangle it. Rather we must strike its neck from behind (*PhM Bekhorot* 1:7).

... and every firstborn human of your sons you shall redeem. — God said, "and the firstborn donkey... and every firstborn human of

---

61. M. *Bekhorot* 1:7 (BT *Bekhorot* 13a). *Yibbum* and *halitzah* refer, respectively, to levirate marriage or the rejection thereof mentioned in Deut. 25:5-6.

your sons you shall redeem."[62] R. Eliezer says there is a thematic connection between a firstborn donkey and firstborn human.[63] And the Sages learn from what it says, "you shall surely redeem every firstborn human and every impure animal you shall redeem" (Num. 18:15). The meaning is the firstborn donkey, as has been explained in the *Sifrei*. And they say, "I have connected it [the firstborn donkey] to redemption, but no other animal" (*PhM Eduyot* 7:1).

FURTHER: It is stated in the Torah, "And the firstborn of a donkey you shall redeem with a sheep" (Exod. 34:20), and it is stated, "whatever opens the womb of the children of Israel, of man and of beast," and it is said to Aaron, "and every firstborn of an impure animal you shall redeem" (Num. 18:15), which is a reference to the donkey, since the only non-kosher animal that needs to be redeemed is the donkey (*PhM Bekhorot* 1:1; see also 1:6).

FURTHER: The law that the firstborn of a donkey was to have its neck broken [in case it is not redeemed] (Exod. 13:13) will only ensure the redemption of the donkey [by giving it to the priest] (*Guide* 3:39; see extended passage quoted at Exod. 13:3).

13:14. And it shall be that when your son asks you tomorrow, saying, "What is this?" that you shall say to him, "With a mighty hand the Lord brought us out from Egypt from the house of bondage." — See Exod. 13:8, where Maimonides understands this is the simple son of the Haggadah.

13:15. And it shall be that when Pharaoh's heart was hardened and would not let us go, that the Lord killed all of the firstborn

---

62. Kapach notes that this is a splice of Exod. 13:13 and 34:20. See there.
63. Rashi quotes two reasons for this: (1) The firstborn of Egypt are compared to donkeys (see Exod. 23:19-20; the commentaries there understand the verse differently). (2) When the Jews left Egypt, each left with many donkeys laden with gold and silver (BT *Bekhorot* 5b); see *Guide* 3:39

in the land of Egypt, from the firstborn of man to the firstborn of beast; therefore I sacrifice to the Lord everything that opens the womb of the males, and all of my firstborn sons I shall redeem. — See at Exod. 13:1-2.

13:16. And it shall be a sign on your hand and a frontlet between your eyes, for with a mighty hand the Lord brought us out of Egypt. — See at Exod. 13:9.

PARASHAT BESHALLAH

13:17. And it was that when Pharaoh sent away the nation and God did not lead them through the land of the Philistines, though it was close, for God said perhaps the nation will regret when they see war and they will return to Egypt. — ... the Exodus took place in the beginning of the year 2448 (*Epistle to Yemen*, §16; based on *Seder Olam Rabbah*).

FURTHER: True, they had matured to some extent in the affairs of the world, but He [=God] anticipated that they would return to Egypt, and would forfeit what was planned for them. Likewise, He also anticipated that they would not accept this principle, I mean the return of the soul to the body, and as a result would forfeit the ultimate goal provided for them. They will surely mature and accept the doctrines as well, seeing that the Leader and the Developer is the same (*Essay on Resurrection*, p. 230).

> Abraham Halkin notes, "Realizing that it is God who redeemed them and revealed the Torah to them, they will recognize that He is also the Author of the hopes and promises laid before them."

13:18. And God led the people through the wilderness to the Sea of Reeds, and the children of Israel went out from the land of Egypt prepared. — ... the Israelites would not have been able to conquer the land and fight with its inhabitants, if they had not previously undergone the trouble and hardship of the wilderness. Scripture says in reference to this: "for God said perhaps the nation will regret when they see war and they will return to Egypt. And God led the people through the wilderness to the Sea of Reeds, and the children of Israel went out from the land of Egypt prepared" (Exod. 13:17-18). Ease destroys bravery, while trouble and care for food create strength; and this was [also for the Israelites] the good that ultimately came out of their wanderings in the wilderness (*Guide* 3:24).

Kapach points out that this verse is central to Maimonides' understanding of the spiritual and psychological development of the Jewish people. At the beginning of the sojourn in the wilderness, the Jews were not ready to fight and defend themselves, which is why they needed to be led in a circuitous route.

FURTHER: Here God led the people about, away from the direct road which He originally intended, because He feared they might meet on that way with hardships too great for their ordinary strength; He took them by another road in order to obtain thereby His original object. In the same manner God refrained from prescribing what the people by their natural disposition would be incapable of obeying, and gave the above-mentioned commandments as a means of securing His chief object, namely, to spread a knowledge of Him [among the people], and to cause them to reject idolatry. It is contrary to man's nature that he should suddenly abandon all the different kinds of Divine service and the different customs in which he has been brought up, and which have been so general, that they were considered as a matter of course; it would be just as if a person trained to work as a slave with mortar and bricks, or similar things, should interrupt his work, clean his hands, and at once fight with real giants. It was the result of God's wisdom that the Israelites were led about in the wilderness till they acquired courage.[64] For it is a well-known fact that travelling in the wilderness, and privation of bodily enjoyments, such as bathing, produce courage, while the reverse is the source of faint-heartedness: besides, another generation rose during the wanderings that had not been accustomed to degradation and slavery. All the travelling in the wilderness was regulated by Divine commands

---

64. In the Aristotelian model, courage is the mean between cowardice and foolhardiness, and the courageous man is afraid but acts despite that fear; see *Nicomachean Ethics* 3.6-9. Compare: "Who is strong? He who conquers his impulse" (*Avot* 4:1).

through Moses; e.g., "At the commandment of the Lord they rested, and at the commandment of the Lord they journeyed; they kept the charge of the Lord and the commandment of the Lord by the hand of Moses" (Num. 9:23). In the same way the portion of the Law under discussion is the result of divine wisdom, according to which people are allowed to continue the kind of worship to which they have been accustomed, in order that they might acquire the true faith, which is the chief object [of God's commandments].

You ask: What could have prevented God from commanding us directly, that which is the chief object, and from giving us the capacity of obeying it? This would lead to a second question: What prevented God from leading the Israelites through the way of the land of the Philistines, and endowing them with strength for fighting? The leading about by a pillar of cloud by day and a pillar of fire by night (see Exod. 13:21-22) would then not have been necessary. A third question would then be asked in reference to the good promised as reward for the keeping of the commandments, and the evil foretold as a punishment for sins. It is the following question: As it is the chief object and purpose of God that we should believe in the Law, and act according to that which is written therein, why has He not given us the capacity of continually believing in it, and following its guidance, instead of holding out to us reward for obedience, and punishment for disobedience, or of actually giving all the predicted reward and punishment? For [the promises and the threats] are but the means of leading to this chief object. What prevented Him from giving us, as part of our nature, the will to do that which He desires us to do, and to abandon the kind of worship which He rejects?

There is one general answer to these three questions, and to all questions of the same character; it is this: Although in every one of the signs [related in Scripture] the natural property of some individual being is changed, the nature of man is never changed by God by way of miracle. It is in accordance with this important principle that God said, "O that there were such a heart in them, that they would fear Me..." (Deut. 5:26).

It is also for this reason that He distinctly stated the commandments and the prohibitions, the reward and the punishment. This principle as regards miracles has been frequently explained by us in our works: I do not say this because I believe that it is difficult for God to change the nature of every individual person; on the contrary, it is possible, and it is in His power, according to the principles taught in Scripture; but it has never been His will to do it, and it never will be. If it were part of His will to change [at His desire] the nature of any person, the mission of prophets and the giving of the Law would have been altogether superfluous (*Guide* 3:32).

13:19. And Moses took the bones of Joseph with him, for he had surely made the children of Israel swear, saying, "God will surely take notice of you, and you shall carry my bones out from here with you." — One who is ritually defiled to the dead, and even a corpse itself, may enter to Temple mount, as it says, "And Moses took the bones of Joseph with him,"— *with him* in the Levite camp (*Bi'at ha-Mikdash* 3:4; based on T. *Keilim* 1:7, BT *Nazir* 45a; see also *PhM Keilim* 1:8).

> This scheme is based on the congruity of the Levite camp with the Temple mount; see also *Bet ha-Beḥirah* 7:11

13:21-22. The Lord went in front of them in a pillar of cloud by day, to lead them along the way, and in a pillar of fire by night, to give them light, so that they might travel by day and by night. Neither the pillar of cloud by day nor the pillar of fire by night left its place in front of the people. — See at Exod. 13:18, where Maimonides explores why it was necessary for God to lead the Israelites by a pillar of cloud and a pillar of fire.

Exodus 14

14:3. For Pharaoh will say of the children of Israel, they are astray in the land[65]; the wilderness has shut them in. — [Maimonides uses Pharaoh as an archetype for future critics of the Israelites' journey:]... they [the detractors] might think that the Israelites stayed in the wilderness in a place not far from inhabited land, where it was possible for man to live [in the ordinary way]; that it was like those deserts in which Arabs live at present; or that they dwelt in such places in which they could plow, sow, and reap, or live on some vegetable that was growing there; or that manna came always down in those places as an ordinary natural product [and not as a miracle]; or that there were wells of water in those places.

In order to remove all these doubts and to firmly establish the accuracy of the account of these miracles, Scripture enumerates all the stations, so that coming generations may see them, and learn the greatness of the miracle which enabled human beings to live in those places forty years. For this very reason Joshua cursed him who would ever build up Jericho (Josh. 6:26); the effect of the miracle was to remain forever, so that anyone who would see the wall sunk in the ground would understand that it was not in the condition of a building pulled down by human hands, but sunk through a miracle.

---

65. Hebrew for "astray" is *nevukhim*, which is usually translated as "entangled" or "perplexed." It has also been translated as *metorafim*, "perplexed" (*Mekhilta*, "Beshallaḥ" 2). This translation is based on Maimonides' comments quoted here. However, most Hebrew commentaries understand it as meaning "locked up" or "trapped" (Rashi, Rashbam).

The use of the Hebrew title *Moreh Nevukhim*, (English, *Guide of the Perplexed*) conjures up this verse, where the generation of Maimonides, like the generation of the Exodus, was in need of being led out of the wilderness, one literal, one intellectual. (See *Maimonides Between Philosophy and Halakhah: Rabbi Joseph B. Soloveitchik's Lectures on the Guide of the Perplexed*, ed. Lawrence Kaplan [New York: Ktav/Urim, 2016].) However, I have not consulted if such an allusion exists in the original Arabic title.

In a similar manner the words, "At the commandment of the Lord the children of Israel journeyed, and at the commandment of the Lord they pitched" (Num. 9:18, 20) would suffice as a simple statement of facts; and the reader might at first sight consider as unnecessary additions all the details which follow, e.g., "And when the cloud tarried long... And so it was when the cloud was a few days.... Or whether it were two days..." (Num. 9:19-22).

But I will show you the reason why all these details are added. For they serve to confirm the account, and to contradict the opinion of the nations, both of ancient and modern times, that the Israelites lost their way, and did not know where to go; that "they are astray in the land," wherefore the Arabs unto this day call that desert Al-Tih ("the Desert of Going Astray") imagining that the Israelites erred about, and did not know the way. Scripture, therefore, clearly states and emphatically declares that it was by God's command that the journeyings were irregular, that the Israelites returned to the same places several times, and that the duration of the stay was different in each station; while the stay in one place continued for eighteen years,[66] in another place it lasted one day, and in another one night. There was no going astray, but the journey was regulated by "the rising of the pillar of cloud" (Num. 9:17). Therefore all these details are given. Scripture clearly states that the way was near, known, and in good condition; I mean the way from Horeb, whither they came intentionally, according to the command of God, "You shall serve God upon this mountain" (Exod. 3:12), to Kadesh Barnea, the beginning of inhabited land, as Scripture says, "Behold, we are now in Kadesh, a city in the uttermost of thy border" (Num. 20:16). That way was a journey of eleven days; as it says, "Eleven days' journey from Horeb, by the way of mount Seir, unto Kadesh Barnea" (Deut. 1:2). In such a journey it is impossible to err about for forty years;

---

66. Likely a reference to Kadesh Barnea; however Rashi says they encamped there nineteen (not eighteen) years. See Deut. 1:46.

rather the reason for it is stated in Scripture (Numbers 13-14). In like manner there is a good reason for every passage the object of which we cannot see. We must always apply the words of our Sages: "'It is not a vain thing for you' (Deut. 32:47) — and if it seems vain, it seems your fault" (*Guide* 3:50; This phrase appears at JT *Shabbat* 1:4, JT *Ketuvot* 8:11; however, Maimonides' application appears to be original).

14:4. And I will harden Pharaoh's heart... — See at Exod. 4:21.

14:10. And Pharaoh approached [*hikriv*]... — Maimonides explains that the words *karav*, *naga*, and *nagash* have a literal and a metaphoric meaning. As a literal meaning, they mean "contact" or "nearness in space." Metaphorically, they mean "the approach of man's knowledge to an object, as if resembled the physical approach of one body to another." Maimonides quotes the present verse, *u-Far'oh hikriv*, "And Pharaoh approached," as an example of the literal meaning of the verb *karav* (see *Guide* 1:18).

Since Maimonides cites this verse as well as Exod. 32:19, it appears that he does not differentiate between the *kal* (*karav*) and the *hif'il* (*hikriv*) in the first signification of the verb. Shadal similarly writes, "The Hebrew is an intransitive verb, 'became near.'" Other commentaries, however, take note of the shift in this verse; Rashi quotes that Pharaoh "brought himself near," meaning he led the army from the front, not the rear (here and on v. 6). Ibn Ezra explains that Pharaoh brought his army near (i.e., the verse omits the direct object), and this approach is followed by Sforno. Radak prefers reading it as transitive verb (פועל יוצא), referring to the army, but then adds that it might be an intransitive verb (פועל עומד). *BDB* quotes several meanings of *hikriv*: "bring near, bring, present" (transitive), "make an approach" (intransitive, quoting the present verse, "bring near" (transitive, concerning an offering), "make an offering." Thus

Maimonides has backing from rishonim and modern scholarship that *hikriv* is synonymous with *karav*.

14:11. And they said to Moses, "Are there not enough graves in Egypt that you took us to die in the desert? What have you done to us by taking us out of Egypt?" — [Maimonides will say that this is the first of ten times that the Jews tested God in the wilderness, based on Num. 14:22, *Avot* 5:4, BT *Arakhin* 15a-b:] The ten times that our ancestors tested God in Egypt are all in the verses:

- The first is at the Sea of Reeds, when they said, "Are there not enough graves in Egypt..." (Exod. 14:11);
- The second is at Marah, as it says, "And the people complained to Moses, saying, 'What shall we drink?'" (Exod. 15:24);
- The third is in the wilderness of Sin when they asked for manna, saying, "Would that we had died by the hand of God" (Exod. 16:3);
- The fourth is when they rebelled by leaving the manna to the next day, as it says, "But they did not listen to Moses" (Exod. 16:20);
- The fifth is when they rebelled by looking to collect manna on the Sabbath, as it says, "some of the people went out to collect [manna] and found none" (Exod. 16:27);
- The sixth is at Rephidim when the demanded water ["And the people quarreled with Moses and said, 'Give us water,' and Moses said to them, 'Why do you quarrel with me? why do you tempt the Lord?'" (Exod. 17:2);
- The seventh is at Horeb with the sin of the Golden Calf (Exod. 32);
- The eighth is at Taberah when they expressed their doubts in that place about God and rebelled, as it says, "And it was, when the people complained" (Num. 11:1);
- The ninth is at Kibroth Hattaavah, when they demanded meat, as it says, "And the mixed multitude in their midst lusted..." (Num. 11:4);

- The tenth is in the wilderness of Paran regarding the spies; and there is says, "and they have tried Me ten times" (Num. 14:22) (*PhM Avot* 5:4).[67] (See chart on next page.)

14:13. And Moses said to the people, "Do not fear. Stand firm and see the salvation of the Lord which He will do for you this day, for the Egyptians whom you have seen today, you shall never see again forever." — We are forbidden from ever living in the land of Egypt, so that we should not learn from their heresy and we not follow in their obscene ways. And this is what God, may He be exalted, said [regarding a king], "[However he may not have too many horses, and he may not return the nation to Egypt, for which reason he may not have too many horses, and the Lord has said to you,] 'You shall never return that way again'" (Deut. 17:16). And this prohibition is repeated three times [in Scripture]. The Sages said, "In three places the Holy One, blessed is He, warned Israel against returning to Egypt. Three times they returned, and three times they were punished" (JT *Sukkah* 5:1, *Mekhilta* "Beshallaḥ" 3).

Of the three places, of them is what we have mentioned (Deut. 17:16). And the second is what He, may He be exalted, said, "by the way that I have told you to never see again" (Deut. 28:68). And the third is "for the Egyptians whom you have seen today, you shall never see again forever" (Exod. 14:13). And even though it appears that these words are narrative, the oral tradition teaches that it is a prohibition.... However, it is permitted to travel there for commerce or to travel to another land. And in explaining this, the Sages said in the Jerusalem Talmud (*Sanhedrin* 10:8), "You cannot return there to live, but you may return there to do commerce or business or to conquer the land" (*ShM*, Neg. 46).

---

67. The Hebrew phrase *eser pe'amim* literally means "ten times," which prompts a discussion of what those ten tests are. However, Ibn Ezra and Rashbam understand it as "many," as does Jacob Milgrom, *Numbers*, p. 113.

Ten Times the Israelites tested God in the Wilderness According

	BT *Arakhin* 15a-b	*Avot de-Rabbi Natan* (based on Deut. 1:1)
1	"Because there were no graves in Egypt" (Exod. 14:11)	In the wilderness, where they made the Golden Calf, as it is said, "They made a calf in Horeb" (Ps. 106:19)
2	"But they were rebellious at the sea, even at the Red Sea; nevertheless He saved them for His name's sake" (Ps. 106:7)	At Arabah, where they clamored for water, as it is said, "And the people thirsted there fore water" (Exod. 17:3)
3	[Marah] "And when they came to Marah they could not drink... And the people murmured against Moses" (Exod. 15:23-24)	Over against Suph [i.e., at the Sea of Reeds] is a reference to their being rebellious at the Red Sea. Rabbi Judah says: They were rebellious at the sea, they were rebellious at the sea, as it is said, "But they were rebellious at the sea, even at the Red Sea" (Ps. 106:7)
4	[Rephidim] "They encamped at Rephidim and there was no water to drink" (Exod. 17:1)	In the neighborhood of Paran refers to the incident of the spies, as it is said, "And Moses sent them fron the wilderness of Paran" (Num. 13:3)
5	"Do not go out" whereas they did go out (no verse)	And Tophel refers to the slanderous words which they uttered over the manna (cf. Num. 21:5)
6	"Do not leave over" but they did leave over (cf. Exod. 16:19-20)	And Laban refers to the controversy of Korah (Numbers 16)
7	"When we sat by the fleshpots" (Exod. 16:3)	And Hazeroth refers to the incident of the quail (Numbers 11)
8	"And the mixed multitude that was among them" (Num. 11:4)	And at Taberah (Num. 11:1)
9	As it happened (Exodus 32)	And at Massah (Exod. 16:4)
10	In the wilderness (i.e., spies) (Numbers 13-14)	Kibroth Hattaavah (Num. 11:4; thus there are three tests in this chapter)

to the Talmud, *Avot de-Rabbi Natan*, Maimonides, and R. Yonah

Maimonides	R. Yonah
The first is at the Sea of Reeds, when they said, "Are there not enough graves in Egypt…" (Exod. 14:11)	"Are there not enough graves in Egypt…" (Exod. 14:11)
The second is at Marah, as it says, "And the people complained to Moses, saying, 'What shall we drink?'" (Exod. 15:24);	"And the people complained to Moses, saying, 'What shall we drink?'" (Exod. 15:24);
The third is in the wilderness of Sin when they asked for manna, saying, "Would that we had died by the hand of God" (Exod. 16:3);	"Would that we had died by the hand of God" (Exod. 16:3);
The fourth is when they rebelled by leaving the manna to the next day, as it says, "And they did not listen to Moses" (Exod. 16:20);	"Is God in our midst or not" (Exod. 17:7)
The fifth is when they rebelled by looking to collect manna on the Sabbath, as it says, "some of the people went out to collect [manna] and found none" (Exod. 16:27);	Leaving over the manna (Exod. 16:20)
The sixth is at Rephidim when the demanded water ["And the people quarreled with Moses and said, 'Give us water,' and Moses said to them, 'Why do you quarrel with me? why do you tempt the Lord?'" (Exod. 17:2);	"And there was no water for the congregation" (Num. 20:2)
The seventh is at Horeb with the sin of the Golden Calf (Exodus 32);	Horeb with the Golden Calf, as it says, "and the people gathered to Aaron and they said to him, 'Come, make for us a god'" (Exod. 32:1)
The eighth is at Taberah when they expressed their doubts in that place about God and rebelled, as it says, "And it was, when the people complained" (Num. 11:1);	"And the people complained to God… and a fire of the Lord burned them and and consumed those in the border of the camps" (Num. 11:1)
The ninth is at Kibroth Hattaavah, when they demanded meat, as it says, "And the mixed multitude in their midst lusted…" (Num. 11:4);	At Kibroth Hattaavah when they said, "who will feed us meat" (Num. 11:4)
The tenth is in the wilderness of Paran regarding the spies; and there is says, "and they have tried Me these ten times" (Num. 14:22).	In the wilderness of Paran when they sent the spies, and there it is stated, "And they have tried Me these ten times" (Num. 14:22)

Nahmanides in his commentary renders the verse, "you shall never see again forever of your own free will [*bi-retzonkhem*] from now on [*me-attah* in place of *od*]" (on Exod. 14:13), which explains why this verse is a commandment rather than a prophecy. Rashi, however, probably understood this verse as a prophetic future, rather than a commandment.

FURTHER: It is permitted to return to the land of Egypt for commerce or business or to conquer other lands. The only prohibition is to settle there. And one is not liable for lashes for violating this prohibition, because at the time he entered, it was permitted, and if he decides to dwell and settle there, he has not committed an action.[68] And it seems to me that if a king of Israel conquers the land of Egypt with the consent of the court, then it is permitted [to live in Egypt], for the Torah only prohibited individuals from settling there, or to dwell there while in the hands of Gentiles, because its deeds are the most abhorrent of all nations, as it says, "As the ways of the land of Egypt [among whom you have dwelled, and as the ways of the land of Canaan whither I bring you, you shall not do; and you shall not go according to their statutes]" (Lev. 18:3) (*Melakhim* 5:8).

Historically, Maimonides lived in Egypt from about 1168 until his death in around 1204. According to Rabbi Ishtori ha-Parhi, in his compendium *Kaftor va-Feraḥ*, chapter 5, Maimonides would sign his letters "Moses son of Maimon, who transgresses three commandments every single day," a reference to the three times the prohibition is mentioned (Exod. 14:13, Deut. 17:16, Deut. 28:68). This begs the question of why he did so.

---

68. One is generally not punished for a *lav she-ein bo ma'asah*, a prohibition that is violated but not by the performance of an affirmative action. Here, once he settles in Egypt, there is no physical act at the moment of transgression.

The Radvaz quotes a first answer that perhaps it is only forbidden to voyage on the exact route that the Jews took leaving Egypt; he rejects this answer. Then he suggests that going to Egypt for commerce is permissible; the only prohibition is travelling to Egypt with the intent to settle there. The Radvaz also asks why Maimonides dwelled in Egypt long term, and he suggests Maimonides may have been forced to stay because of royal duress because he was physician to the king and his advisors. He uses this as an archetype for himself, since he opened a yeshiva there to teach and learn Torah.

Alternatively, Rav Hezekiah da Silva (1659-1698), in his *Mayim Ḥayyim*, points out that elsewhere Maimonides writes that during the conquest of Sennacherib, all of the nations were relocated (*Issurei Bi'ah* 15:25), so the people who currently live in Egypt are not the biblical Egyptians (see Frankel's *Sefer Likkutim*). Perhaps the prohibition is only when the biblical Egyptians live within their ancient borders.

14:21. And Moses stretched his hand over the sea and the Lord made the sea move because of a strong east wind all that night, and He made it into dry land, and the waters were divided. — [Maimonides is commenting on the Mishnah that ten miracles were performed for our forefathers at the Sea of Reeds:] The ten [miracles] at the sea are known by way of oral tradition.

1.   The first is the splitting of the sea, according to the plain meaning of the verse, "and the waters were divided" (Exod. 14:21),
2.   The second miracle is that after the sea split, the waters formed a domed roof, neither flat nor sloped, and a path like a tunnel through the water was formed, with water to the left, right, and

155

above, and this is was Habakkuk said, "You have pierced the heads of his villages with spears" (Hab. 3:14).[69]

3. And the third is that the ground became hard and firm for them, as it is said, "and [the children of Israel] walked through on dry land" (Exod. 14:29), and it did not remain like a river bed that has sediment and mud.

4. And the fourth is that when the Egyptians trod on it, the ground became muddy and sticky, as it says, "the heap of mighty waters" (Hab. 3:15).[70]

5. And the fifth is that the water split into many [i.e., twelve] paths in accordance with the tribes, semi-circles within semi-circles, like this [see drawing],[71] and this is what is said, "To Him who divided the Sea of Reeds into pieces..." (Ps. 136:13).[72]

6. And the sixth is that the water grew hard and firm like stones, as it is stated, "... You shattered the heads of sea dragons [i.e., Pharaoh][73] in the waters" (Ps. 74:13).

7. And the seventh is that the sea did not congeal into ice in one large mass, but into discrete and separate like stones piled one over the other, as it is said, "You divided the sea by Your might" (Ps. 74:13).[74]

---

69. The Targum on Hab. 3:14 records such a tradition. Rashi however sees this verse as referring to Sennacherib.
70. Hebrew homer, which literally means "matter."
71. Drawing scanned from Kapach edition.
72. Rashi quotes a similar tradition on that verse—namely that each tribe traversed on its own path. Radak there adds that this is a more orderly progression.
73. Hebrew tannin, lit., "dragon" or "sea monster," but also used as a reference to Pharaoh, based on Isa. 27:1. Targum, Rashi, Radak, and Malbim also understand this verse as a reference to the Egyptians. The firmness is likely a pun on al ha-mayim, which is normally translated "in the waters," but literally means "on [or against] the waters."
74. Possibly because Hebrew porarta, "you divided," is related to Rabbinic Hebrew peirer, "to crumble" (transitive) and peirurim, "crumbs."

8. And the eighth is that it became firm like glass or sapphire, meaning it was clear, so they could see each other when they passed through, as it says, "a gathering of waters, thick clouds of the skies" (2 Sam. 22:12), meaning the waters crystallized like the firmament of the heavens above.
9. The ninth is that fresh drinking water flowed from the sea.
10. The tenth is that the water would solidify (after flowing so they would take water to drink), so that they would not sink into the ground, as it is stated, "the surging waters were firm like a wall, [and the depths] congealed [in the heart of the sea]" (Exod. 15:8) (see next page, comparing Maimonides' list to others; the Midrash's list appears to have eleven items; see resolutions of Rabbenu Bahya and Netziv).

And the oral tradition also teaches that at the sea, the Egyptians suffered greater plagues than in Egypt. However all [of the plagues at the sea] were akin to the plagues in Egypt, but they were divided into different sub-groups at the sea, and this is hinted to by the verse, "This is the God who struck Egypt with *every kind of plague* in the wilderness" (1 Sam. 4:8), which refers to the wilderness at the Sea of Reeds (*PhM Avot* 5:3).

14:27. And Moses stretched out his hand over the sea, and the sea returned in the morning to its normal state; and the Egyptians were fleeing from it, and the Lord overturned the Egyptians in the sea. — See on Exod. 4:4, where Maimonides explains that a miracle is not completed until the natural order is restored, based on the phrase "and the sea returned in the morning to its normal state." The word *le-eitano* has either been translated "to its strength" (*Mekhilta*, Rashi, R. Saadiah; cf. Gen. 49:24), or "its original state" (Maimonides, Sforno). Shadal writes, "It seems to me that the basic meaning of this root refers to something permanent and unchanging, but it was later transferred to mean anything strong or hard that is also permanent and unchanging."

Ten Miracles that Happened at the Splitting of the Sea (Maimonides, *Mekhilta*, R. Yonah)

Maimonides	*Mekhilta**	R. Yonah
The first is the splitting of the sea, according to the plain meaning of the verse, "and the waters were divided."	The sea was broken through and made like a fault, as it is said, "You have pierced through because of his tribes" (Hab. 3:14). It was divided into two halves as it is said, "Stretch out your hand over the sea and divide it" (Exod. 14:16).	The first is *va-ya'er et ha-lailah* (Exod. 14:20), which Onkelos translates, "There was darkness for the Egyptians, but for Israel there light the whole night" (R. Yonah's version of Onkelos is not the standard version).
The second miracle is that after the sea split, the waters formed a domed roof, neither flat nor sloped, and a path like a tunnel through the water was formed, with water to the left, right, and above, and this is was Habakkuk said, "You have pierced the heads of his villages with spears" (Hab. 3:14).	Dry land was formed in it, as it is said, "But the children of Israel walked upon dry land in the midst of the sea" (v. 29)	The second and third are "And the Lord looked down on the Egyptian army from a pillar of file and a cloud" (Exod. 14:24) — A cloud descended and made it like mud, and the pillar of fire heated it and the hooves of the horses got stuck.
And the third is that the ground became hard and firm for them, as it is said, "and they walked through on dry land" (Exod. 14:29), and it did not remain like a river bed that has sediment and mud.	It became like mud, "You have trodden the sea with Your horses, the clay of mighty waters" (Hab. 3:15)	
And the fourth is that when the Egyptians trod on it, the ground became muddy and sticky, as it says, "the heap of mighty waters" (Hab. 3:15).	It crumbled into pieces, as it is said, "You broke the sea in pieces by your strength" (Ps. 74:13)	The fourth is "He locked the wheels of the chariots" (Exod. 14:25) — He locked the wheels on the chariots, so the Egyptians fell and were injured.
And the fifth is that the water split into many [i.e., twelve] paths in accordance with the tribes, semi-circles within semi-circles, like this [drawing], and this is what is said, "To Him who divided the Sea of Reeds into pieces..." (Ps. 136:13).	It turned into rocks, as it is said, "You shattered the heads of the sea-monsters upon the water" (Ps. 74:13)	The fifth is "and they moved forward with difficulty" (v. 25) — after they fell and got injured, they could not stand up, and they remained where they had fallen.

The six is that they wanted to flee but could not, as it says, "And the Egyptians said, 'Let us flee from the children of Israel'" (cf. v. 25)....	The seventh is "and the Lord overturned the Egyptians in the sea" (v. 27), like the Targum *ve-shan-nik*, from the language of "destruction," meaning He overturned them like a man stirs a pot, the top went to the bottom and the bottom to the top.	The eighths is that the ground at the bottom of the sea swallowed them, as it says, "You extended Your right hand, and the earth swallowed them" (Exod. 15:12).	The ninth is that they descended to the depth of the sea like lead, as it says, "they sank like lead in the mighty waters" (Exod. 15:10).	The tenth is that the water spat them out, as it says, "And Israel saw the Egyptians dead on the shore of the sea" (Exod. 14:30).
It split into parts, as it is said, "To Him who divided the Sea of Reeds into parts" (Ps. 136:13)	It was piled up into stacks, as it is said, "And with the blast of Your nostrils the waters were piled up" (Exod. 15:8)	It formed a sort of a wall, as it is said, "The floods stood upright as a heap" (Exod. 15:8)	He extracted for them sweet water from the salt water, as it is said, "He brought streams also out of the rock and caused waters to run down like rivers" (Ps. 78:16)	The sea congealed on both sides and became a sort of glass crystal, as it is said, "The deeps were congealed in the heart of the sea" (Exod. 15:8) * The *Mekhilta* appears to quote eleven miracles; see R. Bahya and Netziv
And the sixth is that the water grew hard and firm like stones, as it is stated, " ... You shattered the heads of sea dragons in the waters" (Ps. 74:13).	And the seventh is that the sea did not congeal into ice in one large mass, but into discrete and separate like stones piled one over the other, as it is said, "You divided the see by Your might" (Ps. 74:13).	And the eighth is that it became firm like glass or sapphire, meaning it was clear, so they could see each other when they passed through, as it says, "a gathering of waters, thick clouds of the skies" (2 Sam. 22:12), meaning the waters crystallized like the firmament of the heavens above.	The ninth is that fresh drinking water flowed from the sea.	The tenth is that the water would solidify (after flowing so they would take water to drink), so that they would not sink into the ground, as it is stated, "the surging waters were firm like a wall, [and the depths] congealed [in the heart of the sea]" (Exod. 15:8).

159

14:29. And the children of Israel walked through on dry land, and the water was a wall for them to their right and left. — See on Exod. 14:21, where Maimonides lists this as the third miracle at the Sea of Reeds.

14:31. And Israel saw the mighty hand of the Lord... — For Maimonides' understanding of "hand of God," see *Yesodei ha-Torah* 1:9, quoted at Exod. 9:3. But even if "hand of God" is a metaphor, as all these authorities believe, then what is it a metaphor about? On this point, Maimonides is to the best of my knowledge silent. However, other commentaries have offered their interpretations:

- **Rashi** says that the phrase has many meanings, but the phrase "And Israel saw the great hand" (Exod. 14:31) means strength (*gevurah*), based on Rabbi Shela in BT *Berakhot* 58a.
- **Ibn Ezra** says it refers specifically to the death of the first born (on Exod. 13:15, long).
- **Nahmanides** says that according to mystical tradition, "hand of God" refers to *middat ha-din*, "attribute of justice" (on Exod. 14:31, 17:16).
- **Sforno** says that it means God changed nature (on Exod. 13:9)
- **Rabbi Abraham Isaac Hakohen Kook** believes "the 'strong hand' (Exod. 13:9) is symbolic of the actual; the 'outstretched arm' — the potential."[75]

---

75. See Rabbi Bezalel Naor's comment in Rav Kook's *Orot*, trans. Bezalel Naor, English only edition, pp. 339-340, note 445.

Exodus 15

15:1. Then Moses and the children of Israel sang this song to the Lord, and they said, saying... — [Maimonides is commenting on double use of *amar*, "say"] R. Nehemiah says that when it says *va-yomru* ("and they said"), it implies that they all participated in the song, but that Moses began reciting it first by himself, just as the prayer leader does when reciting the *Shema*. And according to R. Akiva, they only said the first lines after him, as is done when reciting *Hallel* (*PhM Sotah* 5:4; see BT *Sotah* 30b).

15:4. The chariots of Pharaoh and his armies He hurled into the sea, and his best officers were drowned in the Sea of Reeds. — [Maimonides is commenting on the phrase *markevot Par'oh*, "chariots of Pharaoh"]: [*merkavah*] is a collective noun denoting animals used for riding (*Guide* 1:70).

15:6. Your right hand, O Lord, is majestic in power; Your right hand, O Lord, has shattered the enemy. — See on Exod. 14:31 for a discussion of the anthropomorphism "God's hand."

15:8. And with the blast of Your nostrils the waters were piled up... — See on Exod. 9:3 for a discussion of anthropomorphisms, which is relevant to the phrase "Your nostrils," though Maimonides does not quote this example explicitly.

... the surging waters were firm like a wall, and the depths congealed... — See on Exod. 14:21, where Maimonides lists this as the tenth miracle at the Sea of Reeds. (Maimonides explains *kaf'u* as *karshu*; both words mean "congeal" (*PhM Terumot* 4:11); also Ibn Ezra [long].)

... in the heart of the sea. — For the meaning of "heart" as "center," see on Exod. 3:2.

15:10. You blew with Your breath and the sea covered them; they sank like lead in the mighty waters. — ... motion of the air is, as a rule, ascribed to God (*Guide* 2:30).

> It is possible that Maimonides is minimizing the "miracle" of the splitting of the sea by saying that any motion of air is ascribed to God and there might not be anything miraculous about the wind blowing, but he surely notes that the sea returning to its original state is a miracle. Maimonides maintains that a miracle is not completed until the natural order is restored (see on Exod. 4:4 and 14:27).

15:18. The Lord shall reign forever and ever. — [Maimonides is discussing the fact that on Rosh Hashanah, we recite blessings in the themes of *Malkhiyyot* (Kingship), *Zikhronot* (Remembrance), and *Shofarot* (Trumpets). He discusses which verses can be included in the blessing of *Malkhiyyot*:] All of these verses express the idea of God's kingship: "Hear O Israel, God is our Lord, God is one" (Deut. 6:4); "To you, it has been revealed that you may know..." (Deut. 4:35); and "And you shall know today and draw it close to your heart..." (Deut. 4:39). Although they do not mention "kingship," they are equivalent to "The Lord shall reign forever and ever" (Exod. 15:18); and "When He became King in Jeshurun." (Deut. 33:5) (*Shofar* 3:9).

Further: [Maimonides rejects Aristotle's opinion that the universe is eternal, i.e., that the universe existed stretching backwards for all of eternity; however he fully endorses the opinion that once the world was created, it will exist forever forward:] There are, however, in the book [of Ecclesiastes], some passages which imply the indestructibility of the Universe, a doctrine that is true; and from the fact that the indestructibility of the Universe is taught in this book, some persons wrongly inferred that the author believed in the eternity of the Universe. The following are the words that refer to the indestructibility of the Universe: "And the earth remains forever" (Eccl. 1:4). And those who do not agree with me as regards the above distinction [between the indestructibility and the Eternity of the Universe] are compelled to explain the term *le-olam* [forever] to mean "the time fixed for the existence of the earth." Similarly they explain the words of God, "Yet all the days of the earth" (Gen. 8:22) to signify the days fixed for its existence.

But I wonder how they would explain the words of David: "He laid the foundations of the earth, that it should not be moved forever" (Ps. 104:5). If they maintain here also that the term *le-olam va-ed* ["forever"] does not imply perpetuity, they must come to the conclusion that God exists only for a fixed period, since the same term is employed in describing the perpetuity of God, "The Lord will reign forever" (Exod. 15:18; Ps. 10:16). We must, however, bear in mind that *olam* only signifies perpetuity when it is combined with *ad*: it makes no difference whether *ad* follows, as in *olam va-ed*, or whether it precedes, as in *ad olam* (*Guide* 2:28).

Nahmanides understands the verse not as a reference to an abstract notion of kingship, but as the relationship between God and Israel: "Moses is saying that just as He has no shown that He is King and Ruler by having brought deliverance to His servants and destruction upon those that rebel against Him, so may it be His will to do so for future generations." In other words, it is a prayer that God will continue to act like a *just* King.

It is worth noting that like on the phrase *Ehyeh Asher Ehyeh* (Exod. 3:13-14), a similar debate can be observed on the current verse. For Maimonides, both phrases refer to God's eternality in the abstract, while for Nahmanides, they refer to eternal relationship between God and Israel.

15:22. ... and they went three days in the desert and did not find water. — Maimonides does not quote the famous halakhic midrash that water here represents Torah. However he does quote the derivate law that Moses established having public Torah readings at least every three days, specifically on Monday, Thursday, and the Sabbath so people would not go three days without hearing Torah (see *Tefillah* 12:1, and *Kesef Mishneh* there, and *Torah Temimah* on the present verse).

Rabbi Ari Kahn in personal communication pointed out that Moses likely instituted the reading on Monday, Thursday, and Shabbat, after the revelation at Sinai, which had not happened yet, so perhaps this is why Maimonides did not cite the current, pre-Sinaitic verse as the source for that practice.

15:24. And the people complained to Moses, saying, "What shall we drink?" — This is the second time the Israelites tested God in the wilderness (quoted at Exod. 14:11).

15:25. — ... there [at Marah] He made for them a statute and an ordinance [*ḥok u-mishpat*]... — According to the true traditional explanation, Sabbath and civil laws were revealed at Marah: "statute" [*ḥok*] alludes to Sabbath, and "ordinance" [*mishpat*] to civil laws (*Shabbat* 87b, *Sanhedrin* 56b), which are the means of removing injustice. The chief object of the Law, as has been shown by us, is the teaching of truths; to which the truth of the *creatio ex nihilo* belongs. It is known that the object of the law of Sabbath is to confirm and to establish this principle, as we have shown in this treatise (see *Guide* 2:31).[76] In addition to the teaching of truths the Law aims at the removal of injustice from mankind (*Guide* 3:32).

The *Mekhilta* quotes several opinions about the meaning of *hok u-mishpat*; the midrash is probably prompted by the seeming superfluousness of that phrase (i.e., the law of "omnisignificance"). In other words, since either "*hok*" or "*mishpat*" would have sufficed, the double locution must come to teach something else.

R. Joshua's opinion is that *hok* refers to the Sabbath, and *misphat* refers to the commandment to honor one's father and mother. R. Elazar of Modi'im believes that *hok* refers to forbidden sexual practices, and *mishpat* refers to laws of robbery, fines, and injury.

The Talmud says at Marah, the Jews received *dinim* (monetary laws), the Sabbath, and the obligation to honor one's father and mother. (The latter two are based on an exposition of the phrase, "as the Lord your God commanded you" (Deut. 5:15) that appears in the Ten Commandments, meaning they were already commanded before coming to Sinai, making Marah the obvious candidate.) R. Nahman, in the name of Rabbah b. Abbuha, says that no new laws were given at Marah; only now a conviction required a Sanhedrin, two witnesses, and formal warning. Rava says that the laws of fines were added (BT *Sanhedrin* 56b; see, e.g., Deut.

76. There Maimonides says that the Sabbath is the first step in overthrowing a foreign yoke.

22:19, 29). Rashi believes this refers to the Sabbath, the Red Cow, and monetary law.[77]

Nahmanides believes that the words *ḥok* and *mishpat* both refer to "custom" (*minhag*); the phrase *ḥok u-mishpat* may just be an idiom. Nahmanides writes, "It may mean that Moses instructed them in the ways of the wilderness, namely to be ready to suffer hunger and thirst and to pray to God, and not to complain. He taught them ordinances whereby they should live, to love one another, to follow the counsel of the elders, to be discreet in their tents with respect to women and children, to deal in a peaceful manner with the strangers that come into the camp to sell them various objects. He also imparted moral instruction, i.e., that they should not become like bands of marauders who do all abominable things and have no sense of shame...."

See also Radak and Malbim on Josh. 24:25, which uses the phrase *va-yasem lo ḥok u-mishpat bi-Shekhem*, "and he [Joshua] made for them a statute and an ordinance in Shechem." The commentaries understand the phrase more generically at Josh. 24:25 than they do on the current verse.

15:26. And he said, "If you will surely listen to the voice of the Lord your God, and do what is just [*yashar*] in His eyes... — [Maimonides does not quote this verse in this context, but he says that the meaning of *yashar*, "just," is] that man must not depart from his given word, nor deviate from what he agreed upon; but he must give to others all that is due to them (*Guide* 3:49).

---

77. Some believe that Rashi's original list was "Sabbath, honoring parents, and monetary law," which would bring it closer in line with the *Mekhilta*; the assumption is that "honoring parents" was abbreviated כ"א (for *kibbud av*), and a later scribe read it as פ"א (*parah adumah*); see *Torah Temimah* on Exod. 15:25, n. 36. In his commentary on Deuteronomy, Rashi writes, "Even regarding honoring parents they were commanded at Marah, as it says, 'there He made for them a statute and an ordinance'" (on Deut. 5:15).

Plato writes: "no one shall have what belongs to others or be deprived of his own" (*Republic* 4.433). Similarly we encounter the phrase, *iustitia suum cuique distribuit*, "justice renders to everyone his due" (Cicero, *De Natura Deorum*); this was canonized at the beginning of the Justinian Code (sixth century C.E.): "Justice is the constant and perpetual wish to render every one his due." Maimonides' definition of *yashar*, "just," appears very similar to the Greco-Roman definition. Similarly, Maimonides defines *tzedakah* from the word *tzedek*, writing, "it denotes the act of giving every one his due, and of showing kindness to every being according as it deserves" (*Guide* 3:53). Compare this to his definition of *mishpat*: The noun *mishpat* denotes the act of deciding upon a certain action in accordance with justice which may demand either mercy or punishment (*Guide* 3:53). It is possible that Nahmanides, by way of distinction, defines justice as not acting out of either *ahavah* or *sin'ah*, love or hatred (see on Gen. 2:9).

… and hearken to His commandments, and observe all His statutes, then any of the diseases which I inflicted on Egypt I will not inflict on you, for I am the Lord your Healer. — [On the phrase *kol hukkav*, "all of His statutes," Rashi explains that *hukkim* are "matters that are decrees of the King without any reason, and the evil inclination criticizes them, saying, 'What is the prohibition in these? Why were they prohibited? For example, wearing *sha'atnez*, eating swine, the Red Cow, and the like" (based on BT *Yoma* 67b). However, Maimonides does not adopt Rashi's understanding of *hukkim*:] There are commandments which are called *hukkim* ["ordinances"] like the prohibition of wearing garments of wool and linen (*sha'atnez*), boiling meat and milk together, and the sending of the goat [into the wilderness on the Day of Atonement]. Our Sages use in reference

167

to them phrases like the following: "These are things which I have fully ordained for you; and you dare not criticize them"; "Your evil inclination is turned against them"; and "non-Jews find them strange."

But our Sages generally do not think that such precepts have no cause whatever, and serve no purpose; for this would lead us to assume that God's actions are purposeless. On the contrary, they hold that even these ordinances [*hukkim*] have a cause, and are certainly intended for some use, although it is not known to us; owing either to the deficiency of our knowledge or the weakness of our intellect. Consequently there is a cause for every commandment; every positive or negative precept serves a useful object; in some cases the usefulness is evident, e.g., the prohibition of murder and theft; in others the usefulness is not so evident, e.g., the prohibition of enjoying the fruit of a tree in the first three years (Lev. 19:23), or of a vineyard in which other seeds have been growing (Deut. 22:9).

Those commandments whose object is generally evident are called "judgments" [*mishpatim*]: those whose object is not generally clear are called "ordinances" [*hukkim*]. Thus they say [in reference to the words of Moses], "for it is not a vain thing for you" (Deut. 32:74) — "It is not in vain, and if it is in vain, it is only so through you." That is to say, the giving of these commandments is not a vain thing and without any useful object; and if it appears so to you in any commandment, it is owing to the deficiency in your comprehension (*Guide* 3:26).

Here the perspectives of Rashi and Maimonides are extremely far apart. Rashi says that *hukkim* "are decrees of the King without any reason," while Maimonides maintains that "there is a cause for every commandment," even if the purpose is not immediately apparent.

Exodus 16

16:3. And the children of Israel said to them, "Would that we had died by the hand of God when we sat by the fleshpots, when we ate bread until we were full, rather than you taking us out to this wilderness to kill the entire congregation with hunger." — This is the third time the Israelites tested God in the wilderness (quoted at Exod. 14:11).

16:4. And the Lord said to Moses, "Behold I rain bread for you from Heaven, and the nation will go out and collect its ration every day, so that I may test them—if they will follow My teaching or not." — [In the *Guide* 3:24, Maimonides quotes six times that God imposed a test: Gen. 22:1. Exod. 16:4 (the current verse), 20:16, Deut. 8:2, 8:16, 13:4:] The doctrine of trials is open to great objections: it is in fact more exposed to objections than any other thing taught in Scripture. It is mentioned in Scripture six times, as I will show in this chapter. People have generally the notion that trials consist in afflictions and mishaps sent by God to man, not as punishments for past sins, but as giving opportunity for great reward. This principle is not mentioned in Scripture in plain language, and it is only in one of the six places referred to that the literal meaning conveys this notion. I will explain the meaning of that passage later on.

The principle taught in Scripture is exactly the reverse; for it is said, "He is a God of faithfulness, and there is no iniquity in Him" (Deut. 32:4). The teaching of our Sages, although some of them approve this general belief [concerning trials], is on the whole against it. For they say, "There is no death without sin, and no affliction without transgression" (BT *Shabbat* 55a). Every intelligent religious person should have this faith, and should not ascribe any wrong to God, who is far from it; he must not assume that a person is innocent and perfect and does not deserve what has befallen him. The trials mentioned in Scripture in the [six] passages *seem* to have been tests and experiments by which God desired to learn the intensity of the faith and the devotion of a man or a nation. [If this were the case] it would be very difficult to comprehend the object of the trials, and yet the sacrifice of Isaac seems to be a case of this kind, as none witnessed it, but God and the two concerned [Abraham and Isaac]. Thus God says to Abraham, "For now I know that you fear God" (Gen. 22:12). In another passage it is said, "For the Lord your God test you to know whether you love..." (Deut. 13:4). Again, "And to prove you to know what was in your heart..." (Deut. 8:2). I will now remove all the difficulties.

The sole object of all the trials mentioned in Scripture is to teach man what he ought to do or believe; so that the event which forms the actual trial is not the end desired; it is but an example for our instruction and guidance. Hence the words "to know [*la-da'at*] whether you love" do not mean that God desires to know whether they loved God; for He already knows it; but *la-da'at* ["to know"] has here the same meaning as in the phrase "to know [*la-da'at*] that I am the Lord that sanctifies you" (Exod. 31:13), i.e., that all nations shall know that I am the Lord who sanctifies you.

In a similar manner Scripture says: If a man should rise, pretend to be a prophet, and show you his signs by which he desired to convince you that his words are true, know that God intends thereby to prove to the nations how firmly you believe in the truth of God's word, and how well you have comprehended the true Essence of God; that you cannot be misled by any tempter to corrupt your faith in God. Your religion will then afford a guidance to all who seek the truth, and of all religions man will choose that which is so firmly established that it is not shaken by the performance of a miracle. For a miracle cannot prove that which is impossible; it is useful only as a confirmation of that which is possible, as we have explained in our *Mishneh Torah* (see *Yesodei ha-Torah* 8:1-3).

Having shown that the term "to know" means "that all people may know," we apply this interpretation to the following words said in reference to the manna: "To humble you, and to prove you, to know what was in your heart, whether you would keep his commandments, or not" (Deut. 8:2). All nations shall know, it shall be published throughout the world, that those who devote themselves to the service of God are supported beyond their expectation. In the same sense it was said when the manna commenced to come down, "so that I may test them—if they will follow My teaching or not" (Exod. 16:4), i.e., let everyone who desires try and see whether it is useful and sufficient to devote himself to the service of God. It is, however, said a third time in reference to the manna: "Who fed you in the wilderness with manna, which your fathers knew not, that He might humble you, and that He might prove you, to do you good at your latter end" (Deut. 8:16). This might induce us to think that God sometimes afflicts man for the purpose of increasing his reward. But in truth this is not the case.[78]

We may rather assume one of the two following explanations: either this passage expresses the same idea as is expressed in the first and second passages, namely, to show [to all people] whether faith in God is sufficient to secure man's maintenance and his relief from care and trouble, or not. Or the Hebrew term *le-nassotekha* means "to accustom you": the word is used in this sense in the following passage: "She has not accustomed [*nissetah*] the sole of her foot to set it upon the ground" (Deut. 28:56). The meaning of the above passage would then be: "God has first trained you in the hardships of the wilderness, in order to increase your welfare when you enter the land of Canaan." It is indeed a fact that the transition from trouble to ease gives more pleasure than continual ease....[79]

---

78. Maimonides ascribes this theory to the Mu'tazila and roundly rejects it (see *Guide* 3:17).
79. The omitted section here is reproduced at Exod. 13:18.

The passage, "For God is come to prove you, and that his fear may be before your faces, that you sin not" (Exod. 20:16), expresses the same idea as is expressed in Deuteronomy (13:4) in reference to a person who prophesies in the name of idols, namely in the words: "For the Lord your God tests you to know whether you love the Lord." We have already explained the meaning of the latter passage. In the same sense Moses said to the Israelites when they stood round Mount Sinai: "Do not fear; the object of this great sight which you perceived is that you should see the truth with your own eyes. When the Lord your God, in order to show your faithfulness to Him, will prove you by a false prophet, who will tell you the reverse of what you have heard, you will remain firm and your steps will not slide. If I had come as a messenger as you desired, and had told you that which had been said unto me and which you had not heard, you would perhaps consider as true what another might tell you in opposition to that which you heard from me. But it is different now, as you have heard it in the midst of the great sight" (*Guide* 3:24).

The idea of God testing man is an old one, and there are several issues that need to be addressed. The first is the meaning of *anassennu*, from the root *n-s-h*, which can mean either "test" (like *nissayyon*, "trial"), or "raise up" (like *nes*, "banner"). According to Maimonides, it can mean "to test," or it can also mean "to accustom," based on Deut. 28:56. If it means "test," then what is the nature of the test? Maimonides offers two answers: either it is an opportunity for the people experiencing the test to determine if the struggle is worthwhile so that they might continue the religious path, or so that a third party, specifically the nations of the world, should know.

Nahmanides, however, rejects this reading, since according to Maimonides the verse should say *le-ma'an*

yenasseh la-da'at, but it says *le-ma'an anassennu ha-yelekh.*
Therefore, Nahmanides argues, "[The manna itself][80] was a
trial to them, since they had no food in the wilderness and
were without recourse to any sustenance except the manna,
which they knew not from before and had never heard of
from their fathers. Each day's quantity came down on its day,
and they were eagerly desirous for it. Yet with all this, they
hearkened to walk after God to a place of no food." In other
words, Nahmanides believes the "test" is whether the Jews
would follow God through the desert, surviving on nothing
but manna. For Maimonides, the test was an examination by
the Jews to see if it was rewarding to follow God (see also
Nahmanides on Gen. 22:1).

I think Maimonides' position can be presented more
simply: suppose that all of a sudden, an individual or a group
of individuals did not have to go to work anymore. They had
no professional responsibilities, did not have to worry about
their safety, and did not even have to worry about where
their food would come from. The quotidian responsibilities
of the world were relieved. Would these people use their
newfound free time for idle pursuits, or would they use that
time to develop and grow religiously, spiritually, emotionally,
intellectually? That is the opportunity that the Jews in the
wilderness had—to have all their needs provided for them
so they could mature in their connection to God.

**16:7. And in the morning you will see the glory of the Lord
because He has heard your complaint against the Lord...** — See
on Exod. 6:9, where Maimonides explains the phrase "[God] heard"
(*Guide* 1:45).

---

80. These words are included in brackets in the Chavel translation.

... and what are we that you complain against us? — [Maimonides uses this phrase as a precedent: just as Moses and Aaron acted with humility, so all Israelite kings should act humbly:] Just as Scripture ascribes honor and greatness to [a king], and everyone is obligated to honor him, so too the king himself is obligated to be humble and modest in his heart and his innards, as it says, "My heart is stricken within me" (Ps. 109:22). And he should not conduct himself against Israel with a haughty heart more than necessary, as it says, "that his heart not be above his brethren" (Deut. 17:20). Rather he should be gracious and merciful with the small and the great. And he should come and go in the goodness for their welfare, and he should show pity even on the lowest of low. And when he addresses the entire community, he should speak with tenderness, as [David] said, "Hear me, my brethren and her people" (1 Chron. 28:2; see T. *Sanhedrin* 4:2). Similarly, [God] says [to Solomon], "If you will be a servant to this people" (1 Kings 12:7). And he should always conduct himself with excessive humility.

We had no leader greater than Moses, our teacher, and he said, "... what are we that you complain against us?" (Exod. 16:7; see BT *Ḥullin* 89a). He should suffer the nation's hardships, burdens, complaints, and wrath as a nursemaid who raises an infant. And Scripture calls him a shepherd, "to pasture Jacob, His nation" (Ps. 78:71). And the way of a shepherd is mentioned explicitly in Scripture, "He will feed his flock like a shepherd; He will gather the lambs in his arms, and carry them in His bosom, and gently lead the mother sheep" (*Melakhim* 2:6; see also *PhM Avot* 4:4).[81]

16:8. And Moses said, "When God gives you meat to eat in the evening and bread in satiety in the morning, because the Lord has heard your complaining which you utter against Him, and what are we? Your complaints are not against us but against the Lord." — [Maimonides uses this as a rationale that contesting with

81. The humility of Moses, according to Maimonides, lies in the fact that he says "and what are we?" meaning, "Are we so powerful that you direct your complaint towards us?"

leaders is like contesting with God:] The Sages have explained that
it is forbidden for a student to dispute his teacher (BT *Sanhedrin*
56), meaning it is forbidden to reject his authority, to give separate
interpretations, and to teach or issue rules without his permission.
It is not permitted to quarrel with him, or to strive with him, or to
suspect him, meaning to attribute to him, in action or words, any
kind of [negative] motivation, since it is possible that that was not his
intention. And in the chapter *Ha-Ḥeilek* it is stated:

- "Whoever engages in disputation with his teacher is like one
  who disputes the Divine Presence, as it says, '[who contented
  against Moses and Aaron in the company of Korah] when they
  contended against the Lord' (Num. 26:9) (BT *Sanhedrin* 110a)."
- And whoever fights against his teacher is like one who fights
  against the Divine Presence,[82] as it says, "These are the waters
  of Meribah where the children of Israel quarreled with the
  Lord..." (Num. 20:13).
- And whoever complains against his teacher is like someone
  who complains against the Divine Presence, as it says, "Your
  complaints are not against us but against the Lord" (Exod.
  16:8).[83]
- Whoever doubts his teacher is like someone who doubts the
  Divine Presence, as it says, "And the people spoke against God
  and Moses" (Num. 21:5).

This is all clear from Korah's rebellion, and from Israel's quarrels,
complaints, evil thoughts, and suspicions against Moses, who was
the leader of all Israel. Yet Scripture presents every case as if it were

---

82. Maimonides defines this as establishing a competing school without the
permission of his rabbi (*Talmud Torah* 5:2, based on BT *Sanhedrin* 5b). However
elsewhere he says, "to reject his authority, to give separate interpretations, and
to teach or issue rulings without his permission" (*ShM*, Pos. 209).
83. Rashi understands מַלִּינָם as a *hif'il*, "cause others to complain," an
interpretation Maimonides appears to not adopt.

committed against God. And in their explanation, the Sages said, "Your fear of your teacher should be like the fear of Heaven" (*Avot* 4:12). And all of this is derived from Scripture's commandment to honor Sages and parents, as have been explained in many places in the Talmud (*ShM*, Pos. 209; see also *Hil. Talmud Torah* 5:1).

16:18. And they measured it with an omer; he who gathered much had nothing left over, and he who gathered little had no lack; they gathered as much as they needed to eat. — [Maimonides interprets this verse in an ethical and allegorical manner:] It is no wrong or injustice that one has many bags of finest myrrh and garments embroidered with gold, while another has not those things, which are not necessary for our maintenance; he who has them has not thereby obtained control over anything that could be an essential addition to his nature, but has only obtained something illusory or deceptive. The other, who does not possess that which is not wanted for his maintenance, does not miss anything indispensable: "He who gathered much had nothing over, and he who gathered little had no lack; they gathered as much as they needed to eat" (*Guide* 3:12).

Maimonides might be building off the midrash quoted by Rashi: "Some collected a lot, and some collected a little, but when they each came home, they measured it with an omer, and they found that he would had gathered a lot did not have more than an omer per person in his tent, and he who gathered a little did not have less than an omer per person. And this was a great miracle done for them" (on vv. 17-18). It is possible that Maimonides is trying to answer the problem of theodicy in the sense of poverty—namely, that even someone exceedingly poor still has sufficient ability to meet at least his scantest needs, if necessary by miracle.

Alternatively, he might be coming from the other direction, namely that one should not engage in hoarding; condemning this practice, John Locke wrote: "He that gathered a hundred bushels of acorns or apples, had thereby a property in them, they were his goods as soon as gathered. He was only to look, that he used them before they spoiled, else he took more than his share, and robbed others. And indeed it was a foolish thing, as well as dishonest, to hoard up more than he could make use of" (*Second Treatise of Civil Government*, Chap. V sec. 46). Just at Locke condemned hoarding that led to spoilage, the Israelites were not permitted to hoard manna, which would become worm-infested.

16:19. And Moses said to them, "Let no man leave any of it over until morning." — Maimonides explains that this is not included in the 613 biblical commandments, since it does not apply for all generations (*ShM, Shoresh* 3).

16:20. But they did not listen to Moses, and some of the men left it over until morning... — This is the fourth time the Israelites tested God in the wilderness (quoted at Exod. 14:11).

... and it became infested [*va-yarum*] with worms, and it stank; and Moses was angry with them. — *rimmah* refers to worms that emerge in dead meat when it begins to decay [as in] *va-yarum tola'im* [it became infested with worms] (*PhM Oholot* 2:2).

The word *va-yarum* appears only once in Tanakh. The majority believes the word comes from *rimmah*, "worms" (Maimonides, R. Abraham, Rashi, Ibn Ezra, Shadal). However, there is an opinion in the *Eitz Yosef* (*Shemot Rabbah* 25:10) that *va-yuram* comes from *romemut*, "lifting up, exaltation."

Another question is whether the manna became infested with worms and then stank, or vice versa, since is says "it became infested with worms, and it stank." The Midrash (*Mekhilta*, "Va-Yissa" 4), Rashi, and R. Saadiah assume that the verse is written out of order; i.e., the manna first stank and then became worm-infested. However, Nahmanides maintains this was a miracle (hence the *romemut*), in order to expose this wickedness of Dothan and Abiram: "But since the manna became wormy in a miraculous way, it is possible that it bred worms first, and there is no need to invert the verse." I have not found indication whether or not Maimonides accepted that the verse was written out of order or not.

16:25. And Moses said, "Eat it today, for today is a Sabbath to the Lord; today you will not find it in the field." — The Sages based the obligation of eating three meals on the Sabbath on what God, may He be exalted, said, "Eat it today [*ha-yom*], for today [*ha-yom*] is a Sabbath to the Lord; today [*ha-yom*] you will not find it in the field." The word [*ha-yom*] is repeated three times" (*PhM Pe'ah* 8:7; BT *Shabbat* 117a; the Sabbath meals are a remembrance of the manna in the wilderness; Maimonides does not quote this halakhic midrash at *Hil. Shabbat* 30:9.).

16:27. And on the seventh day, some of the people went out to collect [manna] and found none. — This is the fifth time the Israelites tested God in the wilderness (quoted at Exod. 14:11)

16:29. See that the Lord has given you the Sabbath; therefore on the sixth day He gives you two days' supply of bread; each person must remain in his place... — In a public domain, a person is permitted to move objects within a four-cubit by four-cubit square,[84] based on where he is standing. He is allowed to move objects within

---

84. A cubit is approximately a foot and a half.

this square.... And according to oral tradition, this is what is meant when the Torah says, "every person must remain in his place," meaning that he may not carry outside of this square, only within this square, which represents the span of a person when he extends his hands and feet; in that area alone is he allowed to carry (*Hil. Shabbat* 12:15, based on BT *Eruvin* 48a; the *Shulḥan Arukh* accepts this ruling (*Oraḥ Ḥayyim* 349:1); see also *Mishnah Berurah* there).

... no man shall go out of his place on the seventh day. — ... we are forbidden to travel outside of the city confines on the Sabbath, as God, may He be exalted, said, "no man shall go out of his place on the seventh day." And the oral tradition defines prohibited "travel" as in excess of 2000 cubits outside of the city, even by one cubit. However, it is permitted to walk 2000 cubits in any direction. The language of the *Mekhilta*: "'no man shall go out of his place on the seventh day' — these are the 2000 cubits." And we learn in *Eruvin* (17b), "One who violates the *teḥum* is liable to the biblical punishment of lashes" (*ShM*, Neg. 321).

FURTHER: Someone who goes beyond the city's Sabbath limit is liable to receive lashes, as it says, "no man shall go out of his place on the seventh day." [The word] *makom* ["place"] means the city limits [*teḥum ha-ir*]. The Torah did not state the length of this limit, but the Sages related that this "limit" is twelve *mil*, which was the size of the Israelite camp. Hence Moses, our teacher, said to them, "do not go outside of the camp." And the Sages said that a person should not go more than 2000 cubits outside the city, and it is forbidden to go more than 2000 cubits beyond the city limits, since 2000 cubits represents the suburbs of the city (cf. Num. 35:5) (*Hil. Shabbat* 27:1).

In the Talmud (BT *Eruvin* 17a), Rabbi Akiva believes the prohibited distance is given from the Torah, while Rabbi Eliezer says the general prohibition is biblical, while the exact measurement is rabbinic. Maimonides, in his early writings, adopts this ruling, siding with Rabbi Eliezer (see *PhM Sotah* 5:3). In the *Mishneh Torah* as well, he interprets the measurement as rabbinic, writing, "And the Sages said that a person should not go more than 2000 cubits outside the city." Similarly, Nahmanides and Rashba understand it is a rabbinic prohibition, as does the *Shulḥan Arukh* (*Oraḥ Ḥayyim* 404:1) and *Mishnah Berurah* (404:5). However, some believe that in the ShM, Maimonides adopts the opinion that the exact measurement of 2000 cubits is also biblical, siding with Rabbi Akiva over Rabbi Eliezer.

16:33. And Moses said to Aaron, "Take a jar and put an omerful of manna in it, and place it before the Lord, to be kept for your generations." — Maimonides explains that this is not included in the 613 biblical commandments, since it does not apply for all generations (*ShM, Shoresh* 3). Elsewhere, he says that a vial of manna, along with Aaron's staff, were placed before the Temple ark (*Bet ha-Beḥirah* 4:1). For the meaning of *melo*, "full," see *Guide* 1:19, quoted at Exod. 35:35 and 40:34.

Exodus 17

17:2. And the people quarreled with Moses and said, "Give us water to drink," and Moses said to them, "Why do you quarrel with me? why do you tempt the Lord?" — This is the sixth time the Israelites tested God in the wilderness (quoted at Exod. 14:11).

17:5. And God said to Moses, "Pass before the people, and take the elders of Israel with you, and take the staff which you have used to hit the river in your hand and go." — The Hebrew *avar*, "to pass," refers to the motion of a body in space, and is chiefly applied to living creatures moving at some distance in a straight line, e.g., "And he passed [*avar*] before the" (Gen. 33:3), "Pass before the people..." (Exod. 17:5) (*Guide* 1:21, see further meanings of *avar* quoted at Exod. 12:12).

Nahmanides suggests the meaning of *avar* is the same as *halakh*, "go."

17:6. Behold I [=God] will be standing [*omed*] there... — Maimonides does not quote this verse, but he says that when *omed*, "stand," applies to God, it means, "permanent and everlasting" and "the events of which He is the cause, will remain efficient" (see *Guide* 1:13, quoted at Exod. 18:23).

But how does *omed* mean "permanent and everlasting" at the current verse? Here Nahmanides fills in the blank: "Since the wonder with the water in this place was not to become a permanent feature as long as they would be in the wilderness, as our Rabbis have said, this was why the Divine Glory was revealed upon it at this place...."

... and you shall strike the rock [*tzur*] ... — Maimonides says that the primary meaning of *tzur* is "hard stone like flint" (see *Guide* 1:16, where he quotes other meanings of this word). The *Mekhilta* also says *tzur* in this verse means "hard stone" (see Rashi).

17:7. And he called the name of the place Massah and Meribah, because of the quarrelling of the children of Israel and because they tested the Lord, saying, "Is the Lord in our midst or not?" — Once the prophecy of a prophet has become known and his words have been affirmed time after time, or that another prophet has testified about him, and he continues in the path of prophecy, then it is forbidden to doubt him or to suspect that his prophecy is untrue. And it is forbidden to test him more than necessary, and we are forbidden to test him continually, as it says, "Do not test the Lord your God as you tested Him at Marah" (Deut. 6:16) and "Is the Lord in our midst or not?" (Exod. 17:7). Rather, once it is known that this person is a prophet, they must affirm him and know that God is in their midst, and not suspect him or doubt him, as it says, "And they shall know that a there was a prophet among them" (Ezek. 2:5) (*Yesodei ha-Torah* 10:5).

> Nahmanides similarly writes, "He prohibited for all generations to test the Torah or the prophets because it is not proper to worship God by being skeptical or by requesting a wonder or some test, since it is not God's will to perform miracles for all men at all times. Nor is it fitting to serve Him in order to receive a reward" (on Deut. 6:16).

17:13. And Joshua assailed Amalek and its people with the edge of a sword. — Maimonides makes tangential reference to "Joshua assailed Amalek" at *PhM Arakhin* 9:4.

17:14. And the Lord said to Moses, "Write this as a memorial in a book and place it in the ears of Joshua, for I will utterly destroy

the memory of Amalek from under heaven." — A commandment that can be performed—and is not limited to a specific time—is considered applicable for all generations, because if it would be possible to fulfill the commandment, then it would be applicable. Would you think that when God completely destroys the seed of Amalek and removes them to the last, as God, may He be exalted, promised us, "I will utterly destroy the memory of Amalek," would we then say that this commandment does not apply for all time? This should not be said; rather it applies in every generation (see Deut. 25:17-18). Whenever the seed of Amalek is found, it is a commandment to wipe them out (*ShM*, Pos. 187).

It must be noted that Maimonides counts the commandment to destroy the seed of Amalek and the commandment to remember what Amalek did to the Jews as separate commandments (*ShM*, Pos. 188 and 189 respectively; see also the introduction to *Hilkhot Melakhim*). According to Maimonides, the war with Amalek can only be pursued when the Jews enter the land and appoint a king (*Hil. Melakhim* 1:1-2), and this opinion is adopted by Nahmanides and others, since the war with Amalek did not commence until Saul was appointed king (1 Samuel 15). Additionally, the Temple cannot be rebuilt until Amalek is destroyed (see on Exod. 17:15-16 where the *Lehem Mishnah* is quoted).

Is Amalek a racial status or a moral one? In other words, is Amalek a question of who your parents are, or based on what moral decisions you make? Rabbi Ari Kahn quotes from Rabbi Chaim Soloveitchik, who "formulated his answer to this question by carefully examining the various passages in which Rambam discusses the laws regarding Amalek. Rav Chaim's careful reading and comparison of these passages, as well as his sensitivity to how Rambam phrased the prohibition and what he did not say regarding Amalek, led him to answer in the affirmative: Anyone can 'achieve' the status of Amalek" (see Rabbi Ari Kahn, "Amalek: A Question of Race? (Updated 2014)."

Similarly, Rabbi Joseph B. Soloveitchik, quoting Maimonides *Melakhim* 5:1 and 5:5, writes, "From Maimonides' words, it appears that Amalek still exists in the world... One wonders why Maimonides did not employ the rule of R. Joshua that 'Sennacherib came and intermingled all the nations' with relation to Amalek. The answer to this question is very simple. The Bible testifies that Amalek still exists in this world. Go and see what the Torah says: 'The Lord will have war with Amalek from generation to generation' (Exodus 17:16). Accordingly, it is impossible for Amalek to be blotted out of the world until the coming of the Messiah. So said our Sages, 'God's name and throne will not be complete until the children of Amalek are blotted out' (Rashi to Exodus 17:16). But where is Amalek? I heard the answer from my father of blessed memory. Every nation that conspires to destroy the Jewish people is considered by the halakhah [=Jewish law] to be Amalek" (*Kol Dodi Dofek: Listen—My Beloved Knocks*, pp. 112-113).

FURTHER: *Parashat Shofetim* includes... the commandment to blot out the memory of Amalek (Deut. 25:17-19). In the same way as one individual person is punished, so must also a whole family or a whole nation be punished, in order that other families shall hear it and be afraid, and not accustom themselves to practice mischief. For they will say, we may suffer in the same way as those people have suffered; and if there be found among them a wicked, mischievous man, who cares neither for the evil he brings upon himself nor for that which he causes to others, he will not find in his family any one ready to help him in his evil designs. As Amalek was the first to attack Israel with the sword (Exod. 17:8-16), it was commanded to blot out his name by means of the sword; while Ammon and Moab, who have not been friendly simply from meanness, and have caused them injury by cunning, were only punished by exclusion from intermarriage with the Israelites, and from their friendship. All these things which God has commanded as a punishment are not excessive nor inadequate, but, as is distinctly stated, "according to the fault" (Deut. 25:2) (*Guide* 3:41).

FURTHER: God distinctly commanded the Israelites concerning Amalek to blot out his name (Exod. 17:14-16, Deut. 25:17-19). Amalek was the son of Eliphaz and Timna, the sister of Lotan (Gen. 36:12). The other sons of Esau were not included in this commandment. But Esau was by marriage connected with the Seirites, as is distinctly stated in Scripture: and Seirites were therefore his children: he reigned over them; his seed was mixed with the seed of Seir, and ultimately all the countries and families of Seir were called after the sons of Esau who were the predominant family, and they assumed more particularly the name Amalekites, because these were the strongest in that family. If the genealogy of these families of Seir had not been described in full they would all have been killed, contrary to the plain words of the commandment. For this reason the Seirite families are fully described, as if to say, the people that live in Seir and in the kingdom of Amalek are not all Amalekites: they are the descendants of some other man, and are called Amalekites because the mother of Amalek was of their tribe. The justice of God thus prevented the destruction of an [innocent] people that lived in the midst of another people [doomed to extirpation]: for the decree was only pronounced against the seed of Amalek (*Guide* 3:50).

17:15-16. And Moses built and altar and called it Y-H-W-H-Nissi. And he said, "For a hand is on the throne of God [kes Y-ah]... —

185

R. Hisda in the name of R. Yohanan says the Hebrew letters כ'ס'י'ה should be written as one word, but Rabbah implies it is two words (BT *Pesaḥim* 117a), and those two words are an abbreviated form of the phrase "throne of God." Rashi writes, "The Holy One, Blessed be He, swore that His throne will not be complete, and His name will not be complete, until the name of Amalek will be completely blotted out" (Rashi on the current verse and on Isa. 12:2).

Therefore, it is not surprising that Maimonides rules that the Temple cannot be built until Amalek is destroyed (*Melakhim* 1:2). However, he does not use this verse, but instead he derives it from, "Now when the king [David] was settled in his house, and the Lord had given him rest from all his enemies around him, the king said to the prophet Nathan, 'See now, I am living in a house of cedar, but the ark of God stays in a tent'" (2 Sam. 7:1-2), which is when David started to build the Temple. The use of this verse is questionable for several reasons: (1) It is not the verse the Talmud uses, (2) It is not from a legalistic passage, (3) Maimonides himself says that law cannot be derived from biblical books besides the Pentateuch. Why then did Maimonides use verses from the book of Samuel, rather than the current verse which is the actual legal source that the Temple cannot be built after the war with Amalek?

The *Leḥem Mishnah* (*Melakhim* 1:2) explains that Maimonides' methodology is to not feel beholden to how the Talmud sources the law, and is not bothered by offering a different source, whether that source is from a different rabbinic source, or "from another place," which might be a euphemism for the fact that it is Maimonides' own derivation. According to the *Leḥem Mishnah*, Maimonides' greatest concern is clarity, so he quotes the clearest and simplest source for the law, even if that means breaking with precedent. In this case, the narrative in Samuel explains that after David was delivered from his enemies, he began to build the Temple, and that source is simpler than the linguistic feat of explaining how כ'ס י'ה is an abbreviated from of בסא י'ה'ו'ה. This principle is important for understanding how and why Maimonides chose certain verses and not others when quoting biblical laws. In this case, he might not necessarily disagree with Rashi, but thought that it did not belong in the *Mishneh Torah*.

FURTHER: God is incorporeal... how, then, can He be said to occupy any space, or rest on a body? The fact which I wish to point out is this: every place distinguished by the Almighty, and chosen to receive His light and splendor, as, for instance, the Sanctuary or the Heavens, is termed "throne"; and, taken in a wider sense, as in the passage "For a hand is on the throne of God" (Exod. 17:16): "the throne" here denotes the Essence and Greatness of God.[85]

These, however [the Essence and Greatness of God] need not be considered as something separate from the God Himself or as part of the Creation, so that God would appear to have existed both without the throne, and with the throne: such a belief would be undoubtedly heretical. It is distinctly stated, "You, O Lord, remain forever; Your throne from generation to generation" (Lam. 5:19). By "Your throne" we must therefore understand something inseparable from God. On that account, both here and in all similar passages, the word "throne" denotes God's Greatness and Essence, which are inseparable from His Being (*Guide* 1:9).

FURTHER: ... Onkelos keeps free from the idea of the corporeality of God, and from everything that leads thereto, even in the remotest degree. For he does not say, "and under His throne": the direct relation of the throne to God, implied in the literal sense of the phrase "His throne," would necessarily suggest the idea that God is supported by a material object, and thus lead directly to the corporeality of God.

---

85. Joseph Albo says the altar was named Y-H-W-H-Nissi for two reasons, "because the altar is an instrument by means of which miracles of performed, and also because it points to God, who performs the miracles" (*Ikkarim* 2:28).

He therefore refers the throne to His glory, i.e., to the Divine Presence [*Shekhinah*], which is a light created for the purpose. Similarly he paraphrases the words, "For a hand is on the throne of God" (Exod. 17:16) as "An oath has been uttered by God, whose Divine Presence is upon the throne of His glory." This principle found also expression in the popular phrase "the throne of the Glory" (*Guide* 1:28).

PARASHAT YITRO

Exodus 18

18:1. And Jethro, the priest of Midian Moses' father-in-law, heard everything that God had done... — [R. Abraham, the son of Maimonides, writes:] This passage occurs after the revelation at Mount Sinai; and this is the opinion of some of the Sages, as well as R. Saadiah,[86] and R. Abraham ibn Ezra, may their memory be a blessing. And my father and teacher, may his memory be a blessing, also explained it this way.

His proof is that between the revelation at Mount Sinai and the Exodus from Egypt, there were fifty days, and there was not enough time for word to spread to Jethro, and for him, and Moses' wife, and his children to arrive at the Israelite camp (cf. v. 5), and to give advice about appointing judges, and that Moses would send him away and he returned to his place (cf. v. 27), unless this all unfolded with great haste, and this would be a far-fetched explanation.

And there is no proof that this passage (Exodus 18) should precede "on the third month" (Exodus 19), since it is well known that the Sages said, "There is no chronological sequence [in the Torah" (cf. *Pesaḥim* 6a). though a minority did say the Torah is written in chronological sequence]. The reason for these two opinions is the same; the meaning of "there is neither early nor late" is that just because something is written first, that does not mean it occurred first, and just because it is written later, that does not mean it occurred later. And the explanation of "there *is* chronological sequence in the Torah" means that [is the case] unless by necessity we are forced to admit that what is written first occurred later.

The Talmud records different opinions of the phrase *va-yishma Yitro*, "and Jethro heard" — what did Jethro hear? R.

---

86. According to Ibn Ezra, R. Saadiah believed that Jethro came before the theophany at Sinai.

Joshua says Jethro heard about the battle with Amalek, since that episode immediately precedes the current chapter. R. Eleazar of Modim says Jethro heard of the giving of the Torah (Rabbi Abraham's quoting of R. Saadiah, Ibn Ezra, and his father Maimonides). R. Eleazar says Jethro heard about the parting of the Sea of Reeds (BT *Zevaḥim* 116a, *Mekhilta*; the splitting seems to have been a famous event, e.g., Josh. 2:10).

Rashi records two of the three opinions, "What report did he hear [to make him] come? The splitting of the Sea of Reeds and the war with Amalek." See Nahmanides' lengthy comment on this verse, where he entertains the possibility that Jethro came after the revelation at Sinai, but writes, "The most likely explanation seems to me to be to follow the sequence of the sections in the Torah, i.e., that Jethro came before the giving of the Torah when the Israelites were still in Rephidim...."

18:4. And the name of the other was Eliezer, for the God of my father was my help and saved me from the sword of Pharaoh. — [R. Abraham, son of Maimonides, writes:] My father and teacher, may his memory be a blessing, said that when "the messenger" [Moses] named his second son "Eliezer" because of the circumstance of saying "the God of my father was my help..." it revealed that in his heart Moses did not trust (his heart wasn't settled), and still had fear that Pharaoh was trying to kill him, until he heard the news that Pharaoh had died.

18:13. ... and the people stood before Moses from morning until evening. — It should not be the case that one litigant sit and one stand. Rather, they should both stand. However, if the court wishes for them to be seated, they may both sit. And one [litigant] should not sit higher than the other; rather they should both sit at the same level. When does this apply? When arguments are being presented. However when the verdict is announced, everyone should stand, as it says, "and the people stood before Moses...." (*Hil. Sanhedrin* 21:3, based on BT *Shevuot* 30b; see however 21:5).

18:20. And you shall teach them statutes and teachings, and you shall make known to them the path that they should follow in it and the work which they must do. — [Here a bit of background is in order. Many commandments are explicitly mentioned in Scripture; in addition, there are many commandments that are derived from seemingly superfluous letters, words, or phrases in biblical verses. There is a third category, namely commandments that are entirely rabbinic in origin without scriptural support. Maimonides in the first principle of his *Sefer ha-Mitzvot* explains that rabbinic commandments do not qualify to be counted among the 613 commandments. His second principle is that when the Sages derive a law from a superfluous letter, word, or phrase in a biblical verse, that rabbinic derivation should not be counted in the 613 commandments. Maimonides uses a rabbinic derivation on the current verse as an example:] ... when there is a homily on a verse that obligates someone to perform an action or avoid something, without question these laws are rabbinic, and they[87] mistakenly count them among the 613 commandments, even though the simple reading of the verse does not teach one of those things when using the principle that we said about them [to not count rabbinic homilies of biblical verses as separate commandments]. The Sages said, "A verse never departs from its plain meaning," and therefore the Talmud always asks, "What is the context of the verse?" When they find a verse, they learn many things from it as explanations and proofs.

And those who rely on this (mistaken) thought count among the commandments visiting the sick, comforting mourners, and

---

87. A reference to earlier attempts to delineate the 613 commandments, perhaps the *Behag* specifically.

burying the dead, based on the homily. God, may He be exalted, said, "And you shall teach them statutes and teachings, and you shall make known to them the path that they should follow in it and the work which they must do" (Exod. 18:20). And the Sages said, "the path" [*ha-derekh*] means acts of kindness; "follow" [*yeilkhu*] means visiting the sick; "in it" [*vah*] means burying the dead; "the actions" [*ha-ma'aseh*] means monetary law; "to do" [*ya'asun*] means going beyond the letter of the law (this is the opinion of Rabbi Eliezer ha-Modaï in *Mekhilta de-Rashbi*; see also BT *Bava Kamma* 100a and *Bava Metzia* 30b). The foolish ones thought that each and every one of these actions is a separate commandment, and they did not realize that these actions, along with similar ones, count as only one of the commandments written in the Torah, namely "And you shall love your neighbor as yourself" (Lev. 19:19)[88] (*ShM*, Shoresh 2).

18:21. And you should look from among the people... — [Maimonides is commenting on the Mishnah that says "courts for the tribes can only be established based on a court of seventy-one" (M. *Sanhedrin* 5:1)] ... "courts for the tribes can only be established based on a court of seventy-one" — Only Moses and his court made them, as it says, "And you should look from among the people" (*PhM Sanhedrin* 5:1; based on BT *Sanhedrin* 16b).[89]

And you should look from among the people for valorous men who fear God, men of truth who hate gain, and you should set them as leaders of thousands, leaders of hundreds, leaders of fifties, and leaders of tens. — [Every judge] must have seven qualities: wisdom, and fear, and humility, and hatred of money, and love of truth, and he

88. Maimonides says that tending to the sick is not a specific rabbinic commandment, but is a fulfillment of the commandment of a general nature, "you shall love your neighbor as yourself" (see *Avel* 14:1-2).

89. The implication is that Moses had the status of a court of seventy-one judges.

194

must be beloved by people, and he must have a good reputation. All of these qualities are explicit in the Torah. As it says:

- **"men of wisdom and understanding"** (Deut. 1:13), which refers to men of wisdom;
- **"known among your tribes"** (ibid.) are individuals who the people finds desirable. And how do they become beloved by the people? When they conduct themselves pleasantly and in humble spirit, and of good company, and their conduct and speech is pleasant with the people.
- And earlier when it says, **"men of valor"** (Exod. 18:21), this refers to people who are mighty in their observance of the commandments, and are punctilious, and who conquer their evil inclination until they have no shamefulness and no evil, and even in adolescence they were cordial. Included in the phrase "men of valor" means that they should have a courageous heart to save a victim from his oppressor, as it says on the matter, "but Moses arose and came to their defense" (Exod. 2:17).
- And just as Moses our teacher was **humble**, so too every judge needs to be humble.
- **"Men who fear God"** (ibid.) — this is obvious.
- **"Who hate gain"** (ibid.) — they are not concerned even about their own money, and they do not run to accumulate money, for whoever is concerned with wealth will come to be lacking (cf. Prov. 28:22).[90]
- **"Men of truth"** (ibid.) — that they should pursue justice on their own, and because of their own desire, who love truth, hate violence, and run from all forms of iniquity (*Hil. Sanhedrin* 2:7).

---

90. Elsewhere, Maimonides writes, "It is proper that a judge not increase in his pursuit of pleasures of the world and love of money and self-importance, as it says 'who hate gain'" (Introduction to *PhM*; in *Kehati*, p. י, based on BT *Ketubot* 105b). Maimonides appears to understand *betza* simply as "money" rather than "bribery/unjust gain." See Nahmanides for an analysis of this word.

In the Midrash (*Deuteronomy Rabbah* 1:10), Rabbi Berakhiah in the name of Rabbi Hanina says that a judge requires seven traits. Three of those traits are *hakhamim*, "wise," *nevonim*, "understanding," and *yedu'im* (either "knowledgeable" or "reputable"), mentioned in Deut. 1:13. And there are four implied, but not mentioned explicitly from the current verse, which are likely *anshei ḥayil* (men of valor), *yer'ei Elokim* (God-fearing), *anshei emet* (men of truth), and *sonei batza* (hating gain).

However, the *Sifrei* derives three different traits from Deut. 1:13: *anashim*, which refers to venerated and revered individuals, *hakhamim u-nevonim*, where *hakhimim* refers to the ability to apply what one has learned, while *nevonim* refers to the ability to derive one principle logically from another, and *yedu'im le-shivteikhem* means they are familiar (recognizable).

The main difference between the two lists is that Rabbi Berakhiah counts *hakhamim* and *nevonim* as separate traits, while the *Sifrei* likely counted them as one trait (Rashi followed the *Sifrei*). Furthermore, Rashi only counts three traits on the current verse: *anshei ḥayil*, *anshei emet*, and *son'ei betza*, while Maimonides counts four: *anshei ḥayil*, *yer'ei Elokim*, *anshei emet*, and *son'ei betza*, following *Deuteronomy Rabbah* 1:10. However Maimonides does not accept all of Rabbi Berakhiah's derivations on Deut. 1:13.

Here are three lists of the seven traits required for a judge:

Maimonides	Rashi (on Exod. 18:21 and Deut. 1:13)	R. Berakhiah
Men of wisdom and understanding	Anshei ḥayil = rich men	Wise
Known among your tribes	Anshei emet = inspiring confidence	Understanding
Men of valor (anshei ḥayil)	Hating gain = willing to part with money before going to court	Knowledgable or reputable
Humble	Men = righteous men	Men of valor
God-fearing	Wise (likely not counted by Rashi) = knows how to apply the rules	God-fearing
[Men] who hate gain	Understanding = derives one thing from another logically	Men of truth
Men of truth	Known to your tribes = familiar and recognizable	Men who hate gain

Dr. Isadore Twersky adds, "Maimonides' interesting typology of the moral-intellectual traits required for appointment to a court of law is avowedly based on explicit Scriptural statements, but analysis reveals that much of the exegesis is novel" (*Introduction to the Code of Maimonides (Mishneh Torah)*, p. 146).

18:22. And they shall judge the nation at all times... — According to Torah law, monetary cases can be adjudicated any day, as it says, "And they shall judge the nation at all times." However according to rabbinic law, we do not judge cases on Friday before the Sabbath (*Hil. Sanhedrin* 11:3; based on BT *Sanhedrin* 34b).

... and every major case they will bring to you, but the smaller cases they can judge themselves, and it will be lighter for you, and they will bear your burden for you. — [Maimonides is commenting on the Mishnah that states that a high priest can only be judged by a court of seventy-one judges (M. *Sanhedrin* 1:5)]: A high priest based on what it says "every major case they will bring to you" [lit., "every great matter they will bring to you"], meaning a matter of a great man (see *Sanhedrin* 16a), and we have none greater than the high priest, as it says, "and the high priest" (Lev. 21:10) (*PhM Sanhedrin* 1:5).[91]

FURTHER: Capital cases against [a high priest] are only judged by a high court, as it says, "every major case they will bring to you" (*Klei ha-Mikdash* 5:8).[92]

---

91. The Talmud does not quote Lev. 21:10 as a rationale. Kapach points out that Maimonides' rationale would exclude a prince.
92. Normally capital cases are judged by a court of twenty-three judges, not seventy-one.

FURTHER: A king can only be enthroned by a high court of seventy-one judges. And a minor court for each tribe and each city can only be made by a high court of seventy-one judges. A tribe is not judged to have completely apostatized, a false prophet, and a capital case of a high priest, are only judged by a high court. (However, financial cases regarding the high priest can be judged by a court of three judges.)[93] Similarly, a rebellious elder, an apostate city, and the waters of a suspected adulterous are only judged by a high court (BT *Sanhedrin* 15b-16b). And the borders of Jerusalem and the limits of Temple courts, and the declaration of a voluntary war, and measuring the distance from a corpse can only be done by a high court of seventy-one judges (BT *Sanhedrin* 14b), as it says, "every major case they will bring to you" (*Hil. Sanhedrin* 5:1).

> The Ramakh (quoted in the *Kesef Mishnah*) points out that the Talmud brings this verse regarding a high priest, but not regarding a king or any of the other matters mentioned in this passage, "and this matter requires further examination." The Brisker Rav understands *davar gadol* as matters that differ not just in degree but also in kind, i.e., matters that are categorically different. Based on that, it would make sense why Maimonides extended from matters of the high priest to other matters that are categorically different.

18:23. If you do this, and God commands you, then you will be able to endure [*amod*], and all these people will also go home in peace. — The term *amad* ["he stood"] is a homonym signifying:

1. In the first instance "to stand upright," as "When he stood [*be-omdo*] before Pharaoh" (Gen. 41:46); "Though Moses and

___
93. Similarly, cases of lashes, even for a high priest, are administered by a court of three (*Klei ha-Mikdash* 4:22).

Samuel stood [*ya'amod*]" (Jer. 15:1); "He stood by them" (Gen. 18:8).[94]

2. It further denotes "cessation and interruption," as "but they stood still [*amedu*] and answered no more" (Job 32:16); "and she ceased [*va-ta'amod*] to bear" (Gen. 29:35).

3. Next it signifies "to be enduring and lasting," as, "that they may continue [*ya'amedu*] many days" (Jer. 32:14); "then you will be able to endure [*amod*]" (Exod. 18:23); "His taste remained [*amad*] in him" (Jer. 48:11), i.e., it has continued and remained in existence without any change; "His righteousness stands [*omedet*] forever" (Ps. 111:3), i.e., it is permanent and everlasting.

The verb applied to God must be understood in this latter sense, as in, "And his feet shall stand [*ve-amedu*] in that day upon the Mount of Olives" (Zech. 14:4), [meaning] "His causes, i.e., the events of which He is the cause, will remain efficient," etc.... In the same sense is this verb employed in, "But as for you, stand here by Me," (Deut. 5:27), and "I stood between the Lord and you" (Deut. 5:5) (*Guide* 1:13).

---

94. The Talmud acknowledges this meaning at BT *Kiddushin* 32b.

Exodus 19

19:3. And Moses went up [*alah*] to God, and the Lord called to him from the mountain, saying, "Thus shall you say to the house of Jacob and tell the children of Israel." — [Maimonides explains the meanings of *alah*, "go up," and *yarad*, "go down." On the present verse, Maimonides says that "Moses went up to God" has both a physical and intellectual meaning.] We shall thus proceed in our treatment of the terms *alah* ["went up"] and *yarad* ["went down"]. These two words, *alah* and *yarad*, are Hebrew terms used in the sense of "ascending" and "descending." When a body moves from a higher to a lower place, the verb *yarad*, "to go down," is used; when it moves from a lower to a higher place, *alah*, "to go up," is applied.

These two verbs were afterwards employed with regard to greatness and power. When a man falls from his high position, we say "he has come down," and when he rises in station, "he has gone up." Thus the Almighty says, "The stranger among you shall rise higher and higher, and you will sink lower and lower" (Deut. 28:43). Again, "The Lord your God will set you on high [*elyon*] above all nations of the earth" (Deut. 28:1); "And the Lord highly exalted [*le-ma'aleh*] Solomon" (1 Chron. 29:25). The Sages often employ these expressions, as "In holy matters men must ascend [*ma'alin*] and not descend [*moridin*]."

The two words are also applied to intellectual processes, namely, when we reflect on something beneath ourselves we are said to go down, and when our attention is raised to a subject above us we are said to rise.

Now, we occupy a lowly position, both in space and rank in comparison with the heavenly sphere, and the Almighty is Most High not in space, but with respect to absolute existence, greatness, and power. When it pleased the Almighty to grant to a human being a certain degree of wisdom or prophetic inspiration, the divine communication thus made to the prophet and the entrance of the Divine Presence into a certain place is termed *yeridah* ["descending"], while the termination of the prophetic communication or the departure of the divine glory from a place is called *aliyah* ["ascending"].

The expressions "to go up" and "to go down," when used in reference to God, must be interpreted in this sense. Again, when, in accordance with the divine will, some misfortune befalls a nation or a region of the earth, and when the biblical account of that misfortune is preceded by the statement that the Almighty visited the actions of the people, and that He punished them accordingly, then the prophetic author employs the term "to descend": for man is so low and insignificant that his actions would not be visited and would not bring punishment on him, were it not for the divine will: as is clearly stated in the Bible, with regard to this idea, "What is man that You should remember him, and the son of man that You should visit him" (Ps. 8:5).

The design of the Deity to punish man is, therefore, introduced by the verb "to descend," e.g., "Come, let us go down and there confound their language" (Gen. 11:7); "And the Lord came down to see" (Gen. 11:5); "I will go down now and see" (Gen. 18:21). All these instances convey the idea that man here below is going to be punished.

More numerous, however, are the instances of the first case, namely, in which these verbs are used in connection with the revelation of the word and of the glory of God, e.g., "And I will come down and talk with you there" (Num. 11:17); "And the Lord came down upon Mount Sinai" (Exod. 19:20); "The Lord will come down in the sight of all the people" (Exod. 19:11); "And God went up from him" (Gen. 35:13); "And God went up from Abraham" (Gen. 27:22).

When, on the other hand, it says, "And Moses went up unto God" (Exod. 19:3), it must be taken in the third signification of these verbs, in addition to its literal meaning that Moses also ascended to the top of the mount, upon which a certain material light (the manifestation of God's glory) was visible; but we must not imagine that the Supreme Being occupies a place to which we can ascend, or from which we can descend (*Guide* 1:10).

Maimonides identifies five meanings of *alah* (go up) and *yarad* (go down):

1. the motion of physical bodies,
2. with regard to greatness and power (e.g., Deut. 28:43),
3. intellectual processes,
4. the appearance of the Divine Presence is described as "go down," and the removal is described as "go up,"
5. God is described as "descending" in order to mete out punishment.

On the present verse, Rashi understands *u-Mosheh alah*, "and Moses went up," as referring to physical ascent (based on BT *Shabbat* 88a). However, Maimonides adds a second component: the physical ascent is accompanied by an intellectual elevation.

19:4. You have seen what I did to Egypt, and how I carried you on the eagles' wings and I brought you to Myself. — The [Lawgiving] was the aim an object of the Exodus from Egypt, and thus God said, "I brought you to Myself." As that great revelation took place on one day, so we keep its anniversary [i.e., the holiday of Shavuot] only one day (*Guide* 3:43).

Onkelos translates the end of this verse as *ve-kareivit yatkhon le-fulḥani*, "I brought you near to My service," an interpretation that Rashi accepts. Kapach footnotes Onkelos' translation in his edition of the *Guide* (n. 13), suggesting this is Maimonides' understanding as well.

19:6. And you shall be to Me a kingdom of priests and a holy nation; these are the words you shall speak to the children of Israel. — God sent Moses to make [the Israelites] a kingdom of priests and a holy nation by means of knowledge of God (*Guide* 3:32).[95]

The Hebrew word *kohanim*, here translated as "priests," does not have a ritual signification. Rashi understands it as *sarim*, "ministers" (see also Rashi on Gen. 47:22), and Ibn Ezra (short) understands it as *shammashim*, "attendants." Here it seems Maimonides understands that the Jews become ministers or attendants of God by achieving knowledge of God.

[R. Abraham son of Maimonides writes:] The explanation of a "nation of priests" is that the priest of the entire congregation is the leader—meaning he is its most honored person and role model, since the people of the assembly follow him. They find his upright glory in him, saying, "You will be the leaders of the world in keeping my Torah; your relationship to them [the other nations of the world] is like the relationship of the priest to his congregation. The world will follow you and they will affirm your actions and follow in your ways. This is the explanation I received for this verse from my father, may his memory be a blessing, about what will happen if they make sure to listen (i.e., follow the Torah). As it says, "And you will listen and you will do, because it is your wisdom and understanding" (Deut. 4:6). And God promised that this will be fulfilled in the future, as He said though Isaiah, "And many nations will go and say, 'Let us go up to the mountain of the Lord to the house of the God...'" (Isa. 2:3).

---

95. Malbim says that holiness includes an external component and a holiness hidden in proper understanding and character traits (*bi-kedushah ha-tzefunah ba-de'ot u-ve-middot*) (see on Exod. 19:10).

19:9. And the Lord said to Moses, "Behold, I come [*ba*] to you...
— In Hebrew, the verb *bo* signifies "to come" as applied to a living being, i.e., its arrival at a certain place, or approach to a certain person, as "Your brother came [*ba*] with guile" (Gen. 27:35). It next denotes (with regard to a living being) "to enter" a certain place, e.g., "And when Joseph came [*va-yavo*] into the house" (Gen. 43:26); "When you enter [*tavo'u*] into the land" (Exod. 12:25). The term was also employed metaphorically in the sense of "to come" applied to a certain event, that is, to something incorporeal, as "When your sayings come to pass [*yavo*]" (Judg. 13:17); "Of that which will come [*yavo'u*] over you" (Isa. 47:13). Nay, it is even applied to privatives,[96] e.g., "Yet evil came [*va-yavo*]" (Job 30:26); "And darkness came [*va-yavo*]" (ibid.).

Now, since the word has been applied to incorporeal things, it has also been used in reference to God, to the fulfillment of His word, or to the manifestation of His Divine Presence [the *Shekhinah*]. In this figurative sense it is said, "Behold, I come [*ba*] to you in a thick cloud" (Exod. 19:9); "For the Lord the God of Israel comes [*ba*] through it" (Ezek. 44:2). In these and all similar passages, the coming of the Divine Presence is meant, but the words, "And the Lord my God shall come [*u-va*]" (Zech. 14:5) are identical with "His word will come," that is to say, the promises which He made through the Prophets will be fulfilled; therefore Scripture adds "all the holy ones that are with you" (ibid.) that is to say, "The word of the Lord my God will be performed, which has been spoken by all the holy ones who are with you, who address the Israelites" (*Guide* 1:22).

Maimonides identifies three meanings of *ba*, which is usually translated "come." First, it means "come," as applied to a physical body. Second it means "enter," also as applied to a

---

96. Privatives are the absence of removal of some quality. Qualities like darkness (absence of light) and evil (absence of goodness) are considered privatives. See also on Exod. 4:11.

physical body. (This distinction is already made by Onkelos, who translates ba sometimes as *kaneis* and sometimes as *ul* (עול), e.g. Exod. 10:1.) Third, metaphorically it means that a certain event occurs. In this metaphorical sense, when it says "God comes," it refers to the Divine Presence and means that His word is fulfilled. But what "word of God" is being fulfilled in this verse? It is likely the fact that God will fulfill His word of giving the Law. It appears that Maimonides here does not follow Onkelos, who translates *ba eilekha* as *mitgeli lakh*, "revealed to you." Both authorities seek to explain away the anthropomorphization, but do so in different ways.

... in a thick cloud... — [Maimonides does not quote this phrase, but his writings explains that "thick cloud" can be a reference to a metaphor of prophecy:] The corporeal element in man is a large screen and partition that prevents him from perfectly perceiving abstract ideals: this would be the case even if the corporeal element were as pure and superior as the substance of the spheres; how much more must this be the case with our dark and opaque body. However great the exertion of our mind may be to comprehend the Divine Being or any of the ideals, we find a screen and partition between Him and ourselves.

Thus the prophets frequently hint at the existence of a partition between God and us. They say He is concealed from us in vapors, in darkness, in mist, or in a thick cloud, or use similar figures to express that on account of our bodies we are unable to comprehend His essence. This is the meaning of the words, "Clouds and darkness are round about Him" (Ps. 97:2). The prophets tell us that the difficulty consists in the grossness of our substance; they do not imply, as might be gathered from the literal meaning of their words, that God is corporeal, and is invisible because He is surrounded by thick clouds, vapors, darkness, or mist. This figure is also expressed in the passage, "He made darkness His secret place" (Ps. 18:12).

The object of God revealing Himself in thick clouds, darkness, vapors, and mist was to teach this lesson; for every prophetic vision contains some lesson by means of allegory; that mighty vision, therefore, though the greatest of all visions, and above all comparison, namely, His revelation in a thick cloud, did not take place without any purpose; it was intended to indicate that we cannot comprehend Him on account of the dark body that surrounds us. It does not surround God, because He is incorporeal.

A tradition is current among our people that the day of the revelation on Mount Sinai was misty, cloudy, and a little rainy[97]: "Lord, when You went forth from Seir, when You marched out of the field of Edom, the earth trembled, and the heavens dropped water" (Judg. 5:4). The same idea is expressed by the words "darkness, clouds, and thick darkness" (Deut. 4:11). The phrase does not denote that darkness surrounds God, for with Him there is no darkness, but the great, strong, and permanent light, which, emanating from Him, illuminates all darkness, as is expressed by the prophetic simile, "And the earth shined with His glory" (Ezek. 43:2) (*Guide* 3:9).

---

97. There are several allusions to rain associated with Mount Sinai. Besides the two that Maimonides quotes (Deut. 4:11, Judg. 5:4), there is also: "The earth quaked, the heavens poured down rain at the presence of God, the God of Sinai, at the presence of God, the God of Israel. Rain in abundance, O God, you showered abroad; you restored your heritage when it languished" (Ps. 68:9-10); see also how the Talmud understands this passage (*Shabbat* 88b). The abundance of verses is probably what he means in writing, "tradition is current among our people."

Is Maimonides here giving a weather report (i.e., a historical fact about the atmospheric conditions on the day of revelation) or is he using it as a metaphor? It seems that he is giving a metaphor, based on the traditional sources that allude to rain. However, while he explains that *anan ve-arafel* ("clouds") is a metaphor for prophecy, he does not explain the meaning of "rain" in this metaphor. Here the traditional commentaries pick up the narrative: Crescas and *Shem Tov* both write that in writing "rain," Maimonides means *hassagah*, "attainment," of prophecy. The rest of the nation experienced the revelation at Sinai as "cloud" (i.e., opaque), while Moses experienced the prophecy fully, and that is described by the metaphor of "a little rain."

... so that the people will hear when I speak with you, and believe in you forever, and Moses told the words of the people to the Lord.
— [Maimonides is addressing the question of why the Israelites will believe in Moses:] The Israelites did not believe in Moses because of the signs that he performs. For one who believes because of signs has falsehood [*dofi*] in his heart that perhaps it is possible to perform that sign through magic or witchcraft. Rather, all the signs that Moses performed in the wilderness were for a specific purpose, and not for the purpose of brining a proof concerning his prophecy.

It was necessary to submerge the Egyptians, so he split the sea and drowned them in it. We needed manna, so he brought down the manna for us. They were thirsty, so he split the rock. The cohort of Korah denied him, so the earth swallowed them, and similar with other signs.

And why did they believe in him? At the standing at Mount Sinai, our eyes saw and not a foreigners, our ears heard and not those of another. The fire, the thunder, the lightning, and he approached the cloud, and the voice spoke to him and we heard, "Moses, Moses, go say to them such-and-such." Therefore it is stated, "Face to face, God spoke to you" (Deut. 5:4) and it is stated, "it is not with your fathers that God made this covenant [but with us who are all alive here today]" (Deut. 5:3).

And how do we know that standing at Mount Sinai alone is the proof that his prophecy is truth and not vain? As it says, "Behold, I will come to you in a thick cloud, so that the people will hear Me speaking to you, [so that] they will believe in you forever" (Exod. 19:9). It seems that before this event, they did not believe in him with a belief that would endure forever, rather with a belief that had doubt and skepticism.

Those to whom [Moses] was sent were witnesses that his prophecy was truth, and it was not necessary to perform another sign for them. It is like two witnesses that saw one event together, and each one of them is a witness to his fellow that he is speaking the truth, and neither one of them needs to bring a proof to his fellow.

Similarly, regarding Moses, all of Israel were witnesses for him after standing at Mount Sinai, and it was not necessary to perform a sign for them. And this is what the Holy One, Blessed is He, said to him at the beginning of his prophecy at the time He gave him the signs to perform in Egypt and said, "And they will listen to your voice" (Exod. 3:18). Out teacher Moses knew that someone who believes on account of signs has uncertainty, and doubts, and is skeptical, and he refused to go, and he said, "They will not believe me" (Exod. 4:1), until the Holy One, Blessed is He, informed him that these signs were only until the departed from Egypt, and then once they departed and stood at this mountain all doubt that they expressed about you would be removed: "For I give you here this sign so that they will know that I truly sent you from the beginning, so that no doubt would remain in their hearts, as Scripture says, "This will be your sign that I sent you: When you take the people out of Egypt, you will serve God on this mountain" (Exod. 3:12) (*Yesodei ha-Torah* 8:1-2; see Rashi at Deut. 4:34).

FURTHER: God has given assurance—He is an adequate guarantor—and informed them that not only did all the persons who were present at the Sinaitic revelation believe in the prophecy of Moses and in his Law, but that their descendants would likewise do so until the end of time. He declares, "I will come to you in a thick cloud, in order that the people may hear when I speak with you and so trust you ever after." Consequently, let everyone who spurns the religion that was revealed at that theophany that he is not an offspring of the fold that witnessed it. This is what the sages of Israel of blessed memory said of those who entertain scruples concerning the divine message: They are not the scions of the race that was present at Mount Sinai (*Epistle to Yemen*, p. 103).

FURTHER: "and believe in you forever" — [Moses] informed us that no teaching [i.e., no other Torah] will come from God besides this one... (Introduction to *PhM*).[98]

19:10. And the Lord said to Moses, "Go to the people and sanctify them today and tomorrow... — God commanded [Moses] to sanctify the people for the receiving of the Law, and said, "And sanctify them today and tomorrow" (Exod. 19:10), Moses [in obedience to this command] said to the people, "Come not at your wives" (Exod. 19:15). Here it is clearly stated that sanctification consists in absence of sensuality (*Guide* 3:33).

... and let them wash their clothes. — There was immersion in the wilderness before the Torah was given, as it says, "... and sanctify them today and tomorrow and let them wash their clothes" (*Issurei Biah* 13:3; see at Exod. 12:48, where it is explained that this is one of the three acts by which the Jews entered into the covenant with God).

FURTHER: Wherever it is said in the Torah "washing flesh" or "laundering garments" from impurities, this means immersion of the entire body in an immersion pool (*Mikva'ot* 1:2).

> Maimonides appears to understand the Hebrew root *k-d-sh* as "sanctify." However, some other commentaries take different approaches. Onkelos, Rashi, and Rashbam understand it as *z-m-n*, "prepare." R. Saadiah and Nahmanides understand it as *t-h-r*, "purify." (See my *A Theology of Holiness*, pp. 42-45.)

19:11. And be ready on the third day, for on the third day the Lord will come down [*yered*] in the sight of all the people on Mount Sinai. — See *Guide* 1:10, quoted at Exod. 19:3; there

_____

98. Kapach, p. 4; i.e., the people can only believe "forever" if the Torah will not be superseded.

Maimonides explains five meanings of "going up" [*aliyah*] or "going down" [*yeridah*]. In this verse, as applied to God, it likely means the appearance of the Divine Presence. This is also the interpretation of Onkelos, R. Saadiah, and Nahmanides.

FURTHER: Onkelos the Proselyte, who was thoroughly acquainted with the Hebrew and Aramaic languages, made it his task to oppose the belief in God's corporeality. Accordingly, any expression employed in the Pentateuch in reference to God, and in any way implying corporeality, he paraphrases inconsonance with the context. All expressions denoting any mode of motion, are explained by Him to mean the appearance or manifestation of a certain light that had been created [for the occasion], i.e., the *Shekhinah* [Divine Presence], or Providence. Thus he paraphrases "the Lord will come down" (Exod. 19:11) as "The Lord will manifest Himself"; "And God came down" as "And God manifested Himself" and does not say "And God came down"; "I will go down now and see" (Gen. 48:21), he paraphrases, "I will manifest Myself now and see" (*Guide* 1:27; in the sequel Maimonides quotes the exception is Gen. 46:4).

19:13. No hand shall touch it; rather he shall surely be stoned or cast down,[99] whether man or beast, it shall not be allowed to live.' When the trumpet blasts long, they shall come up the mountain."
— [This verse is used as the basis of a legal principle:] How is the commandment of stoning fulfilled [as a form of execution]? Four cubits from the place of execution, we strip off the clothes of the convict but we covers his private region. And a woman is not executed naked; rather she is [covered] by a garment. The place of execution is a height of two stories. The witnesses and the convict ascend, with his hands tied together. One of the witnesses pushes him at his loins from behind, and he flips over to the ground [landing] on

99. Hebrew *yaroh yiyyareh* here means "cast down," i.e., thrown to the ground, and not "shot with arrows."

211

his heart. If he dies, the obligation has been fulfilled, as it says, "he shall surely be stoned or cast down," which equates a person who has a stone fall on him with one who falls to the ground himself (*Sanhedrin* 15:1, based on BT *Sanhedrin* 44b-45a, quoted again at *PhM Sanhedrin* 7:4).

> Rashi quotes the same halakhic interpretation as Maimonides: *"yaroh yiyyareh* — from here it is learned that those who are executed by stoning are pushed down from the place of execution, which is two stories high."
>
> Hizkuni raises a question on Rashi that applies to Maimonides as well: based on this, the verse should not say that he is first cast down and then stoned. Therefore he concludes that the Hebrew word אֹ, which normally means "or," here means *asher*, "which," and he concludes the verse means: "you shall surely stone [the person] which was cast down" (see also *Gur Aryeh*).

19:15. And he said to the people, "Be ready for the third day... — On the phrase "Be ready for the third day," Maimonides explains that this is not included in the 613 biblical commandments, since it does not apply for all generations (*ShM, Shoresh* 3).

... do not go near your wives." —The Torah states, "Be ready on the third day; do not go near your wives." And there is a debate when this command was given, and this is not the place to assess the appropriateness of each argument (*PhM Mikva'ot* 8:3, based on the debate between Rabbi Akiva and Rabbi Elazar b. Azariah at BT *Shabbat* 86a; see Rashi on this phrase).

FURTHER: God commanded [Moses] to sanctify the people for the receiving of the Law, and said, "And sanctify them today and tomorrow" (Exod. 19:10), Moses [in obedience to this commandment] said to the people, "... do not go near your wives" (Exod. 19:15). Here it is clearly stated that sanctification consists in absence of sensuality (*Guide* 3:33).

19:17. And Moses brought the people out of the camp to meet God... — Long ago Solomon compared our community with a beautiful woman having a perfect figure, marred by no defect, in the verse, "Every part of you is fair, my darling; there is no blemish in you" (Cant. 4:7). He further depicted the adherents of other religions and faiths, who strive to entice us and win us over to their convictions, as beguiling seducers who lure virtuous women for their lewd purposes. Similarly they seek devices to trap us into embracing their religions, and subscribing to their doctrines. To those who endeavor to decoy her into avowing the superiority of their creed, he in his wisdom answered in the name of the community: "Why do you take hold of me, can you confer upon me something like the felicity of the two companies?" She challenges them, saying: "If you can furnish me with something like the theophany at Sinai, in which the camp of Israel faced the camp of the Divine Presence, then I shall espouse your doctrine" (see *Shir ha-Shirim Rabbah* 7:1). This is metaphorically expressed in the verse, "Turn back, turn back, O Shulammite! Turn back, turn back, that we may gaze upon you. Why will you gaze at the Shulammite in the Mahanaim dance?" (Cant. 7:1). "Shulammite" signifies the Perfect One; the "Mahanaim dance" the joy of the revelation at Mt. Sinai that was shared by the camp of Israel, as He states, "Moses led the people out of the camp towards God" (Exod. 19:17), and the camp of God, as He explained saying: "God's chariots are myriads upon myriads, thousands upon thousands" (Ps. 68:18) (*The Epistle to Yemen*, ch. 1, pp. 104-105).

... and they gathered [*va-yityatzevu*] at the foot of the mountain. — Maimonides says that the roots *y-tz-b* and *n-tz*-b mean "to gather" or "to place oneself." See *Guide* 1:15.

213

19:19. And the sound of the trumpet grew louder and louder; Moses spoke, and God answered him by voice. — Maimonides uses the phrase "Moses spoke" in *Guide* 1:65, where he explains three meanings of "speak" (*medabber*) and "say" (*omer*); see at Exod. 2:4. This verse is also one of Maimonides' proofs that Moses and the nation of Israel had different experiences at Sinai; see *Guide* 2:33, quoted at Exod. 20:1. Nahmanides writes on this verse, in part, "The Israelites heard the Voice of God answering Moses and commanding him, but they did not understand what He said to him. Thus He commanded Moses the precepts mentioned further on in the section."

... by voice. — [Maimonides is commenting on the Mishnah which addresses which formal declarations must be in Hebrew and which can be in the vernacular. According to the Mishnah, the declaration of first fruits, *ḥalitzah*, the blessings and curses, the priestly blessings, the blessing of the high priest, the recitation of the king, the recitation of the eglah arufah, and anointing the king for battle must be recited in Hebrew:] It says, "And the Levites shall speak, and say unto all the men of Israel with a loud voice" (Deut: 27:14).[100] And it says, "Moses spoke, and God answered him by voice." Just as there it was in the Holy Language, so too this must be in the Holy Language (*PhM Sotah* 7:2; see also *PhM Sotah* 8:1; based on BT *Sotah* 33b and 42a).

On the phrase *lashon ha-kodesh* (or *leshon ha-kodesh*), Maimonides says the term is used because Hebrew "has no special name for the organ of generation in females or in males, nor for the act of generation itself that generates offspring, nor for semen, nor for secretion and feces. The Hebrew has no original expressions for these things, and only describes them in figurative language and by way of hints, as if to indicate thereby that these things should not be

---

100. The Levites there recite a series of curses against people who commit specific sins.

mentioned" (*Guide* 3:8). Nahmanides disagrees, and writes, "because "the words of the Torah and of the prophets and all sacred utterances were spoken in that language.... [He used it when] He created His universe, gave names to heaven and earth and all therein" (on Exod. 30:13). In an entirely different vein, Gesenius writes that regarding Hebrew as the holy language "as being the language of the sacred books in opposition to the lingua profana, i.e., the Aramaic vulgar tongues" (*Hebrew Grammar* 9).

19:20. And the Lord came down to Mount Sinai, to the top of the mountain, and the Lord called to Moses to the top of the mountain, and Moses ascended. — See *Guide* 1:10, quoted at Exod. 19:3, where Maimonides explains the different meanings of "the Lord went up/down." On the present verse, "The Lord came down" likely means the appearance of the Divine Presence.

19:22. And let the priests also, which come near to the Lord, sanctify themselves, lest the Lord break forth upon them. — If such was the case with them [i.e., "'the nobles of the children of Israel'" {who} were impetuous, and allowed their thoughts to go unrestrained"], how much more is it incumbent on us who are inferior, and on those who are below us, to persevere in perfecting our knowledge of the elements, and in rightly understanding the preliminaries which purify the mind from the defilement of error: then we may enter the holy and divine camp in order to gaze: as the Bible says, "And let the priests also, which come near to the Lord, sanctify themselves, lest the Lord break forth upon them" (Exod. 19:22; see *Guide* 1:5 at Exod. 24:10-11, where he criticizes the "nobles of the children of Israel" for their behavior, and uses the current verse as a warning for approaching God in an impetuous and unprepared state).

Exodus 20

[Maimonides here addresses the question of whether it is proper to stand for the reading of the Ten Commandments:] It is the practice in many places to stand [for the reading of the Decalogue], and it is necessary to prevent them, as it causes a diminution of faith, because they come to believe that the Torah has different levels, and some are higher than others, and this is extremely terrible. And it is imperative to plug all the holes that bring about this deficient belief (*Teshuvot ha-Rambam*, No. 263; in some editions, No. 43).

According to the Talmud, the Sages wanted to institute the practice of reciting the Ten Commandments every day, but that proposition was voided because of *tar'omet ha-minim*, meaning the heretics would say that only the Decalogue is from Sinai, while the rest of the Torah is made up (BT *Berakhot* 12a; Rema, *Shulḥan Arukh, Oraḥ Ḥayyim* 1:5). Maimonides extends that rationale to standing for the public reading of the Decalogue in the Torah portions of *Yitro* and *Va'etḥannan*, as well as for the holiday of Shavuot, lest someone arrive at the false belief that the Torah has different levels.

However, today there is a widespread practice to stand when the Ten Commandments are read from the Torah. Rabbi Ovadia Yosef (1920-2013) says that this ruling of Maimonides was not well known, and had it been known, it would have been followed; therefore we should actively discourage people from standing (*Yeḥavveh Da'at* 1:29).

Other authorities permit one to stand. Rabbi Samuel Aboab (1610-1694) and Rabbi Chaim Joseph David Azulai (the Hida, 1724-1806) differentiate between a daily recitation and the calendrical readings; the Talmud forbade a daily reading but was silent on the matter of standing for the calendrical reading. Furthermore, standing for the reading of the Decalogue reenacts the theophany at Sinai, and it is appropriate to stand for God's presence. Rabbi Moses Feinstein (1895-1986) also permitted standing, because people stand for other parts of the Torah as well, like the Song of the Sea (Exodus 15) (see Rabbi Gil Student's "The Heresy of the Ten Commandments").

Rabbi Joseph B. Soloveitchik finds another justification to stand: there are two cantillation marks for the Decalogue, the regular or "lower" cantillation marks, and the "upper" marks (*ta'am tahton* and *ta'am elyon*). The lower marks represent Torah reading as a form of study (for which it is proper to sit), while the upper marks represent Torah reading as a form of acceptance, a reenactment of the theophany at Sinai (for which it is proper to stand). Since the three public readings—*Yitro*, *Va'ethannan*, and Shavuot—use the upper marks, it is proper to stand (Rabbi Aharon Ziegler, *Halakhic Positions of Rabbi Joseph B. Soloveitchik*, pp. 111-113).

20:1. And God spoke all of these words, saying. — [Maimonides addresses the when the words *amar* and *dibber* are applied to God. In an earlier part of this chapter, Maimonides says these words have three meanings: speech, thought, and will (quoted at Exod. 2:4):] The two terms [*amar* and *dibber*], when applied to God, can only have one of the two last mentioned significations, namely, "He wills and He desires," or "He thinks," and there is no difference whether the divine thought became known to man by means of an actual voice, or by one of those kinds of inspiration which I shall explain further on (see *Guide* 2:38). We must not suppose that in speaking God employed voice or sound, or that He has a soul in which the thoughts reside, and that these thoughts are things superadded to His essence; but we ascribe and attribute to Him thoughts in the same manner as we ascribe to Him any other attributes. The use of these words in the sense of "will" and "desire" is based, as I have explained, on the homonymity of these terms. In addition they are figures borrowed from our common practices, as has been already pointed out. For we cannot, at a first glance, see how anything can be produced by a mere desire; we think that he who wishes to produce a thing, must perform a certain act, or command someone else to perform it. Therefore the command is figuratively ascribed to God when that takes place which He wishes, and we then say that He commanded that a certain thing should be accomplished. All this has its origin in our comparing the acts of God to our own acts, and also in the use of the term *amar* in the sense of "He desired," as we have already explained (*Guide* 1:65).

FURTHER: It is clear to me that what Moses experienced at the revelation on Mount Sinai was different from that which was experienced by all the other Israelites, for Moses alone was addressed by God, and for this reason the second person singular is used in the Ten Commandments; Moses then went down to the foot of the mountain and told his fellow men what he had heard, e.g., "I stood between the Lord and you at that time to tell you the word of the Lord" (Deut. 5:5). Again, "Moses spoke, and God answered him by voice" (Exod. 19:19).[101]

In the *Mekhilta* our Sages say distinctly that he brought to them every word as he had heard it. Furthermore, the words "In order that the people hear when I speak with you" (Exod. 19:9) show that God spoke to Moses, and the people only heard the mighty sound, not distinct words (see *Guide* 3:9, quoted at Exod. 19:9). It is to the perception of this mighty sound that Scripture refers in the passage, "When you hear the sound" (Deut. 5:20); again it is stated, "You heard a sound of words" (Deut. 4:12), and it is not said "You heard words"; and even where the hearing of the words is mentioned, only

101. Maimonides understands the letter *bet* of יעננו בקול as "by a voice" or "in a voice," i.e., by speaking. Rashi, however, understands *be-kol* as *al devar kol*, "regarding the voice."

the perception of the sound is meant. It was only Moses that heard the words, and he reported them to the people. This is apparent from Scripture, and from the utterances of our Sages in general.

There is, however, an opinion of our Sages frequently expressed in the Midrashim, and found also in the Talmud, to this effect: The Israelites heard the first and the second commandments from God, i.e., they learned the truth of the principles contained in these two commandments in the same manner as Moses, and not through Moses (BT *Makkot* 24a; Rashi here). For these two principles, the existence of God and His Unity, can be arrived at by means of reasoning, and whatever can be established by proof is known by the prophet in the same way as by any other person; he has no advantage in this respect. These two principles were not known through prophecy alone; e.g., "You have been shown to know that..." (Deut. 4:34).

But the rest of the commandments are of an ethical and authoritative character, and do not contain [truths] perceived by the intellect. Notwithstanding all that has been said by our Sages on this subject, we infer from Scripture, as well as from the words of our Sages, that the Israelites heard on that occasion a certain sound which Moses understood to proclaim the first two commandments, and through Moses all other Israelites learned them when he in intelligible sounds repeated them to the people. Our Sages mention this view, and support it by the verse, "God has spoken once; twice have I heard this" (Ps. 62:11). They state distinctly, in the beginning of *Midrash Hazita*, that the Israelites did not hear any other commandment directly from God; e.g., "A loud voice, and it was not heard again" (Deut. 5:19). After this first sound was heard, the people were seized with the fear and terror described in Scripture, and that they said, "Behold the Lord our God has shown us..." "and now why shall we die..." "Come near...."

Then Moses, the most distinguished of all mankind, came the second time, received successively the other commandments, and came down to the foot of the mountain to proclaim them to the people, while the mighty phenomena continued; they saw the fire, they heard the sounds, which were those of thunder and lightning during a storm, and the loud sound of the shofar: and all that is said of the many sounds heard at that time, e.g., in the verse, "and all the people perceived the sounds..." refers to the sound of the shofar, thunder, and similar sounds. But the voice of the Lord, that is, the voice created for that purpose, which was understood to include the diverse commandments, was only heard once, as is declared in the Law, and has been clearly stated by our Sages in the places which I have indicated to you. When the people heard this voice their soul left them[102]; and in this voice they perceived the first two commandments.

It must, however, be noticed that the people did not understand the voice in the same degree as Moses did. I will point out to you this important fact, and show you that it was a matter of tradition with the nation, and well known by our Sages. For, as a rule, Onkelos renders the word *va-yedabber* by *u-mallel* ("and God spoke"); this is also the case with "And God spoke all these words" (Exod. 20:1), which Onkelos translated as *u-mallel Adonai yat kol pitgamayya*.[103] However the words *ve-al yedabber immanu Elohim*, "let not God speak to us" (Exod. 20:19), addressed by the people to Moses, is rendered *ve-la yitmallel immanu min kodam Adonai* ("Let not aught be spoken to us by the Lord"). Onkelos makes thus the same distinction which we made. You know that according to the Talmud, Onkelos received all these excellent interpretations directly from R. Eliezer and R. Joshua, the wisest men in Israel (BT *Megillah* 3a). Note it, and remember it, for it is impossible for any person to

---

102. According to R. Joshua b. Levi's understanding of *nafshi yatze'ah be-dabbero*, lit., "my soul went out when he spoke" (BT *Shabbat* 88b, quoting Cant. 5:6).
103. This example is absent in the Friedlander edition but I have added it based on the Kapach edition.

expound the revelation on Mount Sinai more fully than our Sages
have done, since it is one of the secrets of the Law. It is very difficult
to have a true conception of the events, for there has never been
before, nor will there ever be again, anything like it (*Guide* 2:33).

Maimonides' distinction is that Moses understood God's
actual words, while the rest of the nation could only perceive
unintelligible sounds. Rabbi Abraham, son of Maimonides,
quotes this distinction in his commentary on the present verse.
In the same chapter of the *Guide*, Maimonides also says, "Moses
then went down to the foot of the mountain and told his fellow
men what he had heard, e.g., 'I stood between the Lord and
you at that time to tell you the word of the Lord' (Deut. 5:5)."
This is, in part, Maimonides' proof that Moses and the rest of
the nation experienced the prophecy differently. The Jews only
perceived a *kol* (Exod. 19:19), which Maimonides interprets as
"sound" rather than "voice," because they heard sounds but
did not understand what they were hearing. Moses however
understood what God was saying, and therefore went down
the mountain to tell the rest of the nation what God had said.

Maimonides also addresses whether the first two
commandments were heard directly from God, or if the
Moses served as an intermediary even for the first two. He
quotes the rabbinic teaching that the first two were heard
directly from the Almighty (see BT *Makkot* 24a), writing, "For
these two principles, the existence of God and His Unity, can
be arrived at by means of reasoning, and whatever can be
established by proof is known by the prophet in the same way
as by any other person; he has no advantage in this respect."
Efodi, in his commentary, explains, "they can be proven by
human logic without a person needing to be a prophet—
that is the meaning of the rabbinic description of *mi-pi*

ha-gevurah, i.e., through human intelligence the existence and unity of God can be attained by demonstration."[104] Here, Efodi understands ha-Gevurah not as "the Almighty," as it is usually translated, but as "the force of logic," since Maimonides believes the first two commandments can be ascertained by logical demonstration alone.

However, Maimonides seems to qualify that interpretation: "the Israelites heard on that occasion a certain sound which Moses understood to proclaim the first two commandments, and through Moses all other Israelites learned them when he in intelligible sounds repeated them to the people." Ultimately, even though the first two commandments are logically demonstrable, the ordinary Israelite would not have been strong enough to withstand the power of hearing God; that strength was only possessed by Moses, who had to serve as an intermediary, even for the first two commandments.

20:2. I am the Lord your God who brought you out of the land of Egypt, out of the house of bondage. — [It is a positive commandment] to believe in God,[105] which is that we believe that there is a source and cause of existence who brought into being all that exists, as He, may He be exalted, said, "I am the Lord your God..." (Exod. 20:2, Deut. 5:6).

At the end of tractate *Makkot*, the Sages said, "613 commandments were spoken to Moses at Sinai. How do we know this? From the verse, 'Moses commanded us the Torah'" (Deut. 33:4) (*Makkot* 23b-24a). That is to say the count of the commandments is equal to the numerical value of the word *Torah*.[106] But then it is asked, "But is this case? The numerical value of *Torah* is only 611!" The answer is, "They heard

104. Quoted in Nehama Leibowitz, *New Studies in Shemot (Exodus)*, p. 312.
105. This is sometimes translated "to know God"; see next citation.
106. Numerology of the Hebrew alphabet is called *gematria*. The numerical value of the word *Torah* is 611.

two commandments, 'I am the Lord your God' and "Do not have any other gods,' directly from the Almighty." This clarifies that "I am the Lord your God" is included in the 613 commandments, and this is a commandment to believe, as we have explained (*ShM*, Pos. 1).

Nahmanides agrees that this verse constitutes a commandment (see his comments on the current verse, as well as his gloss on *ShM*, Neg. 5), but for him the commandment isn't just to believe in God but to accept the yoke of God's kingship (*kabbalat malkhuto*). But before doing, Nahmanides has a lengthy discourse on the position of the *Behag* (see his gloss on *ShM*, Pos. 1).

Simon Kayyara (the *Behag*) did not count belief in God as a commandment, because the *Behag* only counted commandments that required us to do something (mandatory), or prohibited us from doing something (forbidden). However, to believe in God necessitates neither action nor forbearance; rather belief in God is the preamble to observing the commandments. Similarly, Crescas and Abarbanel do not count this verse as a commandment.

Rabbi J. David Bleich explains the position of the *Behag* as follows: "As Bertrand Russell stated in formulating his Theory of Types, a statement about a class cannot itself be a member of that class. God, a commander, stands outside the system of commandments and constitutes the authority by which commandments must be accepted. Commandments are binding because they are decreed by God. But logically prior to a system of commandments is the principle that God's decrees must be obeyed. A commandment to that effect is not self-validating" (Rabbi J. David Bleich, *The Philosophical Quest*, p. 111).

Even if this is a commandment, following Maimonides, Nehama Leibowitz adds, "Whether we take the first verse

223

of the Decalogue to be a commandment... or merely a preamble... one thing is clear. It is not formulated as a principle as in: 'You shall know this day that the Lord, He is God in heaven above and the earth beneath; there is none else.' It is not stated as an impersonal law as in, 'He who sacrifices to the gods except to the Lord alone shall be utterly destroyed' (Exod. 22:23). It take the form of a personal proclamation, a manifesto of Divine revelation: 'I am the Lord your God who brought you out of the land of Egypt.'"[107]

Ultimately, Maimonides and Nahmanides both count this is a commandment, and the simple reading of the Talmud is that this verse is a commandment, the rationale being as follows: Rav Simlai derives the number 613 from the fact that the alphanumeric value of the word *Torah* is 611; add the verses "I am the Lord" and "You shall have no other gods" to 611 and the result is 613. Thus these two verses are by definition included in the count of 613.[108]

FURTHER: The foundation of foundations and pillar of wisdoms is to know that there is a First Cause who created everything that exists, and whatever exists in heaven and earth and everything in between only exists because of the truth of the Creator.[109] And if it would arise in your mind that He does not exist, then nothing else could exist. And if it would arise in your mind that nothing else besides Him exists, He alone would continue to exist, and He would not be cease to exist if they ceased to exist, for everything that exists has need of Him, and He, may He be blessed, does not need them, not one of them. Therefore His truth is not like the truth of any of them.

---

107. Translation based on *New Studies in Shemot (Exodus)*, p. 306.
108. See also Menachem Kellner, "Maimonides, Crescas, and Abravanel on Exod. 20:2: A Medieval Jewish Exegetical Dispute." *Jewish Quarterly Review* Vol. 69, No. 3 (Jan. 1979), pp. 129-157.
109. For "create," Maimonides uses *himtzi* rather than the more common *bara*.

This is what the prophet said, "the Lord, God, is true" (Jer. 10:10) — He alone is the truth and none other has truth like His truth, and this is what the Torah states, "there is none beside Him" (Deut. 4:35), which means that there is no true existence beside Him that is like Him. This Being is the God of the world and master of the earth, and He guides the sphere with a strength that has no end or finitude; with a strength without interruption, for the sphere constantly turns, and it is not possible for it to turn without one turning it, and He, blessed is He, is the One who turns it, [but] without a hand or a body. And the knowledge of this is a positive commandment, as it says, "I am the Lord your God" (Exod. 20:2, Deut. 5:6). And whoever considers that there is another god besides this violates a negative commandment as it says, "you shall have no other gods before Me" and he denies the fundamental tenet, for this is a great fundamental upon which everything depends" (*Yesodei ha-Torah* 1:1-6).

Rabbi Netanel Weiderblank explains that Maimonides believes the verse "I am the Lord your God" teaches three principles: "(a) there is a First Being (God), (b) who brought into being all existence, (c) such that all other existents are contingent, depending on His existence.... He instructed us to believe in His necessary existence" (*Illuminating Jewish Thought*, vol. 2, p. xxxii).

Rabbi Joseph B. Soloveitchik analyzes the differences between Maimonides formulation in *Sefer ha-Mitzvot* and *Mishneh Torah*: "The differences between the passage in the Code and the one here are easily discernible. First, in the Hebrew translation of *Sefer ha-Mitzvot* Maimonides speaks of *emunah* (faith), instead of knowledge. The term *yedi'ah* (knowledge) does not appear in the Hebrew *Sefer ha-Mitzvot* text. The emphasis is laid upon *emunah*—belief. Second, the principle of unity, in the *Sefer ha-Mitzvot*, is connected to the original covenant between God and Israel, from which the people of Israel derives charismatic endowment and which constitutes the legal basis for the continuation of the community relationship. In other words, the singular historical occurrence of the Jewish people finds both its root and apex, its uniqueness and legitimation, in our faith in the unity of God. While in the *Mishneh Torah* the whole doctrine has been placed on the level of metaphysics or theology, the *Sefer ha-Mitzvot* alters the dominant theme from the metaphysical or theological to the historical" (*Worship of the Heart*, p. 116; see also Malbim on Exod. 20:2, s.v. *ve-ha-Rambam*).

20:3. You shall have no other gods before Me. — … He alone, may He be exalted, is worthy of being worshipped, elevated, in order to publicize His grandeur and renown (*PhM Sanhedrin*, Fifth Principle; Maimonides does not quote this verse in the current passage).

Joseph Albo questions if this should be counted as one of the essential principles of the Torah: "It is… difficult to see why Maimonides included as a principle the dogma that God alone should be worshipped and none else. For, though it is one of the commandments of the Torah, as is written, 'You shall have no other gods before Me… You shall not bow down to them nor worship them' (Exod. 20:3, 5), nevertheless it is not a fundamental principle upon which the entire Torah depends. For if a man believes in God and His law, and introduces a mediator between himself and God, he violates, indeed, the commandment just quoted, but this does not make it a fundamental principle with which the entire law stands and falls" (*Ikkarim* 1:3).

Philo sees one flowing naturally from the other: "in order that the only true God might be honored in truth and simplicity" (*Heir* 169). Were people to engage in syncretistic worship, they would be "like ships without ballast, they are tossed about in every direction for ever... never to be able to anchor firmly in truth" (*Decalogue* 67).

FURTHER: We are forbidden to believe in any god beside Him, may He be exalted, at it says, "you shall have no other gods before Me." This has already been explained at the end of *Makkot* (24a) that this prohibition is included in the 613 commandments... (*ShM*, Neg. 1; see Pos. 1; and on Exod. 20:2).

FURTHER: The primary commandment against idolatry is to not worship any of the created beings—neither angel, nor sphere, nor star, nor any of the four elements, nor anything that is created from them. And even if the worshipper knows that God is the true Lord, yet he still worships this created being in the way that Enosh and the people of his generation did originally, this is still idolatry (*Avodah Zarah* 2:1).

> Ibn Ezra writes, "the meaning of 'jealous God' — this is the judgment because after God created you and gave you life, how can you give honor to another, which can do you neither good nor evil."

FURTHER: ... the commandment not to worship any other being is merely an explanation of the first (*Guide* 2:31).

20:4. You shall not make for yourself any graven idol, or any image of what is in heaven above or on earth below, or in the water below under the earth. — We are forbidden from making an idol to be worshipped. And there is no difference whether he makes it himself or instructs someone else to make it for him, as God, may He be exalted, said, "You shall not make for yourself any graven idol, or any image...." And whoever transgresses this prohibition is liable to receive lashes, which means whether he made an idol for himself or instructs someone to make it for him, even if he did not worship it (*ShM*, Neg. 2; see also *Avodah Zarah* 3:9 and Ra'avad there).

Rashi writes somewhat similarly: "'You shall have no [other gods before Me]' – Why is this stated? since the next verse says, 'You shall not make for yourself,' I only know not to make [an idol]; how do I know [not to worship] an idol that has already been made? As it says, 'you shall have no [other gods before Me].'" Both Rashi and Maimonides highlight two separate prohibitions: the prohibition of making an idol, and a separate prohibition of worshipping an idol that has already been made.

R. Saadiah renders *lo ta'aseh lekha pesel*, "you shall not make for yourself any graven idol" as *lo ta'aseh pesel*, "you shall not make any graven idol," understanding the word *lekha* as extraneous. In other words, it is used merely for emphasis,[110] but does not impact the meaning of the verse. In this case, for Maimonides as well, the word *lekha* is extraneous, since it makes no difference whether one crafts an idol for himself or for someone else.

20:5. You shall not bow down to them... — We are forbidden to bow down to an idol. And it should be clear that when we say "idol" [*avodah zarah*, lit., "foreign worship"] we mean anything that might be worshipped other than God. And He, may He be exalted, said, "You shall not bow down to them nor worship them." And the intention is not merely to only prohibit prostration and nothing else.

---

110. The modern term for this is a "pleonasm," which is "A grammatical element that is redundant or unnecessary; a statement or use of an adjective that is tautological" (Todd Murphy, *Pocket Dictionary for the Study of Biblical Hebrew*, p. 130; see Gesenius 119s, 135a-b).

Rather, the verse mentions one of the forms of worship, indicating prostration, and we are also forbidden to sacrifice to them, and to libate to them, and to burn incense to them. And whoever violates one of these, and prostrates or sacrifices or libates or burns incense is punished by stoning.

And the language of the *Mekhilta*, "'One who slaughters to [another god] shall be destroyed' (Exod. 22:19) — from this we learn the punishment but not the prohibition. Therefore we learn, 'You shall not bow down to them nor worship them' — sacrifices are included [in the phrase 'nor worship them']. It is specified to teach us that just as sacrificing is a way to serve God, and one is guilty whether or not it is the customary way of worshipping [this specific idol], so too concerning any similar form of service to God, one is guilty whether or not this is the customary form of service."

The meaning of this statement is that there are four types of service, and they are prostration, sacrifice, burning incense, and libation, about which He commanded us that we serve God, may He be exalted. Whoever worships a false god with one of these is punished by stoning, even if the god being worshipped is not customarily worshipped in that manner. And this is what is called "non-customary" [*lo ke-darkah*], which means that even if he worshipped it in one of the ways that it is not normally worshipped, once he was worshipped in one of these [four] ways, he is stoned if he did it intentionally, and by punished by *karet* if it was not known or if he was not punished. And if he did it accidentally he must bring an offering. And similarly if he accepts upon him anything else as a god, he is also liable (*ShM*, Neg. 5).

... nor worship them... — We are forbidden to worship an idol, even if it is not one of the four ways of service as has been mentioned earlier (*ShM*, Neg. 5; see above). However this prohibition only applies if the idol is worshipped in a customary manner [*ke-darkah*].

This means worshipping it in the manner than it is customarily worshipped, such as defecating on Peor[111] or throwing stones at Markolis. And God, may He be exalted, said, "nor worship them." And the language of the *Mekhilta* is, "'You shall not bow down to them, nor worship them' — to make guilty the service itself and the prostration itself." Therefore one who throws a stone at Peor or defecates on Markolis is not guilty, since this is not the normal manner of service, and He, may He be exalted, said, "How did these nations serve their gods? and I shall do the same" (Deut. 12:3) (*ShM*, Neg. 6; see also *Avodah Zarah* 3:3).

FURTHER: One who hugs an idol or kisses it, or sweeps before it, or mops before it, or washes it, or anoints it, or dresses it, or fits it with shoes, or similar way of showing respect to it violates a negative commandment, as it says, "nor worship them," and these acts are considered forms of worship. Nonetheless, he is not punished with lashes, since these are not mentioned explicitly in the Torah. And if it was the proper manner of worship, and he performed them in order to worship it, then he is liable (*Avodah Zarah* 3:6, based on M. *Sanhedrin* 7:7 (BT *Sanhedrin* 60b); Maimonides states the same idea almost verbatim at *PhM Sanhedrin* 7:6. Nahmanides quotes this in part in his commentary to Exod. 22:19).

...for I the Lord your God am a jealous God... — ... you will not find the expressions "burning anger," "provocation," or "jealousy" applied to God except in reference to idolatry (*Guide* 1:36).

> Rashi writes, "'a jealous God' – jealous to punish and does not waive His attribute [of justice] to forgive the sin of idolatry. Every use of *kannei* [jealous] is *anprenement* [in Old French][112]—setting His heart to exacting out punishment"

---

111. See Rashi on Num. 25:3.
112. An "outburst of rage or frenzy leading to action" (Dayan I. Gukovitzki).

(see also Rashi on Deut. 29:19; However, Rashi elsewhere understands "jealousy of God the Lord of Hosts" as "jealous about Zion regarding the plans of Aram and Pekah" (on Isa. 9:6); see Radak and Malbim on that verse).

Nahmanides accepts what Maimonides writes about "jealousy," but finds verses to refute the application of "burning anger" and "provocation" as limited to idolatry (see on Exod. 20:3). He continues, "In my opinion, jealousy is mentioned only with reference to idolatry in Israel. The reason for the jealousy is that Israel is the treasured possession of the Glorious Name, which He has separated to Himself, as I have explained above (on Exod. 19:4). Now if His people, His servants, turn to other gods, God is 'jealous' of them even as a man is jealous of his wife when she goes to other men, and of a servant who makes another master for himself. But Scripture uses no such term of jealousy with reference to other peoples to whom He has allotted the hosts of heaven" (on Exod. 20:3). Shadal, after quoting both disputants, writes:

I say, however, that even this is not true, for we find, "The Lord is a jealous [kanno] and avenging God" (Nahum 1:2), where the prophet is speaking against Assyria, which did evil to Israel; it was for this evil that there was jealousy and vengeance, not on account of the idolatry that Assyria had committed, for (as per Nachmanides himself) Scripture records "jealousy" on the part of God only in connection with Israel's idolatry, not with that of the other nations. Even though the present verse [Exod. 20:5] speaks of idolatry, it nevertheless seems to me that the phrases "a jealous God" and "demands account of the sins of the fathers" refer not only to idolatry, but are used in a general way, so as to say that He is an avenging and wrathful God; that is, a person who commits grievous sins is punished by Him with grievous blows, as if He were a human being whose anger was aroused (trans. Klein).

Maimonides quotes Nahum 1:2 not too much later in the *Guide* (1:54), where he uses this verse as an example of his thesis that "He performs acts similar to those which, when performed by us, originate in certain psychical dispositions, in jealousy, desire for retaliation, revenge, or anger; they are in accordance with the guilt of those who are to be punished, and not the result of any emotion, for He is above all defect!"

The dispute hinges on the meaning of Nah. 1:2. Rashi and Radak assume the verse does not refer to idolatry (*à la* Shadal), while R. Joseph Kara (Mahari Kara) writes, "'The Lord is a jealous and avenging God' – since they backslid to idolatry therefore the prophet said about them: the Holy One, Blessed is He, acts jealously with the wicked idolators and punishes them and keeps hostility to those who hate Him." According to Nehama Leibowitz, Maimonides' interpreters "iron out the difficulty by limiting Maimonides' statement to the Almighty's relations with the nation as a whole" (see *New Studies in Shemot (Exodus)*, p. 395).

... visiting the sins of the fathers on the sons... — When a person or a people of a country sin, and committed the sin knowingly and voluntarily, as we have made known that it is appropriate to be punished, and the Holy One, Blessed is He, knows how he should be punished. Some people are punished in their body or their money, or their minor children—for a minor child does not have mental capacity and has not included in the commandments—rather they are like his property, as it is written, "Each man [*ish*] shall be put to death for his own sin" (Deut. 24:16) — [he is not punished] until he becomes an *ish* (*Teshuvah* 6:1; see next entry).

... unto the third or fourth generation of those that hate Me.
— When it is said that God visits the iniquity of the fathers upon
the children, this refers exclusively to the sin of idolatry, and to no
other sin. That this is the case may be inferred from what is said in
the Ten Commandments, e.g., "upon the third and fourth generation
of those that hate Me," none except idolaters being called "enemy,"
also "every abomination to the Lord, which He hates" (Deut. 12:31).
It was, however, considered sufficient to extend the punishment to
the fourth generation, because the fourth generation is the utmost a
man can see of his posterity; and when, therefore, the idolators of a
place are destroyed, the old man worshipping idols is killed, his son,
his grandson, and his great-grandson, that is, the fourth generation.
By the mention of this attribute we are, as it were, told that His
commandments, undoubtedly in harmony with His acts, include the
death even of the little children of idolators because of the sin of their
fathers and grandfathers. This principle we find frequently applied
in the Law, as, e.g., we read concerning the city that has been led
astray to idolatry, "destroy it utterly, and all that is therein" (Deut.
13:15). All this has been ordained in order that every vestige of that
which would lead to great injury should he blotted out, as we have
explained (*Guide* 1:54).

Maimonides' interpretation is troubling; the Talmud
assumes that God only visits the sins on children who
continue in their parents' wickedness (BT *Berakhot* 7a;
Sanhedrin 27b; quoted by Onkelos, Rashi, Nahmanides,
Sforno). Despite this, Maimonides says that for the sin of
idolatry, God's punishments "include the death even of the
little children of idolators because of the sin of their fathers
and grandfathers." Maimonides derives this law from the *ir
haniddaḥat*, the perverted city (see Deut. 13:13-19), which
must be entirely wiped out (*Avodah Zarah* 4:6).

The answer must be that righteous children are not included in the punishment. Rabbi Chaim Soloveitchik says that this only applies to children who have also sinned, not "those who are still suckling at the bosom." In general, people are not liable for punishment until the age of halakhic maturity, but in the case of *ir ha-niddaḥat* even a minor who practiced idolatry is liable (see *Rambam la-Am* on *Avodah Zarah* 4:6).

20:6. And showing steadfast love [*ḥesed*]... — See on Exod. 34:6, where Maimonides explains there are two types of kindness: "first, we show kindness to those who have no claim whatever upon us; secondly, we are kind to those to whom it is due, in a greater measure than in due them" (*Guide* 3:53).

... to the thousands that love Me and keep My commandments. — For Maimonides' understanding of "loving God," see *ShM*, Pos. 3, *Yesodei ha-Torah* 2:1-2, *Teshuvah* ch. 10, *Shemonah Perakim* ch. 5, *Guide* 1:39, 3:28, to be quoted at Deut. 6:5.

On the current verse, Nahmanides makes allusion to Maimonides, writing, "Now many scholars have explained that 'His lovers' are those who worship Him without the intention of receiving a reward. Just as our Sages have mentioned" (see *Avot* 1:3, Rashi on BT *Sotah* 31a). However, Nahmanides himself understands "His lovers" as those who are willing to face martyrdom rather than violate the Torah.

20:7. You shall not take the name of the Lord your God in vain... — [The prohibition of taking a] vain oath is divided into four categories: The first is if he swears about something that is known to be untrue. How so? For example, he swears about a man that he is a woman, or that a woman is a man, or that a wall of stone is made of gold, or anything similar. The second is if he swears about something

234

over which there is no doubt. For example, if he swears that the heavens are the heavens, or that this stone is stone, or that these two objects are two objects, and everything similar. For this is a matter about which there is no doubt to a reasonable person for which it would be necessary to reinforce the matter with an oath. The third is one who swears to violate a commandment. How so? For example one who swears to not wear a fringed garment, or to not wear *tefillin*, or to not dwell in a *sukkah* on Sukkot, or to not eat matzah on the eve of Passover, or to fast on the Sabbath or holidays, or anything similar. The fourth is one who swears about something that he does not have the strength to do. How so? For example one who swears not to sleep for three days, for three consecutive nights and days, or to not eat a morsel for seven consecutive days, or anything similar. Whoever takes a vain oath in one of these four [categories of] oaths violates a negative commandment, as it says, "You shall not take the name of the Lord your God in vain." And if he did so intentionally he receives lashes, and if he did no unintentionally he is fully exempt (*Shevuot* 1:4-7; see also *ShM*, Neg. 61-62).

FURTHER: Whoever makes a blessing which is not necessary is like one who takes the Name in vain, and is like one who has sworn in vain... (*Hil. Berakhot* 1:15).

> This comment is based on *Berakhot* 33a; however some authorities assume this is fundamentally a rabbinic prohibition. In the *Guide*, he writes, "Know that in some instances by the phrase 'the name of the Lord,' nothing but the name alone is to be understood, e.g., 'You shall not take the name of the Lord your God in vain'" (*Guide* 1:64).

FURTHER: [Maimonides does not quote the present verse in the following citation, but it is necessary in order to observe the ensuing debate between him and Nahmanides:] It is not just a vain oath that is forbidden; rather, it is even prohibited to needlessly mention any of the names that are specific to God, even when one is not taking an oath. Behold the verse that gives the commandment, saying, "to fear the glorious and awesome Name" (Deut. 28:58), and included in this verse is to not mention God's name without need. Therefore, if one's tongue erred and the Name was mentioned without need, he should quickly praise and exalt and glorify Him, so that the name not be mentioned without need. How so? If he said, "God," he should say, "may He be blessed forever and ever," or "great is He and exceedingly praised," or the like, in order that it not be for naught (*Shevuot* 12:11).

> Nahmanides explains that according to the Sages, the present verse prohibits swearing in vain, but then continues: "By way of the plain meaning of Scripture, the verse also prohibits the taking of the Glorious Name in vain upon one's lips [even without taking an oath]." Nahmanides believes the prohibition of speaking God's name for naught is a violation of the present verse, while for Maimonides, it is a violation of Deut. 28:58.

... for the Lord will not cleanse one who takes His name in vain...
— [Maimonides explains the procedure for preparing someone about to take an oath:] How to we admonish someone who is taking an oath? We say to him: Know that the entire world trembled when the Holy One, blessed is He, said, "You shall not take the name of the Lord your God in vain." Concerning all of the transgressions in the Torah it is stated, "He will cleanse," and here it is stated, "He will not cleanse." Concerning all of the commandments in the Torah, he alone is punished, but here he and his family are punished for concealing the issue for him. Furthermore, he causes punishment

to be meted out to "the enemies of the Jews," since all the Jews are responsible for one another, as it says, "Swearing, and lying, and murdering... for this the land will mourn and all who inhabit it will be forlorn" (Hos. 4:2-3). Concerning all the commandments in the Torah, [punishment] is deferred for two or three generations if they are meritorious, but here they are punished immediately, as it says, "'I will bring it [the curse] forth,' says the Lord of Hosts, and it will enter the house of the thief, and into the house of he who swears falsely by My Name" (Zech. 5:4). "I will bring forth" means "immediately"; "and it will enter the house of the thief" means one who deceives people, i.e., one who does not have the money another owes him but files a complaint against him for no reason and makes him take an oath; "he who swears falsely by My name" is understood literally. [The verse concludes:] "... shall consume it, its timber and its stones" — things which cannot be destroyed by fire and water will be destroyed by a false oath (*Shevuot* 11:16).

FURTHER: Even though one who swears in vain or falsely receives lashes, and one who swears an oath of testimony or an oath of deposit brings an offering, he is not entirely forgiven for his sinful oath, as it says, "the Lord will not cleanse." There is no cleansing from the judgment of Heaven until he is punished for desecrating the Great Name, as it says, "[You shall not take a false oath in My name, for] you will desecrate the name of your God" (Lev. 19:12). Therefore, a person must be exceedingly cautious about this sin, even more than with other transgressions. This sin is considered one of the severe transgressions, as we have explained in *Hilkhot Teshuvah* (1:2). Even though it does not carry the penalty of *karet* or execution by the court, it involves the desecration of the sacred Name, which is worse than all other sins (*Shevuot* 12:1-2).

20:8. Remember the Sabbath day to sanctify it. — It is a positive commandment that we are commanded to sanctify the Sabbath and to recite words when it enters and when it departs. We must mention the greatness of the day and its exaltedness, and how it is distinct from the days before it and those that come after it. And He, may He be exalted, said, "Remember the Sabbath day to sanctify it," which means remember it by remembering [=mentioning] its sanctity and its greatness. This is the commandment of Kiddush. And the language of the *Mekhilta* is, "'Remember the Sabbath day to sanctify it' — sanctify it with a blessing." And in explaining it, the Sages said, "Remember it over wine" (BT *Pesaḥim* 106a). And they said, "Sanctify it when it enters and sanctify it when it departs," which is a reference to *havdalah*,[113] which is also a part of properly remembering the Sabbath (*ShM*, Pos. 155; he makes the same point at *Shabbat* 29:1).[114]

> The *Maggid Mishneh* (*Shabbat* 29:1) observes that according to Maimonides, both Kiddush and *havdalah* are biblical commandments, and this might be based on his manuscript version of the Talmud. Modern printed versions of the Talmud only inlcude Kiddush.

FURTHER: Four things have been said about the Sabbath: two from the Torah, and two from the scribes and explained by the prophets. In the Torah, it says "remember" and "observe." And those that are explicated by the prophets are "honor" (*kavod*) and "delight" (*oneg*), as it says, "And you shall call the Sabbath a delight, the holy of the Lord, honored" (Isa. 58:13) (*Shabbat* 30:1).

---

113. Lit., "separation," but refers to the ritual of marking the end of the Sabbath with blessings, wine, spices, and a multi-wick candle.
114. The printed edition of the Talmud does not mention the *yetzi'ah* [departure] of the Sabbath [=*havdalah*]. However, Rashi appears to have had it in his manuscript as well (see BT *Nazir* 4a, s.v. *ve-harei*).

20:9. Six days shall you labor and do all of your work. — [R. Bahya quotes the following in the name of Maimonides:] He should say: All six days it is possible for you to serve God, may He be blessed, by performing your labors, just as the patriarchs served God, may He be blessed, with shepherding and other physical matters. However the seventh day is entirely a day of rest for the Lord your God; you shall do no labor on it at all. This I heard in the name of Maimonides, may his memory be a blessing.

20:10. But the seventh day is a Sabbath to the Lord your God; you shall not do any work, you, or your son, or your daughter, or your manservant, or your maidservant, or your cattle, or the stranger within your gates. — [Maimonides criticizes the *Behag* for his analysis of this verse:] The *Behag* counts desecrating the Sabbath among those who are liable for stoning, and then he counts "you shall not do any work." And the only thing possible to say is that they considered the fulfillment of the punishment as a negative commandment. But how could they count the punishment [as a commandment] as well as the underlying matter that made this punishment necessary? (*ShM*, Principle 14).

FURTHER: We are prohibited from doing work on the Sabbath, as He said, "you shall not do any work." And [concerning] one who transgresses this prohibition, Scripture specifies [the punishment] of *karet*, if the judge did not know about it. However, if witnesses testified about it, then he is punished by stoning—this is all if it was done intentionally. And if it was done unintentionally, then he brings a fixed sin offering (*ShM*, Neg. 320).

FURTHER: Resting from work on the seventh day is a positive commandment, as it says, "you shall rest on the seventh day" (Exod. 23:12). Anyone who performs labor on it nullifies a positive commandment and violates a negative commandment, as it says, "you shall not do any work" (*Shabbat* 1:1; see further at Exod. 23:12).

... or your cattle... — there is an explicit prohibition in the Torah as it says, "you shall not do any work, you, or your son, or your daughter, or your manservant, or your maidservant, or your cattle," which applies to plowing and everything that is similar to plowing. However since this is a prohibition that is connected to capital punishment by the court, one does not receive lashes for violating it (*Shabbat* 20:2).

20:11. For in six days the Lord made the heaven and earth, the sea, and all that is in them... — It is perhaps clear why the laws concerning Sabbath are so severe that their transgression is visited with death by stoning (Exod. 31:14-15), and that the greatest of the prophets put a person to death for breaking the Sabbath (Num. 15:35-36). The commandment of the Sabbath is the third from the commandment concerning the existence and the unity of God. For the commandment not to worship any other being is merely an explanation of the first. You know already from what I have said,[115] that no opinions retain their vitality except those which are confirmed, published, and by certain actions constantly revived among the people. Therefore we are told in the Law to honor this day; in order to confirm thereby the principle of Creation which will spread in the world, when all peoples keep Sabbath on the same day. For when the question is asked, why this is done, the answer is given, "For in six days the Lord made..." (Exod. 20:11).

Two different reasons are given for this commandment, because of two different objects. In the Decalogue in Exodus, the following reason is given for distinguishing the Sabbath: "For in six days...." However in Deuteronomy the reason is given: "And you shall remember that you were a slave in the land of Egypt... therefore the Lord your God commanded you..." (Deut. 5:15). This difference

---

115. Kapach assumes this means orally to his student for whom the work was written.

can easily be explained. In the former, the cause of the honor and distinction of the day is given: "Therefore the Lord blessed the Sabbath day and sanctified it" (Gen. 2:3), and the cause for this is, "For in six days...." But the fact that God has given us the law of the Sabbath and commanded us to keep it, is the consequence of our having been slaves; for then our work did not depend on our will, nor could we choose the time for it; and we could not rest. Thus God commanded us to abstain from work on the Sabbath, and to rest, for two purposes; namely, (1) That we might confirm the true theory, that of the Creation, which at once and clearly leads to the theory of the existence of God. (2) That we might remember how kind God has been in freeing us "from the burden of the Egyptians" (cf. Exod 6:7). The Sabbath is therefore a double blessing: it gives us correct notions, and also promotes the well-being of our bodies (*Guide* 2:31).

FURTHER: The object of the Sabbath is obvious, and requires no explanation. The rest it affords man is known; one seventh of the life of every man, whether small or great, passes thus in comfort, and in rest from trouble and exertion. This the Sabbath effects in addition to the perpetuation and confirmation of the grand doctrine of the Creation (*Guide* 3:43).[116]

... and He rested [*va-yanaḥ*] on the seventh day, therefore the Lord blessed the Sabbath day and sanctified it. — ... "to rest" has likewise been figuratively applied to God in reference to the Sabbath day, on which there was no creation; it is therefore said, "And he rested [*va-yishbot*] on the seventh day" (Gen. 2:2).... Our Sages, and some of the commentators, took, however, *nuaḥ* in its primary sense

---

116. See Shadal's comment on the current verse, p. 307 in the Klein translation.

"to rest," but as a transitive form (*hif'il*),[117] explaining the phrase thus: "and He gave rest to the world on the seventh day" (*Genesis Rabbah* 10:9), i.e., no further act of creation took place on that day. It is possible that the word *va-yanaḥ* is derived either from *yanaḥ*, a verb of the class *pe-yod*, or *naḥoh*, a verb of the class *lamed-he*, and has this meaning, "he established" or "he governed" the Universe in accordance with the properties it possessed on the seventh day; that is to say, while on each of the six days events took place contrary to the natural laws now in operation throughout the Universe, on the seventh day the Universe was merely upheld and left in the condition in which it continues to exist... (*Guide* 1:67).

20:12. Honor your father and mother, so that your days may be long on the land which the Lord your God gives you. — We are commanded to honor father and mother, and that is what He, may He be exalted, said, "Honor your father and mother...." And the language of the *Sifra*, "What does 'honoring' mean? Providing them with food and drink, clothing and cover, and to bring them inside and take them out" (*ShM*, Pos. 210).[118]

FURTHER: Honoring father and mother is a great positive commandment, as is fearing one's father and mother. Scripture equated the honoring and fearing [parents] with [honoring and fearing] Him. It is written, "Honor your father and mother," and it is written, "Honor the Lord with your wealth" (Prov. 3:9). And regarding one's father and mother it is written, "A person shall fear his father and mother" (Lev. 19:3),

---

117. This is the interpretation of R. Saadiah, and Kapach quotes that he gives the same interpretation in *Emunot ve-De'ot* 2:12. According to Dr. Richard Steiner, this is one of the "theologically problematic passages that Saadia wished to purify" (see *A Biblical Translation in the Making: The Evolution and Impact of Saadia Gaon's Tafsir*, 121-122). In other words, Saadiah translated "He rested" as "He caused others [=Creation] to rest," since the literal translation would ascribe deficiency to God.
118. Maimonides counts "fearing" one's parents as a separate commandment (Pos. 211).

and it is written, "And you shall fear the Lord your God" (Deut. 6:13). Just and He commanded us to honor and fear His great name, He also commanded us to honor and fear them....

What is meant by "honor"? Providing them with food and drink, clothing and cover—from the father's own resources. If the father has no money and the son does, we compel him to sustain his father and mother according to his ability. He should bring them out and bring them in, and serve Him in all the ways that one serves a teacher. And he should stand before him in the way that one stands before a teacher.... How far does the honor of father and mother go? Even if they took a purse gold and threw it into the sea when he was standing there, he should not embarrass them nor yell at them or get angry at them. Rather he should accept the scriptural decree and remain silent....

Even though we have commanded in this, it is prohibited for someone to set a heavy yoke on his son and to be exacting about his honor with them, so that he not serve as a stumbling block. Rather he should waive [his honor] and ignore [offenses], since if a father waives his honor, his honor is waived[119].... (see *Mamrim* chapter 6; see also *ShM*, Principle 2).

FURTHER: ... [Commandments like:] "Honor your father and mother" (Exod. 20:12), "You shall not turn aside from what they tell you" (Deut. 17:11) are to remove the attributes of stubbornness and to achieve the attribute of humility (*Shemonah Perakim*, ch. 4).

20:13. You shall not murder... — Whoever kills an Israelite violates a negative commandment, as it says, "You shall not murder." And if he killed intentionally, in front of witnesses, he is executed by the sword, as it says, "he shall surely be avenged" (Exod. 21:20), and from the oral tradition we learn that this refers to the sword. Whether he kills the person with iron or burns him with fire, he is executed by the sword (*Rotze'ah* 1:1; see also *ShM*, Neg. 289).

---

119. A father has the right to waive the honor due him.

FURTHER: Although there are sins more severe than murder, there is none that destroys habitation of the world like murder. Even idolatry—and needless to say sexual sins and Sabbath desecration—are not like murder, for these are sins between man and the Holy One, blessed is He, but murder is among the sins that are interpersonal. And whoever has committed this sin is completely wicked, and all of the commandments that he performs are not equal to this sin and will not save him from judgment, as it says, "A man who does violence to the blood of any person [shall flee to the pit; let nobody assist him]" (Prov. 28:17).[120]

Go and learn from Ahab the idolater of whom it is said, "But there was none like Ahab [who gave himself to work wickedness in the eyes of the Lord]" (1 Kings 21:25), but when his sins and merits were set before the Lord of spirits, no sin that made him worth of death or was offset by a merit, except the blood of Naboth, as it says, "And the spirit came forth and stood before the Lord" (1 Kings 22:21) — this is the spirit of Naboth. And it is stated, "You shall persuade him and also prevail" (1 Kings 22:22). And behold, this sinner did not murder with his own hands; he merely caused [Naboth's death]. All the more so someone who kills with his own hands (*Rotze'ah* 4:9).

… you shall not commit adultery… — Tradition teaches that this is a prohibition regarding a married woman (ShM, *Shoresh* 7).

---

120. Maimonides here gives a more physical understanding of the verse. Rashi, however, writes, "'A man who does violence to the blood of any person' — one who has the crime of blood. This is one who causes his friend to sin, and his soul is lost because of his actions; 'shall flee to the pit' — until the day he dies he shall flee for assistance, that it should be atoned for him; 'let nobody assist him' — from Heaven to give him the strength to repent, so that he will not be in the Garden of Eden and his student in Hell; thus was taught in tractate *Yoma* [87a]." It is possible that Malbim, in his commentary on this proverb, makes reference to Maimonides.

FURTHER: We are forbidden to reveal the nakedness of a married woman, as He, may He be exalted, said, "And you shall not lie carnally with your neighbor's wife" (Lev. 18:20). And there are different forms of punishment for one who violates this prohibition. If she is a married woman or a betrothed maiden, then they are both executed by stoning, as the verse explains (Deut. 22:24). And if she was the daughter of a priest, then she is executed by burning and he by strangulation. And if she is the daughter of an Israelite, they are both executed by strangulation. This all applies when the testimony was admitted. However if the testimony was not admitted, then the penalty is *karet*. This all applies if it was done intentionally. However, if it was done unintentionally, then a fixed sin offering must be brought.

This prohibition has been repeated in the Ten Commandments, "you shall not commit adultery," which means not to have relations with a married woman. And the language of the *Mekhilta* is, "'you shall not commit adultery' — why is this written? Since it says, 'the adulterer and the adulteress shall be put to death' (Lev. 20:10), which teaches us the punishment, but not the prohibition, therefore it says, 'you shall not commit adultery.'"

And in the *Sifra* it says, "'who commits adultery with a married woman, and she is the wife of his neighbor' teaches us only the punishment but not the prohibition. Therefore is says 'you shall not commit adultery' [which teaches the prohibition] for both the man and the woman."

And [these Midrashim] do not employ the verse "And you shall not lie carnally with your neighbor's wife" (Lev. 18:20) as the prohibition, since it does not apply to the adulterer and adulteress, but only to the adulterer. And similarly regarding other sexual prohibitions, it was necessary to extend the prohibition to the woman as well [as the man], as the Sages said, "the verse 'you [plural] shall not approach [to uncover nakedness]' (Lev. 18:6), which applies to two—to prohibit the man through the woman and the woman through the man."

245

And the Talmud in *Sanhedrin* (51b) the Sages said, "everything is included in the word 'adulterer' and 'adulteress,' though the verse excluded the daughter of a *kohen* for execution by burning and a betrothed maiden for stoning." And this explanation has already been explained for us in the introduction (*ShM*, Neg. 347).

... you shall not steal... — Whoever steals property worth at least a *perutah* [an object of minimal value] violates a negative commandment, as it says, "you shall not steal."[121] One does not receive lashes for violating this punishment, since one is required to make [financial] restitution, since the Torah obligated the thief to pay [back what he stole], whether he stole from an Israelite or from a Gentile who practices idolatry, whether he stole from an adult or from a child. The Torah prohibited one to steal even the smallest amount, and it is forbidden to steal in a playful way, or to steal on the condition of returning, or to steal with the intent to repay. This is all forbidden, so that one not habituate himself in such behavior.

Who is a thief? One who takes another's property secretly, without the owners' knowledge, like someone who slips his hand into another's pocket and takes coins and the owners do not notice, and anything similar to this. However, if he takes openly and publicly, by force, then he is not a thief [*gannav*] but a robber [*gazlan*]. Therefore, an armed bandit who commits theft is not considered a robber [*gazlan*], but a thief [*gannav*], even though the owners know when the theft is occurring (*Geneivah* 1:1-3).

FURTHER: We are commanded not to commit kidnap [lit., *lignov ish me-Yisrael*, "to steal an Israelite person"], as it is stated in the

---

121. The standard editions of Maimonides have *lo tignov*, "you [sing.] shall not steal," which is a quotation from the Ten Commandments. However, the Frankel edition has *lo tignovu*, "you [pl.] shall not steal," which would be a quotation from Lev. 19:11. Even if the standard editions of Maimonides are correct, it is Maimonides practice to quote the simplest verse when teaching a law (see *Leḥem Mishnah* on *Melakhim* 1:1-2, quoted at Exod. 17:15-16).

Ten Commandments, "you shall not steal." And the language of the *Mekhilta* is, "'You shall not steal' — this is a prohibition of stealing a person [Hebrew *nefesh*, lit., 'soul']." And the Talmud in *Sanhedrin* (86a) states, "What is the course of the prohibition of kidnapping? Rabbi Yoshiah says it is from "you shall not steal," and Rabbi Yohanan says it is from the verse, "they may not be sold as slaves" (Lev. 25:42). However, they are not really arguing; one [verse] refers to kidnapping, and the other refers to selling [a person who has been kidnapped]." [These are mentioned together because] a person only incurs punishment when he kidnaps and sells [the person]. And if he violates both of these commandments, the punishment is strangulation, as He, may He be exalted, said, "And someone who steals a person and sells him and is found in his hand, he shall be put to death" (Exod. 21:16) (*ShM*, Neg. 243; see also *Geneivah* 9:1-2, 6; and on Exod. 21:16).

The root *ganav* means "kidnap" at Gen. 40:15. There appears to be an assumption, quoted by Rashi on the current verse, that the redundancy between this verse and "you shall not steal" (Lev. 19:11) means one verse teachings the generic prohibition of theft and one teaches the prohibition of kidnapping; the only question is to determine which verse teaches which prohibition.

... you shall not bear false witness against your neighbor... — We are forbidden to give false testimony, as God, may He be exalted, said, "you shall not bear false witness [*ed sheker*] against your neighbor." And this prohibition has already been repeated elsewhere in different words: *ed shav* (Deut. 5:20). And if someone violates this prohibition, the Torah decreed the punishment, "and you shall do to them as they schemed to do to their brother" (Deut. 19:19). And the language of the *Mekhilta* is, "'you shall not bear [false witness] against your neighbor' is the prohibition of false witnesses [*edim zomemim*]." And included in this prohibition is the punishment of lashes, as explained at the end of *Makkot*... (*ShM*, Neg. 285).

FURTHER: Whoever testifies based on what others said is considered a false witness [*ed sheker*], and violates a negative commandment, as it says, "you shall not bear false witness against your neighbor" (*Edut* 17:1).

> Jewish tradition does not admit testimony *ed mi-pi ed*, "a witness from the mouth of another witness," which seems to be an early instance of the prohibition on hearsay. While today the prohibition of hearsay is well accepted, it took a long time to develop. John H. Wigmore wrote, "The history of the Hearsay Rule, as a distinct and living idea, begins only in the 1500's, and it does not gain a complete development and final precision until the early 1700's"; see "The History of the Hearsay Rule" *Harvard Law Review* Vol. 17, No. 7 (May 1904), pp. 437-458. Thus while this rule might seem pedestrian to a modern reader, it is remarkably modern, predating its secular equivalent by more than a thousand years.

20:14. You shall not covet your neighbor's house, you shall not covet your neighbor's wife, nor his slave, his bondmaid, his ox, his donkey, or anything that belongs to him. — ... we are forbidden from setting our mind to scheming ways to acquire something that belongs to our brother, and this is what God, may He be exalted, said, "you shall not cover your neighbor's house." And the language of the *Mekhilta* is, "'you shall not covet [*taḥmod*]' — perhaps this means even coveting an object. Rather another verse states, 'you shall not covet [*taḥmod*] silver and gold and take it for yourself' (Deut. 7:25). Just as the later verse refers to performing an action, so too this verse applies to performing an action." Here it is demonstrated to you that this prohibition prohibits any cunning to acquire for ourselves an object that we desire belonging to our brethren. And even buying at an excessive price is included in the prohibition "you shall not covet" (*ShM*, Neg. 265).

FURTHER: [According to Maimonides, there are two different prohibitions: *lo taḥmod*, "you shall not covet" (Exod. 20:14) and *lo titavveh*, "you shall not desire" (Deut. 5:17)] — These two prohibitions do not have the same meaning. Rather, the first prohibition, which is "you shall not covet [*lo taḥmod*]," forbids one to purchase someone else's property, and the second prohibition [*lo titavveh*] forbids us to even desire the object in our hearts. And the language of the *Mekhilta* is, "'You shall not covet your neighbor's house' and later it says 'you shall not desire,' which forbids coveting and desiring as separate prohibitions." It also says there, "From where do we know that a person's desire will result in coveting? As it says, 'you shall not desire' and 'you shall not covet.' From where do we know that coveting will result in theft? As it says, 'And they coveted fields and stole them' (Mic. 2:2). The explanation is that if he sees a beautiful object in his brother's possession, his thoughts might overpower him and he come to desire it, he transgresses what He, may He be exalted, said, "you shall not desire." And if his love for that object grows strong to the point that he tries to bring the object into his possession and does not relent in pestering him and pressuring him to sell it to him or to exchange it for something better or more expensive; and if he succeeds in his quest he also violates "you shall not covet," since he acquired the object from his friend who did not wish to sell, but he pressured him or finessed him until he sold the object so that it belonged to him, he has violated the two prohibitions of "you shall not covet" and "you shall not desire," as we have explained. However, if the owner refuses to sell or trade the object because he loves the object, he will take it by force and compulsion by the strength of his soul's love for the object, in which case he has also violated "you shall not steal."[122] And you can understand all of this from the story of Ahab and Naboth (1 Kings 21). Thus it is explained to you the difference between what He said "you shall not covet" and what He said "you shall not desire" (*ShM*, Neg. 266).

FURTHER: Whoever covets his colleague's slave or bondmaid or house or possessions, or any object that can be purchased from him, and pressures him with schemes, and urges him until he sells it, even if he pays a lot of money, violates a negative commandment, as it says, "you shall not covet." And he does not receive lashes for this violation, since it has no deed. And one does not violate this commandment until he purchases the object he coveted, as it says, "you shall not covet silver and gold and take it for yourself" (Deut. 7:25) — a coveting that also has an action. And whoever desires his colleague's house or wife or possessions, or the like of anything else, which it is possible to acquire from him, as soon as he thought in his heart how he will acquire the object, and his heart is seduced by the object, he has violated a negative commandment, as it says, "you shall not desire," and desire refers only to the heart. Desire brings about coveting, and coveting brings about theft, since if the owners do not want to sell, even if he offers more money and entreats him cunning, he will come to theft, as it says: and they coveted houses and stole (cf. Mic. 2:2). And if the owners stand before him to save their property to prevent him from stealing, he will come to bloodshed. Go and learn from the incident of Ahab and Naboth. Thus you have learned that one who desires violates one prohibition and one who acquires an object of desire by pressuring the owners and making requests of them violates two prohibitions. Therefore it says

122. The *Ḥinnukh* adds that if the person tries to steal the object from its owner, the owner might defend his property and be killed; even if this bloodshed is justified, it is tragic and could have been avoided.

"you shall not covet" and "you shall not desire." And if he steals [the object], he violates three prohibitions (*Gezeilah ve-Aveidah* 1:9-12).

FURTHER: ... desire [*ta'avah*] is denounced because it leads to coveting [*ḥimmud*], and the latter is prohibited because it leads to robbery, as has been said by our Sages (*Guide* 3:40).

According to Rashi (on Deut. 5:17), the prohibition on *ta'avah* (desire) and *ḥimmud* (coveting) are one commandment, but he does not explain how one violates the commandment. Ibn Ezra also views them as synonyms, and says that this is a commandment of the heart, meaning that one violates it even by mere desire, without an actional component (see his famous analogy of the pauper and the princess; see further Nehama Leibowitz, *New Studies in Shemot (Exodus)*, "Thou Shalt Not Covet," pp. 342-351).

However, the *Mekhilta* (against Rashi and Ibn Ezra) rules that *ta'avah* and *ḥimmud* are not synonyms; rather the *Mekhilta* explains that *ta'avah* leads to *ḥimmud*, which leads to coercion, which leads to theft; and the *Mekhilta* clarifies that one does not violate *lo taḥmod* without taking an action. Maimonides, following the *Mekhilta*, counts them as separate commandments: *ta'avah* is a sin of the heart, while *ḥimmud* is only violated by action; this conclusion is accepted by *Shulḥan Arukh, Ḥoshen Mishpat* 359:10.

By combining his different statements, we can see Maimonides perceived a progression of five parts: *ta'avah* (desire), then *ḥimmud* (coveting), *oness* (coercion, i.e., pestering someone who refuses to sell), theft, and murder.[123] This is based on the *Mekhilta*, which says that *ta'avah* leads to *ḥimmud*, which leads to coercion, which leads to theft.

---

123. In Goethe's *The Sorrows of Young Werther*, the inability to have the woman he desires leads not to murder, but to suicide.

Maimonides' approach is reminiscent of Aristotle, who writes, "he who acts incontinently [i.e., uncontrollably, without restraint] does not fancy that the act is good till the passion is upon him" (*Ethics*, 1145b). In other words, a person might think it is permitted to "only" desire, or "only" covet, etc., because it will not lead to a worser sin; however Aristotle observes that once the passion takes hold, he will not be restrained: he might coerce, steal, or even kill to capture his quarry. In a similar vein, Nahmanides concludes "he who does not covet will never harm his neighbor."

However, one could construct the opposite argument: desire is inherently bad. Even if an individual could somehow guarantee that his desire and coveting would not escalate to more, it is doubtless pernicious to the soul to spend one's life fixated on others' possessions is not spiritually elevating. Maimonides does not stress the inherent perniciousness of coveting, but only on the tragic and avoidable end result.

20:15. And the entire nation was seeing the sounds and the lightning and the noise of the trumpet, and the mountain smoking, and the nation saw and they moved and stood afar. — You thus find in Hebrew instances in which the perception of the one sense is named instead of the other; thus, "See the word of the Lord" (Jer. 2:31), in the same meaning as "Hear the word of the Lord," for the sense of the phrase is, "Perceive what He says." Similarly the phrase, "See the smell of my son" (Gen. 27:27) has the same meaning as "smell the smell of my son," for it relates to the perception of the smell. In the same way are used the words, "And all the entire nation was seeing the sounds and the lightning" (Exod. 20:15), although the passage also contains the description of a prophetical vision, as is well known and understood among our people (*Guide* 1:46; see also *Guide* 3:32, quoted at Exod. 24:1).

Dr. J.H. Hertz quotes that this is an example of a "zeugma," i.e., a literary device where the context only fits one part; in this case the phrase *ro'im et ha-kolot ve-et ha-lappidim*, 'seeing the sounds and the lightning" is seemingly inconsistent, because "see" only fits "lightning," not "sounds." However, Rashi understands it as an instance of synesthesia, "they saw what was audible, which was impossible at any other place."

20:16. And they said to Moses, "Speak with us that we may hear, but let God not speak with us, lest we die." — It must, however, be noticed that the people did not understand the voice in the same degree as Moses did. I will point out to you this important fact, and show you that it was a matter of tradition with the nation, and well known by our Sages. For, as a rule, Onkelos renders the word *va-yedabber* by *u-mallel* ("and God spoke"); this is also the case with "And God spoke all these word" (Exod. 20:1), which Onkelos translated as *u-malleil Adonai yat kol pitgamayya*.[124] However the words *ve-al yedabber immanu Elohim*, "let not God speak to us" (Exod. 20:19), addressed by the people to Moses, is rendered *ve-la yitmallel immanu min kodam Adonai* ("Let not aught be spoken to us by the Lord"). Onkelos makes thus the same distinction which we made. (*Guide* 2:33; quoted more fully at Exod. 20:1).

Nahmanides disagrees with Maimonides about why Onkelos adopted this translation, writing, "when Onkelos saw here the expression 'but let God not speak with us,' and no 'partition' is mentioned, he did not deem it fit to translate that literally" (on Exod. 20:16; see there).

20:17. And Moses said to the people, "Do not fear, for God has come to prove you... — The passage, "for God has come to prove

124. This example is absent in the Friedlander edition but I added it based on the Kppach edition.

you, so that His fear may be before you, that you not sin" expresses the same idea as is expressed in Deuteronomy (13:4) in reference to a person who prophesies in the name of idols, namely in the words: "For the Lord your God proves you to know whether you love the Lord." We have already explained the meaning of the latter passage.

In the same sense Moses said to the Israelites when they stood round Mount Sinai: "Do not fear; the object of this great sight which you perceived is that you should see the truth with your own eyes. When the Lord your God, in order to show your faithfulness to Him, will prove you by a false prophet, who will tell you the reverse of what you have heard, you will remain firm and your steps will not slide. If I had come as a messenger as you desired, and had told you that which had been said unto me and which you had not heard, you would perhaps consider as true what another might tell you in opposition to that which you heard from me. But it is different now, as you have heard it in the midst of the great sight" (*Guide* 3:24).

FURTHER: [From the "Epistle to Yemen"] Remember, brethren, that this great, incomparable, and unique covenant and faith is attested by the best of evidence. For never before or since has a whole nation heard the speech of God or beheld His splendor. This was done only to confirm us in the faith, so that nothing can change it, and to reach a degree of certainty that will sustain us in these trying times of fierce persecution and absolute tyranny, as He says, "For God has come only in order to test you" (Exod. 20:17). It means that God has revealed Himself thus to give you strength to withstand all future trials. Now, brethren, do not slip or err, be steadfast in your religion and persevere in your faith and its duties (*The Epistle to Yemen*, ch. 1, p. 104).

… so that His fear may be before you, that you not sin." — God has been gracious with this nation—that is to say, the Jews—that they experience shame. And this is what the Sages said that the signs of the stock of Abraham are that they can be embarrassed, and they are merciful, and they are bestowers of kindness.[125] It is stated, "so that His fear may be before you," and they said, "This refers to shame"[126] (*PhM Avot* 5:18).

20:20. You shall not make with Me gods of silver and gods of gold—you shall not make for yourselves. — … we are forbidden to make images of human beings out of wood, stones, metal, or anything similar, even though they are not made to be worshipped. And this is a precaution against making any images so that we should not believe what the fools—the idolators—believe, who believed that the images had powers. And this is what God, may He be exalted, said, "You shall not make with Me gods of silver and gods of gold."

The language of the *Mekhilta* is: The prohibition "You shall not make with Me gods of silver and gods of gold—you shall not make *for yourselves*," means, "So that a person not say, 'Behold I will make them for decoration just as other people make them in other lands,'—so we come to learn 'you shall not make for yourselves.'" Someone who violates this prohibition is punished by lashes.

The details of this commandment have already been explained—which type of images may be fashioned and which may not be fashioned, and what they can look like—have already been explained in the third chapter of *Avodah Zarah* (42b-43b). In *Sanhedrin* (7b), it is explained that this prohibition also means "'You shall not make with me any gods of silver or gods of gold' includes other prohibitions as well emerging from this commandment."[127] However the simple

---

125. BT *Yevamot* 79a; Maimonides quotes this at *Issurei Bi'ah* 19:17. R. Abraham, the son of Maimonides, quotes this teaching at Exod. 2:20.

126. BT *Nedarim* 20a; Kapach quotes that written manuscripts omit this passage.

127. There the Talmud understands *elohei khesef* not as "gods of silver," but as "judges of silver," meaning judges who committed bribery to achieve their position. Maimonides however does not accept this as the simple meaning of the verse (*pashteih di-kra*), but he quotes it at *Sanhedrin* 3:8.

meaning of the verse is in accordance with what we have said from the *Mekhilta* (*ShM*, Neg. 4).

FURTHER: It is forbidden to make images [even] for beauty, even if they are not false gods, as it says, "You shall not make with Me gods of silver and gods of gold," which refers to images [made] of silver or of gold for ornamental purposes. [This is so that] people do not make the mistake of believing those images are for idolatry.[128] The prohibition on decorative objects only applies to the likeness of human beings. Therefore we should not use wood, cement, or stone to craft the likeness of a human. This only applies when the image protrudes, like sculptures [*ha-tziyyur ve-ha-kiyyor*] in a palace, and the like. And one who makes such images receives lashes. However, if the image was sunken, or was made with paint, like an image on a board or tablet, or images embroidered in cloth, these are permitted....

And similarly it is prohibited to form a likeness of the sun, moon, stars, and constellations, and angels, as it says, "You shall not make with Me," — you shall not make images of servants who serve before Me on high, even on a [flat] board.

It is permitted to make images of other of other animals and living beings—except for human beings—such as images of trees, plants, and anything similar, even if the images protrude (*Avodah Zarah* 3:10).

The Raavad writes, "It seems that he makes a distinction between the image of a person and the image of servants who serve on high. Images of servants that serve on high— even if they are level and neither protrude or are recessed— are prohibited, but images of people are permitted if they do not protrude, and I do not know why or from where [he made this distinction]."

128. From here it appears Maimonides viewed this prohibition as preventative of the sin of idolatry, but not inherently wrong in its own right.

The *Kesef Mishnah* however suggests a possible rationale: angels do not have bodies, and the other celestial bodies are not perceived as having three dimensions; therefore even making their likeness on a flat surface is prohibited, since it is not substantively different than how they are perceived in real life. However, human beings are only perceived in three-dimensional space, and therefore nobody would think that a two-dimensional rendering is an actual person. The *Tur*, however, rules that this prohibition applies "specifically to a whole image with all of its limbs; however if an image of a head without a body, or a body without a head, then there is no prohibition at all in owning it [*be-motz'o*] or making it [*be-oseh*]" (*Tur* 141 [end]).

20:21. An altar of earth shall you make for Me… — … Regarding the verse "an altar of earth shall you make for Me" — this verse might be considered a separate commandment besides the commandment to construct the Temple, but the meaning is as I will relate to you. The simple meaning of the verse is that it speaks of a time when it was permissible to bring offerings outside of the Temple, so that it was permitted to construct an altar of earth anywhere and bring offerings on it. And the Sages, peace be upon them, have already said that the verse means that He commanded us to build an altar, which must be attached to the earth (*Mekhilta*), and that it not be replicated and transported as it was in the wilderness (*ShM*, Pos. 20).

FURTHER: We do not make the altar from anything but a structure of stone. And what the Torah says, "you shall make Me an altar of earth" (v. 20), means that it must be attached to the earth—and not be built on an arch or in a cave (*Bet ha-Beḥirah* 1:13; based on BT Zevaḥim 58a; also Rashi here).

FURTHER: [God] transferred to His service that which had formerly served as a worship of created beings [including]... to have an altar erected in His name, i.e., "an altar of earth you shall make for Me" (*Guide* 3:32).

... and upon it you shall slaughter your burnt offerings and your peace offerings... — ... there is a debate about the meaning of the verse that God, may He be exalted, said, "and upon it you shall slaughter your burnt offerings and your peace offerings." You already know from the previous chapter (i.e., *Zevaḥim* 5) that the burnt offering is one of the most holy offerings and needs to be slaughtered on the north side, and the peace offerings are lesser holy offerings that can be slaughtered anywhere. Rabbi Yosi says the entire altar is suitable for slaughtering the burnt offering and peace offering. Rabbi Yosi b. Rabbi Yehudah says that half of it is for the burnt offering and half for the peace offering (*PhM Zevaḥim* 6:1; based on *Zevaḥim* 58a).

FURTHER: When most holy offerings are slaughtered on top of the altar, it is as if they were slaughtered in the north [of the Temple courtyard], as it says, "and upon it you shall slaughter your burnt offerings and your peace offerings," which teaches that the entire altar is suitable for slaughtering the burnt offerings and peace offerings (*Pesulei ha-Mukdashim* 3:1).[129]

FURTHER: If the altar is damaged, then all of the offerings are invalidated if they were slaughtered but their blood was not yet poured on the altar, since there is no altar upon which to pour the blood, and it says, "and upon it you shall slaughter your burnt offerings and your peace offerings," which means that you will slaughter when the altar is in proper form and undamaged (*Pesulei ha-Mukdashim* 3:22).

---

129. Burnt offerings are the paradigm for other most holy offerings. Peace offerings are of lesser holiness but they still may be offered on top of the altar, as this verse indicates. Despite their lesser sanctity they are not prohibited from the greater holiness of the top of the altar.

... in every place where I mention My name I will come to you and I will bless you. — In the first chapter of *Berakhot* (6b), how do we know that if someone is sitting [alone] and engaged in Torah study that the Divine Presence is with him? As it says, "in every place where I mention My name I will come to you and I will bless you" (*PhM Avot* 3:2).

FURTHER: [From Maimonides' discussion of which names are mentioned in in the priestly blessing. According to the Mishnah, the inexpressible name may be mentioned in the Temple, while the *kinnui'im*, "nicknames," are used outside the Temple:] "His nicknames" refers to what we recite today. And you must know that it is forbidden to express the inexpressible Name and we are not to mention it all, and that is the *yud, hei, vav, hei*, except in the Temple. A hint of this exists in the Torah, where it is stated, "in every place where I mention My name...." And the Sages said: Invert the verse, and explain it "in every place where I will come to you and I will bless you, I will mention my name" (*PhM, Sotah* 7:4; based on BT *Sotah* 38a).

20:22. And if you will make for Me an altar of stone ... — And it is explained in the *Mekhilta de-Rabbi Yishmael* in the explanation of this verse: "when you will enter the land, make an altar for Me attached to the ground" (based on v. 21). In this way, it becomes a commandment application for all generations, yet it is part of the commandment of the Temple, meaning that the altar must necessarily be built of stones. And in the *Mekhilta* it is stated in an explanation of what God, may He be exalted, said, "'And if you will make for Me an altar of stone' — R. Ishmael says: every *im* ["if"] in the Torah refers to something discretionary, with three exceptions. One exception is 'And if [you will make for Me] an altar of stone,' which is an obligation. How do you know this is obligatory or discretionary? Learn from the verse,

'You shall build the altar of the Lord your God of whole stones'" (Deut. 27:6) (*ShM*, Pos. 20; also *Bet ha-Beḥirah* 1:13).

... you shall not build it of hewn stone, for if you wave your sword over it you will have defiled it. — ... we are forbidden from building an altar of stones that have been touched by iron, as He, may He be exalted, said, "you shall not build it of hewn stone, for if you wave your sword over it you have defiled it." And if one built an altar with them, it is invalid and one may not offer sacrifices upon it (*ShM*, Neg. 79; also *Bet he-Beḥirah* 1:15).

FURTHER: The commandment that the stones of the altar shall not be hewn and that no iron tool shall be lifted up upon them (Deut. 27:5) has been explained by our Sages as follows: It is not right that the tool that shortens man's life should be lifted up upon that which gives length of life (*Mekhilta*, Rashi). As an aggadic explanation this is good, but the real reason is this: the heathen used to build their altars with hewn stones, and we ought not to imitate them. For this reason we have to make an altar of earth: "An altar of earth shall you make for Me" — if it should be impossible to dispense altogether with stones, they must not be hewn, but employed in their natural state. Thus the Law also prohibits from worshipping over painted stones (see Lev. 26:1), or from planting any tree near the altar of the Lord (Deut. 26:21). The object of all these commandments is the same, namely, that we shall not employ in the worship of God anything which the heathen employed in the worship of their idols. In general terms this is repeated in the following passage: "Take heed, that you not inquire after their gods, saying: How did these nations serve their gods? even so will I do likewise" (Deut. 12:30) — the Israelites shall not do this, because, as is expressly added, "every abomination unto the Lord, which He hates, have they done unto their gods" (*Guide* 3:45).

Nahmanides quotes this Maimonides' reason, "that this is an extraordinary precaution against making stones into certain shapes, thus being hewn stones, for such was the custom of the heathens." Nahmanides rejects this reason, because stones are only invalid if they are cut with iron, but not if they are cut with other tools, like those of silver or the *shamir*. Therefore Nahmanides suggests that iron instruments— unlike other cutting instruments—represent destruction, and for that reason there was no iron anywhere in the Tabernacle or the Temple, with the exception of the ritual knives; furthermore the act of slaughter is not considered "service" (*avodah*) in the technical sense. Based on this, Nahmanides concludes that the *Mekhilta*, quoted by Rashi, is the proper explanation of the verse.

20:23. And you shall not ascend by steps to My altar, so that your nakedness not be revealed on it. — We are forbidden to ascend to the altar with stairs, in order to avoid taking large steps when ascending. Rather, one should walk "heel to toe." And this is what God, may He be exalted, said, "And you shall not ascend by steps to My altar, so that your nakedness not be revealed on it."

The language of the *Mekhilta* is, "What does 'so that your nakedness not be revealed on it' mean? — That when you ascend to the altar, you should not take large steps, but should instead walk 'heel to toe.'" And the design of the ramp, and how it is built, is explained in the third chapter of *Middot*. And whoever walks with large steps to the altar so that his nakedness is revealed is punished with lashes (*ShM*, Neg. 80).

FURTHER: It is forbidden to make steps to the altar, as it says, "And you shall not ascend by steps to My altar." Rather, we are to build a ramp [*tel*] on the south of the altar, descending gradually from the top of the altar to the earth—and this is called a "ramp" [*kevesh*].

And one who ascends to the altar with steps receives lashes (*Bet ha-Beḥirah* 1:17).

FURTHER: The mode of worshipping Peor, then very general among the heathen, consisted in uncovering the nakedness. The priests were therefore commanded to make breeches for themselves to cover their nakedness during the service (Exod. 28:42), and, besides, no steps were to lead up to the altar, "so that your nakedness not be revealed on it" (*Guide* 3:45).

> Nahmanides offers a much more pedestrian reason: "The reason for [the prohibition against ascending the altar with] steps is that the fear of the altar and its enhancement is for the glory of God."

PARASHAT MISHPATIM

Exodus 21

21:1. And these are the judgments which you shall set before them. — Whoever is judged with the laws of the gentiles and their courts—even if their laws are the same as Israelite laws—is considered a wicked person and as if he has disgraced and rebelled against the Torah of Moses our teacher, as it says, "And these are the judgments which you shall set before them" — before them and not before gentiles; before them, and not before commoners (*Sanhedrin* 26:7; Maimonides here combines both opinions at BT *Gittin* 88b, that of Rabbi Tarfon and an anonymous teaching).

... judgments [*mishpatim*]... — [Maimonides does not quote this verse in this passage but does define the word *mishpat*:] The noun *mishpat* denotes the act of deciding upon a certain action in accordance with justice which may demand either mercy or punishment (*Guide* 3:53; see also the discussion of the meaning of *yashar* at 15:26).

21:2. If you buy a Hebrew servant... — We are commanded concerning the law of the Hebrew servant, as God, may He be exalted, said, "If you buy a Hebrew servant...." And the majority of laws of this commandment has already been explained explicitly in the Torah, and the details of this commandment are fully explained at the beginning of *Kiddushin* (14b, ff.) (*ShM*, Pos. 232).

> The phrase *ki tikneh*, which literally means "if you buy," is here understood not as a mere conditional, but as a conditional commandment.

FURTHER: The Hebrew servant mentioned in the Torah refers to an Israelite who was forcibly sold by the courts or who voluntarily sold himself. How so? If he stole [something] and does not have the means to repay the principle, the court sells him, as we have explained in *Hilkhot Geneivah*. And the only Israelite whom the court sells into slavery is a thief. And regarding the fact that the court sells him, the verse states, "If you buy a Hebrew servant..." (Exod. 21:2). And regarding him it says in Deuteronomy, "When your Hebrew brother will be sold to you..." (15:12).

How does he sell himself? If an Israelite has become extremely impoverished, the Torah has given him permission to sell himself, as it says, "When your brother will become impoverished and be sold to you" (Lev. 25:39). And it is not proper to sell oneself and to hoard his property or buy merchandise or vessels or give the money to creditors. He may only sell himself when he needs money to eat. And it is not proper to sell oneself unless he has no possessions remaining, not even clothing—then he may sell himself (*Avadim* 1:1).

> Aristotle beleived that slavery was a natural condition for some people (see the beginning of *Politics*). While the Torah sanctioned slavery, it was not the ideal state and there were strict limitations on how a master could treat his slave. Maimonides writes, "[T]he attribute of piety and the way of wisdom is for a person to be merciful and to pursue justice, not to make his slaves carry a heavy yoke, nor cause them distress"(*Avadim* 9:8).

... six years shall he serve... — ... that is to say, six years of service from the day that he is sold until the completion of six years, even if there is a sabbatical year within those six years. And that is what is said, "six years *shall* he serve," and *sometimes* on the seventh [as well].[130] And if the Jubilee year falls within those six years, then he goes free (*PhM Kiddushin* 1:2).

---

130. BT *Arakhin* 18b, *Niddah* 48a; JT *Kiddushin* 1:2; *Mekhilta*. See also *Avadim* 2:2.

... and on the seventh he shall go free for nothing. — It is a commandment to say to him, "Depart!" when he leaves. Even if he [the master] does not say this, he still goes free and he does not need a writ of manumission. Even if the slave had been sick and the master had spent significant funds [to heal him], the slave still owes him nothing, as it says, "he shall go free for nothing" (*Avadim* 2:12).

21:3. If he came in my himself, he shall go out by himself; if he was married, then his wife shall go out with him. — A master is obligated to provide sustenance for the wife of every Hebrew servant. This is when his wife is a *nesu'ah*, but not if she is an *arusah* or a *shomeret yavam*. However, if she was among the forbidden marriages, even if she is only among the secondary prohibitions, then the master is not obligated to sustain her, as it says, "his wife [shall go out] with him" — meaning a woman who is suitable to be married to him. The master is also obligated to provide the servant's sons and daughters with their sustenance. When a court sells him, it is stated, "If he was married, then his wife shall go out with him." And would you think that once he was acquired, then his wife should also be indentured? Rather this phrase teaches [something else, namely] that the master is obligated to sustain her. And regarding someone who sold himself, it is stated, "And he shall depart from you, he and his children with him" (Lev. 25:41). And regarding a servant sold to a Gentile, it is stated, "and he shall go out in the Jubilee year—he and his children with him" (v. 54).

This applies to whether he had a wife and children at the time he was sold, or if he acquired a wife and children after he was sold— so long as he married with the master's consent. However if he got married without the master's consent, then he is not obligated to provide her with sustenance (*Avadim* 3:1).

21:4. If his master will give him a wife... — If the court has sold someone into slavery, then his master has to give him a Canaanite bondmaid as a wife. This applies to the master, as well as the master's son if the master dies—he is supposed to give him a Canaanite bondmaid. And we compel him to do this, so that he will give birth to slaves through her. And she is permitted to him all the days of his servitude, as it says, "If his master will give him a wife...." And if someone sells himself into slavery, he is not permitted to take a Canaanite bondmaid—just like any other Israelite (*Avadim* 3:3; see also *PhM Kiddushin* 1:2).

FURTHER: If he [the servant] has a wife and children, even if it was his master who gave him a Canaanite bondmaid, he may not separate him from his wife and children, as it says, "his wife *with him.*"... [A master] may not give him two bondmaidens, and he may not give one bondmaid to two of his Hebrew servants in the way he gives them to Canaanite servants, as it says, "will give him a [=one] wife"[131] (*Avadim* 3:5).

... and she gives birth to sons or daughters, the wife and her children shall belong to her master and he will go forth alone. — Regarding a maidservant, it states, "the woman and her children will belong to her master," which teaches that her children have the same status as she does (*Yibbum ve-Ḥalitzah* 1:4; see also *PhM Yevamot* 2:5).

21:5. And if the servant plainly says, "I love my master, and my wife, and my children, and I do not want to go out free." — "If the servant plainly says [*amor yomar*]" — until he says it and repeats it; "the servant" — while he is still a servant. However, if he makes the declaration after six years, his ear is not pierced (see v. 6), unless he makes the statement and repeats it at the end of six years of servitude, at the beginning of the last *perutah* [of his servitude].

131. The Hebrew word *ishah* can be translated as either "woman" or "wife," so the phrase *im adonav yitten lo ishah* can mean "If his master will give him a wife" of "will give him a woman" — "a woman" implies *one* wife, not more.

How so? For example, if there is still the value of a *perutah* left in the day of the servant's time, or a little bit more [then the declaration and repetition is valid]. However if there is less than *perutah*'s worth of time left [in the time of his service], then it is as if he made the declaration after six years [have elapsed] (*Avadim* 3:10; see also *PhM Kiddushin* 1:2).

FURTHER: [His ear should only be pierced:] If his master has a wife and children, but if he does not have a wife and children, his ear should not be pierced, as it says, "I love my master, and my wife, and my children" (*Avadim* 3:11).

21:6. And his master shall bring him to the judges, and he shall bring him to the door or to the doorpost... — How is the ear pierced? The master brings him to a court of three judges, and he says his words in their presence, and the master brings him at the end of six years to the door or to the doorpost when they are standing [as part] of a building—either the master's own door or doorpost, or belonging to anyone else. And the master pierces the servant's right ear, in the earlobe, with a metal awl until it reaches the door, as it says, "and you shall thrust it through his ear at the door" (Deut. 15:17). And the doorpost is only mentioned [to teach] that the servant may be standing either next to the door or next to the doorpost. And just as the doorpost must be standing, so too the door must be standing. However the piercing must be through to the door (*Avadim* 3:9).

... and his master shall pierce his ear with an awl... — The master himself does the piercing, as it says, "his master shall pierce" — [the master] and not his son, and not his emissary, and not the emissary of the court. And we do not pierce the ears of two servants at once, since we do not discharge the commandments in bundles[132] (*Avadim* 3:9).

---

132. I.e., hastily and without appreciating each opportunity to do a mitzvah individually, based on, e.g., *Berakhot* 49a.

... and he shall serve him forever. — Even if the master [dies and] leaves a son, a servant whose ear is pierced does not serve the son. From the oral tradition, this is learned from "and he shall serve *him*" — and not his son; "forever" — for the length of the Jubilee. Thus we learn that the servant whose ear is pierced can only acquire himself through the Jubilee or through the death of the master (*Avadim* 3:7).

21:7. And if a man sells his daughter as a bondmaid... — In a lengthy series of examples, Maimonides derives that only a man may sell his daughter, but a woman may not sell her daughter, since it says "*his* daughter" (see *PhM Sotah* 3:6).[133]

FURTHER: [Maimonides cites this verse among others to describe how the six orders of the Mishnah[134] are arranged:] He [Rabbi Yehudah ha-Nasi] began with the order of *Zera'im* ("Agriculture"), since it deals with commandments that are specific to the growth of the land, and the growth of the land provides food for every living thing. And whenever somebody does not have food, it is impossible for him to serve God in any manner of service. Therefore he began to speak with the commandments concerning the growth of the land. And he then proceeds to the order of *Mo'ed* ("Festivals"), for this is the order of the verses, as it says, "And for six years you shall sow the land, and you shall gather its produce. And on the seventh you shall surely let the earth lie fallow..." (Exod. 23:10-11). And afterwards it is stated, "For six days you shall do your labors" (v. 12) and "Three times a year you shall keep a feast to Me" (v. 14). And after that he saw fit to

---

133. Today, no doubt, the notion that a man can sell his daughter into slavery is reprehensible. However, it has been argued that it allows for upward mobility since a daughter from a poor family can marry into a wealthy family, and there are many safeguards in place to reduce the risk of her being maltreated. Nonethless, Maimonides adds, "A father is not permitted sell his daughter as a bondmaid unless he became destitute and owns nothing, neither land or movable property, and not even the shirt he is wearing. Nonetheless, we compel a father to redeem his daughter after he sold her, because this is a defect of the family" (*Avadim* 4:2).
134. The Mishnah was codified in the second century of the common era; it is the skeleton over which the Talmud is built.

place the order of *Nashim* ("Women") before other laws of fighting [*rivot*], modeled after the order of Scripture, since God has already written, "And if a man sells his daughter as a bondmaid..."; "And if men fight and hurt [a woman who is pregnant]" (Exod. 21:22); and after it, "If an ox gore a man [or a woman]..." (Exod. 21:28). Therefore he placed *Nashim* before *Nezikin* ("Torts"), since the book of Exodus includes all four of these matters—that is to say, *Zeraim*, *Mo'ed*, *Nashim*, and *Nezikin*. And after that he passed from Exodus to Leviticus, in order of the Torah, and after the order of *Nezikin* he fixed the laws of *Kodashim* ("Holy Things") and then the order of *Taharot* ("Purity"), since this is the arrangement in Scripture: the laws of offerings precede the laws of purity and impurity, since the laws of purity and impurity do not begin until *Parashat Shemini* (*PhM*, Introduction to *Zera'im*).

The Talmud offers a different source for the divisions of the Mishnah and Talmud:

Reish Lakish said: What is the meaning of that which is written: "And the faith of your times shall be a strength of salvation, wisdom, and knowledge [the fear of the Lord is his treasure]" (Isaiah 33:6)? "Faith" [*emunat*] — this is the order of *Zera'im* [Agriculture].[135] "Your times" [*ittekha*] — this is the order of *Moed* [Festivals]. Strength [*hosen*] — that is the order of *Nashim* [Women]. Salvations [*yeshu'ot*] — is the order of *Nezikin* [Torts]. Wisdom [*hokhmat*] — that is the order of *Kodashim* [Consecrated Items]. And knowledge [*da'at*] — that is the order of *Taharot* [Items of Purity] (*Shabbat* 31a).

... she shall not go out as the menservants do. — [Maimonides explores whether or not this verse should be considered a separate

---

135. Because a person has faith in God when he plants.

commandment:] It has been hidden from us whether or not we should count "she shall not go out as the menservants do" as a separate commandment or as a limitation of a previous commandment. And the explanation of this is as I will relate: God had already said that if someone strikes his manservant or Canaanite bondmaid such that they lose one of the twenty-four body parts, the servant goes free.

It might occur to you that if a Canaanite slave goes free on this account, all the more so regarding a Hebrew bondmaid, so that if she loses one of the twenty-four limbs, then she too goes free. However, the limitation of this law is what He said, "she shall not go out as the menservants do." It is as if it was stated that it does not become obligatory to set her free if she loses one of these twenty-four body parts, and this is a limitation of a [previous] law, not a new prohibition.

This is also how the masters of tradition explained it, as it says in the *Mekhilta*: "'she shall not go out as the menservants do' — she does not go out [for losing one of the twenty-four] limbs like Canaanites go out." Behold it is clear to you that it is a limitation on a law, not a new prohibition (*ShM, Shoresh* 8).

Chavel, in his translation of Nahmanides on the current verse, adds, "Maimonides dedicated the eighth principle to the clarification of this distinction between a negation and a prohibition, and without mentioning the name of the author of the 'Hilchoth Gedoloth,' differs with him on the interpretation of this verse, which in his opinion merely states that there is no obligation on the part of the master to let her go free where he causes her the loss of one of her organs... In his notes to Maimonides' Book of Commandments, Ramban came to the defense of the 'Hilchoth Gedoloth.'"

FURTHER: A Hebrew bondmaid does not go free [if she loses one of her twenty-four] body parts, as it says, "she shall not go our as the menservants do." Similarly, if the master knocks out the tooth or eye of a Hebrew manservant, he pays like the damage for injuring his fellow, as we explained in *Hilkhot Ḥovel u-Mazzik*.

Thus we learn that a Hebrew bondmaid is acquired by two methods: through money or a legal document; and she acquires her freedom through six methods: through the passage of six years, at the Jubilee year, paying a pro-rated price, writ of manumission [=being freed by his master in a written document], the death of her master, and the appearance of signs of physical maturity (*Avadim* 4:6).

21:8. And if she is displeasing to her master, who has designated her for himself, then he must let her be redeemed... — ... a person is commanded to marry his female Jewish servant—either he himself or to have his son marry her; and this is the commandment of *yi'ud* ("designation") [This can only be done with her consent (*Avadim* 4:8).] And the Sages have already explained: the commandment of *yi'ud* takes precedence over the commandment of *pediyah* ("redemption"), as God, may He be exalted, said, "who has designated her for himself, then he must let her be redeemed" (BT *Bekhorot* 13a, *Mekhilta*). And know that the laws of the Hebrew servant and Hebrew bondmaid are only practiced when the Jubilee is observed (*ShM*, Pos. 233).

FURTHER: ... we are commanded regarding the redemption of a Jewish bondmaid, as God, may He be exalted, said, "then he must let her be redeemed." This redemption has many details, conditions, and laws, which have been explained in the tractate *Kiddushin*, where the laws of a Jewish bondmaid are explained in entirety. And in the *Mekhilta*, it is explained that "And if he does not do one of these three things" (v. 11) means "either he must designate her to himself, to his son, or allow her to be redeemed" (*ShM*, Pos. 234; see also *PhM Kiddushin* 1:2).

There are several verses that give options about how to handle a specific situation. For example: "And the firstborn of every donkey you shall redeem with a sheep, and if you do not redeem it you shall break its neck" (Exod. 13:13). Similarly, "And if she is displeasing to her master, who has designated her for himself, then he must let her be redeemed" (Exod. 21:8). Maimonides counts both options as separate commandments. In regard to the donkey, he counts redemption as one commandment, and decapitation as a second commandment. Similarly, he counts *yi'ud* as one commandment and *pediyah* as a second commandment. One final case: he counts levirate marriage (*yibbum*) as one commandment (*ShM*, Pos. 216) and *halitzah* as a separate commandment (*ShM*, Pos. 217).

FURTHER: If a man designates a Hebrew bondmaid for himself or for his son, then she is like any other betrothed woman, and she does not go free in any of the ways mentioned above,[136] except by the death of the husband or [receiving a] bill of divorce. And the commandment of "designation" takes precedence over the commandment of "redemption."

How is the commandment of "redemption" performed? He says in the presence of two witnesses, "Behold, you are consecrated to me" or "Behold, you are betrothed to me," or "Behold, you are my wife" — even after six years as sunset approaches. And he need not give her any monies, since the original monies [at the time of purchase] were given for the sake of marriage. And in all matters, he must treat her as a wife and not as a slave. And one is not to perform *yi'ud* [designation] on two women, as it says, *ye'adah* ("designate her") (*Avadim* 4:7).

------

136. The passage of six years, the onset of Jubilee, paying a pro-rated purchase price, a writ of manumission, the death of the master, or reaching the signs of maturation (*Avadim* 4:6).

... he may not sell her to a different man[137] **to have dominion over her, for he has dealt treacherously with her.**[138] — A master is not permitted to sell a Jewish bondmaid or to gift her to another man, regardless of whether he is a relative or non-relative. And if he sells her or gifts her, the sale is invalid, since it says, "he may not sell her to a different man to have dominion over her, for he has dealt treacherously with her." Similarly, a master is not permitted to sell or gift a Jewish manservant.

And it seems to me that Scripture only needed to prohibit this action regarding a bondmaid because he was supposed to designate her for himself or for his son. Therefore it is needs to say, "he may not sell her to a different man to have dominion over her" (*Avadim* 4:10; see also *ShM*, Neg. 261).

21:9. And if he designates her for his son... — How does a master designate for his son? If his son is of the age of majority, and the father gives permission to "designate" her, then the father says to her, in the presence of two witnesses, "Behold you are consecrated to my son" (*Avadim* 4:7; see also *PhM Kiddushin* 1:2).

Rashi, in his biblical commentary, writes that if the bondmaid is to be designated to the master's son, then it is the son who makes the declaration, "You are designated to me [to be a wife] by the money that your father received as a price [from my father]." Maimonides, on the other hand, seems to assume that the *yi'ud*-marriage is transacted by the father, not the son.

The *Leḥem Mishnah* assumes that there is no disagreement. By default, the son transacts the marriage (à la Rashi). According to the *Leḥem Mishnah*, Maimonides is

---

137. Hebrew *am nokhri*, literally, "foreign nation."
138. The antecedent of *be-vigdo*, "he dealing treacherously with her," is ambiguous; Rashi writes the treachery is the master's failure to fulfill the commandment of *yi'ud*.

only writing about a case where the son appoints his father as an emissary to transact a the *yi'ud*-marriage on his behalf.

... then he shall deal with her in the manner of daughters. — See on next verse.

21:10. If he takes another wife, then he may not diminish her food, her clothing, or her marital rights. — All of these [i.e., not to diminish her food, clothing, or marital rights] are counted as one commandment [and not three separate commandments] (*ShM*, Principle 9).

FURTHER: ... someone who purchases a Jewish bondmaid is forbidden from afflicting her. When I say "from afflicting her," it means that he shall not allow her to lack food or clothing, and he shall not withhold her marital rights to the point of affliction and anguish. This is what God, may He be exalted, said, "he may not diminish her food, her clothing, or her marital rights."

And this same prohibition applies to anyone who marries a daughter of Israel[139]: he may not afflict her in any of these three ways that causes anguish and discomfort. And that which God, may He be exalted, said regarding a Jewish bondmaid—that He forbade a man from withholding her food, her clothing, and her marital rights in "the manner of daughters" (v. 9). It has already been made known to us that "the manner of the daughters" means that he may not diminish food, clothing, and marital rights. And this is what they said in the *Mekhilta*, "The phrase 'in the manner of daughters' appears to expound something but is actually expounded upon."[140] There it is explained that *she'eirah* refers to "her food," *kesutah*

---

139. I.e., not just someone who marries a bondmaid.
140. "By saying that a maidservant must be treated like a regular married woman, it would seem that we know something about the regular woman that we don't know about the maidservant. In reality, however, the opposite is true: we learn from verse 10 that a maidservant's food, clothing, and conjugal relations may not be diminished. By saying in verse 9 that the maidservant is treated like a regular woman, we learn that the same applies to a regular woman" (Rabbi Berel Bell, Chabad website).

refers to "her clothing," and *onatah* refers to *derekh eretz* [conjugal rights] (*ShM*, Neg. 262).[141]

FURTHER: It is forbidden for a man to withhold marital rights from his wife, and if he trangresses and withholds it in order to cause her pain, then he violates a negative commandment in the Torah, as it says, "he may not diminish her food, her clothing, or her marital rights." And if he becomes sick or exceedingly weak and is not able to have relations, he should wait six months to recover, for there is no span greater than this that she has to wait. And after six months, she may decide if she wants to stay married, or to be divorced and collect her *ketubah* (*Ishut* 14:7; see also 15).

21:11. And if he does not do one of these three things for her... — ... in the *Mekhilta*, it is explained that "And if he does not do one of these three things" means "either he must designate her to himself, to his son, or allow her to be redeemed" (vv. 8-9) (*ShM*, Pos. 234; i.e., the three things in this verse are *not* food, clothing, and marital rights).

... then she shall go out free without money. — A Hebrew bondmaid has an advantage [over a Hebrew manservant] since she goes free when she shows signs of sexual maturation. How so? Once she shows signs of maturation and becomes an adolescent she goes free without having to pay money. Even if she matures the day after the master purchased her, she goes out to her freedom, as it says, "then she shall go out free without money" — the verse included another way that she goes free, in addition to when the manservant

---

141. This is based on *Mekhilta*, which quotes three opinions. R. Josiah's opinion is codified by Maimonides and quoted by Rashi on this verse.

Second, R. Jonathan says *she'eirah kesutah* is one phrase, meaning clothing that is befitting her (if she is young, he should give her clothing worn by young people, and if she is old, clothing worn by older people); he continues that *onatah* means clothing for the right season: summer clothing in the summer and winter clothing in the winter. He derives the obligations of food and maritial intimacy from an argument *a fortiori* (see there).

Third, Rabbi Judah ha-Nasi says *she'eirah* refers to intimacy, *kesutah* refers to clothing, and *onatah* refers to food. (See *Mekhilta*, Nezikin 3.)

goes free. According to oral tradition, we learn that this refers to
signs of physical maturation. And [in such a case] she returns to her
father's domain until she matures further,[142] at which point she leaves
her father's domain (*Avadim* 4:5).

**21:12. One who strikes a man so that he dies, shall surely be put
to death.** — [Maimonides focuses on the phrase *makkeh ish*, which
literally means, "one who strikes a *man*."] ... the word *ish* [man]
is here used in the same sense as *adam* [human being], for "man"
in a general sense is sometimes expressed in Scripture by *ish*, e.g.,
"One who strikes a man [*ish*] so he dies, shall surely be put to death"
(*Guide* 3:13).

**21:13. But if he did not lie in waiting, but God brought it about to
his hand, then I will appoint for you a place to where he shall flee.**
— There are three [categories] of people who kill without intention
[*be-lo kavvanah*]:

- There is a person who kills accidentally and completely
  inadvertently [*bi-shegagah ve-ha'alamah gemurah*], about
  whom it is said, "But if he did not lie in waiting [*va-asher lo
  tzadah*]," and the law is that he is exiled to a city of refuge,
  where he will be saved [from the blood redeemer]....
- And there is a person who kills accidentally, but this accident is
  beyond his control [*ha-shegagah kerovah la-oness*], i.e., this death
  was caused by an exceptional occurrence that is not a common
  occurrence at all, and the law is that he is exempt from exile, and
  if the blood redeemer kills him, he is killed on that account.
- There is one who kills accidentally, but this accident is close
  to intentional [*ha-shegagah kerovah la-zadon*], i.e., and this is

142. Her servitude ends when she becomes a *na'arah*, at which point she
returns to her father's domain. She leaves her father's domain when she
becomes a *bogeret*.

like a reckless act, or regarding something he was supposed to be cautious but he was not cautious. And the law is that he is not exiled. And since his sin is so severe, exile does not atone for him. And the cities of refuge do not receive him, since they only receive those who are obligated to go into exile. Therefore, if the blood redeemer finds him in any place and kills him, he is exempt [from punishment] (*Rotze'ah* 6:1-4).

It is clear from vv. 13-14 that the *sui generis* protection of asylum is only available to people who commit manslaughter (i.e., unintentional homicide). Asylum is not a suitable protection for any other offense, whether lesser or greater. See further Pamela Begaj, "An Analysis of Historical and Legal Sanctuary and a Cohesive Approach to the Current Movement" *John Marshall Law Review* 42 (2008), 135-163.

FURTHER: A person who killed another person unknowingly must go into exile (Exod. 21:13, Num. 35:11-28), because the anger of "the avenger of blood" (Num. 35:19) cools down while the cause of the mischief is out of sight.[143] The chance of returning from the exile depends on the death of [the high priest], the most honored of men, and the friend of all Israel. By his death the relative of the slain person becomes reconciled (see Num. 35:25), for it is a natural phenomenon that we find consolation in our misfortune when the same misfortune or a greater one has befallen another person. Amongst us no death causes more grief than that of the high priest (*Guide* 3:40).

---

143. There is a debate among the Tannaim: Rabbi Yosi b. Yehudah says, "At first, both the intentional and inadvertent killer would flee to the city of refuge [i.e., before the trial]" (M. *Makkot* 2:6, *Sifri*). However according to Rebbi, even from the beginning the cities of refuge were only asylum for inadvertent killers. Maimonides rules like Rabbi Yosi b. Yehudah (*Rotze'ah* 5:7). This is consistent with the opinion that "The Torah's purpose is to amend the primitive practice of blood vengeance" (Umberto Cassuto, *A Commentary on the Book of Exodus*, p. 270).

Maimonides suggests that when the high priest dies, the common grief throughout Israel will serve as a unifying force; when the manslayer is in mourning for the death of the high priest, that grief is shared by the "blood redeemer," whose anger is therefore cooled. The national mourning for death of the high priest will serve as a binding event for the nation of Israel, upon which the animosity of the blood redeemer toward the manslayer will be mitigated. Philo, not dissimilarly, says the high priest is the "nearest of kin to the whole nation" (*Special Laws* 3.131). For other explanations, *Makkot* 11, Rabbenu Bahya on Num. 16:1, and Shadal on Num. 35:25.

21:14. But if a man comes intentionally against his neighbor to kill him deliberately... — Originally, if a person killed a resident alien he would not be executed in court, as it says, "But if a man comes intentionally against his neighbor." And needless to say he would not be executed for killing an idolator. Whether he killed his own Canaanite servant or the servant of someone else, he is executed, for a servant has accepted upon himself the heritage of God (*Rotze'aḥ* 2:11).

... then you shall take him from My altar to die. — The altar serves as an asylum [for unintentional killers], since it says regarding a deliberate killer, "then you shall take him from My altar to die," from which we derive that one who has killed accidentally is not killed from the altar. Therefore, if someone kills unintentionally and is received on the altar, and then the blood redeemer kills him there, then he [the blood redeemer] is to be executed as if he killed him in the city of refuge.

Only the top of the altar of the Eternal House serves as refuge. And it only serves as refuge when a priest is performing his service. However, regarding a non-priest, or a priest who is not engaged in service, or a priest is engaged in service but is not on top of the altar just merely next to it or holding its horns, the altar does not serve as refuge (*Rotze'aḥ* 5:12-13; see also Nahmanides on Num. 35:29).

The *Kesef Mishnah* quotes Maimonides' source: Rav Judah said in the name of Rav: Joab committed two errors [when Solomon sent Benaiah to execute Joab], as it is written, "... and [Joab] fled to the tent of the Lord and took hold of the horns of the altar" (1 Kings 2:28). He erred since only the top of the altar serves as refuge, but he grasped it by the horns. He erred [again] since only the altar of the Eternal House serves as refuge, but he grasped the altar at Shiloh. Abaye says: He also erred in the following — he erred in [not knowing] that it only serves as refuge when the priest is performing his service, but he was a non-priest (BT *Makkot* 12a). Maimonides rules that all three conditions must be present: the fugitive must be on top of the altar, must be in the Jerusalem Temple, and must be during the priestly service.

Rabbi Bezalel Naor develops the idea that the altar serves as refuge and that it saves (*mizbeaḥ kolet u-mizbeaḥ matzil*); see his *Shod Melakhim: Iyyunim ba-Sefer Mishneh Torah* [Hebrew], pp. 117-156.

FURTHER: … when sinners and evildoers seek our help, it must not be granted; no mercy must be shown to them, and the course of justice must not be interfered with, even if they claim the protection of that which is noblest and highest: for "you shall take him from My altar to die" (Exod. 21:14). Here a person comes to seek the help of God, and claims the protection of that which is devoted to his name; God, however, does not help him, and commands that he be delivered up to the prosecutor, from whom he fled. Much less does any one of us need to help or pity his fellow-men [under such circumstances]: because mercy on sinners is cruelty to all creatures. These are undoubtedly the right ways designated as "righteous statutes and judgments" (Deut. 4:8), and different from the ways of the fools, who consider a person praiseworthy when he helps and protects his fellow-men, without discriminating between the oppressor and the oppressed. This is well known from their words and songs (*Guide* 3:39).

> A similar idea is expressed by Rabbi Elazar: "Whosoever is merciful towards the cruel will ultimately be cruel to the merciful" (*Tanḥuma*, "Metzora").

21:15. And one who strikes his father or his mother shall surely be put to death. — ... we are forbidden to strike our father or mother. This specific prohibition is not explicitly mentioned in Scripture, but its punishment is mentioned, as it says, "one who strikes his father or his mother shall surely be put to death." And we learn this prohibition in the same way we learn the prohibition of cursing one's father. And we have already explained this in the three-hundredth negative prohibition, in which we are forbidden to strike any Jew, which includes the prohibition of striking one's father.

And the language of the *Mekhilta* is, "'one who strikes his father or his mother shall surely be put to death' — we have learned the punishment, but we have not learned the prohibition. Therefore we come to learn 'Forty times he will strike him and not exceed...' (Deut. 25:3). This verse teaches a lesson *a fortiori*: if one who is commanded to strike someone [i.e., a judge] is forbidden to strike [more than forty times], then one who is not commanded to strike is certainly forbidden to strike." And one who violates this prohibition—meaning one who strikes his father or mother intentionally and draws blood—is punished by strangulation (*ShM*, Neg. 319; also *PhM Shevuot* 4:6).

FURTHER: If someone strikes his father or mother, he is executed by strangulation, as it says, "one who strikes his father or his mother shall surely be put to death." And it is necessary that there be witnesses and warning, just like all other people executed by the court. This applies to both a man and a woman, and also to a *tumtum* and an androgynous individual, so long as they have reached [the age of majority and liable] to punishment. One is not liable for strangulation until he causes injury to his parents. If he does not cause injury, then he is like one who strikes another Jew. And if he strikes them after death, he is not liable (*Mamrim* 5:5).

> Maimonides also uses this verse to assert that a presumption (*ḥazzakah*) is sufficient rather than an explicit proof (*rayah berurah*) is sufficient to establish the individual as a parent, even to administer capital punishment (see *Issurei Bi'ah* 1:20, and *Maggid Mishneh* there, which traces it to JT *Kiddushin* 4:10).

21:16. One who kidnaps [lit., "steals"] a man and sells him, or if he is found in his hand... — [The following are not liable for capital punishment for kidnapping:] A person who kidnaps his son or brother who is a minor, as well as a guardian who kidnapped orphans who are in his care, and the head of a household who kidnapped one of his dependent family members, and a teacher who kidnaps one of the students who learn from him. Even if he makes use of the person he kidnapped, or sells him, he is still exempt, as it says, "found in his hand" — which excludes individuals that are regularly found in his hand (*Geneivah* 9:5).

... he shall surely be put to death. — ... we are commanded to execute by strangulation those who violate certain of the commandments, as God, may He be exalted, said, "he shall surely be put to death" (e.g., Exod. 21:15-16, Lev. 20:10). And we will indicate which negative commandments are punished by strangulation (Neg. 26, 27, 243, 312, 319, 347) (*ShM*, Pos. 227).

In the *Minyan ha-Mitzvot*, Maimonides explains this commandment: "for the court to execute by strangulation, as it says, 'the adulterer and adulteress shall surely be put to death' (Lev. 20:10)." The salient point is that according to the *Minyan ha-Mitzvot*, this commandment applies to the court (*bet din*), not the individuals.

According to the Rabbis, there are four forms of execution; stoning, burning, decapitation, and strangulation (M. *Sanhedrin* 7:1). Maimonides counts these as four separate commandments (*ShM, Principle* 14). Decapitation is based on Exod. 21:20 (*ShM*, Pos. 226). Strangulation is based on the phrase *mot yumat*, "he shall surely die," which appears in several places, including the current verse (*ShM*, Pos. 227). Burning is based on "[If a man takes a wife and her mother also, it is depravity;] they shall be burned to death, both he and they, [that there may be no depravity among you]" (Lev. 20:14, *ShM*, Pos. 228). Stoning is based on "[If there is a young woman, a virgin already engaged to be married, and a man meets her in the town and lies with her you shall bring both of them to the gate of that town] and stone them to death" (Deut. 22:23-24, *ShM*, Pos. 229). However, Nahmanides counts all four methods of execution as one commandment, under the verse "and you shall purge the evil from your midst" (Deut. 17:7; see his comments on Exod. 22:17). I do not know if there is a practical difference (*nafka mina*) whether this is counted as one or four commandments.

FURTHER: [The punishment for kidnapping is execution...] because he is also prepared to kill him whom he steals (*Guide* 3:41).

21:17. And one who curses his father and mother shall surely be put to death. — ... we are forbidden to curse a father or mother. Indeed in the language of the Torah, the punishment is mentioned explicitly, as it says, "And one who curses his father and his mother shall surely be put to death," and his punishment is stoning. And even if he only cursed one of them using the Name after their death, if he did so intentionally, he is stoned. Nonetheless, this prohibition is not clearly expressed in Scripture, since it never says, "you shall not curse your father." However, it comes to us as part of the prohibition to curse any person of among Israel, including one's father or anyone else.

And in the *Mekhilta* it is stated, "'one who curses his father and mother shall surely be put to death' — we have learned the punishment, but we have not learned the prohibition! We should learn from 'You shall not curse judges [*elohim*]'[144] (Exod. 22:27) — if your father is a judge [*dayyan*], then he is included in 'judges' [*elohim*]. And if he is a prince, then he is included as a prince. And if he is a commoner, then he is included in 'You shall not curse the deaf' (Lev. 19:14). From these three sources, you can derive a common principle that these three are 'among your people' [*be-ammekha*], and you are forbidden to curse them; even your father 'among your people' you are forbidden to curse."

And in the *Sifra*, it is stated, "'For whoever curses his father or mother shall surely be put to death' (Lev. 20:9) — we have learned the punishment, but we have not learned the prohibition! We should learn from 'You shall not curse judges,'" just as in the *Mekhilta* (*ShM*, Neg. 318; see also *Mamrim* 5:4).

FURTHER: A *shetuki*[145] is liable for cursing his mother but not his father. Even if his mother is interrogated and she says, "He is the

---

144. This Hebrew word is a sign of prominence and can either refer to "judges" in a secular sense (Maimonides, *Hil. Sanhedrin* 26:1, Onkelos, R. Ishmael [*Sanhedrin* 66a], Saadiah, Sforno), or "God" (R. Akiva [*Sanhedrin* 66a]), or a reference to both blasphemy and cursing judges (Rashi, see also Maimonides *ShM*, Neg. 60). See *Kesef Mishnah* to *Mamrim* 5:4.

145. A person, male or female, who does not know who their father is.

son of so-and-so," he is not stoned or strangled based on her word. However, a son who is the product of a maidservant or from a Gentile woman is not liable for either his father or his mother (*Yevamot* 22a). Similarly, a convert who was conceived when his parents were not Jewish, even if he was born after they converted,[146] he is not liable for striking or cursing his father. Just as he is not liable on account of his father, neither is he liable on account of his mother, as it says, "one who curses his father and mother" — one who is liable on account of his father is liable on account of his mother, and one who is not liable on account of his father is not liable on account of his mother (*Mamrim* 5:9-10).

21:18. And if men are quarreling and one strikes another with a stone or with his fist, and he does not die but is confined to bed. — If someone strikes his colleague with a small stone that does not have the wherewithal to cause injury, or with a small piece of wood, and causes injury that he did not wish to cause, he is exempt, as it says, "with a stone or with a fist" — something that is capable of causing injury. Rather he is only liable for shaming [the other person], for one is liable for causing shame even if he had spat on the other person. Therefore, the witnesses must know what caused the injury, and they must bring the object to court for it to be evaluated, and judge based on it (*Ḥovel u-Mazzik* 1:18; see also *Rotze'aḥ* 2:14, 4:3).

21:19. If he arises and walks around outside with his staff, then the person who struck him will be exempt... — When the Torah states "with his staff," it does not mean that he walks while leaning on a staff or another person, for even someone about to die can walk using a crutch. The phrase "his staff" means that he can walk under his own power and does not rely on someone else's strength to be able to walk (*Rotze'aḥ* 4:4).

---

146. A somewhat loose and contextual translation.

The standard printings of Maimonides use the phrase *mishenet boryav*, "the power [lit., 'staff'] of his own health." The current translation follows the Frankel edition, which reads *mishenet koho*, "the 'staff' of his own strength," though the consequence of the phrase remains effectively unchanged. In both cases, the biblical mention of "staff" does not mean "crutch," but refers to the regular manner in which people would walk—while carrying a staff.

The phrase *mishenet boryav* is based on Onkelos, who translates *al mishanto* as *al baryeih* (his health); likewise the *Mekhilta* quotes that R. Ishmael interpreted the phrase *ke-min mashal*, "figuratively" (*Mekhilta*), and this interpretation is also adopted by Rashi. On the other hand, Nahmanides understands *al mishanto* as "crutch," writing, "even though he is weak and leans on a staff [*mishenet*], the person who struck him will be exempt." The *Torah Temimah*—against Nahmanides and in support of Rashi (and by extension, support of Maimonides)—writes, "it is not written *al mishenet* [on a staff], but *al mishanto* [on his staff], which implies his own staff that is 'the staff of his body' and under his own control" (note 139). (See also Malbim and *Mekhilta de-Rashbi*.)

... he will only pay for lost time, and he shall surely heal him. — From where do we know that an assailant must pay for lost wages and medical costs independently? As it says, "he will only pay for lost time, and he shall surely heal him" (*Hovel u-Mazzik* 1:8).

FURTHER: If a person injures someone else on Yom Kippur, even intentionally, he is obligated to pay, even though he violated a commandment for which he is liable to receive lashes. But is it not the case that if someone commits a crime whose punishment is lashes and payment, then he is to receive lashes but does not have to pay, since nobody ever receives lashes and has to pay? This is the case for everything except someone who injures his colleague, in which case he must pay, since the Torah explicitly added that someone who injures his colleague must pay, as it says, "he will only pay for lost time, and he shall surely heal him" (*Hovel u-Mazzik* 4:9).

FURTHER: The punishment of him who sins against his neighbor consists in the general rule that there shall be done unto him exactly as he has done: if he injured any one personally, he must suffer personally; if he damaged the property of his neighbor, he shall be punished by loss of property.... I have, however, an explanation for the interpretation given in the Talmud, but it will be communicated *vivâ voce*. Injuries that cannot be reproduced exactly in another person are compensated financially: "he will only pay for lost time, and he shall surely heal him" (*Guide* 3:41).

> Maimonides develops the concept that the ideal form of punishment is "measure for measure," which should be imposed whether on the Divine or mortal plane. However, there are times when that it not possible, due to the circumstances of the perpetrator or limitations of human justice, and this is one of those cases. So while the general rule is "that there shall be done unto him exactly as he has done," this cannot be applied without exception, and when the injury cannot be reciprocated in kind, then "Injuries that cannot be reproduced exactly in another person are compensated for by payment," and Maimonides' proof for this principle is the current verse.

21:20. And if a man strikes his manservant or his bondmaid with a rod [*sheivet*] and he dies under his hand... — It seems to me that if someone strikes his servant with a knife, a sword, a stone, or a fist, or anything similar, and it was assessed that he would die, and in fact the servant died, this is not included in the law of "a day or two days" (v. 21; see there). Even if the servant died [from his injuries] a year later, he is executed. Therefore it is stated, "with a rod," because the Torah only gave permission to strike a servant with a rod, a staff, a strap, or something similar, and not with a lethal blow (*Rotze'aḥ* 2:14).

Rabbi Eleazar Rokeach, in his *Ma'aseh Roke'aḥ*, writes, "It appears that our master follows the Targum [Onkelos], who translates *sheivet* as *shaltan*, meaning in the manner of lording and mastery, which is with a rod, stick, or strap, but not with a sword, stone, or fist, which is the way of punishment, despite the end of the verse which says 'and he dies under his hand, he shall surely be punished.' This implies that even if it does not have the capacity to kill, since it is a rod that is light, nonetheless if he dies, 'he shall surely be punished.' And this is the opposite of the *Mekhilta* there, which requires the capacity to kill, and with a limb that has the capacity to kill...."

... he shall surely be punished. — ... we are commanded to execute with a sword those who transgress certain specific commandments, as He, may He be exalted, said, "he shall surely be punished." And this refers to negative commandments for which one is liable for decapitation (*ShM*, Pos. 226; see also *Rotze'aḥ* 1:1).

21:21. However if he survives for a day or two days, he shall not be punished, for the slave is his property. — What is the difference between his slave and a slave belonging to others? He has permission to strike his own slave. Therefore if he strikes him hard enough to kill him and comes close to death but lives for twenty-four hours and then dies, he is not executed, even though the slave died because of the blow, as it says, "he shall not be punished, for the slave is his property." And why does it say "a day or two days"? Since it is like two days, [since we measure the twenty-four hours] from the minute it happened (*Rotze'aḥ* 2:12).

> The *Mizraḥi* explains "And in the *Mekhilta*: A day that is like two days, and two days that is like one day — How so? From moment [of the first day] to moment [of the second day], whose length is one day [one twenty-four hour period], which is two days, part in this day and part in this day." (Rashi and Maimonides are operating from the same passage in the *Mekhilta*; the *Mizraḥi*'s commentary on Rashi can be applied here to explain the legal/exegetical derivation.)

21:22-23. If men quarrel and strike a pregnant woman and her child leaves yet no fatality [*ason*] follows, he shall surely be punished, according to the woman's husband will lay upon him, and he shall pay as much as the judges determine. If any fatality [*ason*] follows, then you shall give life for life. — And that which God said, "yet no *ason* follows" (v. 22), means that there was no fatality [*ason*] between the quarreling men,[147] and the one who struck [the woman] will surely be punished [financially]. And if there is fatality [*ason*] between the two fighters—meaning if one of them dies—the killer will be executed, and there will be no [financial] punishment at all, as it says, "and you shall give life [for life]" (v. 23). And this cancels the financial penalty, since a person is not executed and forced to pay, even if he did so accidentally and is not liable for execution. This is because any transgression that could be punished with execution in court does not require financial payment [as well], even if he committed the crime by accident (*PhM Ketubot* 3:2).

FURTHER: If someone strikes a woman and she miscarries [*ve-yatze'u yeladeha*] and [the fetus] dies, even if he did it unintentionally, he is exempt from making payment, and he does not pay anything, as

---

147. In *Hilkhot Na'arah Betulah* 1:13, Maimonides rules that *ason* refers to the death of the woman, not one of the combatants

it says, "yet no fatality [*ason*] follows, he shall surely be punished [financially]." The verse does not differentiate between intentional and unintentional about a matter that could [theoretically] lead to a court execution to exempt him from payment (*Ḥovel u-Mazzik* 4:5).

Elsewhere, Maimonides writes, "If an ox gored a woman and she miscarried [*yatze'u yeladeha*], even if the ox is 'warned' [*mu'ad*] concerning goring, the owners are exempt from [paying] *demei veladot*, because the Torah only obligated *demei veladot* [when the damaged was committed] by a person" (*Nizkei Mamon* 11:3).

FURTHER: If she was among those women who are forbidden to him under penalty of execution by the court, like his daughter, his son's wife, or the like, then regardless of whether or not he was warned, he is exempt from paying a fine, as it says, "yet no fatality [*ason*] follows, he shall surely be punished." Thus if there was a fatality [*ason*], there is no [financial] punishment. And even if he killed the woman unintentionally, since they did not intend [to harm] her, as it says, "If men quarrel and strike a woman who is pregnant...." Thus you learn that there is no difference between unintentional and intentional to exempt him from payment.... And this is the case for any transgression that can be met with execution by the court—that there is no financial payment (*Na'arah* 1:13-14).

Verses 22 and 23 are fraught with exegetical ambiguity. We will need to address the meaning of several questions: (1) What is the meaning of *yazte'u yeladeha*—miscarriage or premature delivery? (2) What is the meaning of *ason*—injury or fatality? (3) Who suffers the *ason*—one of the combatants or the pregnant woman? (4) Why does the assailant pay?

1. The meaning of *yatze'u yeladeha*: The standard rabbinic and halakhic interpretation is "miscarry"; also Josephus (*Antiquities* 4.8.30.3), Philo,[148] and Shadal. Cassuto understood it as premature delivery, as do some modern translations (NIV). Maimonides follows the standard interpretation that *yatze'u yeladeha* means "miscarry" (*Hovel u-Mazzik* 4:5).

2. The meaning of *ason*: The general meaning is "mischief, evil, harm" (*BDB*). As a matter of *halakhah*, the *Mekhilta* says it means "death" (*Mekhilta de-Rabbi Yishmael*), as does Ibn Ezra (Gen. 42:4). Shadal says it is an unnatural death (here and Gen. 42:4). "Death" is the logical meaning of "If any fatality [*ason*] follows, then you shall give life for life." Here capital punishment would most likely be prescribed for understanding ason as fatality, not mere injury. Similarly, the Mishnah states, "anyone who is liable [to pay] with his life does not [also] pay monetary [penalties], as it is stated, '... no *ason* follows, he shall surely be punished [by fine]'" (M. *Ketubot* 3:2). Again, Maimonides follows the standard interpretation that ason means "death" rather than "injury."

3. Who is the victim of the *ason*—the fighting men or the pregnant woman? The *Mekhilta*, Talmud (*Sanhedrin* 79b), Rashi, Rashbam, Ibn Ezra, and *Bekhor Shor* write

---

148. Philo also understands this phrase as miscarriage. However, he distinguishes as says that if the fetus is viable, then the attacker pays a fine, while if the fetus is viable:

> But if the child which was conceived had assumed a distinct Shape in all its parts, having received all its proper connective and distinctive qualities, he shall die; for such a creature as that is a man, whom he has slain while still in the workshop of nature, who had not thought it as yet a proper time to produce him to the light, but had kept him like a statue lying in a sculptor's workshop, requiring nothing more than to be released and sent out into the world (*Special Laws* 3.108-109).

that *ason* refers to the woman. In *PhM*, Maimonides breaks with the traditional interpretation, and writes that *ason* refers to the death of one of the <u>combatants</u>. His motivation is likely as follows: according to the other interpreters, killing an unintended victim (the woman) would lead to execution. However, Maimonides rules, "If a person intended to kill one person and killed another, he is exempt from execution by the court, and from payment, and from exile" (*Rotze'aḥ* 4:1). In keeping with this ruling, Maimonides concludes that the *ason* refers to one of the original combatants, not a bystander.[149] Nonetheless, in *Hil. Na'arah* 1:13, he reverts to the standard interpretation that *ason* refers to the woman.

4. Why should the assailant pay? The Torah added a specific law of *demei veladot*, which refers to compensation for the death of the fetus. Here the question can be asked in two possible ways: why should the assailant be forced to pay anything at all, or alternatively why should the assailant pay and not be executed? It is possible that Rabbenu Bahya understands it as a form of property damage: the assailant has caused a damage to the husband's possessions.[150] However, *Mizraḥi* (s.v. *ve-lo yihyeh ason ba-ishah*) quotes from Maimonides: "If someone kills an adult, or a child that is at least a day old, whether male or female, he is executed if he killed him intentionally.... And this is a case where the child was full

---

149. Maimonides holds *ha-mitkavven la-harog et zeh ve-harag et zeh patur*, "If someone intended to kill one person and he killed another, he is exempt." In legal parlance, this is called "transferred intent," and there is a common doctrine in American law that "intent follows the bullet." In Jewish law, the culpability of transferred intent is debated between the Sages and Rabbi Shimon (*Sanhedrin* 79a), and Maimonides follows Rabbi Shimon that in a case of transferred intent there is no culpability.

150. He writes, "the legal position of a woman and her children is similar to the legal position of a man to whom an object or animal has been entrusted for safe-keeping..." (on 21:23, s.v. *ka-asher yashit alav ba'al ha-ishah*).

term. However, if the baby was born prematurely, it is like a stillborn [for purposes of punishment] until it lives for thirty days" (*Rotze'aḥ* 4:5). Killing a premature baby, a baby less than 24 hours old, or a *tereifah* are prohibited acts of murder but for technical reasons do not carry a punishment of execution.

The assailant pays *demei veladot* to the husband either because the assailant has destroyed the property of the husband (R. Bahya), or because it is a form of homicide for which there is no capital punishment (*Mizraḥi*); *Mizraḥi* believes the latter is Maimonides' rationale.

Hence Maimonides reads the verses as follows: "If men quarrel and strike a woman who is pregnant and she miscarries [*yatze'u yeladeha*] yet no fatality [*ason*] follows to one of the combatants, he shall surely be punished for causing the miscarriage, according as the woman's husband will lay upon him, and he shall pay as much as the judges determine. If any fatality [*ason*] follows to one of the combatants, then you shall give life for life [but if one of the combatants causes a fatality of the pregnant woman then there is no execution because one is not executed when there is transferred intent]."

21:24-25. An eye for an eye, tooth for a tooth, hand for hand, foot for foot. Burn for burn, bruise for bruise, wound for wound.
— How does one assess damages? If he cut off the hand or foot of his colleague, we imagine that he was a slave being sold on the market. How much would he have been worth before, and how much is he worth now, and the damager pays the difference that he caused from among his property, as it says, "An eye for [*taḥat*] an eye." And according to oral tradition, we learn that the word *taḥat* refers to a monetary payment (*Ḥovel u-Mazzik* 1:2).

FURTHER: And how do we know that what is said regarding body parts, "an eye for an eye," etc., refers to monetary compensation? As it says, "wound for wound." Yet it says explicitly, "one who strikes another with a stone or with his fist... he will only pay for lost time, and he shall surely heal him" (cf. Exod. 21:18-19). Thus you learn that *tahat* mentioned regarding a "wound" [*habburah*] refers to money. And this is also true for the word *tahat* in reference to "eye" and every other body part.

And even though these words are implied in the written Torah, they were all explained from the mouth of Moses at Mount Sinai, and they are all law from Moses in our hand. And this is how all of our forebears saw fit to rule this way. This is how the court of Joshua ruled, and the court of Samuel the Ramathite, and each and every court that has stood since the days of Moses until today (*Hovel u-Mazzik* 1:5-6).

FURTHER: The punishment of him who sins against his neighbor consists in the general rule that there shall be done unto him exactly as he has done: if he injured any one personally, he must suffer personally; if he damaged the property of his neighbor, he shall be punished by loss of property. But the person whose property has been damaged should be ready to resign his claim totally or partly. Only to the murderer we must not be lenient because of the greatness of his crime; and no ransom must be accepted of him: "And the land cannot be cleansed of the blood that is shed therein but by the blood of him that shed it" (Num. 31:33). Hence even if the murdered person continued to live after the attack for an hour or for days, was able to speak and possessed complete consciousness, and if he himself said, "Pardon my murderer, I have pardoned and forgiven him," he must not be obeyed. We must take life for life, and estimate equally the life of a child and that of a grown-up person, of a slave and of a freeman, of a wise man and of a fool. For there is no greater sin than this. And he who mutilated a limb of his neighbor, must himself lose a limb: "...as he has caused a blemish in a man, so shall it be done to him again" (Lev. 24: 20). You must not raise an objection from our practice of imposing a fine in such cases. For we have proposed to ourselves to give here the reason for the precepts mentioned in the Law, and not for that which is stated in the Talmud. I have, however, an explanation for the interpretation given in the Talmud, but it will be communicated *vivâ voce*. Injuries that cannot be reproduced exactly in another person, are compensated for by payment (*Guide* 3:41).

The idea of "an eye for an eye" is ancient, and the earliest known source is Hammurabi's Code, which reads, "If a man put out the eye of another man, his eye shall be put out. If he break another man's bone, his bone shall be broken." However the Talmud vehemently stresses that "an eye for an eye" is not *lex talionis*, but monetary compensation for the value of the eye (*Bava Kamma* 84a).

Nahmanides shows how, internally, "an eye for an eye" cannot literally refer to physical punishment. First, he shows that the Hebrew word *tahat* means monetary compensation in the verse, "And he that smites a beast mortally shall pay for it, life *tahat* life" (Lev. 24:18). Then he shows that "an eye for an eye" *must* mean monetary compensation, since the assailant "will only pay for lost time, and he shall surely heal him" (Exod. 21:19). Nahmanides' intention is therefore to prove that monetary compensaiton is not just legal casuistry, but is actually the original meaning (*peshat*) of the verse.

However, Sforno writes that there is an underlying *talion* since technically the assailant deserves to lose his eye, but it is impossible to estimate the eye relative to the assailaint and victim; this appears consistent with *Guide* 3:41.

Similarly, Daniel A. Klein, in explaining the view of Shadal, writes, "According to Maimonides... the Torah's intention in using such terminology was not that the court should actually injure the guilty party in the same way that he injured his neighbor, but rather to express the thought that it would have been morally fitting to amputate his limb or injure him, just as he did to the injured party" (p. 337).

Furthermore, Rabbi Joseph B. Soloveitchik passionately wrote, "The time has come for us to fulfill the law of 'an eye for an eye' in its plain sense. I am certain that everyone who knows me knows that I am a believer in the Oral Law and, consequently, that I do not doubt that the verse refers to monetary compensation, in accordance with the halakhic interpretation. However, with regard to Nasser or the Mufti I would demand that we interpret the phrase 'an eye for an eye' in a strictly literal sense—as referring to the removal of a concrete, actual eye" (*Fate & Destiny*, pp. 31–32). This is in line with the thinking that in some deep sense, an eye for an eye is a legitimate, just punishment.

Additionally, it has been pointed out that Maimonides appears to contradict himself between the *Mishneh Torah* and the *Guide*. Isadore Twersky writes, "While there are thus many instances in which Maimonides quietly bypasses the Talmudic interpretation and actually presents the literal Biblical view, only with regard to the lex talionis... does he explicitly state that his goal is to confront the Biblical text" (*Introduction to the Code of Maimonides (Mishneh Torah)*, p. 437, n. 198).

21:26-27. And if a man strikes the eye of his servant or the eye of his bondmaid and destroys it, then he shall send him free on account of his eye. And if he knocks out the tooth of his slave or his bondmaid, then he shall send him free on account of the tooth. — ... we are commanded regarding the law of the Canaanite slave, about which it says that we should have him serve us forever, since he does not go free except by means of tooth or eye. And this applies to other body parts that do not grow back, in accordance with the received tradition (*Kiddushin* 25a).

And this is what God, may He be exalted, said, "they shall serve you forever" (Lev. 25:46), and it is stated, "And if a man strikes..." (Exod. 21:26). And the language of the Talmud in *Gittin* is, "Whoever frees his [Canaanite] slave violates a negative commandment, as it says, 'they shall serve you forever'" (38a). And it is written in the Torah that he is freed on account of his tooth or his eye (*ShM*, Pos. 235).

FURTHER: How [does a Canaanite slave go free on account of] limbs? If someone strikes his slave intentionally so that he loses one of the twenty-four limbs that do not grow back, the slave goes free but he requires a writ of manumission. If so, why does the Torah only mention "tooth" and "eye"? In order to derive the following principle: just as a tooth and an eye are observable and do not regenerate, so too [on account of] any blemish that is observable and does not regenerate, the slave goes free. However, if someone castrates his slave or cuts of his tongue, the slave does not go free, since these [parts of the body] are not exposed. Similarly, if someone knocks out a child's tooth, he does not go free, since it will regenerate (*Avadim* 5:4; see also 5:1).

Like Rashi, Maimonides understands this verse as applying to a Canaanite slave; see *Kesef Mishnah*. Maimonides adds that the act must be intentional (*Avadim* 5:11). To me, it seems that because the Hebrew *hippil*, lit., "caused to fall," is used, which was understood by the Sages as a verb of intentionality, since the simpler form *nafal*, "fall," could have been used.

FURTHER: The precepts contained in the laws concerning slaves likewise prescribe only acts of pity, mercy and kindness to the poor. It is an act of mercy to give liberty to a Canaanite servant for the loss of one of his limbs (Exod. 21:26-27), in order that he should not suffer from slavery and illness at the same time. The law applies even to the case that a tooth of a slave has been knocked out, and certainly to the mutilation of other [non-regenerating] limbs. He could only be corrected with a rod or reed or the like, as we have stated in *Mishneh Torah*. Besides, if the master strikes the slave too hard and kills him, he is punished with death as for ordinary murder. Mercy is also the object of the law, "You shall not deliver unto his master the servant that is escaped from his master" (Deut. 23:16); but it teaches besides a very useful lesson, namely, that we must always practice this virtue, help and protect those who seek our help, and not deliver them unto those from whom they flee; and it is not sufficient to give assistance to those who are in need of our help; we must look after their interests, be kind to them, and not hurt their feeling by words. Thus the Law says, "He shall dwell with you, even among you, in that place which he shall choose in one of your gates, where it pleases him best; you shall not vex him" (Deut. 23:17). This we owe to the lowest among men, to the slave; how much more must we do our duty to the freeborn, when they seek our assistance? (*Guide* 3:39).

21:28. And if an ox gores [*yiggaḥ*]... — ... goring [*negihah*] refers only to [damage done by a] horn (*PhM Bava Kamma* 1:4).

... a man or a woman that they die... — ... we are commanded to judge an ox according to the law, as God, may He be exalted, said, "And if an ox gores..." and "And if [one man's] ox injures..." (v. 35) (*ShM*, Pos. 237).

299

FURTHER: If someone uses oxen for sport and trains them to gore each other, they are not considered *mu'adim* to each other. Even if they kill a person they are not liable, as it says, "if [*ki*] an ox gores" — but not if others make it gore (*Nizkei Mamon* 6:5; see also Raavad).

> As an aside, Maimonides says that many people engage in "bullfighting," i.e., setting two bulls against each other to see which one is stronger (also with chickens, and people who do this are fools (*tipshei bnei adam*, PhM *Bava Kamma* 4:2, 4).

FURTHER: [Maimonides is commenting on the following in Mishnah: The Sadducees say, "We take issue with you, you Pharisees, for you say: 'If my ox or my donkey causes damage, they are liable, but if my manservant or bondmaid causes injury, they are not liable.' If in the case of my ox or my donkey, about which no commandments are laid upon me, I am responsible for the injury that they cause, how much more so in the case of my manservant or bondmaid, about whom certain commandments are laid upon me, should I be responsible for the injury that they cause!" They said, "No! As you argue concerning my ox or my donkey, which have no understanding, would you also argue concerning my manservant or bondmaid, who have understanding? — For if I provoke him to anger, he may go and set fire to another's stack of corn, and it is I that must make restitution" (*Yadayim* 4:7).] — And you already know that according to our Law, if a slave causes damage, the owners are not obligated to pay at all, as explained in *Bava Kamma* that it is unfortunate to knock into women, slaves, and minors, for if they cause damage, they are exempt (Mishnah *Bava Kamma* 8:4).[151] However if that man's animal causes damage, it is explicit in the Torah that he is liable, as it says, "if an ox gores," "if a man causes [a field or vineyard] to be consumed" (Exod. 22:4). "For if I provoke him to anger" — if I cause him anguish and I enrage him (*PhM Yadayim* 4:7).

---

151. However if someone causes damage to them, he is liable.

... then the ox shall surely be stoned and its flesh shall not be eaten, but the owner of the ox shall be guiltless. — ... we are forbidden to eat the flesh of a condemned ox [lit., "an ox that is to be stoned"], even if it was slaughtered before it was stoned. Since from the time that the judgment is rendered, it is forbidden to be eaten, even if the slaughter is proper. And this is what God, may He be exalted, said, "and its flesh shall not be eaten." And the language of the *Mekhilta* is: "If an ox was being brought out to be stoned, and the owners preemptively slaughtered it, its flesh may not be eaten; therefore it says, 'and its flesh may not be eaten' [even in a case of preemptive slaughter]." And if someone eats an olive's measure of flesh, he receives lashes (*ShM*, Neg. 188).

FURTHER: It is one of the principles of our Torah that wherever it is stated, "it shall not be eaten," it teaches there is a prohibition to either eat it or derive benefit from it unless Scripture specifies [otherwise] as it does in the case of *neveilah*.[152] And whenever we are forbidden to eat something but are permitted to benefit from it, we require a clear proof to permit benefiting from it, whether it is a verse or derived from one of the [thirteen hermeneutical] principles.... It is stated regarding a condemned ox, "its flesh shall not be eaten" (Exod. 21:28) (*PhM Kiddushin* 2:9).

FURTHER: Regarding a condemned ox, it is stated, "and its flesh shall not be eaten." But why would it be permitted to eat it when it is *neveilah*. Rather, this verse only comes to inform you that as soon as judgment is rendered, it becomes forbidden and becomes like an unclean beast. And even if someone preemptively slaughters it with a proper ritual slaughter, one may not derive benefit from it. If someone eats an olive's measure of flesh, he is liable to receive

---

152. "You shall not eat any *neveilah* [an animal that dies on its own]; you may give it to the stranger in your gates and he may eat it, or you may sell it to the foreigner" (Deut. 14:21). Here the Torah prohibits a Jew from *eating* the flesh of *neveilah* but then permits other forms of benefit (gifting, selling).

lashes. And similarly, once it is stoned, it may not be sold, and one may not give it to dogs, nor to Gentiles. Therefore it says, "its flesh may not be eaten" (*Ma'akhalot Asurot* 4:22; also *PhM Bava Kamma* 4:8, based on, e.g., *Bava Kamma* 41a).

FURTHER: The killing of an animal that has killed a human being (Exod. 21:28-29) is not a punishment to the animal, as the dissenters insinuate against us, but it is a fine imposed on the owner of that animal. For the same reason the use of its flesh is prohibited.[153] The owner of an animal will, therefore, take the greatest possible care in guarding it: he will know that if any person is killed by the animal, whether that person be grown up or young, free or in bondage, he forfeits at least the animal; and in case he has already received a warning concerning it, he will have to pay a ransom in addition to the loss of the animal (Exod. 21:30). This is also the reason why a beast is killed that has been used by a human being for an immoral purpose (Lev. 20:15-16); its owner will be more careful as regards his beast, will guard it, and never lose sight of it, just as he watches his household: for people fear the loss of their property as much as that of their own life: some even more, but most people hold both in the same estimation, e.g., "and to take us for bondmen, and our donkeys" (Gen. 43:18) (*Guide* 3:40).

21:29. And if the ox was wont to gore in the past, and it has been testified to its owner, and he has not guarded him, but that it has killed a man or a woman; the ox shall be stoned...— A *shor ha-mu'ad* [literally, "an ox that was testified about"] is the subject of the verse, "and it has been testified to its owner" that it had frequently gored in the past (*PhM Bava Kamma* 1:4).[154]

---

153. Cf. Philo, "... it is inconsistent with the law of God that man should take the food or for a seasoning to his food the flesh of an animal which has slain a man" (*Special Laws* 3.144).

154. A *shor mu'ad* is in contradistinction to a *shor tam*, an ox that has not habitually gored in the past.

FURTHER: Warning [*ha'adah*] is only in the presence of the witnesses and in the presence of the court, as it says, "and it has been testified [*ve-hu'ad*] to its owner" — and there is no warning except in court (*Nizkei Mamon* 6:2).

Maimonides says that testimony can only be received by a court of three *semukhim* (i.e., judges who have ordination that concatenates back to Moses), and only in the land of Israel (*Sanhedrin* 5:12). Since today we lack this ordination, these procedures are no longer observed.

... and its owner also shall be put to death. —It is stated in the Torah, "and its owner also shall be put to death," which according to oral tradition, we learn refers to death at the hands of Heaven (*Nizkei Mamon* 10:4).

Rashi and Nahmanides follow the rabbinic understanding that this phrase means death at the hands of Heaven; Nahmanides also analyzes why Onkelos translates *yumat* as *yitkil*, which suggests the owner is executed in court; see there. Ḥizkuni and Shadal, however, say the simple meaning is that he is executed in court. Ibn Ezra (long) says that this verse is like "an eye for an eye" — on some level he is deserving of death, which the ransom payment counters.

21:30. If a fine [*kofer*] is laid on him... —And if he pays a fine [*kofer*] for the victim, then he is acquitted on his behalf. And even though the fine is an atonement, we seize it from the person who is obligated to pay it, even against his will (*Nizkei Mamon* 10:4).

Rashi also appears to understand that the fine is extracted, even involuntarily. However, Nahmanides writes, "Since this fine is an atonement [*kofer kapparah*], just like offerings, and if he does not desire it, we do not compel him to come to court to obligate him in it. And even if the court ordered him to pay it, we do not seize it, since it says 'if' [*im*]." However, Rashi and Maimonides state that we can compel a person to pay the fine.

... then he shall give for the ransom [*kofer*] of his life whatsoever is laid upon him. — How much is the fine [*kofer*]? As much as the judges assess the value of the victim. Everything is according to the value of the victim, as it says, "then he shall give for the ransom of his life whatsoever is laid upon him." And the ransom for slaves, whether adults or minors, males or females, is a penalty fixed in the Torah: thirty *sela'im* or fine silver, whether the slave was worth a hundred *maneh* or worth only one *dinar* (v. 32). And if a servant only lacks his writ of manumission, there is no penalty, since he has no master, since he has already attained freedom.

And to whom does one give the ransom? To the heirs of the victim. And if he has killed a woman, the ransom is paid to her heirs from her father, and not to the husband. If he killed someone who was half free and half slave, he gives half of the penalty to his master, and the other half is appropriate to give, but there is none to receive it (*Nizkei Mamon* 11:1-2).

21:31. Whether it has gored a boy, or gored a girl, like this judgment [*ka-mishpat ha-zeh*] shall it be done to him. — Rabbi Akiva and the Sages debate the meaning of this verse (*Bava Kamma* 33a). The Sages say, "According to the judgment of an ox against an ox [*ka-mishpat shor ba-shor*], so is the judgment of an ox against a person [*ka-mishpat shor ba-adam*]," meaning that in such a case, he is obligated to pay half damages; and if it is a *mu'ad*, then he pays full damages [for injuring either a person or another ox]. (And we have already learned that a person is always considered "warned" — Mishnah *Bava Kamma* 2:6 [and therefore always must pay full damages].)

And Rabbi Akiva says, "*ka-mishpat ha-zeh* refers to a *mu'ad* ox, which is the original context of the verse, so too this is always the case regarding an ox that injured a person, whether it is *mu'ad* or *tam*." And the law does not follow Rabbi Akiva (*PhM Bava Kamma* 3:8).

21:32. If the ox pushes a manservant or bondmaid, he shall give thirty shekels of silver to their master, and the ox shall be stoned.
— [See end of verse 30.]

FURTHER: The compensation for a slave is uniformly estimated at half the value fixed for a free man. For in the law concerning the valuation you find the highest valuation at sixty shekels,[155] while the money to be paid for a slave is fixed at thirty shekels of silver (*Guide* 3:40).

... shekels... — Maimonides says that the biblical word *shekel* or *kesef* is equal to the rabbinic word *sela* (see *PhM Bekhorot* 8:8).

21:33. And if someone uncovers a pit or digs a pit and does not cover it... — ... we are commanded to judge the laws of the pit, as God, may He be exalted, said, "And if someone uncovers a pit...." (*ShM*, Pos. 238).[156]

FURTHER: Whether he digs a pit or uncovers a place that had been covered, as it says, "And if someone uncovers a pit or digs a pit and does not cover it."[157] However, if he covered it appropriately, even if it rotted from the inside so that an ox falls in and dies, he is exempt, since it says, "and does not cover it" — so if he covers it, he is exempt (*Nizkei Mamon* 12:4).

---

155. The verse actually says "fifty" not "sixty" (Lev. 27:3). The Kapach note says, "It is possible that our rabbi meant approximately half."
156. In other words, judging the laws of the pit qualifies as a separate entry in the roster of 613 commandments.
157. Hebrew *yiftah* means "will open" a pit; Maimonides appears to understand this as "uncover" (*megalleh*); which is also how Saadiah, Rashi, and Shadal understood it.

FURTHER: [This applies] whether he digs a pit, a ditch, a cave, or a trough. And why does it say "pit"? Because it must be something capable of causing death. And when is it considered something that can cause death? At a depth of ten handbreadths. However if it is less than ten handbreadths, and an ox or other animal, beast, or bird falls in and dies, he is exempt. And if the animals are injured, then the one who created the item that caused damage is liable to pay full damages (*Nizkei Mamon* 12:10).

... and an ox or a donkey falls in. — If vessels have fallen into a pit and get broken, the owner of the pit is exempt, as it says, "and an ox or a donkey falls in" — according to oral tradition we learn, "'ox' and not a person, 'donkey' and not vessels." Even if an ox falls in with vessels, so that the ox dies and the vessels break, he is liable for the ox and exempt [for damages relating to] the vessels (*Nizkei Mamon* 13:1; see also *PhM Bava Kamma* 5:6).

21:34. The owner of the pit shall pay... — If someone digs a pit in a public area, and an ox or a donkey falls in, and it dies, even if the pit was filled with cotton gauze or the like, the owner of the pit is liable to pay damages in full, as it says, "the owner of the pit shall pay...." [This applies] whether it is an ox, a donkey, other livestock, beasts, or fowl; "ox or donkey" are only mentioned because they are common.

Whether one digs a pit in a public area, or he digs it on his own property that opens to a public area, or it opens to his neighbor's property, or he digs it or opens it on his own property but declares his property—but not the pit—to be ownerless, then he is liable for the damages. However, if he declares his property and his pit to be ownerless, or he declares the pit on his property to be ownerless, or he dedicates it to the Temple, then he is exempt, as it says, "the owner of the pit shall pay" — [a pit] that has an owner, while this is ownerless. And he started to dig legally, because he started to dig on his property.

Whether he dug the pit, or it was dug [indirectly] by him, or a beast or fowl dug it, since he is obligated to fill it or cover it, and did not do so, he is liable for its damages. Whether he dug it, or purchased it, or it was given to him as a gift [he is liable], as it says, "the owner of the pit shall pay" — whatever has an owner, regardless [of how he acquired it] (*Nizkei Mamon* 12:1-3).

... he shall return money to its owner, and the carcass shall belong to him. — It is incumbent on the person who caused the damage to carry the carcass until he brings it to the victim. How so? For example, if the ox fell into a pit and died, he must lift it out of the pit and give it to the victim, and then measure the devaluation of the carcass, as it says, "he shall return money to its owner and the carcass shall belong to him," which teaches that he is obligated to return the carcass, and the difference belongs to the victim, and if it is a *tam*, then the owner pays half of the impairment, as we have explained (*Nizkei Mamon* 7:13).

FURTHER: If an ox that was consecrated and then invalidated fell into [a pit], and dies, he is exempt, as it says, "and the carcass shall belong to him" — provided the carcass has an owner [lit., "the carcass belongs to him"], which excludes this case, since one cannot benefit from this animal, and by law it must be buried (*Nizkei Mamon* 12:17).

21:35. And if one man's ox injures his neighbor's ox, and it dies...
— [Maimonides explains the Hebrew phrase *ve-khi yiggof shor ish,* "And if one man's ox injures..."] *Negifah* is with one of the limbs of the body (*PhM Bava Kamma* 1:4; in contrast to *negihah* at 21:28).

Rashi similarly writes, "'And if [one man's ox] injures [*yiggof*]' — 'It will push [*yidhof*],' whether with its horns, its body, its feet, or bit it with its teeth, these are all considered *negifah*, since *negifah* only means striking [*makkah*]."

FURTHER: Whatever animal is under a person's control and causes damage, the owner is obligated to pay, since his property caused damage, as it says, "if one man's ox injures his neighbor's ox," which applies to an ox, or any other animal, whether beast or fowl. And Scripture only mentions "ox" because that is commonplace (*Nizkei Mamon* 1:1; see also *ShM*, Pos. 237, quoted at v. 28).

FURTHER: The ox of a Jew that gored a consecrated ox, or if a consecrated ox gored an ox owned by a Jew, there is no liability, as it says, "his neighbor's ox" [and not a consecrated ox]. And anything for which one is liable for trespass, then there is no liability of damages. And animals invalidated as offerings are liable for damages, whether they inflict damage or suffer damage, since they are subject to redemption and have become non-sacred (*Nizkei Mamon* 8:1).

FURTHER: And similarly, an ownerless ox that causes damage is exempt, as it says, "his neighbor's ox," which means that it is property designated to owners. How so? If an ownerless ox gored, and before the victim takes hold of it, someone else stands up and acquires it, he is exempt. Furthermore, if an ox designated to its owners that caused damage—and after it caused damage, they consecrated it or declared it ownerless—he is exempt, until it has the same owner at the time of the damage and the time of standing trial (*Nizkei Mamon* 8:4).

... then they shall sell the living ox and divide its money, and the carcass shall belong to him. — And how much does he pay? If it caused damage in a manner that it habitually damages in accordance with its nature, for example an animal that eats straw or fodder, or damages with its foot while walking, he is obligated to pay the full amount from the best of his property, as it says, "from the best of his field or the best of his vineyard he shall pay" (Exod. 22:4).

And if it deviates [from its nature] and performs actions that it does not habitually perform, and causes damage thereby, for example if an ox gores or bites, then he is obligated to pay half of the damages from the animal that caused damage itself, as it says, "then they shall sell the living ox and divide its money…" (*Nizkei Mamon* 1:2).

21:36. Or if it be known that the ox has gored in the past… — If an animal does something that it frequently does in accordance with its nature, then it is called "warned" [*mu'ad*, for that action]. And if it deviates and does something that its species is not accustomed to do, like an ox that gored or bit, then it is called "simple" [*tam*].[158] And if it becomes habituated in those changes many times, then it becomes *mu'ad* for that action in which it is accustomed, as it says, "or if it be known that the ox has gored" (*Nizkei Mamon* 1:4).

… and the owners did not guard him, he shall surely pay ox for ox… — If the owner of an ox tied it with a rope or locked it up properly, and it escaped and caused damaged: If it is *tam* then he pays half damages. And if it is *mu'ad*, then he is exempt, as it says, "and has not guarded him," meaning that if he guarded it, he is exempt, and in this case the ox was guarded.[159] And similarly if it caused damage in a way that for which it is *mu'ad* about originally—for example, if it ate things that are appropriate to eat or caused damage with its feet while walking—then he is exempt from paying (*Nizkei Mamon* 7:1).

… and the carcass shall be his. — We appraise the amount of damage caused. How so? If his colleague's vessel was broken, whether by himself or by his animal, we do not say to the damager, "Take this broken vessel and pay this person the price of the vessel." Rather, we appraise the loss of the vessel, and he pays the [full] difference if the

---

158. "*Tam* is a term for something that does not habitually cause damage in that way and for such damages to arise from it, rather it occurs as happenstance" (*PhM Bava Kamma* 1:4).
159. This ruling is somewhat paradoxical, because it emerges that the law for a *mu'ad* is more lenient than for a *tam*. Therefore, the Rosh rules that for a *mu'ad*, as for a *tam*, the owner pays half damages.

damager was *mu'ad*, and half the damages if it was a *tam*, as it says, "and the carcass shall be his" — [i.e., belong] to the victim (*Nizkei Mamon* 7:8; see also *PhM Bava Kamma* 3:9).

21:37. If a man steals an ox or a sheep and slaughters it or sells it, he shall pay five oxen for the ox, and four sheep for the sheep. — ... we are commanded regarding the law of the thief, that we fine him twofold, fourfold, or fivefold, or that we kill him if he is breaking in, or we sell him. And all of this is included in the commandment regarding the thief, as Scripture has explained (*ShM*, Pos. 239).

FURTHER: And we have a principle that there is no difference whether he slaughters the animal himself, or whether he has an agent do it for him for the purposes of repayment. And this is hinted at with God's statement *o mekharo* ["or sells it"], and according to tradition the word *o* ["or"] comes to include an agent (*PhM Bava Kamma* 7:2).

FURTHER: It is right that the more frequent transgressions and sins are, and the greater the probability of their being committed, the more severe must their punishment be, in order to deter people from committing them; but sins which are of rare occurrence require a less severe punishment. For this reason one who stole a sheep had to pay twice as much as for other goods, i.e., four times the value of the stolen object: but this is only the case when he has disposed of it by sale or slaughter (Exod. 21:37). As a rule, the sheep remained always in the fields, and could therefore not be watched so carefully as things kept in town. Therefore the thief of a sheep used to sell it quickly before the theft became known, or to slaughter it and thereby change its appearance. As such theft happened frequently, the punishment was severe. The compensation for a stolen ox is still greater by one-fourth, because the theft is easily carried out. The sheep keep together when they feed, and can be watched by the shepherd, so that theft when it is committed can only take place by night. But oxen when feeding are very widely scattered, as is also mentioned in the *Nabatean Agriculture*, and a shepherd cannot watch them properly; theft of oxen is therefore a more frequent occurrence (*Guide* 3:41).

Ibn Ezra (long) says it is easier to hide a sheep than an ox. Nehama Leibowitz observes, "Maimonides differs from Ibn Ezra on two counts: on a matter of fact, and on the rationale of punishment. Ibn Ezra maintains that the stealing of sheep is easier than that of oxen, whereas Maimonides holds the reverse. Ibn Ezra regards the penalty as retributive— commensurate with the crime. Ox stealing involved greater 'professional' skill, so the penalty is stiffer. Maimonides regarded punishment as a deterrent. Since ox stealing, in his opinion, was easier to carry out and therefore more prevalent, the penalty had to be stiffer to deter people."[160]

---

160. Translation based on *New Studies in Shemot (Exodus)*, vol. 2, p. 368. For other opinions of why this case involves fourfold and fivefold payment, see there, pp. 361-371.

Exodus 22

22:1. If a thief be found breaking in and is struck and dies, there is no bloodguilt for him. — If someone is breaking in, whether in the day or at night, there is no bloodguilt for him. Rather, if the homeowner or anyone else kills him, they are exempt. And anyone has permission to kill him—whether on the weekday or on the Sabbath—by inflicting any form of death by which it is possible to kill him, as it says, "there is no bloodguilt for him [*ein lo damim*, lit., 'he has no blood']."

And whether he breaks in, or the thief is found on a person's roof, or in someone's courtyard, or his enclosed area, whether day or night. And why does it say "breaking in" [*mahteret*]? Because the majority of thieves break in at night.

And why did the Torah permit the blood of a thief, even though he only came concerning money? Because it is assumed that if the homeowner stood against him and prevented him, he will kill him, and thus the person who entered his colleague's house to commit theft is considered like someone pursuing his colleague to kill him. And therefore he can be killed, whether he is an adult or a minor, whether man or woman (*Geneivah* 9:7-9).[161]

22:2. And if the sun shines on him, then there be bloodguilt for him... — If the matter was clear to the homeowner that this thief that is entering will not kill him, and only comes to rob him, then it is forbidden to kill him. And if he kills him, then he is a murderer, as it says, "if the sun shines on him," meaning if it *as clear to you as the sun* that he is at peace with you, then you may not kill him. Therefore if a father breaks into his son's home he may not be killed, since he

---

161. Elsewhere Maimonides writes, "desire [*ta'avah*] is prohibited because it leads to coveting [*himmud*], and the latter is prohibited because it leads to robbery, as has been said by our Sages" (*Guide* 3:40); theft leads to murder; see on Exod. 20:14.

certainly will not kill him, but if a son breaks into his father's home, he may be killed (*Geneivah* 9:10).

> Raavad writes, "I will not refrain from expressing my opinion: it appears to me that even though the Sages expounded 'If the sun shines upon him' metaphorically to mean if the matter is as clear [*barur*] to you as the sun that he does not come with lethal intentions [*iskei nefashot*], nonetheless, a verse does not depart from its plain meaning: in the day it is not proper to kill him, because a thief does not come during the day [to kill]; rather if he can escape, he escapes and runs away and does not tarry to steal much wealth and stand up against its owner to kill him. But a thief [who comes] at night, because he knows that the homeowner is home, he is coming either to kill or be killed. With regard to a thief [who comes] during the day, though, the homeowner is not around, and he is coming only to escape [at stealing]. And I swear that this should suffice for any understanding person."[162]
>
> Hayim Tawil notes that Rabbi Ishmael (*Mekhilta*), Onkelos, Rashi, and Maimonides understand the verse metaphorically, while Targum Neofiti, Saadiah, Ibn Ezra, Rashbam, Nahmanides, Hizkuni, Shadal, and Cassuto understand the verse literally (like Raavad). Dr. Tawil then attempts to show, based on ancient Near Eastern texts, that *peshat* could be metaphorical.

... he shall surely pay; if he has nothing, then he shall be sold for his theft. — The law is that a thief must pay the principle and twofold, fourfold, or fivefold, from his moveable property. And if he does not have fourfold or fivefold from his moveable property, the court evaluates his assets and seizes the entire amount from the finest

---

162. Translation based on Hayim Tawil, *Lexical Studies in the Bible and Ancient Near Eastern Inscriptions*, p. 240.

of his assets, as in the case with other torts, as it says, "the best of his field or the best of his vineyard he shall pay" (Exod. 22:4). And if he does not have real property or moveable property, then the court sells him and gives the money to the victim, as it says, "if he has nothing, then he shall be sold for his theft."

A man is sold for his theft, but a woman is not sold, and this matter is learned from the oral tradition. And a thief is only sold [to repay] the principle. However, for the penalties of twofold, fourfold, or fivefold, he is not sold; rather it remains as a lien until he has the money (*Geneivah* 3:11-12).

22:3. If the stolen property is surely found in his hand, whether ox or donkey or sheep, still alive, then he shall pay double. — If two valid witnesses testified against a thief that he committed theft, then he is obligated to pay double to the victim. If he stole one *dinar*, he must repay two. If he stole a donkey or clothing or a camel, he repays twice its value. Thus he loses the amount by which he tried to damage the victim (*Geneivah* 1:4).

FURTHER: [Maimonides gives a philosophical answer why the thief should pay double:] If any one damaged the property of another, he must lose exactly as much of his own property: 'whomever the judges convict shall pay double to his neighbor'; namely, he restores that which he has taken, and adds just as much [to it] of his own property (*Guide* 3:41; see also *ShM*, Neg. 244).

22:4. If a man lets a field or vineyard to be grazed... — ... we are commanded concerning the laws of grazing, as God, may He be exalted, said, "If a man lets a field or vineyard be grazed..." (*ShM*, Pos. 240).

... or releases his animal in another's field... — Every *mu'ad* pays full damages from the best of his property, and every *tam* pays half damages from itself. What is this concerning? When the animal enters the victim's property and damages it. However if the victim enters the damager's property and the animal of the owner's property causes damage, then he is exempt for all damage, since he can say to him, "If you had not entered my property, this damage would not have befallen you." And this is explicit in the Torah, "or releases his animal into another's field" (*Nizkei Mamon* 1:7).

... then from the best of his field or the best of his vineyard he shall make restitution. — See *Nizkei Mamon* 1:2, quoted at Exod. 21:35, and *Geneivah* 3:11, quoted at verse 2.

FURTHER: An animal is considered *mu'ad* ["warned"] for eating fruits and vegetables and the like. Therefore if it enters onto the victim's property and eats things that it customarily eats, he pays full damages, as it says, "or releases his animal in another's field, then from the best of his field... [he shall make restitution]." And if it ate those things in a public area, he is exempt; and if it derived benefit from them, then he pays for what it benefitted but not for the damage it caused (*Nizkei Mamon* 3:1).

FURTHER: And what the Lord said, "from the best of his field or the best of his vineyard he shall make restitution" has fallen into debate if this refers to the victim or the damager. And even according to the opinion that it refers to the victim, because of *tikkun ha-olam* the victim may collect damages from the finest property that the damager possesses, so as not to increase damages and retaliation between people (*PhM Gittin* 5:1; see also *PhM Bava Kamma* 1:1).

22:5. If a fire breaks out and encounters thorns and a stack of corn or standing corn be consumed, then the person who kindled

the fire shall surely pay restitution. — ... we are commanded regarding damage caused by fire, as it says, "If a fire breaks out..." (*ShM*, Pos. 241).[163]

FURTHER: If someone kindles a fire in his friend's field, and the fire spreads and causes damage, he is obligated to pay full damage, as it says, "if a fire breaks out... the person who kindled the fire shall surely pay restitution." And damage caused by fire is one of the primary categories of damages (*Nizkei Mamon* 14:1).

FURTHER: If a fire spread and consumed branches, [or scorches] stones or earth, he is obligated to pay, as it says, "and encounters thorns" in a field (*Nizkei Mamon* 14:8).

22:6. If a man give his neighbor money or vessels to guard... — ... we are commanded regarding the *shomer ḥinnam* ("unpaid watchman"), as God, may He be exalted, said, "If a man give his neighbor money or vessels to guard..." (*ShM*, Pos. 242).

FURTHER: There are four types of watchmen mentioned in the Torah, and there are three sets of laws relating to them. And these are the four watchmen: an unpaid watchman, a borrower, a paid watchman, and a renter. And these are the three laws about them: If an entrusted object is stolen from an unpaid watchman, or is destroyed, or a major calamity befalls the object, like if it dies or is taken captive, then he takes an oath that we watched it in a way proper to watchmen [*derekh ha-shomrin*], and he is exempt, as it says, "and they are stolen from the man's house... then the homeowner shall approach the judges" (vv. 6-7).

163. In the *Guide*, Maimonides explores the meanings of *yatza*, and uses this verse as a literal usage of the word, "The term *yatza* is applied to the motion of a body from a place in which it had previously rested, to another place (whether the body be living or not), e.g., "And when they were gone out [*yatze'u*] of the city" (Gen. 44:4); "If a fire break out" (Exod. 22:5) (*Guide* 1:23).

And a borrower makes full restitution, whether the borrowed object was destroyed or stolen, or even if a major calamity befell it, such as the borrowed animal died, or was injured, or was taken captive, since this is what is written regarding a borrower: "and it is hurt or dies, the owner not being present, full restitution shall be made" (v. 13).

A hired worker and a renter—there is one law for the two of them. If an object that is rented or someone paid to watch it, and if it is stolen or destroyed, then they make restitution, and if a major calamity befalls it, such as if the animal died, was injured, was taken captive, or was mauled, then they take an oath that the calamity occurred and they are exempt, as it says, "it dies or is injured, or is driven away, and nobody sees it, then an oath of the Lord shall be between them" (vv. 9-10). And it is said, "if it surely be stolen from him, he shall make restitution to its owner. And if it be torn to pieces..." (vv. 11-12).

We thus find that an unpaid watchman takes an oath for all [types of damage]. And the borrower pays for everything unless the animal dies while it is being worked as we will explain. A hired watchman and renter make restitution for a lost or stolen object, and takes an oath if major calamities occurred, for example if it was injured, driven away, died, or mauled, or if the object was lost on a ship that sunk in the sea or taken captive by armed bandits, and any other major calamity like these (*Sekhirut* 1:1-2; see also *PhM Bava Metzia* 7:8).[164]

FURTHER: And these are the objects over which the Torah does not require one to take an oath [if their status is disputed]: land, slaves, and written documents, and consecrated property. Even if he made a partial admission, or there is one witness who testified against him, or he guarded it and made a claim of guardianship he is exempt

164. To summarize, the four guardians are: (1) *shomer ḥinnam* (unpaid watchman), (2) *sho'el* (borrower), (3) *nosei sekhar* (paid watchman), (4) *sokher* (renter).

[from taking an oath], as it says, "If a man give his neighbor," which excludes consecrated property, "money or vessels," which excludes land as well as slaves (which are considered like land). And it also excludes written documents, since they have no inherent value like money or vessels, but are only an indicator for them.

In all of these cases [i.e., land, slaves, written documents, and consecrated property], he takes a consuetudinal oath (*shevuat hesset*) if the plaintiff makes an affirmative claim, with the exception of consecrated property. And even though the Torah did not obligate him to take an oath, the Sages instituted that he take an oath similar to a biblical oath, so that consecrated property should not be disgraced (*To'en ve-Nit'an* 5:1; see also *PhM Kiddushin* 1:5, *Shevuot* 6:5).

FURTHER: If someone claims that an article entrusted to him by a minor was stolen, even if he entrusted it when he was a minor and demanded it back when he was an adult, and [the watchman] made an oath, and then witnesses came, he is exempt from paying double, as it says, "If a man give his neighbor," and giving to a minor is meaningless. Rather, the entrusting and demanding both must be when he is an adult (*Geneivah* 4:9).

... money or vessels... — There are three laws mentioned in the Torah regarding four types of watchmen, which only apply to moveable property, belonging to a Jew, and unconsecrated, as it says, "money or vessels or any animal" (cf. Exod. 22:6, 9), which excludes land, and excludes slaves, since they have the same law as land, and excludes written documents, since they are not actual property. And it is stated, "If a man give his neighbor" (Exod. 22:6) which excludes consecrated property and the property of gentiles. Accordingly, the

Sages said that an unpaid watchman need not take an oath regarding slaves, written documents, land, and consecrated property, and a hired watchman and renter need not pay [if they are destroyed], but if they acquired them [with a formal acquisition], then they are responsible [if those objects are destroyed] (*Sekhirut* 2:1).

FURTHER: ... "money or vessels" — all vessels are like money [for the purpose of compelling an oath] (*To'en ve-Nit'an* 3:5; see there).

... to guard... — If money was entrusted to someone for the poor or to redeem captives, and he was negligent with the money or it was stolen, he is exempt, as it says, "to guard" [*lishmor*] — but not to distribute to the poor (*She'eilah u-Fikkadon* 5:1).

... and they are stolen from the man's house... — [Maimonides is commenting on the phrase *ganav ve-hikdish ve-aḥar kakh tavaḥ u-makhar*, "if he stole an animal and then consecrated it, and then slaughtered it or stole it." Maimonides argues that the Mishnah should not be interpreted literally:] The debate between Rabbi Simeon and the Sages is not regarding someone who stole [an animal] and consecrated it. Rather it is about someone who stole a consecrated animal and slaughtered it or sold it. The Sages say: "and stolen from the man's house" — and not from Temple property. Rabbi Simeon says: if these are consecrated items that must be replaced [if lost or stolen], then they belong to the owners, and we consider it as "stolen from the man's house..." ... And the law does not follow Rabbi Simeon (*PhM Bava Kamma* 7:4).

FURTHER: If someone steals from a gentile or consecrated property, he only pays the principle, as it says, "he shall pay twice to his colleague" (v. 8) — "to his colleague," but not to the Temple treasury, "to his colleague," but not to a gentile. And similarly, if someone steals consecrated property from the donor's house, whether it is most holy property or lesser holy property, whether it is consecrated property which has to be replaced [if lost or stolen], whether it is consecrated property which must be replaced, he is exempt from paying double, fourfold, or fivefold, as it says, "stolen from a man's house" — and not from Temple property.

And similarly, if someone steals slaves, written contracts, or land, he does not pay double, since the Torah only obligated double-payment for something that is moveable and has inherent worth, as it says, "an ox, a donkey, a sheep, a garment," but not slaves, which are considered like land, as it says, "and you shall give them as an inheritance to your children" (Lev. 25:46), and written contracts do not have inherent value (*Geneivah* 2:1-2).

... if the thief is found... — if someone claimed that [an entrusted object] was stolen, and it was he who stole it, he is obligated to pay twofold, since the Lord said, "if the thief is found," meaning if he is found to be the thief, then he pays double if there are witnesses. And if he admits it himself, he pays the principle, and a one-fifth [penalty], and an *asham* (*PhM Shevuot* 8:3).

... he shall pay double. — If any one damaged the property of another, he must lose exactly as much of his own property: "whomever the judges convict shall pay double to his neighbor" (Exod. 22:8); namely, he restores that which he has taken, and adds just as much [to it] of his own property (*Guide* 3:41; Maimonides does not quote the verse in this context but his rationale is applicable here).

22:7. And if the thief is not found, then the homeowner shall approach the judges to determine if he has not used his neighbor's property for himself.[165] — [The Mishnah says, "If

165. Hebrew *im lo shalaḥ yado bi-melekhet rei'eihu*, lit., "if he did not send his hand in his neighbor's property."

someone was contemplating using an entrusted item for personal use, Bet Shammai says he is liable [for unforeseen damage], and Bet Hillel says he is not liable [for unforeseen] until he actually uses the property himself, as it says, "if he did not use his neighbor's property for himself" (M. *Bava Metzia* 3:12). Maimonides explains:] The debate… is over the meaning of the verses. Bet Shammai says, "'In any case of wrongdoing' (v. 8) — even if he commits a wrong in his thoughts," and Bet Hillel says, "'if he did not use his neighbor's property for himself' (v. 7) — until he actually uses the property" (*PhM Bava Metzia* 3:12).

FURTHER: If someone entrusts his colleague without remuneration, and the object is stolen or destroyed, then the watchman takes an oath and is exempt from liability, as it says, "and they are stolen from the man's house… then the homeowner shall approach the judges to determine if he has used his neighbor's property for himself" (vv. 6-7). And included in this oath is that (1) he was not negligent, rather he guarded it the way watchmen do [*derekh ha-shomrin*][166]; (2) that he did not use it first and then it was stolen, for if it was stolen after he used the entrusted object, then he is obligated to replace it (*She'eilah u-Fikkadon* 4:1; also *Sekhirut* 1:2).

What exactly does the watchman swear to? According to Rashi, the watchman swears that he did not use his neighbor's property for his personal use (*she-lo shalaḥ yado be-she-lo*). Nahmanides rejects this opinion, and says that the watchman swears that the object was stolen (*nignav*); see *Maggid Mishneh*.

---

166. See next *halakhah* for a definition of this phrase.

22:8. In any case of wrongdoing, regarding an ox, a donkey, a sheep, a garment, or any lost object... —They said in the *Sifra*:[167] "In any case of wrongdoing" — this is the general statement, "regarding an ox, a donkey, a sheep, a garment" — this is the specific statement, "or any lost object" — this returns to the general statement. This is a general statement, followed by a specific statement, followed by a general statement, for which you derive a law about things that resemble the specific statement: just as the specific is an example of something that is moveable and has inherent value, so too [the verse applies] to anything that is moveable and has inherent value, to the exclusion of land, which is not moveable, and to the exclusion of slaves, which are connected to the land; to the exclusion of contracts, since although they are moveable, they do not have inherent value. And based on this law, it is clear to you that the payment of double applies to something that is living and also to inanimate objects (*PhM Bava Kamma* 7:1). (See also *PhM Shevuot* 6:5 and *Geneivah* 2:1-2, quoted at v. 6.)

... or any lost object... — If someone claimed that a lost article was stolen, and takes an oath to that effect, and then witnesses come [saying] the lost object is on his property and that he swore falsely, then he pays double, as it says, "*any* lost object" (*Geneivah* 4:4).

... about which someone claims to belong to him... — ... we are commanded concerning claims and counterclaims, as God, may He be exalted and His name be blessed, said, "In any case of wrongdoing... about which someone claims to belong to him...." And the *Mekhilta* says, "'about which someone claims to belong to him' — this refers to someone who makes a partial admission." And this commandment includes any claims that people make about admission or denial (*ShM*, Pos. 246).

---

167. This is not in our version of the *Sifra*, and perhaps he meant to write it is in the *Mekhilta* (see Kapach's edition of *PhM*).

FURTHER: If someone makes a claim against his colleague regarding moveable property, and he admits to owing part of it, then he pays what he admits to owing, and according to the Torah he takes an oath that he does not owe the rest, as it says, "about which someone claims to belong to him"[168] (*To'en ve-Nit'an* 1:1; see also 3:1).

... the matter of them both shall come to the judges... — [Maimonides gives a law derived from the Hebrew phrase *ad ha-elohim*, here translated as "to the judges":] And know that we have a principle among the principles of our Torah that we do not impose fines in Babylonia, nor any other place in the world, except for the land of Israel alone, since God, may He be exalted, said, *ad ha-elohim* ("to the judges"), and we do not have judges that are called *elohim* except the judges that were ordained in the land of Israel (*PhM Bava Kamma* 8:1).

> Rashi similarly writes, "And in Babylonia there is no [formal] ordination" (*Bava Kamma* 84b, s.v. *elohim ba'inan*). See also *PhM Sanhedrin* 1:1.

FURTHER: The term *elohim* signifies "judges" [in the example of] "the matter of them both shall come to the 'judges'" (*Guide* 2:6).

... and whomever the judges convict shall pay double to his neighbor. — If a thief himself admits that he stole, he pays the principle amount, but is exempt from paying twofold, as it says, "whomever the judges convict shall pay double," but someone who convicts himself does not pay double. And this is the case with all fines that someone who admits is exempt (*Geneivah* 1:5; on the concept of paying double, see at v. 6).

---

168. Hebrew *ki zeh hu*, which can also be translated "this is it."

Also Rashi, "someone who admits to [crime that carries] a penalty is exempt [from paying the penalty] from 'whomever the judges convict' — to exclude someone who convicts himself (*Ketubot* 41a, s.v. *ve-eino meshallem kenas*). Maimonides also quotes this verse at *PhM Terumot* 6:4.

FURTHER: If anyone damaged the property of another, he must lose exactly as much of his own property, "whomever the judges convict shall pay double to his neighbor," namely, he restores that which he has taken, and adds just as much to it of his own property. It is right that the more frequent transgressions and sins are, and the greater the probability of their being committed, the more severe must their punishment be, in order to deter people from committing them; but since they are of rare occurrence, they require a less severe punishment (*Guide* 3:41).

22:9. If a man gives to his neighbor a donkey or ox or sheep or any animal to guard, and it dies or is injured, or is driven away, and nobody sees it. — ... the Torah commands us about the law of a hired watchman and renter, since the laws of both of them are the same, and we have explained and they said: there are three laws for four types of watchmen. And this is what God, may He be exalted, said, "If a man give his neighbor a donkey or ox or sheep..." (*ShM*, Pos. 243; see also v. 6 as well as Rashi on v. 14).

22:10. Then an oath of the Lord shall be between them that he has not used his neighbor's property for himself... — There are only three cases where the Torah commands someone to take an oath: (1) someone who makes a partial admission, (2) someone obligated by one witness; (3) and a watchman, since regarding a watchman it says, "an oath of the Lord shall be between them." ... And in each one of these three cases, he takes an oath and he is exempt from making restitution (*To'en ve-Nit'an* 1:2).

FURTHER: If a guardian claimed that a calamitous event occurred, like that the animal was injured or died; if the calamity occurred in a place where witnesses are present, we force him to bring a proof to his claim that this calamity occurred, and then he is exempt from even making an oath, and if he does not bring a proof, then he must make restitution, as it says, "nobody sees it, then an oath of the Lord shall be between them" (reading vv. 9-10 as a continuous thought). Thus in a place where it is possible to bring a proof, there is no need for an oath; rather [in such a case] he brings a proof or he makes restitution.

However, if he claims the calamity occurred in a place where no witnesses are present, we do not force him to bring a proof; instead he swears that the calamity occurred and he is exempt. And if he brings witnesses that he did not act negligently, then he is even exempt from taking an oath (*Sekhirut* 3:1; see also on v. 7; see also *Shevuot* 11:5).

... then the owner shall take what is his, and shall not make restitution. — Regarding someone who is obligated to take an oath, the Lord said, "the owner shall take what is his, and shall not make restitution." From this we learn that someone who does not make restitution must take an oath; and all the more so someone who takes something [from someone else] on account of his oath (*PhM Shevuot* 7:1).

22:11-12. And if it surely be stolen from him, he shall make restitution to its owner. And if it be torn to pieces, they shall bring it as a witness, and he shall not make restitution on what is torn. — ... It is already known to you that a hired watchman and a renter are exempt from calamities, since in those cases God said, "he shall not make restitution for what is torn," and similarly they are not liable for what is damaged or what is driven away, and therefore these things are considered calamities [for which the hired watchman and renter are exempt] (*PhM Bava Metzia* 7:9).

22:13. And if a man borrow from his colleague and it is hurt or dies, the owner not being present, full restitution shall be made.
— ... we are commanded regarding the laws of the borrower, as God, may He be exalted, said, "And if a man borrow from his colleague" (*ShM*, Pos. 244; see also v. 6).

FURTHER: If someone borrows a vessel or an animal or the like of other moveable property from his friend, and it is damaged or stolen, even if it is because of some major calamity, like that the animal was injured or driven away or died, he is obligated to pay in full, as it says, "And if a man borrow from his colleague and it is hurt or dies, the owner not being present, full restitution shall be made" (*She'eilah u-Fikkadon* 1:1).

22:14. If its owners are with it he shall not make restitution; if he was a hired worker he came for his wages. — If someone deposits an object with his colleague—whether unpaid, hired, borrowed, or rented—if the watchman offers to hire the owners, then the watchman is exempt from everything. Even if he was negligent with the object he was guarding and it was lost because of his negligence, he is exempt, as it says, "If its owners are with it he shall not make restitution; if he was a hired worker he came for his wages" (Exod. 22:14).

When is this the case? When he asked the owners or hired them at the time that he took the object, even if the owners are not there with him at the time of the theft or loss, or when an unavoidable event occurred. However, if he took the object and he first became a watchman and then hired the owners or asked them, even though the owners are standing there at the time that the watchman was distressed, nonetheless he [i.e., the watchman] pays, as it says, "the owner not being present, full restitution shall be made" (Exod. 22:13). According to oral tradition we learn that if he was with him at the time of the borrowing, even if he was not with him at the time of the theft or death, he is exempt; and if he was not with him at the time of borrowing, even if he was with him at the time of theft or death, he is liable. And this is the case for other watchmen: in all cases if they are "with the owners" they are exempt. Even in a case of negligence, if he is "with the owners," he is exempt (*Sekhirut* 1:3; see also *She'eilah u-Fikkadon* 2:1 and *PhM Bava Metzia* 8:1).

22:15. If a man seduces a virgin who is not betrothed and lies with her, he shall surely pay a dowry and she shall be a wife for him. — ... we are commanded concerning the law of the seducer, as God, may He be exalted, said, "If a man seduces a virgin" (*ShM*, Pos. 220).

FURTHER: What is meant by "seduce" [*mefatteh*] and what is meant by "rape" [*oness*]? "Seduction" means with her consent, and "rape" means that he takes her against her will (*Na'arah Betulah* 1:2).

22:16. If her father utterly refuse to give her to him, he shall pay money of the dowry of virgins. — If a man seduces a virgin, he pays a penalty of fifty *sela'im* of fine silver, and this is called a "fine" [*kenas*], and similarly if he rapes her. And [the imposition of] this fine is a positive commandment, as it says, "And the man who lies with her shall give the young girl's father fifty [shekels of] silver" (Deut. 22:29) (*Na'arah* 1:1).

FURTHER: If a seduced woman does not want to marry her seducer, or her father does not want him to marry her, or that he does not want to marry her, then he pays the fine and leaves, and we do not force him to marry her. If they consent and he marries her, he does not pay the fine. Instead, he writes her a marriage document like all other virgins.

However, if either a rape victim or her father does not want [the victim] to marry the rapist, it is in their power [to prevent the marriage] and he pays the fine. If both she and the father consent, and he does not want to, we force him, and he marries her and he pays the fine, as it says, "and she shall be a wife to him" (Deut. 22:29). This is a positive commandment   (Pos. 218).

Even if she is lame, blind, or leprous, we force him to marry her, and he can never initiate divorce proceedings, as it says, "he may not send her away for the rest of his life" (Deut. 22:29). This is a negative commandment (i.e., Neg. 358) (*Na'arah* 1:3).

FURTHER: The seducer pays for embarrassment and damages immediately, but he only pays the fine if he does not marry her, as it says, "If her father utterly refuse to give her to him, he shall pay money of the dowry of virgins." However, the rapist pays all four [financial impositions] immediately and then marries. Therefore is she desires to be divorced or he dies, she does not receive anything (*Na'arah* 2:7).

> Rabbi S. R. Hirsch explains that the fine "is imposed in lieu of the marriage which really should have taken place; and the fine only consists in paying that which ordinarily—whether according to custom or law—is paid at the breaking-up of a marriage by death or divorce, here has to be paid instead of entering into the marriage."

FURTHER: As every maiden expects to be married, her seducer therefore is only ordered to marry her; for he is undoubtedly the fittest husband for her. He will better heal her wound and redeem her character than any other husband. If, however, he is rejected by her or her father, he must give the dowry (Exod. 22:16). If he uses violence he has to submit to the additional punishment, "he may not send her away for the rest of his life" (Deut. 22:29) (*Guide* 3:49).

How can a man be allowed to marry a girl after raping or seducing her? Nahmanides says that men who seduce are usually handsome young men hoping to marry young women from prominent families; however, he should not profit from his sin; he cannot marry the girl against the will of either the girl or her father. At the same time, since she sinned (in the case of seduction, not rape) he does not have to marry her against his will, but in such a case pays fifty shekels. Nahmanides continues rapists are usually from prominent families who victimize less prominent women, and they expect no consequences. Therefore he can be forced to marry her, unless either the woman or her father refuse (e.g., if she is from a more prominent family than he).

22:17. You shall not permit a sorceress to live. — ... we are forbidden let a sorcerer to live, as it says, "You shall not permit a sorceress to live." And if we acquit him[169] we violate a negative commandment. This is not like a positive commandment, as is the case of other cases of capital punishment (*ShM*, Pos. 310).

The original here is slightly unclear, and has been translated according to context. Maimonides makes a similar point at *Sanhedrin* 14:3. Maimonides counts each of the four separate forms of execution of negative commandments; however Nahmanides counts them as one commandment; see Chavel's translation of Nahmanides on Exodus, p. 389, note 274; see also note 275.

169. The verse speaks in the feminine, while Maimonides writes in the masculine. Similarly Rashi writes, "Whether male or female, but the verse speaks about what is more common, since women are more commonly found as sorcerers" (based on *Sanhedrin* 67a). See also the use of masculine "sorcerer" (Deut. 18:10).

FURTHER: A sorcerer is liable to death by stoning, and that is if he commits an act of sorcery. However, if he engages in trickery of the eye, and so that he appears to do something but does not actually do it, then he gets [rabbinic] lashes for rebellion. This prohibition is based on the verse about a sorcerer, "There shall not be found among you [one who passes his son or daughter through fire, or who practices divination, or is a soothsayer, an augur, or a sorcerer]" (Deut. 18:10). And since this prohibition is attached to a capital crime, one does not receive lashes for violating it, as it says, "You shall not permit a sorceress to live" (*Avodah Zarah* 11:15).

FURTHER: It is the object and center of the whole Law to abolish idolatry and utterly uproot it, and to overthrow the opinion that any of the stars could interfere for good or evil in human matters, because it leads to the worship of stars. It was therefore necessary to slay all witches as being undoubtedly idolaters, because every witch is an idolater; they only have their own strange ways of worship, which are different from the common mode of worship offered to those deities. But in all performances of witchcraft it is laid down as a rule that women should be employed in the chief operation; and therefore the Law says, "You shall not permit a sorceress to live." Another reason is the natural reluctance of people to slay women. This is also the cause why in the law of idolatry it is said "man or woman" (Deut. 17:2), and again repeated a second time, "the man or the woman" (v. 5)—a phrase which does not occur in the law about the breaking of Sabbath, or in any other law; for great sympathy is naturally shown to women.

Now the witches believed that they produced a certain result by their witchcraft; that they were able through the above-mentioned actions to drive such dangerous animals as lions, serpents, and the like out of the cities, and to remove various kinds of damage from the products of the earth. Thus they imagine that they are able by certain acts to prevent hail from coming down, and by certain other acts to kill the worms in the vineyards, whereby the latter are protected from injury; in fact, the killing of the worms in vineyards, and other superstitions mentioned in the *Nabatean Agriculture*, are fully described by the Sabeans. They likewise imagine that they know certain acts by which they can prevent the dropping of leaves from the trees and the untimely falling of their fruit (*Guide* 3:37).

> Why does the Torah obligate a sorceress to be killed? Maimonides argues it is because of her involvement with idolatry. This position is also accepted by Shadal. Nahmanides and Rabbi S.R. Hirsch argue—relatedly—that the prohibition uproots man's erroneous belief that he can master nature.[170]

22:18. Whoever lies with a beast shall surely be put to death. — If someone penetrates an animal, or is penetrated by an animal, they are both stoned, as it says, "And you shall not lie with any animal" (Lev. 18:23), whether one penetrates it or is penetrated by it. This applies to any livestock, beast, or fowl; they are all punished by stoning. And Scripture did not specify between a young or old animal, as it says, "any animal" — even on the day it was born. This applies whether one has normal or non-normal intercourse, as soon as the crown penetrates it, or the crown penetrates him, he is liable (*Issurei Bi'ah* 1:16; also *PhM Sanhedrin* 7:4).

22:19. One who sacrifices to gods, except the Lord alone, shall be destroyed. — He has forbidden to do any of these things [that relate to offerings] to any other being, as it says, "One who sacrifices to gods, except the Lord alone, shall be destroyed" (*Guide* 3:32, quoted in fuller form at Exod. 25:8; see also *ShM*, Neg. 5 and *Avodah Zarah* 3:3, both quoted at Exod. 20:5).

---

170. See Philo's unique answer at *Special Laws* 3.95

22:20. And you shall not mistreat the convert [*ve-gerim lo toneh*]
...[171] — ... we are forbidden to mistreat the convert with words, which means *ona'at devarim*, as God, may He be exalted, said, "You shall not mistreat the convert." And the language of the *Mekhilta* is "'You shall not mistreat the convert' — with words." And this prohibition is repeated in the prohibition, "you shall not mistreat him [*lo tonu oto*]" (Lev. 19:33). And the language of the *Sifra* is "That you not say to him: Yestereve you were practicing idolatry and today you have entered under the wings of the Divine Presence" (*ShM*, Neg. 252).

... nor shall you distress him [*ve-lo tilḥatzennu*], for you were strangers in the land of Egypt. — We are prohibited from distressing a righteous convert and in causing him financial harm, as He said, "nor shall you distress him." And the language of the *Mekhilta* is "'nor shall you distress him' — financially." And it has already been explained in *Bava Metzia* (59b) that one who distresses a convert violates the prohibition of "a man shall not mistreat his brother" (Lev. 25:14) and "you shall not mistreat the convert" (Exod. 22:20). And similarly someone who causes him distress violates "nor shall you distress him" in addition to the general prohibition that applies to all Jews (i.e., Neg. 250), which is to cause financial distress (*ShM*, Neg. 253; see also Pos. 207, to be quoted at Deut. 10:19).

FURTHER: Whoever causes distress to a convert, whether financially or verbally, violates three commandments, as it says, "And you shall not mistreat the convert," which refers to verbal mistreatment; "nor shall you distress him," which refers to financial distress. Thus you learn that someone who causes distress to a convert violates three commandments: (1) "A man shall not mistreat his fellow" (Lev. 25:17); (2) "A man shall not mistreat his brother" (Lev. 25:14); and (3) "You shall not mistreat the convert."

171. Hebrew *ger*, which literally means "stranger," but for legal contexts only means "convert."

And similarly if he mistreats him and causes financial distress, he violates three commandments: (1) "A man shall not mistreat his brother" (Lev. 25:14); (2) "A man shall not mistreat his fellow" (Lev. 25:17); and (3) "nor shall you distress him."

Why does a person who takes financial advantage of a person also violate the prohibition of verbal abuse; and if he verbally abuses a convert, why is this considered financial mistreatment? Because Scripture uses the word generic word "mistreat" [hona'ah], and it repeats these prohibitions regarding a convert explicitly: "you shall not mistreat" and "you shall not distress" (Mekhirah 14:15-17, see Maggid Mishneh; see also Avadim 8:11, where the same point is presented differently).

FURTHER: It is not proper to count afflicting the convert as three separate commandments because the warning was repeated. And [despite] that which the Talmud says, "one who mistreats the convert violates three prohibitions, and one who distresses him—three" (Bava Metzia 59b), it is only two commandments: "you shall not mistreat" [lo toneh] and "you shall not distress" [lo tilḥatzennu], and the warning is repeated in them. And this is clear without a doubt. And the meaning of what the Sages said, "Why did the Torah contain thirty-six warnings about the convert? Because he has a strong evil inclination." And is it possible that one might say that this includes thirty-six of the 613 commandments? This is how that statement should not be explained (ShM, Shoresh 9; see Nahmanides on Neg. 256 on the contradiction between here and Mekhirah 14:15-17, quoted above).

22:21-23. You shall not afflict any widow or orphan. If you afflict them in any way, when they will cry out to Me, I will surely hear their cry. And My anger shall flare up and I will kill you with the sword, and your wives shall be widows and your children shall be

orphans. — ... we are forbidden to afflict the orphan and the widow, as God, may He be exalted, said, "You shall not afflict any widow or orphan" (v. 21). And this is a commandment which prohibits afflicting them in either word or deed; rather one should speak with them with pleasant and comforting words, and conduct business dealings with them with excessive kindness. And whoever is lacking in this matter violates this prohibition. And God, may He be exalted, has explained the punishment for violating this commandment is what He, may He be exalted, said, "And My anger shall flare up and I will kill you" (v. 23) (*ShM*, Neg. 256).

FURTHER: One must be cautious [in his treatment of] orphans and widows since their souls are lowly and their spirit is crushed, even if they happen to be affluent. We are even warned concerning the widow of a king, and the orphans of a king, as it says, "You shall not afflict *any* widow or orphan" (v. 21).

And how should we treat them? We should only speak with them softly, and we should treat them only with respect. And we should not pain their bodies with work or their hearts with words. And one should be more considerate with their money than he would be with his own. And whoever distresses them or angers them or causes them pain or distresses them or destroys their property violates a negative commandment, and certainly someone who strikes them or curses them [violates this prohibition]. And even though someone who violates this commandment is not lashed, his punishment is explicit in the Torah, "And My anger shall flare up and I will kill you with the sword" (v. 23). The One who spoke and the world came into being made a covenant with them that whenever they cry out in despair, they are answered, as it says, "when they cry out to Me, I will surely hear their cry" (v. 22).

In which cases does this apply? When someone deprives them of what they need for themselves. However if a teacher afflicts them in order to teach them Torah or a trade, or to lead them on the proper path, this is permitted. Nonetheless, he should not treat them as he would treat anyone else; rather he should make a distinction and guide them with pleasantness and great mercy, for "the Lord will fight their fight" (Prov. 22:23).

This applies whether one is orphaned from his father or orphaned from his mother. And until when is someone considered an orphan for this purpose? Until they no longer need an adult to support on, depend on, and to care for them, rather they can take care of all their needs for themselves like any other adult (*De'ot* 6:10).

Maimonides does not use the phrase *middah ke-neged middah*, "measure for measure," but it is implied from the fact that God will fight their fight against those who sought to oppress the widow and orphan. This phrase is used explicitly by Rashbam, Ḥizkuni, Sforno, as well as Gersonides (Prov. 22:23), and implied by Nahmanides on the present verse. Maimonides, in a different context, writes, "The punishment of him who sins against his neighbor consists in the general rule that there shall be done unto him exactly as he has done: if he injured anyone personally, he must suffer personally; if he damaged the property of his neighbor, he shall be punished by loss of property" (*Guide* 3:41). Hence God's wrath might be kindled against the oppressor because the widow or orphan might feel like the whole world has turned against him.

FURTHER: *Shama* is used homonymously. It signifies "to hear," and also "to obey":[172]

---

172. Kapach translates this as *kabbalah*, lit., "receiving." Rashi says that *shama* can mean "hear" or *kabbalah*, where it is better translated as "to act in response [to a report]" (see Rashi on Isa. 37:9). This verse certainly points to meaning not of obeisance, since the messengers were not commanded by Rabshakeh to act one way or another, but

- As regards the first signification, e.g., "Neither let it be heard out of your mouth" (Exod. 23:13); "And the fame thereof was heard in Pharaoh's house" (Gen. 45:26). Instances of this kind are numerous.

- Equally frequent are the instances of this verb being used in the sense of "to obey": "And they hearkened [*shame'u*] not unto Moses" (Exod. 6:9); "If they obey [*yishme'u*] and serve him" (Job 36:11); "Shall we then hearken [*nishma*] unto you" (Neh. 13:27); "Whosoever will not hearken [*yishma*] unto thy words" (Josh. 1:18)

- The verb also signifies "to know" ("to understand"), e.g., "A nation whose tongue [i.e., its language] you will not understand [*tishma*]" (Deut. 28:49).

The verb *shama*, used in reference to God, must be taken in the sense of perceiving, which is part of the third signification, whenever, according to the literal interpretation of the passage, it appears to have the first meaning, e.g., "And the Lord heard it" (Num. 11:1); "For that He hears your murmurings" (Exod. 16:7). In all such passages mental perception is meant.

When, however, according to the literal interpretation the verb appears to have the second signification, it implies that God responded to the prayer of man and fulfilled his wish, or did not respond and did not fulfill his wish: "I will surely hear their cry" (Exod. 22:22); "I will hear, for I am gracious" (Exod. 22:26); "Bow down Your ear, and hear" (2 Kings 19:16); "But the Lord would not

to inform Rabshakeh; Rabshakeh in turn acted in his perceived best interest based on this act of informing. See also Rashi on Exod. 6:9. Based on this Rashi, *shama* can mean to act in response to what J.L. Austin called "expositive" words (see *How to Do Things with Words*, pp. 161-163, especially the third group on p. 162). It appears to me that Rashi's understanding is closer than Maimonides to the proper meaning, since the latter does not have the meaning "to act in response [to information]."

hearken to your voice, nor give ear unto you" (Deut. 1:45); "Yea, when you make many prayers, I will not hear" (Isa. 1:15); "For I will not hear you" (Jer. 7:16). There are many instances in which *shama* has this sense (*Guide* 1:45).

FURTHER: Whenever the term "to hear" is applied to God in the Torah, Onkelos the proselyte does not translate it literally, but paraphrases it, merely expressing that a certain speech reached Him, i.e., He perceived it, or that He accepted it or did not accept, when it refers to supplication and prayer as its object. The words "God heard" are therefore paraphrased by him regularly as either, "It was heard before the Lord," or "He accepted" when employed in reference to supplication and prayer; [e.g.] "I will surely accept" (Exod. 22:22). This principle is followed by Onkelos in his translation of the Torah without any exception... (*Guide* 1:48).

Maimonides' analysis can be presented in the following chart:

Meaning of *Shama* (General)	When Applied to God
Physical hearing	Perception
Obeisance	Response to prayer or wish
Understanding	Perception

FURTHER: ... in some cases the Law contains a truth which is itself the only object of that Law, as, e.g., the truth of the Unity, Eternity, and Incorporeality of God; in other cases, that truth is only the means of securing the removal of injustice, or the acquisition of good morals; such is the belief that God is angry with those who oppress their fellow-men, as it is said, "My anger shall flare up and I will kill," or the belief that God hears the crying of the oppressed and vexed, to deliver them out of the hands of the oppressor and tyrant, as it is written, "and it shall come to pass that when he cries out to Me, I will hear, for I am gracious" (v. 26) (*Guide* 3:28).

> From this passage, it appears that Maimonides differentiates between truths that are absolute and removed from any human interaction (God's unity, eternity, incorporeality), and truths about how God relates to man (God is angered by those who oppress others, God hears the cries of the oppressed, God delivers them from tyranny).

22:24. When you lend money to any of My people that is poor among you... — ... we are commanded to lend to a pauper in order to distance and lighten his burden. And this commandment is stronger and more obligatory than the commandment of charity. For if someone is already disgraced enough to show his face to ask people for money, then he does not feel his distress as deeply as one who hides his face and wants to be helped, and does not want his condition publicized so that he not be embarrassed.

And the source of this commandment is what God, may He be exalted, said, "When [*im*] you lend money to any of My people that is poor among you." And the language of the *Mekhilta*: "Every *im* in the Torah is discretionary, except for three cases," and one of those is "*Im* you lend money to any of My people." The Sages said, "'*Im* you lend money' — this is an obligation. You say it is an obligation? Maybe it is only an optional activity? Therefore we learn, "you shall surely lend" (Deut. 15:8), which teaches it is obligatory, not discretionary" (*ShM*, Pos. 197).

> Elsewhere Maimonides adds, "And the Torah was exacting with someone who refused to lend to a pauper, as it says, "[Beware lest there be a thought in your wicked heart, saying: The seventh year, the year of release, is approaching]

and your eye be evil against your impoverished brother"
(Deut. 15:9) (*Malveh ve-Loveh* 1:1).

... you shall not be like a creditor [*ke-nosheh*]... — ... we are
commanded that the creditor not demand money from the borrower
when we know that he is unable to repay the loan, as God, may He be
exalted, said, "you shall not be like a creditor." And in *Bava Metzia* it
is stated, "How do we know that if someone has lent a *maneh* to his
friend, and he knows his friend cannot repay it, he may not even walk
in front of him? Because it says, 'you shall not be like a creditor'"
(75b). And in the *Mekhilta*: "'you shall not be like a creditor' — you
shall not be visible to him constantly." And know that this prohibition
also includes someone who asks for a loan on interest. And similarly
the Sages said that someone who lends on interest violates what He
said, "[to any of My people...] you shall not be like a creditor," as I
will explain later (*ShM*, Neg. 234, he makes the same point at *Malveh
ve-Loveh* 1:2; the "later" refers to Neg. 237).

FURTHER: According to Torah law, when a creditor demands
repayment of the loan, if the borrower has property, we set some aside
for him, and we give the rest to the creditor, as we have explained.
And if the borrower has nothing, or only has property set aside for
himself, the borrower goes free and we do not imprison him, and we
do not say to him, "Bring proof that you are poor," and we do not
make him take an oath as we would do to gentiles, as it says, "you
shall not be like a creditor." Rather we say to the creditor, "If you
know that the person who owes you has property, go and seize it"
(*Malveh ve-Loveh* 2:1).

FURTHER: If a person takes an oath that he has no property and all
that he earns is given to the creditors, we do not allow each creditor
to make him swear. Rather, one oath satisfies all of the creditors. And
this is an enactment of the later authorities and we are not punctilious
to be stringent; rather we are lenient.

If someone is known to be poor, and is honest, and walks justly, and this is known and disseminated to the judge and to the majority of people, and a creditor comes and tries to make him take an oath [concerning his poverty] according to this enactment, and it is clear to the plaintiff that he does not doubt his impoverished state, but only wishes to cause him distress with this oath, and to afflict him, and to publicly embarrass him, in order to take vengeance upon him, or to force him to borrow money from gentiles on interest, or to take his wife's possessions to give to him to relieve him of the oath, it seems to me that it is forbidden for a judge who fears Heaven to impose this oath, and if the judge makes him swear, he violates a negative commandment of the Torah [*bittel lo ta'aseh*], as it says, "you shall not be like a creditor" (*Malveh ve-Loveh* 2:3-4).

... you shall not charge interest. — ... we are forbidden from dealing in loans with interest, whether as the creditor or the borrower, nor to be a guarantor to either of them, nor to be a witness for them, and not to write a contract between them in which they reach an agreement that includes interest. And this is what God, may He be exalted, "you shall not charge interest."

And the Talmud in *Bava Metzia* (75b) states: A guarantor and witnesses only violate the prohibition of "you shall not charge interest." And there it is explained that the scribe has the same status as the witnesses and the guarantor [in terms of violating this prohibition].

And there it is explained that this prohibition of "you shall not charge interest," although it includes the intermediaries, meaning everyone who is handling the transaction, includes also the creditor. And therefore, someone who lends on interest violates six prohibitions:

(1) "you shall not be like a creditor" (Exod. 22:24),
(2) "You shall not give your money on interest [*neshekh*]" (Lev. 25:37),

340

(3) "nor lend him your food for profit" (Lev. 25:37),

(4) "Do not take interest [*neshekh*] from him" (Lev. 25:36),

(5) "you shall not charge interest [*neshekh*]" (Exod. 22:24),

(6) "Do not place a stumbling block before the blind" (Lev. 19:14).

And there the Sages said: the borrower, the lender, the guarantor, and the witnesses all transgress a negative commandment. And the Sages said: even the scribe!

They violate "do not give him" and "do not take from him" and "you shall not be like a creditor" and "you shall not charge interest" and "Do not place a stumbling block before the blind."

And in the Talmud, Abaye said the lender violates all of them, and the borrower violates "do not deduct" and "Do not place a stumbling block before the blind," and the guarantor and the witnesses only violate "you shall not charge interest."

And someone who violates this prohibition, if it is definitely interest [i.e., a biblical prohibition], then we take it from him and return to the person from whom it was taken (*ShM*, Neg. 237; similarly *PhM Bava Metzia* 5:12).

22:25. If you take your neighbor's garment as a pledge [*im ḥavol taḥbol*]... — ... the Targum of *im ḥavol taḥbol* is *im mishkona tissav* ["if you take a pledge"] (*PhM Shekalim* 1:3).

... you shall deliver it to him before the sun goes down. — ... we are commanded to return a pledge to its Jewish owners when he has need for it. If it is something that he needs in the day, like the tools of his trade, he must return it during the day and take it as a pledge at night. And if it is something that he needs at night, like clothing or a covering that he sleeps in, he should return it at night and take it as a pledge in the day.

341

And the language of the *Mekhilta* is, "'you shall deliver it to him before the sun goes down' — this refers to daytime clothing that you return to him for the entire day, nighttime clothing that you return to him for the entire night. How do we know this? As it says, 'You shall surely return the pledge again when the sun goes down' (Deut. 24:13). From here we say that we entrust daytime clothing at night and nighttime clothing during the day, and we return daytime clothing in the day and nighttime clothing at night."

And it has already been explained in *Makkot* (16a) that God, may He be exalted, said, "'you shall not enter his house to retrieve the pledge' (Deut. 24:10) — this is a negative commandment (see Neg. 239) connected to a positive commandment, and the positive commandment is 'You shall surely return the pledge again' (v. 13)." And the language of the *Sifra* is, "'You shall surely return the pledge again' teaches that he returns a daytime tool to him in the day and a nighttime tool at night. A quilt is returned at night and a plough during the day" (*ShM*, Pos. 199; see also *Malveh ve-Loveh* 3:5, to be quoted at Deut. 24:13).

22:26. For that is his only clothing, the only covering for his skin; in what shall he sleep? and it shall come to pass that when he cries out to Me, I will hear, for I am gracious. — See *ShM*, Neg. 240. Maimonides uses this phrase regarding the importance of giving charity and making loans accessible to the poor (*Matnot Ani'im* 10:3, to be quoted at Deut. 15:9); he explains the phrase "God heard" (*Guide* 1:45, quoted at Exod. 6:9); he provides a rationale for this commandment (*Guide* 3:28, quoted at Exod. 22:21-23).

22:27. You shall not revile the judges... — ... we are forbidden to curse a judge, as God, may He be exalted, said, "You shall not revile the judges." And someone who violates this commandment receives lashes (*ShM*, Neg. 315; also at *Sanhedrin* 26:1).

FURTHER: ... and in the *Mekhilta* we also learn "You shall not revile *Elohim*" to give the prohibition of blasphemy[173] (*ShM*, Neg. 60, to be quoted in full at Lev. 24:16; see also *Avodah Zarah* 2:7-8).

... nor curse a ruler [*nasi*] of your people. — ... we are forbidden to curse a ruler, as He, may He be exalted, said, "nor curse a ruler of your people." And Scripture uses the word *nasi* ["ruler"] to mean a king who has authority [*ha-melekh asher lo ha-memshalah*], asGod, may He be exalted, said, "When a ruler [*nasi*] sins" (Lev. 4:22). According to the Sages, this refers explicitly to the head of the academy of seventy elders. And the phrases "rulers and heads of the court" and "ruler and head of the court" appear throughout the Talmud and Mishnah. And they have also said that if a ruler waives his honor, his honor is waived, but if a king waives his honor, his honor is not waived.

And know that this prohibition includes both the ruler [*nasi*] and the king, since the commandment means that we are forbidden to curse anyone who has the highest governing authority, whether in civil government, or in Torah, which is the yeshiva. And this is all implied from this commandment. And someone who violates this commandment is liable for lashes (*ShM*, Neg. 316).

FURTHER: Whoever curses a judge of the judges of Israel violates a negative commandment, as it says, "You shall not revile the judges." And similarly if someone curses a ruler—whether it is the head of the great Sanhedrin or a king—he violates a negative commandment, as it says, "nor curse a ruler of your people." ... Since whoever issues a curse against any person is liable (see at Lev. 19:14), why is there a commandment specifically regarding a judge or a ruler? To make him liable for two violations.

Therefore if someone curses a regular Jew, whether man or woman, whether adult or minor, he receives one set of lashes. If he

---

173. The Hebrew word *Elohim* has a sacred meaning ("God") and a secular meaning ("judges"). Maimonides understands the verse to prohibit both cursing God (i.e., blasphemy) as well as cursing judges.

curses a judge, he receives two sets of lashes. If he curses a ruler, he receives three sets of lashes. And the son of a ruler who curses his father violates four separate prohibitions: three just like anybody else [who curses a ruler] and one because the ruler is his father....

... One does not receive lashes until he issues a curse with one of the Names, like the Tetragrammaton, or Shaddai, or Elohim, or one of the appellations of God, like the Merciful One [Ḥannun], the Jealous One [Kanna], or the like. And since one is guilty for using any of the appellations, if he issued a curse in any language, using one of the names by with the nations call the Holy One, Blessed is He, with any of the appellations he is guilty. The word "cursed" [*arur*] can mean an oath, a curse, or a ban of excommunication....

Even though a judge and a ruler can waive their honor, they cannot waive a curse against them. And similarly, if any commoner waived a curse against him, we [nevertheless] lash the one who issued the curse who has already sinned and become guilty (*Sanhedrin* 26:1-3, 6, with abridgments).

22:28. You shall not delay [in offering] your produce offerings and your liquid offerings... — ... we are forbidden from bringing the offerings out of order; rather we should bring them in the proper sequence. And the explanation of this is that wheat, for example, once it is threshed and piled up, has the status of *tevel*. And we should first take *terumah gedolah*, which is one fiftieth. And then we take a tenth of what remains, and that is the first tithe. And then we take a tenth of what remains, and that is the second tithe. And the *terumah gedolah* is given to the priest, and the first tithe is given to the Levite, and the second tithe is eaten by the owners in Jerusalem. And this is the order that is supposed to be followed. And this commandment comes to prohibit us from taking first what should be taken later, or taking later what should be taken first, as God, may He be exalted, said, "You shall not delay your produce offerings and your liquid offerings." It is as if the verse said: You shall not delay what is properly taken earlier of your produce offerings and your liquid offerings.

And the Mishnah in *Terumot* (3:6) it says, "If someone brings *terumah* before *bikkurim*, first tithe before *terumah*, or the second tithe before the first tithe, even though he violates a negative commandment, as it says, 'You shall not delay [in offering] your produce offerings and liquid offerings,' what has been done is valid."

And in the *Mekhilta* is says, "'Your produce [*mele'atkha*]' — this is the *bikkurim*, which are only harvested when ripe [*melai*], 'and your liquid offerings [*ve-dim'akha*]' — this is *terumah*, 'you shall not delay' — you shall not bring the second tithe before the first one, or the first tithe before *terumah*, or *terumah* before *bikkurim*." And there they said: Even though it is stated that if someone brought *terumah* before *bikkurim*, or the second tithe before the first, even though he violates a negative commandment, what has been done is valid (*ShM*, Neg. 154).

Rashi also understands *mele'atkha* as *bikkurim* and *ve-dim'akha* as *terumah*. See however Ibn Ezra (his own opinion and quoting Saadiah), Rashbam, Nahmanides, and Sforno.

... the firstborn of your sons shall you give to Me. — ... we are commanded to redeem the first born males and to give their price to the priest, as He, may He be exalted, said, "the firstborn of your sons shall you give to Me." And the explanation of this "giving" is that he should be redeemed from the priest, since it is like the priest already owns him, and we are acquiring him back for the price of fifty *sela*, and this is what He said, "You shall surely redeem the firstborn male" (Num. 18:15). And this is the commandment of "redeeming the son" [*pidyon ha-ben*]. And women are not obligated in this commandment; it is a commandment concerning the son which is incumbent on the father... (*ShM*, Pos. 80; see also Exod. 13:2).

22:29. Likewise shall you do to your ox and your sheep; seven days it shall be with its mother; on the eighth day you shall give it to Me. — This is in reference to a firstborn animal (*PhM Parah* 1:4).

> This is also the opinion of Ibn Ezra (long) and Sforno. Likewise, according to Kapach, this verse specifically applies to firstborn animals and not other offerings; see *PhM Zevaḥim* 14:2, note 4. Maimonides, in *ShM*, Pos. 60, quotes the prohibition of bringing any offering before its eighth day of life, based on Lev. 22:27, where he quotes this verse as a secondary source. See also *Guide* 3:49, to be quoted at Lev. 22:27.

FURTHER: The circumcision must take place on the eighth day (Lev. 12:3), because all living beings are after birth, within the first seven days, very weak and exceedingly tender, as if they were still in the womb of their mother; not until the eighth day can they be counted among those that enjoy the light of the world. That this is also the case with beasts may be inferred from the words of Scripture, "... seven days shall it be with its mother" (Exod. 22:29, Lev. 22:27), as if it had no vitality before the end of that period. In the same manner man is circumcised after the completion of seven days. The period has been fixed, and has not been left to everybody's judgment (*Guide* 3:49).

22:30. And you shall be men of holiness to Me... — It is not proper to count exhortations that encompass the entire Torah.... Many have already erred in this principle until they have counted "you shall be holy" (Lev. 19:2) as a [separate] positive commandment, and they did not realize that God's statement "you shall be holy," and "you shall sanctify yourselves and be holy" (Lev. 11:44) — these are commandments to fulfill the entire Torah, and it is like saying: Be holy in the state of performing everything which I command you about and take heed about everything I have warned you against.

And the language of the *Sifra* is, "'you shall be holy' — you shall be separate," which means you should be separated from all of the disgusting items that I have warned you about. And in the *Mekhilta* it says, "'And you shall be men of holiness to Me' (Exod. 22:30) — Isi ben Judah says that the Holy One, Blessed is He, instituted a new commandment, He increased their holiness," which means that this directive does not stand on its own; rather one who follows in the commandments he was given, and fulfills the directive will be called "holy." And there is no difference between God saying "you shall be holy" or "perform my commandments." ... And the language of the *Sifra* is, "'and you shall be holy' — this is the holiness of the commandments" (*ShM, Shoresh* 4).

... and you shall not eat any animal mauled in the field; you shall throw it to the dogs. — ... we are forbidden to eat an animal that has been mauled, as He, may He be exalted, said, "and you shall not eat any animal mauled in the field." However, the simple meaning of the verse is how it is mentioned in the *Mekhilta*, as they said that Scripture spoke of the most common case, because the place where most animals are mauled is in the field.

However, the oral tradition has another explanation of this verse: "it is 'an animal mauled in the field,' therefore 'you shall not eat' it." This means that once any [sacral] meat is removed from the walls, it becomes like flesh of an animal that was mauled. For example, flesh of most holy offerings, once it leaves the courtyard, or flesh of the lesser holy offerings, once it leaves the walls [of Jerusalem], or the flesh of the Passover offering, once leaves the group, or once a fetus extends its hand out [of the womb], as was explained in the fourth chapter of *Ḥullin* (68a; see also *PhM Pesaḥim* 7:12, *PhM Zevaḥim* 8:12, *Ma'aseh ha-Korbanot* 11:6). All of these types of flesh are called "mauled" [*tereifah*], and whoever eats an olive's measure receives lashes according to Torah law.

347

And similarly flesh from a living animal is also called *tereifah*, and whoever eats it receives lashes [from the Torah]. In the Talmud, in Ḥullin (102b) they said, "'and you shall not eat any animal mauled in the field' — this refers to the limb of a living animal" (*ShM*, Neg. 181; see *Ma'akhalot Asurot* 4:6-10 and 5:9).

FURTHER: Blood and *neveilah*, i.e., the flesh of an animal that died of itself (Deut. 14:21), are indigestible, and injurious as food: *Tereifah*, an animal in a diseased state (Exod. 22:30), is on the way of becoming a *neveilah* (*Guide* 3:48).

It appears that according to Maimonides, *tereifah* is not prohibited on its own right, but on account of its susceptibility to become *neveilah*.

Exodus 23

23:1. You shall not spread a vain [*shav*] report... — ... a judge is forbidden from hearing the words of one litigant when the other litigant is not present, as God, may He be exalted, said, "You shall not spread a vain report," because most claims that are brought not in the presence of the other litigant are false [*shav*], and it is forbidden for the judge to hear those words, so that improper and untrue ideas not enter his mind.

And the language of the *Mekhilta* is, "'You shall not spread a vain report' — this is a prohibition to the judge to not hear one litigant until the other litigant is present. This is a prohibition that a litigant not make his words heard to the judge until the other one is present. In regards to the same prohibition, it says, "Keep far from a false charge" (Exod. 23:7), as explained in the fourth chapter of *Shevuot* (31a). And included in this commandment is the prohibition against speaking *lashon hara*, receiving *lashon hara*, and giving false testimony... (*ShM*, Neg. 281; see also *Sanhedrin* 21:7, where he quotes Deut. 1:16 for similar effect).

> The Jewish requirement that both litigants be present is similar to the right to confront one's accuser, which is enshrined as a right in the U.S. Constitution: "In all criminal prosecutions, the accused shall enjoy the right... to be confronted with the witnesses against him..." (Sixth Amendment). Its origins are surely earlier, and Christian sources testify to a Roman custom to this effect: "It is not the manner of the Romans to deliver any man up to die before the accused has met his accusers face to face, and has been given a chance to defend himself against the charges" (Apostles 25:16). See further Frank R. Herrmann and Brownlow M. Speer, "Facing the Accuser: Ancient and Medieval Precursors of the Confrontation Clause" 1 34 (1994): 481-552.

... you shall not join hands with the wicked to be a malicious witness. — ... a judge is not permitted to receive testimony from a wicked person and from acting based on his testimony, as God, may He be exalted, said, "you shall not join hands with the wicked to be a malicious witness." The oral tradition explains: "'you shall not join hands with the wicked to be a malicious witness,' which excludes robbers and thieves, who are not eligible to give testimony, as it says, 'When a malicious witness arises against a man...' (Deut. 19:16)" (*ShM*, Neg. 286).

FURTHER: Wicked people are ineligible to give testimony according to the Torah, as it says, "you shall not join hands with the wicked to be a malicious witness." According to oral tradition, we learn, "you shall not allow a wicked person to be a witness." And even if a valid witness knows that his co-witness is wicked, and the judges do not know about his wickedness, then it is forbidden to testify with him, even if the testimony is true, since he is joining together with him, so the valid witness is found joining hands with the wicked so that his testimony be accepted. And needless to say, if a valid witness knows that the testimony of the second witness is false, then it is forbidden for him to testify with him, as it says, "you shall not allow a wicked person to be a witness."

What is meant by "wicked"? Whoever commits a transgression for which one is deserving lashes is wicked and ineligible to give testimony, for the Torah calls someone who is deserving lashes as "wicked," as it says, "And it shall be that if the wicked man is worthy to be beaten" (Deut. 25:2). And needless to say someone who is liable to capital punishment in court is ineligible, as it says, "who is guilty [*rasha*, lit., 'wicked'] to die" (Num. 35:31) (*Edut* 10:1-2).

Maimonides repeats this point at *PhM Sanhedrin* 3:3. See also *PhM Terumot* 6:3, where Maimonides includes violating this prohibition as also a violation of "you shall not place a stumbling block in front of the blind" (see at Lev. 19:14).

In his "Epistle on Martyrdom," Maimonides quotes an opinion that if someone claiming that "anyone who avows that that man [Muhammad] is a prophet, though he does it under compulsion, he is a wicked person, disqualified by Scripture from serving as a witness, since the Torah rules, 'You shall not join hands with the guilty,' that is, do not make a wicked man a witness." However, Maimonides says that this objector has "brought darkness into the hearts of men" (ch. 1). Clearly, Maimonides did not believe Muhammad was a prophet, but one only becomes invalid as a witness when he commits an act for which he is liable for lashes or capital punishment (*Edut* 10:1-2).

23:2. You shall not follow a multitude to do harm, you shall not answer in a dispute, you are not to side with the multitude to pervert justice. — ... a judge is forbidden to follow the majority when there is only a majority of one. And the explanation of this is that when the disagreement between the judges regarding the defendant [lit., "sinner"], and some of them say that he is deserving of capital punishment, and some say he is not deserving of capital punishment, and those voting to convict have a majority of one, then it is not permitted to execute this defendant. And God the true Judge made it forbidden to execute him unless there are at least two more judges to convict than to acquit, as He said, "You shall not follow the multitude to do harm," which means that you should not be drawn after any [simple] majority that happens to issue a capital punishment, and this is the singular meaning of "to do harm [*le-ra'ot*]."

And the language of the *Mekhilta* is: "If eleven acquit and twelve convict, I would think he is guilty. Therefore it says, 'You shall not follow the multitude to do harm.'" And there they said, "Your vote to acquit can be by a majority of one, and to convict by a majority of two" (*ShM*, Neg. 282).

FURTHER: If a court is divided, so that some say [the defendant] is not guilty, and some say he is guilty, we follow the majority, and this is a positive commandment, as it says, "to side with the multitude." When is this the case? In financial suits, and other cases about what is prohibited and permitted, ritually impure and pure, and the like. However, in capital cases if they are divided regarding a sinner whether or not he should be executed, if the majority acquits him he is acquitted, and if the majority convicts him he is not executed unless at least two more vote to convict than to acquit.

According to oral tradition, we learn regarding this that the Torah commands, "you shall not follow a multitude to do harm [*ra'ot*]," which means that if the majority is inclined towards "harm"—to execute [the defendant]—you shall not follow them unless there is a bigger inclination [to convict than to acquit] and there are two additional votes to convict [than to acquit], as it says, "to side with the multitude." Your inclination that he is good can be by the word of one, and that he is evil by the word of two. And all of these matters are part of the oral tradition (*Sanhedrin* 8:1; see also *ShM*, Neg. 282 and *PhM Sanhedrin* 4:1).

FURTHER: … a judge is forbidden to rely on the opinion of another judge beside whom he sits, whether to convict or to acquit, without achieving a full understanding according to Torah law. And this is what He said, "you shall not answer in a dispute… to side [with the multitude to pervert justice]." This means that one should not seek to just follow another's opinion, so that he will follow the majority or the most distinguished judges and remain quiet from what is in your heart in this case.

And the language of the *Mekhilta* is, "'you shall not answer in a dispute… to side' — so that you not say during the time of the vote, "It is enough for me to be like this person." Rather, you should speak what is before you [to say]. You might think this is only in financial cases. Therefore it adds, 'to side with the multitude.'"

And from this prohibition also comes the commandment that after voting to acquit, a judge may not retract and vote to convict, as it says, "you shall not answer in a dispute… to side," which means you should not turn your words towards conviction. And similarly we do not [re-]open a capital case to conviction [after an acquittal], as God, may He be exalted, said, "you shall not answer in a dispute to side" [towards conviction after acquittal]. However, we may retract [a conviction] to acquit, but we may not retract towards conviction. And similarly we do not start [a vote] with the most distinguished judge. And all of these matters are learned from the statement "you shall not answer in a dispute to turn" [away from a senior judge] … (*ShM*, Neg. 283; also *Sanhedrin* 10:1).

FURTHER: Included in this prohibition is that if someone is arguing for acquittal in a capital crime, he cannot change and argue for conviction, as it says, "you shall not answer in dispute… to side." When does this apply? During deliberation. However, at the time of voting, someone who was arguing for acquittal can switch to be counted among those in favor of conviction (*Sanhedrin* 10:2).

FURTHER: It is one of the principles of our Torah that there always must be an odd number of judges, so that if there is a disagreement among the judges on how to rule, there will always be a majority that agrees with one side, and a minority with the opposite, and we will follow the majority opinion, as the Torah has obligated us, in saying, "to side with the multitude." Therefore, a court should not be composed of less than three judges (*PhM Sanhedrin* 1:1).

FURTHER: [Maimonides says that after Moses died, some concepts were universally agreed to, based on the thirteen hermeneutical principles. However, regarding others...] ... there were some which descended into debate between two opinions: one person would make arguments and reach one conclusion, and the other would make arguments and reach a different conclusion, as is the way that different opinions are formed. When these debates arose, and they descended into these debates, they would follow the majority, as Scripture says, "to side with the multitude" (Introduction to *PhM*).

FURTHER: [The following is excerpted from a passage explaining that prophets cannot create new laws:] ... if there are a thousand prophets, all at the level of Elijah and Elisha, who offer one explanation, and a thousand and one sages offer the opposite explanation, then [it is proper] "to side with the multitude" and follow the words of the thousand and one sages and not the words of the thousand distinguished prophets (Introduction to *PhM*).

One might think that prophets, who communicate directly with God, are of a higher stature than mere sages. Here Maimonides is saying that prophets do not have any higher status than sages. Even if a prophet is teaching a law, he is only doing it in his capacity as a sage, not as a prophet.

23:3. And you shall not favor the poor in judgment. — ... a judge is prohibited from showing compassion on the poor in judgment. Rather, he must judge truthfully and not from a place of compassion for him, rather he should treat the poor and rich equally, and force them to pay what they owe. And this is what God, may He be exalted, said, "And you shall not favor the poor in judgment." And this prohibition has been repeated in different language, "you shall not be partial to the poor" (Lev. 19:15).

And the language of the *Sifra* is, "So that you do not say he is poor, and since the rich [defendant] and I are obligated to sustain him, I will rule in his favor so he will be sustained in an honorable way. Therefore it says, 'you shall not be partial to the poor" (*ShM*, Neg. 277; also *Sanhedrin* 20:4).

23:4. If you find your enemy's [*oyvekha*] ox or donkey going astray, you shall surely bring him back again. — It is a positive commandment to return a lost object to its owners as God, may He be exalted, said, "If you find your enemy's ox... you shall surely bring him back again" (Exod. 23:4), "you shall surely return it to your brother" (Deut. 22:1). And in the explanation, the Sages said: Returning a lost object is a positive commandment (*Bava Metzia* 30a, 32a). And further they stated (in the *Mekhilta*) regarding a lost object: it comes out that we learn that he violates a positive commandment and a negative commandment (*ShM*, Pos. 204; see Neg. 269, next).

FURTHER: It is forbidden to ignore a lost object [lit., "to hide oneself from a lost object"]. Rather, we should take it and return it to its owners as God, may He be exalted, said, "you may not hide yourself from it" (Deut. 22:3). And we have already explained (Pos. 204, above) the statement of the Sages in the *Mekhilta* that regarding a lost object [that someone who turns away] violates a negative commandment and a positive commandment. And the language of the Talmud is: "returning a lost object is a positive commandment and a negative commandment" (*Bava Metzia* 30a, 32a). And in the book of Deuteronomy this commandment is repeated and it becomes a separate prohibition, as He said, "You shall not watch your neighbor's ox or sheep straying away and ignore them..." (Deut. 22:1). And in the *Sifrei* it is stated, "'You shall not watch your neighbor's ox' — this is a negative commandment. And later it says, 'If you find your enemy's [*oyvekha*] ox or donkey going astray, you shall surely bring him back again' — this is a positive commandment" (*ShM*, Neg. 269).

Regarding a lost object, Maimonides counts both a positive commandment: "you shall surely bring him back again" (Exod. 23:4) and "you shall surely return it to your brother' (Deut. 22:1). He also sees a negative commandment to not ignore a lost object: "you may not hide yourself from it" (Deut. 22:3). It seems that one would be able to violate one without violating the other: if someone discovered a lost object and collected it with intent to return it, he has not violated "you may not hide yourself from it," but if he subsequently never returned the object he has not fulfilled "you shall surely return."

FURTHER: ... the commandment "you shall surely return" (Deut. 22:3) was instituted to remove the quality of selfishness (*Shemonah Perakim*, ch. 4).

FURTHER: ... the object of the law of restoring lost property to its owner is obvious. In the first instance, it is in itself a good feature in man's character. Secondly, its benefit is mutual: for if a person does not return the lost property of his fellow-man, nobody will restore to him what he may lose, just as those who do not honor their parents cannot expect to be honored by their children (*Guide* 3:40).

Notice that Maimonides here gives what we might call an objective and a relativistic reason. The relativistic reason is that someone should return a lost object, because that person would want his own lost object returned to him. He also gives an objective reason, i.e., it is objectively the right thing to do.

23:5. If you see your enemy's donkey struggling under its load, and consider abandoning him, you shall surely help him. — ...

we are forbidden to abandon someone who is distressed under his load and stalled in his journey. Rather, we should assist him and remove the load from him so that he can adjust it and carry it, or we should carry it with him, whether he carries it himself [lit., "on his back"] or his animal carries it, as is explained in the details of this commandment, as He said, "and consider abandoning him, you shall surely help him."

And the language of the *Mekhilta* is, "'and you consider abandoning him, you shall surely help him' — thus we learn that he violates a positive commandment and a negative commandment." There is a separate prohibition on this topic, as it says, "You shall not watch your brother's donkey [or ox falling on the road and hide yourself from them; you shall surely lift him up]" (Deut. 22:4). And in the *Sifrei* it says, "'You shall not see your brother's donkey' is a negative commandment," and later it says, "'If you see your enemy's donkey' is a positive commandment" ... (*ShM*, Neg. 270).

FURTHER: ... we are commanded to remove the load from an animal that is struggling with its load on the road, as God, may He be exalted, said, "If you see your enemy's donkey... you shall surely help him." And the language of the *Mekhilta* is, "'you shall surely help' — is unloading [*perikah*]." And there they said, "'you shall surely help' — we learn that he violates a positive commandment and a negative commandment." That is to say, we are commanded to remove [the load] from it, and we are also forbidden from leaving it when it is struggling under its load, as will be explained in the section of negative commandments (Neg. 270). And if someone abandon it struggling under its burden, he violates a positive commandment and a negative commandment. Thus it is clear that "you shall surely help" is a positive commandment (*ShM*, Pos. 202; see also *Rotze'aḥ* 13:1-2).

FURTHER: ... we are commanded to load an animal or a person when he is by himself, whether we were the ones to remove the load, or someone else already unloaded it. For just as we are commanded to take the load off, we are also commanded to reload it, as He said, 'you shall surely lift him up' (Deut. 22:4). And the language of the *Mekhilta* is, "'you shall surely lift him up" — this is loading [*te'inah*]." The details of this commandment have been explained in the second chapter of *Bava Metzia*, and there (32a) it is explained that unloading is a commandment from the Torah, and loading up is a commandment from the Torah (*ShM*, Pos. 203).

> Maimonides does not quote our verse in *ShM*, Pos. 203, but quotes Deut. 22:4 instead. However for the sake of completeness it is included here. Thus Maimonides counts three separate commandments regarding someone struggling with a load: the prohibition of abandoning such a person (Neg. 270), *perikah*, the obligation to help unload the animal (Pos. 202), and *te'inah*, the obligation to help reload the animal (Pos. 203).

FURTHER: If he took the load off and put it back on, and it fell off again, one is obligated to take the load off and reload it again, even a hundred times, as it says, "you shall surely help" and "you shall surely lift him up." Therefore one must accompany him for the length of a *parsah* unless the person bearing the load says, "I do not need you."

When does someone become obligated to unload and reload with him? When he sees him in a way that is like "encountering," since it says, "If you see [*tir'eh*]" and then "If you find [*tifga*]" (v. 4). And how much is this? The Sages measured this at 266 2/3 cubits, which is 1/7.5 *mil* [=2/15 *mil*]. If he is farther away than that, he is not beholden to him.

It is a commandment from the Torah to unburden the animal for free. However, to reload the animal is a mitzvah for which he can charge a fee. Similarly, for the time that he accompanies the animal with him for the length of a *parsah*, he may charge a fee.

If he found his colleague's animal struggling, even if the owners are not with it, it is a mitzvah to remove the burden from it and to readjust the burden on it, as it says, "you shall surely help" and "you shall surely lift" — regardless of circumstances. If so, why does it say "with him"? For if the owner of the animal is with it, and goes and sits there and says to the person he meets, "Since this commandment applies to you, if you wish to unload it yourself, then unload it," then he is exempt, as it says, "with him." However, if the owner of the animal is elderly or infirm, then he is obligated to unload and reload it himself (*Rotze'ah* 13:5-8).

FURTHER: The word "enemy" used in the Torah refers to an Israelite and not a gentile. But how is it possible that an Israelite could hate another Israelite, when it says, "You shall not hate your brother in your heart" (Lev. 19:17)? The Sages said this might arise if he sees someone committing a transgression and warns him, yet he did not stop, then it is a commandment to hate him until he repents and returns from his wickedness. And even though he has not yet repented, if he finds him distressed by his load, it is a commandment to unload and reload with him, and not leave him close to death, lest he slow down because of his property and become endangered.

And the Torah was meticulous over the lives of Jews, whether sinners or righteous ones, since they are attached to God and believe in the fundamentals of religion, as it says, "Say unto them, 'As I live,' declares the Lord God, 'Do I desire the death of the wicked? Rather let the wicked man repent his ways and live'" (Ezek. 33:11) (*Rotze'ah* 13:14).

FURTHER: ... the instructions "you shall surely help" (Exod. 23:5) and "you shall surely raise up" (Deut. 22:4) weaken the qualities of wrath and anger (*Shemonah Perakim*, ch. 4).

Concerning this commandment, Rashi writes, "Now who is it who sees his enemy being kind to him, whose heart will not be inspired to embrace and kiss him?" (on Psalm 99:4). There are several issues here. First, Maimonides assumes that one person would only consider another as an *oyev* (enemy) within legal parameters. Therefore he concludes that the only type of *oyev* is a sinner whom one is obligated to hate. However, Rashi seems to imply that the two were rivals for reasons beyond what *halakhah* would permit.

Second, the reason for the commandment is different (and this is significant because Rashi rarely engages in *ta'amei ha-mitzvot*—speculating in reasons for the commandments). For Rashi, the act of kindness in unloading can help mend the broken relationship between two rivals. Maimonides gives two entirely different rationales. In *Shemonah Perakim*, he says the reason is to reduce the quality of anger. (For Rashi, it is an interpersonal commandment, while for Maimonides here it is to reduce the quality of anger in the individual.) However, Maimonides also gives a second answer (*Rotze'ah* 13:14), where he says he must not let the wicked person perish before he has a chance to repent.

23:6. You shall not pervert the justice of the poor in his suit. — If two people come before you in judgment, one is pious and one is wicked, do not say, "Since he is wicked and has the presumption of falsehood, and the other one has the presumption of honesty, I will be show favor against the wicked one. Regarding this it says, "You shall not pervert the justice of the poor in his suit." Even though he is poor in merits, you shall not pervert judgment against him (*Sanhedrin* 20:5; also *ShM*, Neg. 278).

23:7. Keep far from a false matter... — See *ShM*, Neg. 281 and *Sanhedrin* 21:7, both quoted at v. 1.

FURTHER: How do we know that a judge should not advocate for the words [of one of the litigants]? As it says, "Keep far from a false matter." Rather he should say what appears to him [to be true] and then he should be quiet (*Sanhedrin* 21:10).

FURTHER: Similarly, if a student is sitting before his master, and sees a reason to vindicate a pauper or convict a wealthy man, if he remains quiet, then he violates "Do not be afraid of any person" (Deut. 1:17) and "Keep far from a false matter" (Exod. 23:7). And how to we know that if a student sees his master erring in judgment, that he should not say, "I will wait until he renders judgment and then I will refute it and construct it myself so that it will be known by my name"? Since it says, "Keep far from a false matter" (*Sanhedrin* 22:2-3).

FURTHER: And if a judge knows that a claim is fraudulent, how do we know that he should not say, "I will render a decision and it will be the burden around the witnesses' necks"? Because it says, "Keep far from a false matter" (Exod. 23:7). Rather, what should he do? In a capital case, he should examine and question the witnesses with great care and if it appears to him that there is no fraud he should render a decision based on their testimony. However, if his heart is thumping [because of the belief] that there is fraud; or his mind is not convinced by the words of the witnesses even though he cannot disqualify them; or he is inclined to believe that this litigant is fraudulent and deceptive and that he persuaded the witnesses, even if they are reliable and the litigant misled them; or it appears to him that from what was testified there are concealed factors that they do not wish to reveal—in all of these circumstances and in anything similar, if they come to the judge for a ruling, he is forbidden to render a verdict. Instead, he should recuse himself from that case, and someone else whose heart is at peace with the case should judge it. These matters are given over to the person's heart, as Scripture states, "judgment is God's" (Deut. 1:17) (*Sanhedrin* 24:3).

FURTHER: If he owes three people, and denies owing one of them, the other two should not testify [that they are owed more] and when they collect [enough for all three], divide it. Regarding these matters and the like, Scripture warns and says, "Keep far from a false matter" (*To'en ve-Nit'an* 16:10).

FURTHER: If a teacher says to his student, "You know that if they gave me all the money in the world, I would not lie. This person owes me money and I have one witness against him. Go and join with him." If he joins with him, he is a false witness.

If he says to him, "Go and stand with the witness but you do not need to testify. Rather when the borrower sees, he will become afraid because he will think that you are two witnesses and he will admit it himself." It is prohibited for him to stand and appear as if he is a witness, even if he does not testify. And regarding this and the like, it is said, "Keep far from a false matter" (*Edut* 16:5-6).

... and do not execute the innocent or the unconvicted, for I will not vindicate the wicked. — ... we are forbidden to draw unfounded conclusions [about someone's guilt], even if it is almost certain [that he is guilty]. For example if a man is chasing after his enemy to kill him, and in order to escape he enters a house, and the pursuer also enters after him, and we enter after them and the person being chased is found murdered, convulsing, and his enemy who was chasing him is standing over him and the knife is in his hand and the two of them are dripping with blood—even in this case the pursuer is not executed by the Sanhedrin in these circumstances, since there are no witnesses testifying who saw the slaying.

And this prohibition comes from the Torah of truth against executing him, as it says, "and do not execute the innocent or the unconvicted, for I will not vindicate the wicked." And in the *Mekhilta* it says, "If they saw him chasing after his colleague to kill him and they warned him, saying, 'He is an Israelite, he is a son of the covenant. If you kill him you will be killed,' and then they went out of sight, and they found him killed, convulsing, with the sword dripping in blood, I might have thought that he can be found guilty. Therefore it says, 'and do not execute the innocent or the unconvicted.'"

And do not draw back from this ruling and do not be astonished from this law. For among all possible events, there are some which are close to absolute certainty and there are those which are highly doubtful, and there are some in the middle. And the meaning of the word "possible" is very broad. And if the Torah had permitted us to judge capital cases on the standard of "possible" that is close to absolute certainty, as the example above, then we would get gradually farther away from certainty until sometimes we were executing people on minimal evidence and the judge's whim.

Therefore God, may He be exalted, closed this door, and said that no punishment should be administered unless witnesses testify that they know with certainty that this person committed this act— with certainty, without a doubt, and without any speculation.

And just as we do not convict even on strong circumstantial evidence, then we will acquit the sinner. However if we convict based on speculation, then it is possible one day to execute an innocent man. And it is more important and desirable to acquit a thousand guilty men than to one day execute an innocent man.

And similarly if two witnesses testify that he committed two capital offenses, and each one of the two saw him violate one commandment but did not see him violate the other, then he will not be executed. For example if one witness testifies that he performed forbidden labor on the Sabbath, and warned him about it. And the second witness testifies that he engaged in forbidden acts of foreign worship and warned him about it, then he is not executed by stoning. They said, "If one testified that he worshipped the sun, and one testified that he worshipped the moon, I would have thought that they can be combined. Therefore it says, 'and do not execute the innocent or the unconvicted'" (*ShM*, Neg. 290).

23:8. You shall not take a bribe, for the bribe blinds those who can see and subverts the words of the righteous. — ... a judge is forbidden to take a bribe from one of the litigants, even to issue to the proper judgment, as He, may He be exalted, said, "You shall not take a bribe." And this prohibition has been repeated (Deut. 16:19). And in the *Sifrei*, it is written "'You shall not take a bribe' — even to acquit the innocent or to convict the guilty" (*ShM*, Neg. 274; also *Sanhedrin* 23:1; see also Deut. 27:25).

23:9. And you shall not distress the convert, for you know the heart of the stranger, for you were strangers in the land of Egypt. — See on Exod. 22:20.

23:10-11. And six years you shall sow your land and gather your harvest. And on the seventh you shall let it rest and lie still, and the poor of your people may eat, and what they leave the wild animals shall eat. So shall you do to your vineyards and olive orchards. — ... we are commanded to declare as ownerless everything that grows in the earth on the sabbatical year. We are also commanded to declare as ownerless all of the growths of our land for anyone, as God, may He be exalted, said, "And on the seventh you shall let it rest and lie still." And the language of the *Mekhilta* is, "Were vineyards and olive orchards not included? Why were they mentioned explicitly? To relate that just as a vineyard is governed by a positive and negative commandment, so too everything else that related to a positive commandment also has a negative commandment apply to it."

The meaning of this is as I will explain. And what is stated, "And on the seventh you shall let it rest and lie still" includes everything that grows in the earth must be declared ownerless on the seventh year—grapes, figs, olives, peaches, pomegranates, wheat, barley, and everything similar to this. Here it is made known that releasing everything is a positive commandment. Then is the specific statement, when it says, "[so] shall you do to your vineyards and olive orchards." And then is the general principle about whatever grows on the ground, and then the specific commandment regarding only grapes and olives, since Scripture specifically makes a prohibition against gathering produce of the vineyard, as it says, "do not gather the grapes of your unpruned vines" (Lev. 25:5). And just as it is a positive commandment to declare the vineyard as ownerless, withholding it is a negative commandment. Similarly everything that grows on the seventh year that it is explained that they declared ownerless in accordance with a positive commandment, then withholding it is a negative commandment, and the laws of olives should be like the laws of grapes regarding a positive and negative commandment, and the laws of all other fruit are alike.

Thus from everything prior it is clear that declaring as ownerless the growths of the seventh year is a positive commandment.... And this is only an obligation from the Torah regarding fruits of the land of Israel (ShM, Pos. 134).

FURTHER: It is a positive commandment to release everything that grows from the ground on the seventh year, as it says, "And on the seventh you shall let it rest and lie still." And whoever locks his vineyard or fences off his vineyard violates a positive commandment. And the same is also true if he gathers all of his fruits into his house. Rather he should declare it as ownerless, so everyone may have equal claim to it, as it says, "… and the poor of your people may eat." However he is permitted to bring a small amount into his own house, just as one will take from ownerless property: five jugs of oil and fifteen jugs of wine. And if he brings more than that, it is permitted (*Shemittah ve-Yovel* 4:24).

FURTHER: If someone declares his property ownerless only with regard to the poor, Bet Shammai says that it is ownerless and therefore does not need to be tithed. And they learn this from God's statement, "you shall leave them to the poor and to the stranger" (Lev. 19:10). And they said that there is a separate type of "leaving" [*azivah*] that applies to the poor but not to the rich. And Bet Hillel's source is God's statement concerning the sabbatical year "you shall let it rest and lie still" — and what does it mean "lie still" [*u-n'tashtahh*]? There is another *netishah* besides this. [From here, Bet Hillel derives that just as in the sabbatical year, the field must be declared ownerless so that the rich and poor are equal in taking its produce, so to any act of "declaring ownerless" (*hefker*) must be made ownerless to both the rich and the poor. However, Bet Shammai permits partial *hefker*] (*PhM Pe'ah* 6:1; cf. *Eduyot* 4:3).

FURTHER: As to the precepts enumerated in the law concerning the sabbatical and Jubilee year, some of them imply sympathy with our fellow men, and promote the well-being of mankind; for in reference to these precepts it is stated in the Law, "and the poor of your people may eat," and besides, the land will also increase its produce and improve when it remains fallow for some time (*Guide* 3:39).

This short passage contains three separate rationales for the sabbatical year: (1) create sympathy, (2) promote the well-being of mankind, (3) improve and increase the produce of the land in other years.

23:12. Six days you shall do your work, and on the seventh day you shall rest [*tishbot*]... — ... we are commanded to rest on the Sabbath, as He, may He be exalted, said, "and on the seventh day you shall rest," and this commandment has been repeated many times. And God, may He be exalted, explained to us the resting from labor is an obligation upon us, our animals, and our slaves (see Exod. 20:10)... (*ShM*, Pos. 154).

FURTHER: Resting from labor on the seventh day is a positive commandment, as it says, "... and on the seventh you shall rest." And whoever performs labor squanders a positive commandment and violates a negative commandment, as it says, "you shall not do any work" (Exod. 20:10). And when is he liable for performing labor? If it does it voluntarily and intentionally, he is liable for *karet*. And if there are witnesses and he is warned, then he is stoned. And if he did it negligently, he is obligated to bring a fixed sin offering (*Shabbat* 1:1).

FURTHER: It is stated in the Torah "you shall rest" [*tishbot*] — you are even obligated to abstain from acts which are not labor [*melakhah*]. And the Sages prohibited many acts because of *shevut*, some of which are prohibited because they are similar to labor and some of which are prohibited as a [rabbinic] enactment lest one come to commit an act punishable by stoning (*Shabbat* 21:1).

Elsewhere he writes, "The Rabbis said 'because of *shevut*...' which refers to what God said, 'you shall rest,' which includes everything listed here and are called *shevut*" (*PhM Betzah* 5:2). According to the Mishnah, the following acts are prohibited because of *shevut*: climbing a tree, riding an animal, swimming, hand-clapping, dancing, and slapping one's thighs (the latter three lest one tune musical instruments).

More broadly, it seems that Maimonides understood "you shall rest" as a separate positive commandment (see *ShM*, Pos. 154, quoted above; in the *koter* to *Hilkhot Shabbat*, he quotes two separate commandments: "to rest on the seventh day" [which is a positive commandment], and "to not perform labor on it" [which is a negative commandment]). Further support for this position can be gleaned from what he wrote in *Shabbat* 24:12, quoted at the next clause.

Nahmanides writes, "Thus we are not to be engaged the whole day in wearisome tasks: measuring out crops of the field, weighing fruits and gifts, filling the barrels with wine and clearing away the vessels, and moving stones from house to house and from place to place [even though these acts do not violate the biblical commandment to rest].... Therefore the Torah said that it should be a day of solemn rest, meaning that it should be a day of rest and peace, not a day of labor and toil" (on Lev. 23:24).

Nahmanides' comments are regarding the intermediate festival days of Passover and Sukkot, from which he extrapolates to the major festival days and then to the Sabbath. However, this passage develops the idea that the Sabbath is not merely about the abstention of tiresome labor, but about creating a positive, sacred, and restful atmosphere, which seems implied also by Maimonides at *Shabbat* 21:1 and *Shabbat* 24:12. It should be noted the Nahmanides' language in this passage is similar to the language used by Maimonides at *Shabbat* 24:12.

FURTHER: See Exod. 21:7, where Maimonides uses this verse to explain why the order of *Zera'im* precedes the order of *Mo'ed*.

... so that your ox and your donkey may rest... — It is forbidden to bring out a load on an animal on the Sabbath, as it says, "so that your ox and your donkey may rest." This applies to an ox, a donkey, and all other animals, livestock, and birds. And if he brings out a load on an animal, even though he is commanded regarding its rest, he does not receive lashes, since its prohibition is included in a positive commandment. Therefore if someone leads his animal on the Sabbath and it is carrying a load he is exempt (*Shabbat* 20:1).

FURTHER: The Sages prohibited the carrying of certain objects on the Sabbath in the way that one would carry them during the week. And why did they create this prohibition? They said: Just as the prophets warned us and commanded us that our gait on the Sabbath should not be like our gait during the week, and our speech on the Sabbath not like our speech during the week, as it says, "[from] speaking idle words" (Isa. 58:13). Then certainly your manner of carrying on the Sabbath should be different from your manner of carrying during the week, so that [the Sabbath] should not be like a weekday in your eyes, lest you come to lift up articles and repair them, [and carry them] from room to room or house to house, or to set aside stones, or the like, since he is idle and sitting at home, and looking for a way to occupy himself, and ultimately he will not rest and disregard the reason of the commandment, as it says in the Torah, "so that... may rest" (Exod. 23:12, Deut. 5:13) (*Shabbat* 24:12).

At *PhM Pesaḥim* 4:3, Maimonides says that according to the opinion it is forbidden to sell an animal to a gentile, the reason is lest it come to be worked on the Sabbath violating "so that your ox and donkey may rest" (see there).

... and that the son of your handmaid and the stranger may be refreshed. — Just as a person is commanded regarding the rest of his animals on the Sabbath, he is also commanded concerning the rest of his manservants and bondmaids on the Sabbath. Even though they are sentient and by their own volition perform commandments, nonetheless the master must watch them and prevent them from performing labor on the Sabbath, as it says, "so that your ox and your donkey may rest, and that the son of your handmaid and the stranger may be refreshed." ... Regarding whom is it stated "and that the son of your handmaid and the stranger may be refreshed"? This is a resident alien, who is employed by an Israelite, like "the son of his maidservant." He may not work for his Israelite master on the Sabbath, but he may perform labor for himself. And even if this *ger* [alien] is his slave, he may perform work for himself (*Shabbat* 20:14).

23:13. And regarding everything which I have said you shall guard yourselves... — ... it is not proper to count [as separate commandments] general exhortations that include the entire Torah. There are exhortations in the Torah that do not refer to anything specific, but instead include all of the commandments, as if it said, "Perform everything that I have commanded you to do and separate from everything that I have forbidden you" or "Do not perform an act that I have forbidden from you." And there is no reason to count this charge as a separate commandment, since it does not direct us concerning a specific action—whether to perform a positive commandment or to abstain from performing a specific action, i.e., a negative commandment. And this is like what is stated, "And regarding everything which I have said you shall guard yourselves," and "you shall guard My statutes and perform My judgments" (Lev. 19:19), "and you shall keep my charge" (Lev. 18:30), and there are many like this (*ShM, Shoresh* 4).

... and you shall not mention the names of other gods... — .. we are forbidden from swearing in the name of an idol, even with idolators.

Similarly, we may not force them to swear [in the name of an idol], as our Sages explained in their statement, "One may not force a gentile to swear in the name of his [false] god," as God, may He be exalted, said, "and you shall not mention the names of other gods," so we may not force a gentile to swear in the name of his god. And there the Sages said: "'you shall not mention' — one may not take a vow in the name of a false god."

And in *Sanhedrin* (63b), it says, "'you shall not mention' — a man may not say to his colleague, 'Wait for me beside this particular idol.'" If someone violates this prohibition, that is, if he swears in a glorifying manner by one of the created beings by which people stray in believing is a god, then he is liable to receive lashes. The Talmud in *Sanhedrin* (63a) states that, with regards to the prohibition of hugging an idol, or kissing it, or showing honor before it, in any of these actions that show reverence and love, the Sages said that one does not receive lashes unless he takes a vow in its name and fulfills it" (*ShM*, Neg. 14; see also *Avodah Zarah* 5:10-11, and *PhM Sanhedrin* 7:6).

FURTHER: It is permitted to mention the name of any false deity written in the sacred Scripture, such as Peor, and Baal, and Nebo, and Gad, and the like (*Avodah Zarah* 5:10-11).

FURTHER: ...we are forbidden from prophesying in the name of a false god, saying that God commanded one to serve it, or that the idol itself commanded [us] to serve it, and promised reward and imposed punishment, as the prophets of Baal and Asherah did. And there is no clear and specific verse on this subject, that is to say a prohibition against prophesying in its name. However its punishment is explained in Scripture, and that is punishment of death for prophesying in the name of a false god. This is what He, may He be exalted, said, "that speak in the name of other gods, then that prophet shall die"

(Deut. 18:20). And this death is by strangulation, since we have a principle before us that whenever execution is mentioned without specification, it is death by strangulation.

And you already know a principle that I have explained to you in the fourteenth of the introductory principles which precedes this, and they said, "Scripture did not assign a punishment unless it also issued a prohibition." And the prohibition should be what He said, "and you shall not mention the names of other gods." It is not impossible for one prohibition to teach multiple prohibitions and not be among the general commandments, as the punishment is clarified in each and every case (*ShM*, Neg. 26).

FURTHER: How does one prophesy in the name of a false deity? This is if someone says, "This particular false deity, or this particular star, said to me that it is a commandment to do such and such, or to not do such and such. And even if he directs the law properly, to declare the impure as impure or the pure as pure, if they warned him before two people, then he is strangled, as it says, "that speak in the name of other gods, then that prophet shall die" (Deut. 18:20). And this prohibition is included in the verse "and you shall not mention the names of other gods" (*Avodah Zarah* 5:6).

... it shall not be heard in your mouth. — ... we are forbidden from leading people to idolatry—that is, to lead them and speak to them about how to serve an idol and to encourage them [to worship] it, even if the one doing the encouraging does not do any of the [forbidden actions] other than leading [other people] towards it. And if he misleads the majority of people [of a city], he is a *madiah* ["one who causes others to go astray"], as it says, "wicked men from among you have gone out and led the inhabitants of the town astray [saying, 'Let us go and worship other gods', whom you have not known]" (Deut. 13:14). And if he leads any one individual person astray, he is called a *meisit* ["inticer," see Neg. 16], as God, may He be exalted, said, "If your brother from your mother's side... entice you [in secret, saying, 'Let us go and serve false gods whom you and your fathers have not known]" (Deut. 13:7).

However, for the present commandment, we are only concerned with *madiaḥ*, and the prohibition regarding this is what God, may He be exalted, said, "it shall not be heard in your mouth." And the Talmud in *Sanhedrin* says: "They stated: 'it shall not be heard in your mouth' (Exod. 23:13) — this is is a prohibition against being a *meisit*. But a *meisit* is already explicitly forbidden! [As it says:] 'And all of Israel will hear and become afraid and shall no further do [this wicked thing in your midst]' (Deut. 13:12). Rather, it is a prohibition against *madi'aḥ*" (63b). And similarly, in the *Mekhilta* of Rabbi Ishmael, it says, "'it shall not be heard in your mouth' — this is the prohibition of *madi'aḥ*." Whoever violates this prohibition is subject to execution by stoning. And that language of the Talmud is "those who subvert a subverted city [to commit] idolatry are stoned" (*Sanhedrin* 50a, 89b) (*ShM*, Neg. 15).

FURTHER: Those who subvert a city among Israel are executed by stoning, even though they did not commit idolatry [themselves] but rather subverted the residents of their city until they worshipped it. And the residents of the city who have been led astray are executed by beheading, if they committed idolatry or accepted it as a god for themselves. And where is the source against subverting [*madi'aḥ*]? Come and learn, 'it shall not be heard in your mouth'" (*Avodah Zarah* 4:1).

23:14. Three times on the year you shall keep a feast to Me. — The Jewish people are commanded in three positive commandments on each of the three pilgrimage festivals, and they are:

(1) Appearing [before God], as it says, "all your males shall appear [before the Lord God]" (Exod. 23:17, Deut. 16:16),

(2) The festal offering, as it says, "you shall rejoice before the Lord your God" (Deut. 16:15),

(3) And rejoicing, as it says, "and you shall rejoice in your festival" (Deut. 16:14).

The "appearing" mentioned in the Torah is that a person should appear before the Courtyard on the first day of the festival, and bring a burnt offering with him, either a bird or mammals. And if someone comes to the Courtyard on the first day and does not have a burnt offering, it is not just that he has not performed a positive commandment; he has also transgressed a negative commandment, as it says, "nobody shall appear before Me empty-handed" (Exod. 23:15). And someone who violates this prohibition does not receive lashes, since he has not performed an action.

The festal offering mentioned in the Torah is that he should bring a peace offering on the first day of the festival when he comes to be seen. And it is known that a peace offering can only come from mammals. And women are not obligated in these two commandments of "appearing" and [bringing] the festal offering.

The "rejoicing" mentioned on the festivals is that he should bring another peace offering besides the festal offering [*shalmei hagigah*]. And these are called *shalmei simhah* [peace offerings of rejoicing], as it says, "You shall offer peace offerings and you shall eat there, and you shall rejoice before the Lord your God" (Deut. 27:17) (*Hagigah* 1:1; also *ShM*, Pos. 52 and *PhM Hagigah* 1:2).

23:15... and nobody shall appear before Me empty-handed. — ... we are forbidden from ascending on the festival without bringing an offering with us to offer there, as God, may He be exalted, said, "and nobody shall appear before Me empty-handed." Rather, he must have with him a burnt offering and a peace offering…. And women are not obligated in it (*ShM*, Neg. 156; see also *PhM Ḥagigah* 1:2).

FURTHER: [Maimonides comments on the Mishnah which teaches: "Bet Shammai says, 'We bring peace offerings, but we do not lay hands on it (Lev. 3:2), but we do not perform ritual leading on them, but we do not bring burnt offerings.' Bet Hillel says, 'We bring peace offerings and burnt offerings, and lay hands upon it'" (M. *Betzah* 3:2).] There is a dispute between Bet Shammai and Bet Hillel regarding the peace offering of the festival, and the burnt offerings of "appearing" [before God], as God said, "and nobody shall appear before Me empty-handed." Bet Shammai says, "a festival [*hag*] to the Lord" (Exod. 12:14, Lev. 23:41), [implying] on a holiday one only brings a festal offering [*hagigah*], but one brings the burnt offering of "appearing" on the other days of the festival. And Bet Hillel says, "'to the Lord' — everything that is for the Lord." And Bet Shammai learns from "it shall be a solemn assembly for you" (Num. 29:35) — "for you" and not for God. And Bet Hillel learns from what it says, "a solemn assembly for the Lord your God" (Deut. 16:8) — everything that is for God… (*PhM Betzah* 2:3).

FURTHER: If someone comes to the Courtyard on the other days of the festival, he is not obligated to bring a burnt offering whenever he enters, for the verse "and nobody shall appear before Me empty-handed" only applies to the primary celebration of the festival, which is the first day, or the first compensatory day. And if he brings it whenever he comes, we accept it from him and offer it as a burnt offering of appearing, for "appearing" has no limit (*Ḥagigah* 2:6).

23:16. [You shall observe] the feast of harvest, the first fruits of your labors, which you have sown in the field… — [Maimonides is commenting on the Mishnah which says, "All communal and private offerings can be brought from the Land [of Israel] or from outside the Land, from new or old grain, except for the omer and the two loaves, which can only come from new grain and from the Land" (M. Menaḥot 8:1).] — It is explicit in the Torah regarding *omer* and the two loaves that they can only come from the Land [of Israel] and from new [grain]. God said regarding *omer*, "when you come to the land which I give you... then you shall bring an *omer* as a first fruit of your harvest" (Lev. 23:10), and regarding the two loaves, "From your habitations you shall bring two wave offerings" (Lev. 23:17), and it says, "you shall bring a new grain offering" (Lev. 23:16). And it says furthermore, "[You shall observe] the feast of harvest, the first fruits of your labors" (Exod. 23:16) (*PhM Menaḥot* 8:1).

FURTHER: One cannot bring first fruits before Shavuot, as it says, "[You shall observe] the feast of harvest, the first fruits of your labors." And if someone brings them, we do not accept them; rather we leave them until Shavuot comes, when he makes a declaration over them. And similarly we do not bring first fruits after Hanukkah, since what grows after Hanukkah is considered as belonging to the following year, and we leave that for the following Shavuot (*Bikkurim* 2:6).

... and the feast of gathering at the end of the year, when you gather in from the field the fruit of your labors. — The Feast of Tabernacles, which is a feast of rejoicing and gladness, is kept seven days, in order that the idea of the festival may be more noticeable. The reason why it is kept in the autumn is stated in the Law, "when you gather in from the field the fruit of your labors," that is to say, when you rest and are free from pressing labors. Aristotle, in the ninth book of his *Ethics*, mentions this as a general custom among the nations. He says: "In ancient times the sacrifices and assemblies of the people took place after the ingathering of the corn and the fruit, as if the sacrifices were offered on account of the harvest." Another reason is this: in this season it is possible to dwell in tabernacles, as there is neither great heat nor troublesome rain (*Guide* 3:43).

23:17. Three times a year all your males shall appear, before the master, God. — … we are commanded to appear on the festivals, as He, may He be exalted, said, "Three times a year all your males shall appear before the master, God, the Lord of Israel" (Exod. 34:23, cf. Exod. 23:17, Deut. 16:16). And the meaning of this commandment is that someone must ascend to the Temple with every male child with him who is capable of walking on his own and bring a burnt offering when he ascends. And this burnt offering that he brings during his ascent is called an *olat re'iyah* ["burnt offering of appearing"]…. And women are also exempt from this commandment (*ShM*, Pos. 53).

FURTHER: [Maimonides comments on the Mishnah, "Everyone is obligated in 'appearing,' except for a deaf-mute, imbecile, minor, tumtum, androgynus, women, slaves who have not been set free, and a man who is lame, blind, invalid, or elderly so he cannot walk on his own feet" (M. Ḥagigah 1:1)] — The "appearing" is what God said, "all your males shall appear," and therefore women, *tumtum*, and *androgynus* are exempt from this commandment. And He said, "before the master, God," [meaning] one who only has one master, which excludes a slave, and therefore slaves are not obligated. And it says "three times [*regalim*]" (Exod. 23:14), and even though *regel* means a season of time, however since it does not say [the more common word] *pe'amim* as it does in other places (i.e., Exod. 23:17, Exod. 34:23), Tradition says this indicates that this commandment is only incumbent on someone who can walk on his feet, and therefore the lame, invalid, elderly, and minors are not obligated.

And it says further, "to be seen before the Lord" (Deut. 31:11). Therefore it only applies to someone who can see, which excludes someone who is blind. And it says regarding the commandment of *hak'hel*, "that they may hear and that they may learn" (Deut. 31:12) — we learn from this *re'iyah* that on the eighth year to all [uses of] *re'iyah* that does not obligate an imbecile, because he is unable to learn, and a deaf person because he cannot hear. And if one leg, one eye, or one ear becomes paralyzed, he is not obligated in *re'iyah*, since it says *regalim* (Exod. 23:14, in the plural), and regarding *hak'hel* it says, "in their ears" [plural, i.e. with full hearing] (Deut. 31:11), and it says "to be seen" (Deut. 31:11) meaning someone with full vision (*PhM Ḥagigah* 1:1).

FURTHER: [It is said about God, *kanah*, "he acquired"] because God rules over them like a master over his servants. For this reason He is also called "The Lord of the whole earth" (Josh. 3:11-13) and *ha-Adon* ["the Master, Lord"] (*Guide* 2:30; see also *Guide* 3:48, quoted at v. 19).

23:18. You shall not offer the blood of My sacrifice with leaven...
— ... we are forbidden from slaughtering the Passover offering with leaven, as God, may He be exalted, said, "You shall not offer [*tizbaḥ*] the blood of My sacrifice with leaven." And this prohibition has been repeated with the language, "You shall not slaughter [*tishḥat*] [the blood of My sacrifice with leaven]" (Exod. 34:25). And this means that at the time of slaughtering the Passover offering, which is the afternoon [*ben ha-arbayim*], there shall be no leaven in his domain— not of he who sprinkles [the blood], nor of he who slaughters, nor of he who burns [the fat], and not in the domain of any members of the group [that will eat the Passover offering]. And whoever is in possession of leaven at that time is liable to receive lashes. And the *Mekhilta* says, "'You shall not slaughter [the blood of My sacrifice] with leaven' — you shall not slaughter the Passover offering when leaven is present" (*ShM*, Neg. 115).

Maimonides adds two points elsewhere: (1) one only violates this commandment if he has at least an olive's measure of leaven in his possession; (2) nonetheless the Passover offering is valid (*Korban Pesaḥ* 1:5). Maimonides also makes reference to this at *Ḥametz u-Matzah* 2:1. See also *PhM Pesaḥim* 5:4.

... and the fat of My sacrifice shall not remain until morning. — ... we are forbidden to leave the fats of the Passover offering, so that we should not offer them after they have been invalidated by remaining overnight and becoming *notar*, as He said, "and the fat of My sacrifice shall not remain until morning." And this applies to the other fats of the Passover offering. And the language of the *Mekhilta* is, "'the fat [of My sacrifice] shall not remain' — this verse comes to teach regarding the fats that are invalidated by remaining overnight on the floor. And this prohibition has been repeated with other language, 'and the sacrifice of the feast of the Passover shall not remain until morning'" (Exod. 34:25) (*ShM*, Neg. 116).

FURTHER: If someone leaves over fats and does not burn them before they remain overnight and thereby become invalidated violates a negative commandment, as it says, "and the fat of My sacrifice shall not remain until morning." And even though he transgressed, he does not receive lashes since there is no action involved (*Korban Pesaḥ* 1:7).

23:19. You shall bring the first fruits of your land to the house of the Lord your God... — ... we are commanded to take out the first fruits and to bring them to the Temple, as God, may He exalted, said, "You shall bring the first fruits of your land to the house of the Lord your God." And it is clear that this commandment is only practiced when the Temple is standing. And one can only bring fruits from the land of Israel, Syria, and the Transjordan, and only from the seven species…. [They] are the property of the priest (*ShM*, Pos. 125; also *Bikkurim* 2:1).

FURTHER: If someone plants a tree in his field and sinks its shoot into his colleague's field or into a public domain, or if he planted in his colleague's field or a public domain and sinks a shoot into his own field, or if the trunk is in his field and he extended it—and there is a private or public path crossing through—between the trunk and the extended part, [in all of these cases] he does not bring first fruits, neither from this domain, and not from the side in the other domain, as it says, "You shall bring the first fruits of *your* land" — one is not liable unless all of the growth shall be from your land (*Bikkurim* 2:10).

FURTHER: If someone separated his first fruits, and they spoiled, were plundered, lost, destroyed, stolen, or became impure, he is obligated to separate others in their place, as it says, "*You shall bring…* to the house of the Lord your God," which teaches that he is obligated to replace them if he has not brought them to the Temple mount (*Bikkurim* 2:20).

FURTHER: … the first of everything is to be devoted to the Lord, and by doing so man accustoms himself to be liberal, and to limit his appetite for eating and his desire for property (*Guide* 3:39; he says that the *terumah*, "heave offering" (Deut. 18:4), the *ḥallah* (Num. 15:20), first fruit (present verse), and first shearing (Deut. 19:4) are all brought for this reason).

… you shall not cook a kid in its mother's milk. — … we are forbidden from cooking meat in milk, as God, may He be exalted, said, "you shall not cook a kid in its mother's milk" (Exod. 23:19, Exod. 34:26, Deut. 14:21). And whoever cooks it is lashed, even if he does not eat from it, as has been explained in many places in the Talmud (*ShM*, Neg. 186).

FURTHER: … we are forbidden from eating meat and milk, and this is also from what He said "you shall not cook a kid in its mother's milk" a second time, which applies to the prohibition of eating. And the in Talmud, in *Hullin*, the Sages said that one receives lashes for cooking it and for eating it (114a).… The Sages said in *Hullin* that the Torah included the prohibition of "eating" in the prohibition of "cooking" to teach that just as someone receives lashes for cooking, he also receives lashes for eating. And in the second chapter of *Pesahim*, they said, "Regarding meat and milk, the Torah did not use the word 'eating' to teach that one receives lashes even if he did not derive enjoyment" (25b). Remember this.

And here it is appropriate for me to indicate an important principle that has not yet been mentioned. And this is what He said, "you shall not cook a kid in its mother's milk," which is repeated in the Torah three times. And those who expound the verse that each repetition teaches a different prohibition, as they said in the *Mekhilta*, "One teaches the prohibition of eating, one the prohibition of deriving benefit, and one the prohibition of cooking."

And someone could ask the question and say that if you counted the prohibitions of eating and cooking as two separate commandments, you should count the prohibition of deriving benefit as a third prohibition. However the person posing the objection surely knows that it is not necessary to count the prohibition of deriving benefit as a separate commandment, because that prohibition and the prohibition of eating are the same, for eating is one of the ways that one derives enjoyment. And God, may He be exalted, said that something that may not be eaten is included in the types of enjoyment. And the meaning is that one may not derive benefit from it, not by eating, and not in any other form. And this is what the Sages, peace be upon them, said, "Whether it says 'you shall not eat [sing.]' or 'you shall not eat [pl.]' implies a prohibition of eating and a prohibition of benefitting unless Scripture specifies otherwise, as it does regarding *neveilah*" (21b). And there the permission is explicit, since He said, "to the stranger in your gates you shall give it to eat…" (Deut. 14:21).

Based on this principle, it is not appropriate to count the prohibition of eating and the prohibition of benefit as two commandments. And had we counted them as two separate commandments regarding meat and milk, then we would have to do the same thing for leaven, *orlah*, and *kelai ha-kerem*, with each of these four commandments there would have to be a separate commandment of deriving benefit. And in all of these cases, only the prohibition of eating is counted, and the prohibition of benefiting is included, as we have explained, and the same applied to meat and milk.

Yet there is one question that remains. If it is true that the prohibition of benefiting comes via the prohibition of eating as the Sages, peace be upon them, have explained, then we should need to include a third prohibition of benefit regarding meat and milk, as we have explained? The answer to this is that regarding meat and milk it does not say "do not eat from it," from which both eating and benefiting would be prohibited. And therefore we needed a separate prohibition for the prohibition of deriving benefit.

We have already mentioned the circumstance that on this account the Torah did not write "eat" regarding meat and milk, that whenever it says "eat," one is not guilty unless he enjoys his eating, but if he opens his mouth and swallows something prohibited or he ate something so hot that it burns his throat and hurts him as he swallows it, or anything similar to this, he is exempt, except in the case of meat and milk, for which he is liable for eating it, even if he did not derive benefit, as the Sages have said… (*ShM*, Neg. 187).

FURTHER: According to Torah law, it is forbidden to cook meat and milk, and it is forbidden to eat it, and it is forbidden to derive benefit from it, and it needs to be buried, and its ashes are forbidden, just like the ashes of anything that requires burial. And when someone cooks an olive's measure of the two of them, he receives lashes, as it says, "you shall not cook a kid in its mother's milk." And similarly someone who eats an olive's measure of the two of them, of meat and milk, and they are cooked together, is lashed, even if he did not cook it [i.e., someone else cooked it and he only ate it].

Scripture was only silent regarding the prohibition of eating because of the prohibition of cooking, meaning that even the cooking is prohibited, and needless to say eating it [is also prohibited], just like Scripture was silent about the prohibition of [having relations with] one's daughter since it prohibited one's granddaughter.

And the only biblical prohibition of meat and milk regards the meat of a kosher species of domesticated animal with the milk of a kosher species of domesticated animal, as it says, "you shall not cook a kid in its mother's milk." And *gedi* is a general word that includes the offspring of a bovine, a *seh*, or a goat, unless it specifies and says *gedi izzim* (e.g., Gen. 38:17). And Scripture only said "a kid [*gedi*] in its mother's milk" because it spoke of the most common situation.

However, if someone cooked the meat of a kosher animal in the milk of a non-kosher animal, or the meat of a non-kosher animal in the milk of a kosher animal, it is permitted to cook, and permitted to derive benefit, and someone who eats it is does not violate the prohibition of eating meat and milk.

And similarly the meat of a wild mammal, or bird, whether in the milk of a *ḥayah* or the milk of a *behemah* is not biblically prohibited. Therefore it is permitted to cook it and permitted to benefit from it. And according to the Rabbis it is prohibited to eat it, so that it will not become widespread in the nation to violate the biblical prohibition of meat and milk, and eat kosher meat with kosher milk. The only implication of the verse "a kid in its mother's milk" is literal; therefore they prohibited all meat and milk (*Ma'akhalot Asurot* 9:1-4).

Further: [In *Shemonah Perakim*, Maimonides contrasts two types of people: one who has a desire to sin, and one who does not have a desire to sin. He argues that according to the philosophers, the person who has no desire to sin is on a higher level. However, according to the Sages, the person who desires sin but overcomes it is on a higher level, based on the rabbinic dictum, "Whoever is greater than his colleague possesses an evil inclination greater than his colleague" (*Sukkah* 52a). Continuing the Sages' position, Maimonides continues:] Rabban Shimon ben Gamliel said: A person should not say, "It is impossible for me to eat meat and milk" or "It is impossible for me to wear *sha'atnez*" or "It is impossible for me to have forbidden relations." Rather one should say, "It is possible, but what can I do? My Father in Heaven forbade it" (cf. *Sifra*, "Kedoshim"). At first glance two approaches [the philosophers and the Sages] appear to contradict each other.

But this is not the case. Rather, they are both true and there is no controversy between them at all. The evils of which the philosophers spoke are not those for which many people lust, and in that case the person who has no evil desire is on a higher level, like murder, theft, stealing, cheating, injuring someone who has done nothing wrong, reciprocating kindness with injury, disparaging one's parents, and the like. And these are commandments about which the Sages, peace be upon them, said that had they not been written it would be proper to write them (*Yoma* 67b). And some of our later sages who fell amongst the group of Medabrim called them "rational commandments" [*mitzvot sikhliyyot*]. And there is no doubt that the soul that lusts after and yearns for any of these [sins] is on a lower level. And similarly the elevated soul will not desire for any of these evils at all and will not feel distressed in refraining from them.

However, the matters about which the Sages said that the person who conquers his evil inclination is on a higher level and his reward is much greater are the revelational commandments [*mitzvot shimiyyot*].

This is true, for had the Torah not prohibited them, they would not be evil at all. Therefore, the Sages said that a person should continue desiring them and should say that the only thing preventing him is the Torah. You should understand the wisdom of the Sages, peace be upon them, and the example that they employed, for they did not say: "It is impossible for me to kill someone, or steal, or to deceive..." Rather one should say, "It is possible, but what can I do? ..."

Rather, the Sages mentioned commandments that are only *shimiyyot*, such as eating meat and milk together, wearing *shaatnez*, and having forbidden relations. And these commandments, and those similar, are what God called *ḥukkim* ("statutes"), about which the Sages said, "Statutes that I decreed for you [*ḥukkim she-ḥakakti lakh*] and you do not have permission to question them. And the nations of the world question them, and Satan prosecutes about them, such as the red cow and the *se'ir mishtale'aḥ* (cf. *Yoma* 67b, *Numbers Rabbah* 19:3) (*Shemonah Perakim*, ch. 6).

FURTHER: Meat boiled in milk is undoubtedly gross food, and makes overfull; but I think that most probably it is also prohibited because it is somehow connected with idolatry, forming perhaps part of the service, or being used on some festival of the heathen. I find a support for this view in the circumstance that the Law mentions the prohibition twice after the commandment given concerning the festivals, "Three times a year all your males shall appear, before the master, God" (Exod. 23:17, 34:23), as if to say, "When you come before Me on your festivals, do not cook your food in the manner as the heathen used to do." This I consider as the best reason for the prohibition, but as far as I have seen the books on Sabean rites, nothing is mentioned of this custom (*Guide* 3:48).

Cassuto writes, "Maimonides already conjectured that the prohibition of boiling a kid in its mother's milk was intended to keep the Israelites away from idolatrous customs, but he had no proof that the gentiles actually practised such things. Now we know from the Ugaritic texts that the Canaanites prepared such a dish particularly at festal ceremonies pertaining to the fertility of the soil. In the Ugaritic tablet on 'The gods pleasant and beautiful' it is written (line 14): *ṭb[h g]d bḥlb 'annḥ bḥm'at* 'boil a kid in milk, a lamb in butter,' The custom of boiling small cattle in milk has been preserved to this day among Bedouins." However, Jacob Milgrom strenuously objects to this reading (see *Leviticus 1-16*, p. 738).

23:20-21. Behold I will send an angel before you to guard you on the way and to bring you to the place that I have prepared. Be watchful before him, and obey his voice, and do not provoke him, for he will not pardon your transgression, for My name is within him. — [Maimonides addresses the phrase *shem Hashem*, "the name of God." He first says it can simply mean the name, as at Exod. 20:7. He then continues:] Sometimes it stands for "the word of God," so that "the name of God," "the word of God," and "the command of God" are identical phrases, e.g., "for My name is within him" — that is, My word or My command is in him, i.e., he is the instrument of My desire and will (*Guide* 1:64).

FURTHER: [In reference to the present passage as well as Gen. 19:21] — ... these passages show that angels are conscious of what they do, and have free will in the sphere of action entrusted to them, just as we have free will within our province, and in accordance with the power given to us with our very existence (*Guide* 2:7).

FURTHER: The meaning of the scriptural passage, "Behold I will send an angel before you..." is identical with the parallel passage in Deuteronomy which God is represented to have addressed to Moses at the revelation on Mount Sinai, namely, "I will raise them up a prophet from among their brethren" (Deut. 18:18). The words "Be watchful of him, and obey his voice" (Exod. 23:21) said in reference to the angel, prove [that this passage speaks of a prophet]. For there is no doubt that the commandment is given to the ordinary people, to whom angels do not appear with commandments and exhortations, and it is therefore unnecessary to tell them not to disobey him.

The meaning of the passage quoted above is this: God informs the Israelites that He will raise up for them a prophet, to whom an angel will appear in order to speak to him, to command him, and to exhort him; He therefore cautions them not to rebel against this angel, whose word the prophet will communicate to them. Therefore it is expressly said in Deuteronomy, "you shall hearken unto him" (Deut. 18:15), "And it shall come to pass that whoever shall not hearken unto My words which he shall speak in My name" (Deut. 18:19). This is the explanation of the words, "for My name is within him" (Exod. 24:22).

The object of all this is to say to the Israelites: This great sight witnessed by you, the revelation on Mount Sinai, will not continue forever, nor will it ever be repeated. Fire and cloud will not continually rest over the tabernacle, as they are resting now on it: but the towns will be conquered for you, peace will be secured for you in the land, and you will be informed of what you have to do, by an angel whom I will send to your prophets; he will thus teach you what to do, and what not to do. Here a principle is laid down which I have constantly expounded, i.e., that all prophets except Moses receive the prophecy through an angel. Note it (*Guide* 2:34).

23:25. And you shall serve the Lord your God... — ... we are commanded to serve God, may He be exalted, and this commandment has been repeated many times: "And you shall serve the Lord your God," "and you shall serve [*ta'avodu*] Him" (Deut. 13:5), "and you shall serve [*ta'avod*] Him" (Deut. 6:13, cf. Deut. 10:20), "and to serve

Him [*u-le-avdo*]" (Deut. 11:13). And although this commandment is among the general commandments as we have explained in the Fourth Principle, it also includes something specific, and that is prayer [*tefillah*]. And the language of the *Sifrei*, "'and to serve Him' — this is prayer." And the Sages also said, "'and to serve Him' — this is study." In the teachings of Rabbi Eliezer the son of Rabbi Yosi the Galilean, the Sages said, "Where is the source of prayer among the commandments? From here: "And you shall fear the Lord your God, and you shall serve him" (Deut. 6:13). And they said, "Serve Him in His Torah, serve Him in His Temple," which means to travel there and pray there, or in that direction, as Solomon, peace be upon him, explained (1 Kings 8:23, 35; 2 Chron. 6:32) (*ShM*, Pos. 5).

> Nahmanides, in his gloss on the ShM, writes, "And what the Sages explained in the *Sifrei* (Ekev) "'and to serve Him' means 'study'"; alternatively it means prayer is merely an allusion [*ashmakhta*], or it is possible to say that included in 'service' is that we learn Torah and we should pray to Him in a time of distress [*et ha-tzarot*], so that our eyes and hearts should be on Him alone, as the eyes of slaves are on the hands of their masters. And this is the meaning of the verse, 'And when you go to war in your land against the enemy that oppresses you, then you shall sound an alarm with trumpets, and you shall be remembered before the Lord your God [and you shall be saved from your enemies]' (Num. 10:9). And this is a commandment at each and every moment of crisis to join with the community and cry out before Him in prayer and teru'ah."
>
> In other words, Maimondes argues there is a general scriptural obligation to pray every day (see *Tefillah* 1:1), while Nahmanides argues that Maimonides' source is a mere allusion, and the real scriptural commandment is only in a time of distress.

Rabbi Joseph B. Soloveitchik has proposed a reconciliation of these two views, writing, "The views of Maimonides and Nahmanides can be reconciled. Both regarded prayer as meaningful only if it is derived from a sense of *tzarah*. They differ in their understanding of the word" (Abraham R. Besdin, *Reflections of the Rav*, p. 80). He continues by saying that according to Nahmanides, prayer is only obligatory when there is a "surface crisis," i.e., when there is some palpable distress. However, according to Maimonides, there is always a *tzarah* because there is always a "depth crisis," i.e., man is painfully aware of how insignificant he is and how dependent on God he is for protection. See also *Worship of the Heart*, p. 30.

Before I heard of this resolution by Rabbi Soloveitchik, I had proposed a similar synthesis: If someone is about to drown, that is surely a time of distress (*et tzarah*). Assuming nobody else is present to rescue him, he has no option but to pray for salvation. Yet he should not begin with the standard introduction of "God of Abraham, God of Isaac, God of Jacob, the great, mighty, and awesome God...." Rather he should go straight into the "request" (the technical usage of *bakkashah*) section—namely, the request to not drown. A person under normal circumstances does not feel as if he is drowning. Rather, perhaps thinking about the greatness of God, and reciting the words "the great, mighty, and awesome God," will create the same cognitive state as a the experiential state of a man about to drown, and that triggers the biblical obligation of prayer.

FURTHER: It is a positive commandment to pray every day, as it says, "and you shall serve the Lord your God." According to tradition, the Sages said that this "service" means prayer. It is stated, "and to serve Him with all your heart" (Deut. 11:13), and the Sages said, "What is service of the heart? This is prayer." And according to the Torah, there is no fixed number of prayers, and there is no set arrangement of prayers, and there is no set time for prayer. Therefore, women and slaves are obligated in prayer, since it is a positive commandment that is not dependent on time. Rather, the obligation of this commandment is as follows: a person offers prayers and entreaties every day, and relates the praise of the Holy One, blessed is He, and then he asks for the things that he needs in request and supplication, and then he gives praise and thanks to God for the goodness that He has caused to overflow to him. Each person so according to his ability.

If he is eloquent, he would extend his supplications and requests, and if he is inarticulate, he should speak as much as he is able, and whenever he wants. Similarly, regarding the number of prayers, each person would pray in accordance with his ability. Some would pray once a day, and some would pray many times, and everyone—wherever he was—would pray facing the Temple. And this is how things always were from the time of Moses our teacher until Ezra.

When Israel was exiled in the days of the evil Nebuchadnezzar, and they were mingled among the Persians, Greeks, and other nations, and children were born to them in gentile lands, and the language of those children was confused, and everyone's speech was mixed with many languages, and even though they were able to speak, they were unable to make their requests in one language, only in a confusion [of many languages], as it says, "And their children spoke half in the language of Ashdod, and could not speak the Jews' language, but spoke the language of each nation" (Neh. 13:24).

Therefore when one of them prayed, his speech was deficient to ask for his needs or to relate the praise of the Holy One, blessed be He, in the holy language, unless he mixed foreign languages with it. And when Ezra and his court observed this, they arose and instituted for them eighteen blessings in a specific order. The first three are praise to God, and the last three are thanksgiving. The middle ones are requests for things, which are like categories for the desires of each person and for the collective needs of the community. [They did this so the blessings] should be orderly in everyone's mouth, and inculcate them, and so that the prayer of the inarticulate should be as complete as the prayer of those most expressive person. For this reason, they instituted all of the blessings and prayers in an orderly fashion in the mouth of all Israel so that the form of each blessing would be fixed in the mouth of the inarticulate.

And similarly they established a certain number of prayers in accordance with the number of offerings: two prayers every day corresponding the two daily offerings [in the morning and afternoon]. And on every day that there is an additional offering, they established a third prayer corresponding to the additional offering. And the prayer that corresponds to the daily morning offering is called the morning prayer [*tefillat ha-shaḥar*], and the prayer that corresponds with the daily afternoon offering is called the afternoon prayer [*tefillat minḥah*], and the prayer that corresponds to the additional offerings is called the additional prayer [*tefillat ha-musafin*].

And similarly, the Sages instituted that a person should recite a prayer at night, since the limbs of the daily afternoon offering could be incinerated all night long, as it says, "it is the burnt offering [that remains on the hearth all night until the morning]" (Lev. 6:2). And this is the meaning of what it says, "Evening, morning, and afternoon I pray and cry out [and He will hear my voice" (Ps. 55:18).

And the evening prayer is not obligatory like the morning and afternoon prayers. Nonetheless, all of Israel has become accustomed in all the places of their habitation to recite the evening prayer, and they have accepted it upon themselves as an obligatory prayer (*Tefillah* 1:1-6).

FURTHER: [In the following halakhic passage, Maimonides develops the thesis that all mundane activities can be considered "service of the Lord," related to the present verse, "And you shall serve the Lord your God":] A person should direct all of his actions only to know God, may He be blessed. His sitting, his standing, and his speech should all be for this purpose. How so? He conducts business and performs work and takes payment, his mind should not only be concerned with gathering wealth. Rather, these actions should be so that he will obtain matters that the body requires—for eating, drinking, dwelling in a home, and marrying a woman. And similarly, when he eats and drinks and has relations he should not focus on the fact that these actions are enjoyable to the point that he only eats and drinks for the pleasure [lit., "sweetness"] of his palate and has relations for it is enjoyment. Rather he should focus his mind [lit. "heart"] on eating and drinking only so that his body and limbs will be healthy. Therefore he should not eat everything that his palate desires like a dog or a donkey. Rather he should eat things that are healthful [lit., "helpful, effective"] for him, whether they are bitter or sweet. And he should not eat things that are destructive for the body, even if they are sweet to the palate.

How so? If someone has a warm constitution then he should not eat meat or honey, or drink wine. Regarding this, Solomon said by way of parable, "It is not good to eat too much honey" (Prov. 25:27). Rather, he should drink *ulshin* juice, even though it is bitter. Thus he eats and drinks for the only sake of health so that he will be healthy and remain whole, since it is impossible for a man to live without eating and drinking. And similarly, when he has relations he should only do so to make his body healthy and to beget offspring. Therefore he should not have relations whenever he desires, but only at times that he knows that he needs to emit seed for the sake of health or to beget offspring.

Someone who conducts himself accordance to the way of health, if he sets his heart so that his body and all of his limbs should be whole and strong and that he have children who will perform his work and toil on his behalf—this is not the proper way. Rather he should set his heart so that his body is whole and strong so that his soul should be upright to know God, for it is impossible for him to understand and comprehend wisdoms when he is sick or one of his limbs is in pain. And he should be determined to have a son so that perhaps he will be wise and a great man of Israel. Thus someone who goes in this path all of his days constantly serves God, even during business and even during relations, because his thoughts in everything is to fulfill his needs so that his body is whole so that he may serve God (cf. Exod. 23:25).

Even when he sleeps, if he sleeps so that his mind be at ease and his body can rest, so that he does not become sick and he would not be able to serve God when he sick, then his sleep is also for the service of the Omnipresent, may He be blessed. And regarding this, the Sages commanded and said, "And all of your actions should be for the sake of Heaven" (*Avot* 2:12). And regarding this, Solomon in his wisdom said, "In all your ways know Him and He will straighten your paths" (Prov. 3:6) (*De'ot* 3:2-3).

FURTHER: The infidels, however, though believing in the existence of the Creator, attack the exclusive prerogative of God, namely, the service and worship which was commanded, in order that the belief of the people in His existence should be firmly established, in the words, "And you shall serve the Lord your God" (Exod. 23:25). By transferring that prerogative to other beings, they cause the people, who only notice the rites, without comprehending their meaning or the true character of the being which is worshipped, to renounce their belief in their existence of God (*Guide* 1:36; he quotes this verse in passing in *Guide* 3:32).

23:29. I will not drive them out from before you in one year, lest the land be desolate and the beasts of the field increase against

you. — The Holy One, blessed is He, allowed heretics to remain on the land to keep the pious ones company [i.e., from being lonely], as God, may He be exalted and elevated, said, "I will not drive them out from you in one year, lest the land be desolate," and the Sages have also explained the verse "for this is all of man" (Eccl. 12:13) to mean that the entire world was only created for this purpose, meaning to keep them company (Intro to *PhM*, in Kapach ed. p. כד; see Rashi at Exod. 32:7).

23:33. They shall not dwell in your land, lest they cause you to sin against Me and to serve their gods and be a snare for you. — ... we are forbidden from allowing idolators to dwell in our land, so that we not learn from their heresies, as God, may He be exalted, said, "They shall not dwell in your land, lest they cause you to sin against Me...." And if a gentile wishes to dwell in our land, we are not permitted to let him do so unless he accepts upon himself to not practice idolatry, at which point he is permitted to dwell [there]. And this person is called a "resident alien" [*ger toshav*], and he is considered a *ger* only because it is permitted for him to dwell in the land. And the Sages similarly said, "What is a *ger toshav*? This is someone who accepts to not practice idolatry." However, an idolator is not permitted to reside with us [in Israel], and we cannot sell our inheritance to him, or rent it. And this is explicitly explained: "you shall not give them residence in the land" (BT *Avodah Zarah* 20a, based on Deut. 7:2) (*ShM*, Neg. 51; also *Hil. Avodah Zarah* 10:6).

Raavad (*Hil. Avodah Zarah* 10:6) has two objections. First, he says that this verse only applies to the seven Canaanite nations, but not to other peoples. Second, he says that this verse only applies to permanent residence, but not to someone who is passing through. The *Kesef Mishnah* responds that since the verse clearly states the reason for the commandment, namely so that the foreign nations not cause the Jews to sin, Maimonides argued the verse applies to all nations, and even temporary contact (see Rabbi J. David Bleich, *Contemporary Halakhic Problems*, vol. 1, pp. 27-32, esp. p. 30).

Exodus 24

24:1-2. And to Moses He said, "Ascend to the Lord, you and Aaron, Nadab and Abihu, and the seventy elders of Israel, and worship at a distance. And Moses alone shall approach God, but they shall not approach, and the nation shall not ascend with him." — As to the revelation on Mount Sinai, all saw the great fire, and heard the fearful thunderings, that caused such an extraordinary terror; but only those of them who were duly qualified were prophetically inspired, each one according to his capacities. Therefore it is said, "Ascend to the Lord, you and Aaron, Nadab and Abihu." Moses rose to the highest degree of prophecy, according to the words, "And Moses alone shall approach God." Aaron was below him, Nadab and Abihu below Aaron, and the seventy elders below Nadab and Abihu, and the rest below the latter, each one according to his degree of perfection. Similarly our Sages wrote, "Moses had his own place and Aaron his own" (*Guide* 2:32).

FURTHER: [Maimonides comments on the use of the words *karav*, *naga*, and *nagash*, all of which have a basic meaning of "approach" or "draw near":] There can be no doubt respecting the verses "The Lord is close [*karov*] to all them that call upon Him" (Ps. 145:18), "They take delight in approaching [*kirvat*] to God" (Isa. 58:2): "The nearness [*kiravat*] of God is pleasant to Me" (Ps. 73:28). All such phrases intimate a spiritual approach, i.e., the attainment of some knowledge, not, however, approach in space. Thus also "who has God so near [*kerovim*] unto Him" (Deut. 4:7), "Draw you near [*kerav*] and hear" (Deut. 5:23), "And Moses alone shall approach [*ve-niggash*] God; but they shall not approach [*yiggashu*]" (Exod. 24:2).

If, however, you wish to take the words "And Moses alone shall approach" to mean that he shall draw near a certain place in the mountain, whereon the Divine Light shone, or, in the words of the

Bible, "where the glory of the Lord abode," you may do so, provided you do not lose sight of the truth that there is no difference whether a person stand at the center of the earth or at the highest point of the ninth sphere, if this were possible; He is no further away from God in the one case, or nearer to Him in the other; those only approach Him who obtain a knowledge of Him; while those who remain ignorant of Him recede from Him (*Guide* 1:18; see also *Guide* 3:51, and Malbim on Exod. 19:15).

24:5. And he sent the young men of the children of Israel... — Tradition teaches that what is said, "And he sent the young men [*na'arei*] of the children of Israel" refers to the firstborn, for the service had always been [performed] by the firstborn from Adam until Moses our teacher (*PhM Zevaḥim* 14:4).

> This interpretation is based on *Zevaḥim* 115b, and is quoted by Onkelos, Rashi, R. Saadiah, and Rashbam, all of whom say this refers to firstborn (*bekhorot*). However, Ibn Ezra and Ḥizkuni say it refers to *baḥurim*, "young men" (Ḥizkuni says it is to train them in the commandments). See also Nahmanides, who offers rationales for both interpretations, *bekhorot* and *baḥurim*.

... and they brought burnt offerings, and offered peace offerings of oxen to the Lord. — [Maimonides counts this as one of the three acts by which the Jews entered into the covenant with God, i.e., circumcision, immersion, and bringing an offering; see at Exod. 12:48 and 19:10] — And there was an offering, as it says, "And he sent the young men of the children of Israel, and they brought burnt offerings," and they offered them on behalf of all Israel (*Issurei Bi'ah* 13:3).

FURTHER: ... Israel entered into this religion of God by three actions: circumcision, immersion, and bringing an offering [the previous clause is slightly modified]: they were circumcised by the messenger [Moses] in Egypt when he gave them the commandment of the Passover offering, and he warned them that no uncircumcised male may eat from it, and they immersed in the wilderness before the giving of the Torah, and they brought burnt offerings and peace offerings as He said, "and they brought burnt offerings, and offered peace offerings," and then the Torah was given to them (*PhM*, Introduction to *Kodshim*, Kapach p. י׳).

24:7. And Moses took the book of the covenant, and read in the ears of the people, and they said, "All that the Lord has spoken we will do and we will hear." — When Moses was sent to us we signified our acceptance with the words, "All that the Lord has spoken we will do and we will hear" (*Epistle to Yemen*, p. 109).

24:10. And they saw the God of Israel... — In this figurative sense the verb [*ra'ah*, "see"] is to be understood, when applied to God, e.g., "I saw [*ra'iti*] the Lord" (1 Kings 22:19), "And the Lord appeared [*va-yera*] unto him (Gen. 18:1), "And God saw [*va-yar*] that it was good" (Gen. 1:10), "I beseech You, show me [*har'eni*] Your glory" (Exod. 33:18), "And they saw [*va-yiru*] the God of Israel" (Exod. 24:10). All these instances refer to intellectual perception, and by no means to perception with the eye as in its literal meaning: for, on the one hand, the eye can only perceive a corporeal object, and in connection with it certain accidents, as color, shape, etc.; and, on the other hand, God does not perceive by means of a corporeal organ (*Guide* 1:4).

... and there was under His feet as it were like the action of the whiteness of the sapphire stone ... — See *Yesodei ha-Torah* 1:9, quoted at Exod. 9:3.

FURTHER: Onkelos, as you know, in his version, considers the word "his feet" [*raglav*] as a figurative expression and a substitute for "throne": the words "under his feet" [*ve-taḥat raglav*] he therefore paraphrases, "and under the throne of His glory [*u-teḥot kursei yekareih*]." Consider this well, and you will observe with wonder how Onkelos keeps free from the idea of the corporeality of God, and from everything that leads thereto, even in the remotest degree. For he does not say, "and under His throne"; the direct relation of the throne to God, implied in the literal sense of the phrase "His throne" would necessarily suggest the idea that God is supported by a material object, and thus lead directly to the corporeality of God. He therefore refers the throne to His glory, i.e., to the Divine Presence, which is a light created for the purpose....

According to our opinion "under his feet [*raglav*]" denotes "under that of which He is the cause," "that which exists through Him," as we have already stated. They [the young men of the children of Israel, v. 5] therefore comprehended the real nature of the *materia prima*, which emanated from Him, and of whose existence He is the only cause. Consider well the phrase, "like the action of the whiteness of the sapphire stone." If the color were the point of comparison, the words "as the whiteness of the sapphire stone" would have sufficed; but the addition of "like the action [*ke-ma'aseh*]" was necessary, because matter, as such, is, as you are well aware, always receptive and passive, active only by some accident. On the other hand, form, as such, is always active, and only passive by some accident, as is explained in works on Physics. This explains the addition of "like the action" in reference to the *materia prima*. The expression "the whiteness of the sapphire" refers to the transparency, not to the white color: for "the whiteness" of the sapphire is not a white color, but the property of being transparent. Things, however, which are transparent, have no color of their own, as is proved in works on Physics: for if they had a color they would not permit all the colors to pass through

399

them nor would they receive colors: it is only when the transparent object is totally colorless, that it is able to receive successively all the colors. In this respect it (the whiteness of the sapphire) is like the *materia prima*, which as such is entirely formless, and thus receives all the forms one after the other. What they [the young men of the children of Israel] perceived was therefore the *materia prima*, whose relation to God is distinctly mentioned, because it is the source of those of His creatures which are subject to genesis and destruction, and has been created by Him. This subject also will be treated later on more fully. Observe that you must have recourse to an explanation of this kind, even when adopting the rendering of Onkelos, "And under the throne of His glory," for in fact the *materia prima* is also under the heavens, which are called "throne of God," as we have remarked above.

I should not have thought of this unusual interpretation, or hit on this argument were it not for an utterance of R. Eliezer ben Hyrcanus, which will be discussed in one of the parts of this treatise (*Guide* 1:26).

FURTHER: One important thing R. Eliezer taught us here, that the substance of the heavens is different from that of the earth: that there are two different substances: the one is described as belonging to God, being the light of His garment, on account of its superiority; and the other, the earthly substance, which is distant from His splendor and light, as being the snow under the throne of His glory. This led me to explain the words, "And under His feet as like the action of the whiteness of the sapphire stone" (Exod. 24:10), as expressing that the young men of the children of Israel comprehended in a prophetical vision the nature of the earthly *materia prima*. For, according to Onkelos, the pronoun in the phrase, "his feet," refers to "throne," as I have shown. This indicates that the whiteness under the throne signifies the earthly substance. R. Eliezer has thus repeated the same idea, and told us that there are two substances: a higher one, and a lower one; and that there is not one substance common to all things. This is an important subject, and we must not think light of the opinion which the wisest men in Israel have held on this point. It concerns an important point in explaining the existence of the Universe, and one of the mysteries of the Law. In *Bereshit Rabbah* (ch. 12) the following passage occurs: "R. Eliezer says: The things in the heavens have been created of the heavens, the things on earth of the earth." Consider how ingeniously this sage stated that all things on earth have one common substance: the heavens and the things in them have one substance, different from the first. He also explains in the Chapters [of R. Eliezer], in addition to the preceding things, the superiority of the heavenly substance, and its proximity to God; and, on the other hand, the inferiority of the earthly substance and its position (*Guide* 2:26; see also *Guide* 3:4).

... and as if it were the body [*etzem*] of the heaven in clearness. — ... the meaning of *etzem* here [i.e., M. *Bekhorot* 6:9] is one "body" [*guf*] and one piece... as the phrase "and as if it were the body [*etzem*] of the heaven in clearness" (*PhM Bekhorot* 6:9).

24:11. And he did not lay his hands on the nobles of the children of Israel, also they saw God, and did eat and drink. — ... "the nobles of the children of Israel" were impetuous, and allowed their thoughts to go unrestrained: what they perceived was but imperfect. Therefore it is said of them, "And they saw the God of Israel, and there was under his feet..." (Exod. 24:10): and not merely, "and they saw the God of Israel"; the purpose of the whole passage is to criticize their act of seeing and not to describe it. They are blamed for the nature of their perception, which was to a certain extent corporeal—a result which necessarily followed, from the fact that they ventured too far before being perfectly prepared. They deserved to perish, but at the intercession of Moses this fate was averted by God for the time. They were afterwards burnt at Taberah (Num. 11:1), except Nadab and Abihu, who were burnt in the Tabernacle of the congregation (Lev. 10:1-2), according to what is stated by authentic tradition (*Tanḥuma, Leviticus Rabbah*).

If such was the case with them, how much more is it incumbent on us who are inferior, and on those who are below us, to persevere in perfecting our knowledge of the elements, and in rightly understanding the preliminaries which purify the mind from the defilement of error: then we may enter the holy and divine camp in order to gaze: as the Bible says, "And let the priests also, which come near to the Lord, sanctify themselves, lest the Lord break forth upon them" (Exod. 19:22). Solomon, also, has cautioned all who endeavor to attain this high degree of knowledge in the following figurative terms, "Guard your foot when you go to the house of God" (Eccl. 4:17).

I will now return to complete what I commenced to explain. The nobles of the Children of Israel, besides erring in their perception, were, through this cause, also misled in their actions: for in consequence of their confused perception, they gave way to bodily cravings. This is meant by the words, "Also they saw God, and did eat and drink" (Exod. 24:11). The principal part of that passage, i.e., "And there was under his feet as it were a paved work of a sapphire stone" (Exod. 24:10), will be further explained in the course of the present treatise (*Guide* 1:28 and 2:26, both quoted at v. 10; 2:26; see also *Guide* 3:4). All we here intend to say is that wherever in a similar connection any one of the three verbs mentioned above occurs [*ra'ah, hibbit, ḥaza*], it has reference to intellectual perception, not to the sensation of sight by the eye: for God is not a being to be perceived by the eye.

It will do no harm, however, if those who are unable to comprehend what we here endeavor to explain should refer all the words in question to sensuous perception, to seeing lights created [for the purpose], angels, or similar beings (*Guide* 1:5).

Maimonides' negative interpretation is based on the *Tanḥuma*, "Beha'alotekha" 16, and this is the first of two interpretations quoted by Rashi. Rashi's second interpretation is that on Onkelos: bringing offerings is as pleasurable as eating and drinking. It is also worth noting that Maimonides here breaks with, and rejects, the interpretation of Onkelos.

24:12. And the Lord said to Moses, "Ascend to Me on the mountain, and be there, that I may give you the stone tablets, and the law, and the commandment which I have for their instruction. — Know that all of the commandments that were given to Moses were given with their explanations, as it says, "that I may give you the stone tablets, and the law, and the commandment." "Law" [*Torah*] refers to the written Torah, and "commandment" [*mitzvah*] means its explanation. And we are commanded to observe the Torah by its explanation, and this *mitzvah* is called the oral Torah (Introduction to the *Mishneh Torah*).

FURTHER: Know that the Sages said that 613 commandments were related to Moses at Sinai, which teaches that this is the number of commandments that are applicable to all generations. For the commandments that do not apply to all generations have no relevance to Sinai, whether or not they were given there. Rather, the Sages' intention by saying "at Sinai" is that the essence of the Torah was given at Sinai, as God, may He be exalted, said, "Ascend to Me on the mountain, and be there, that I may give you...." And in clarifying this, they said, "What does it mean 'Moses commanded us Torah, an inheritance'? meaning the numerical equivalent of Torah, which is 611, and 'I am the Lord' and 'You shall have no other gods' they heard from the Almighty,' and this completes the count of 613" (*ShM*, Principle 3).

24:16. And the glory of God... — The phrase [glory of God] sometimes signifies "the material light," which God caused to rest on a certain place in order to show the distinction of that place, e.g., "And the glory of God dwelled upon Mount Sinai and the cloud covered it" (Exod. 24:16), "And the glory of the Lord filled the tabernacle" (Exod. 40:35). Sometimes the essence, the reality of God is meant by that expression, as in the words of Moses, "Show me Your glory" (Exod. 33:18), to which the reply was given, "For no man shall see Me and live" (Exod. 33:20). This shows that the glory of the Lord in this instance is the same as He Himself, and that "Your glory" has been substituted for "Yourself," as a tribute of homage... (*Guide* 1:64).

... dwelled [*va-yishkon*] on mount Sinai, and a cloud covered the mountain for six days, and He called to Moses on the seventh day from the midst of the cloud. — [When *shakhen*, "dwell," is applied to God it is employed] to denote the continuance of His Divine Presence (*Shekhinah*) or of His Providence in some place where the Divine Presence manifested itself constantly, or in some object which was constantly protected by Providence, e.g. "And the glory of the Lord dwelled" (Exod. 24:16), "And I will dwell among the children of Israel" (Exod. 29:45), "And for the goodwill of him that dwelled in the bush" (Deut. 33:16). Whenever the term is applied to the Almighty, it must be taken consistently with the context in the sense either as referring to the Presence of His *Shekhinah* (i.e., of His light that was created for the purpose) in a certain place, or of the continuance of His Providence protecting a certain object (*Guide* 1:25).

Rabbi Gil Student writes, "In multiple places, Rambam defines *Shekhinah* as either a created light or continuous guidance (providence). The created light means that when the *Shekhinah* dwells on a place (e.g. the Temple in Jerusalem), a miraculous radiance illuminates the area, a visible marker proving sanctity to all observers. In *Moreh Nevukhim*, Rambam uses the term 'created light' in many places. At the end of 1:5, Rambam says that visions of the supernatural refer to intellectual understanding. However, he adds, if you want to believe that they refer to created light or something similar, there is nothing wrong with that. That strongly implies that he does not believe visions of the *Shekhinah* are created light. However, in 1:27, he praises Onkelos for translating anthropomorphic terms referring to God's motion as meaning the created light, which is the *Shekhinah* or divine guidance. This implies that he believes the visions of the *Shekhinah* are created light" ("What Is the *Shekhinah*?" Torah Musings, November 30, 2017).

FURTHER: [Maimonides uses the past tense verb "dwelled" to prove that Muhammed cannot be a prophet] … the use of the past tense ["dwelled"] indicates that it is an event that has taken place, namely, it describes the revelation at Mount Sinai. It did not descend suddenly like a thunderbolt, but came down gently, manifesting itself gradually, first from the top of one mountain, then from another, until it came to rest on Sinai. Hence He says, "The Lord came from Sinai; He shone upon them from Seir; He appeared from Mount Paran" (Deut. 33:2). Mark well the expression "upon them," i.e., Israel. Note that with Paran, which is further removed from Sinai, he says "appeared [*hofi'a*]"; of Seir, which is nearer, "He shone [*ve-zarah*]," and of the revelation, of the full splendor of God on Sinai, which was the goal of the theophany (as is related), "The glory of God dwelled on mount Sinai." He says *came* from Sinai ("Epistle to Yemen," p. 109).

PARASHAT TERUMAH

Exodus 25

25:1-2. And the Lord spoke to Moses, saying: Speak to the children of Israel that they take for Me an offering [*terumah*], from every man whose heart gives voluntarily shall you take my offering. — Anything that is collected from Israel for the tabernacle is called *terumah*, as it says, "that they take for Me an offering [*terumah*]." And just as none of these five [i.e., a deaf-mute, imbecile, minor, one who donates something that does not belong to him, and a gentile] cannot bring it [for the tabernacle], so too their *terumah* from the threshing-floor is not valid. And they were prohibited from donating *terumah* for the tabernacle, as it says, "Speak to the children of Israel" — which excludes a gentile; "from every man" — which excludes a minor; "whose heart gives voluntarily" — which excludes a deaf-mute and imbecile, since they do not have the capacity to volunteer anything; "which you shall take from them" (v. 3) — which excludes someone who donates something that does not belong to him (*PhM Terumot* 1:1).

.. for Me... — [See at Exod. 28:41. Maimonides is commenting on the word *li*, which can be translated either "to me" or "for me"] The Sages said: Wherever it says "to Me," it means lasting [*kayyam*], such as "to minister to Me," which means enduring, and it is not a temporary commandment; rather it is a commandment for all generations (*ShM*, Pos. 176).

25:4. And *tekhelet*... — The *tekhelet* mentioned anywhere in the Torah is wool dyed light blue, which is the appearance of the firmament that is visible to the eye in the clearness of the firmament (*Tzitzit* 2:1).

Elsewhere, Maimonides writes, "Whenever *tekhelet* is mentioned anywhere, it means wool dyed blue like the

409

clearness of the heavens, which is lighter than [regular] blue (*Klei ha-Mikdash* 8:13), a point he also repeats at *PhM Kela'im* 9:1.

... and *argaman*... — *argaman* is wool dyed red (*Klei ha-Mikdash* 8:13).

Elsewhere, Maimonides says *argaman* refers to something that is blood red (see *PhM Kela'im* 9:1, and Kapach's comment there). Raavad (on *Klei ha-Mikdash* 8:13) writes, "It seems to me that *argaman* is something weaved from two or three colors, therefore it is called *argaman*." Regarding the Raavad's comment, the *Kesef Mishnah* writes, "and his meaning is that *argaman* is a compound word *arug min* ['a type of weave']." R. Saadiah and Ibn Ezra also understand *argaman* as "red." All English translations I have consulted render *argaman* as "purple." See also Jacob Milgrom, *Numbers*, p. 27.

... and *tola'at shani*... — ... *tola'at shani* is wool dyed with a gnat (*Klei ha-Mikdash* 8:13).

Maimonides explains *tola'at* as follows: "*Tola'at* refers to red berries that are like carob seeds. They are like sumac berries. Each berry has an insect that resembles a mosquito [or 'gnat']" (*Parah Adumah* 3:2). Maimonides makes the other following comments about *tola'at shani*: It is a dull red (*PhM Kela'im* 9:1, and Kapach there); the Targum of *tola'at shani* is *tzeva zehori* (*PhM Yoma* 4:2). Jastrow defines *zehori* as either "safran" or "crimson." In other words, Maimonides understands *argaman* and *tola'at shani* as two different shades of red.

... and *shesh*... — Whenever the Torah says *shesh* or *bad*, this is flax, meaning linen (*Klei ha-Mikdash* 8:13).

FURTHER: Whenever the Torah says *shesh* or *shesh mashzar*, the string must be sixfold (*Klei ha-Mikdash* 8:14).

> Regarding the term *bad*, there he writes, "it is valid even if only one string is used, but it is preferable to be sixfold."

25:8. And let them make Me a sanctuary... — ... we are commanded to build a house of service in which we make offerings, bring the eternal flame, and ascend for the festival and gather every year, as will be explained. And this is what God, may He be exalted, said, "And let them make Me a sanctuary." And the language of the *Sifrei* is, "Israel was given three commandments when they entered the land: (1) to appoint a king, (2) to build a Temple, and (3) to destroy the seed of Amalek." Therefore it is clear that building a Temple is a separate commandment. And it has already been explained that this is a general principle which includes separate components, and that the candelabrum, the table, and the altar are all components of the Temple, and together they are called "Temple" even though this commandment includes separate parts (*ShM*, Pos. 20).

> Elsewhere Maimonides writes, "It is not proper to count individually the separate parts that are required to perform a mitzvah.... It says, 'And let them make Me a sanctuary,' and this is one positive commandment among the other commandments, and that is that we build a house that is prepared so they come to it and observe the festivals there, and make offerings there, and gather there for holidays. And then it comes to explain the components of how they shall be made. And it is not proper to count each time it says

411

'and you shall make' as a separate commandment" (*ShM*, Principle 12).

Nahmanides says that the ark is a separate commandment, but the other vessels are included in the commandment of building the Temple (*Hassagot*, Pos. 33).

FURTHER: It is a positive commandment to make a house for the Lord, prepared to bring sacrifices, and observe festivals three times a year, as it says, "and let them make Me a sanctuary." And the tabernacle that Moses made is explained in the Torah. And it was temporary, as it says, "For you have not yet come [to the resting place and inheritance]" (Deut. 12:9). When the Jews entered the land, they established the tabernacle in Gilgal for the fourteen years that they were conquering and dividing the land. And from there they came to Shilo, and they built a house of stones and spread the tabernacle curtains over it, but it did not have a roof. The tabernacle in Shilo stood for 369 years, and it was destroyed when Eli died. Then they came to Nob and built a temple there, and when Samuel died it was destroyed. And they came to Gibeon and built a temple there, and from Gibeon they came to the eternal House, and they were in Nob and Gibeon for 57 years.

Once the Temple in Jerusalem was built, it was forbidden to build a house of God in any other place and to bring sacrifices there. And there is no other house for any future generations except in Jerusalem alone, and on Mount Moriah on which it rests, as it says, "And David said, this is the house of the Lord God, and this is the altar of burnt offerings for Israel" (1 Chron. 22:1), and says, "This is My resting place forever and ever" (Ps. 132:14) (*Bet ha-Beḥirah* 1:1-3).

Curiously, elsewhere, Maimonides says the commandment to build the Temple is based on "you shall seek His Presence and go there" (Deut. 12:5) (see *Melakhim* 1:1). The *Kesef*

Mishnah explains the contradiction as follows: "It appears that he did not want to say that this commandment is because of 'And let them make Me a sanctuary' as our Rabbi wrote, because this verse seems to apply to the tabernacle in the wilderness" (on *Bet ha-Beḥirah* 1:1).

FURTHER: It says, "And let them make Me a sanctuary," and according to tradition, this means "Let them make from what belongs to Me" (*Temurah* 31a), and that is the sacred maintenance offerings (*PhM Temurah* 7:1).

FURTHER: But the custom which was in those days general among all men, and the general mode of worship in which the Israelites were brought up, consisted in sacrificing animals in those temples which contained certain images, to bow down to those images, and to burn incense before them; religious and ascetic persons were in those days the persons that were devoted to the service in the temples erected to the stars, as has been explained by us. It was in accordance with the wisdom and plan of God, as displayed in the whole Creation, that He did not command us to give up and to discontinue all these manners of service; for to obey such a commandment it would have been contrary to the nature of man, who generally cleaves to that to which he is used; it would in those days have made the same impression as a prophet would make at present if he called us to the service of God and told us in His name, that we should not pray to Him, not fast, not seek His help in time of trouble; that we should serve Him in thought, and not by any action. For this reason God allowed these kinds of service to continue; He transferred to His service that which had formerly served as a worship of created beings, and of things imaginary and unreal, and commanded us to serve Him in the same manner; namely, to build unto Him a temple; e.g., "And they shall make Me a sanctuary" (Exod. 25:8); to have the altar erected to His name, e.g., "An altar of earth shall you make for Me" (Exod. 20:21); to offer the sacrifices to Him, e.g., "If any man of you bring an offering unto the Lord" (Lev. 1:2), to bow down to Him, and to burn incense before Him. He has forbidden to do any of these things to any other being, e.g., "One who sacrifices to gods, except the Lord alone, shall be destroyed" (Exod. 22:19); "For you shall bow down to no other God" (Exod. 34:14). He selected priests for the service in the Temple, e.g., "And they shall minister unto Me in the priest's office" (Exod. 28:41). He made it obligatory that certain gifts, called the gifts of the Levites and the priests, should be assigned to them for their maintenance while they are engaged in the service of the temple and its sacrifices. By this Divine plan it was effected that the traces of idolatry were blotted out, and the truly great principle of our faith, the Existence and Unity of God, was firmly established; this result was thus obtained without deterring or confusing the minds of the people by the abolition of the service to which they were accustomed and which alone was familiar to them (*Guide* 3:32).

> Nahmanides does not believe the tabernacle was remedial, but rather optimal: "They are now holy, in that they are worthy that there be amongst them a Sanctuary through which He makes His Divine Glory dwell among them. Therefore He first commanded concerning the Tabernacle, so that He have amongst them a house dedicated to His name, from where He would speak with Moses and command the children of Israel. Thus the main purpose of the Tabernacle was to contain a place in which the Divine Glory rests, this being the ark..." (on Exod. 25:1).

... that I may dwell [*ve-shakhanti*] among them. — Whenever the term [*shakhen*] is applied to the Almighty, it must be taken consistently with the context in the sense either as referring to the

Presence of His *Shekhinah* (i.e., of His light that was created for this purpose) in a certain place, or of the continuance of His Providence protecting a certain object (*Guide* 1:25; see further at Exod. 24:16).

25:9. In accordance with all that I show you concerning the pattern [*tavnit*] of the tabernacle and the pattern [*tavnit*] of all its instrument... — *Tavnit*, derived from the verb *banah* ["he built"], signifies the build and construction of a thing—that is to say, its figure, whether square, round, triangular, or of any other shape, e.g., "the pattern [*tavnit*] of the Tabernacle and the pattern [*tavnit*] of all its vessels" (Exod. 25:9); "according to the pattern [*tavnit*] which you were shown upon the mount" (Exod. 25:40); "the form [*tavnit*] of any bird" (Deut. 4:17); "the form [*tavnit*] of a hand" (Ezek. 8:3); "the pattern [*tavnit*] of the porch" (1 Chron. 28:11). In all these quotations it is the shape which is referred to. Therefore the Hebrew language never employs the word *tavnit* in speaking of the qualities of God Almighty (*Guide* 1:3).

... so shall you [pl.] make it. — God said to Moses, "In accordance with all that I show you... so shall you make it," meaning by this that every sanctuary that will be made in the future shall be made like this. And it is known that Moses was a king and counted among the kings in addition to having prophecy, as it says, "And he was a king in Jeshurun" (Deut. 33:5) (*PhM Shevuot* 2:2).

> Maimonides seems to agree with Rashi, who says that *ve-khen ta'asu*, "and so shall you make it," refers to "future generations." Maimonides, like Rashi, also quotes the teaching that this verse applies *le-dorot* (see *Bet ha-Behirah* 6:11; *PhM Sanhedrin* 1:5).

25:14-15. And you shall put poles in the rings of the side of the ark, by which to carry the ark. And the poles shall be in the

rings of the ark; they shall not be removed from it. — ... we are prohibited from removing the poles of the ark from the rings, as God, may He be exalted, said, "And the poles shall be in the rings of the ark; they shall not be removed from it." And whoever violates this prohibition is liable to receive lashes. And at the end of *Makkot* (22a), the Sages said, "When they mentioned those who are liable for lashes, there is one opinion that omitted someone who removes the poles [from the list], which means that [everyone else agrees] that he is liable to receive lashes." Therefore it is explained to you that it is a negative commandment and someone who violates it is liable to receive lashes (*ShM*, Neg. 86).

FURTHER: When [the Levites] carry [the ark] on their shoulders, they should carry it face to face, and their backs facing outward, and their faces inward. And they are prohibited from removing the poles from the rings. And if someone removes one of the poles from the rings he is liable to receive lashes, as it says, "And the poles shall be in the rings of the ark; they shall not be removed from it" (*Klei ha-Mikdash* 2:13).

> Rabbi Hayyim Angel writes that according to Maimonides, "the people who carried the Ark had to face one another. Their formation parallels the Cherubim, which also faced one another. The Ark represents the mutual covenant between God and Israel. The human side is to bear the burden of the Torah. The poles must be kept attached to the Ark since we must always bear the covenant. The divine side is that God communicates to Israel from between the Cherubim."[174]

25:18. And you shall make two cherubim of gold—you shall make them of hammered gold and the two ends of the ark cover. — ... it is clear that the belief in the existence of angels is connected with the belief in the Existence of God; and the belief in God and angels

---

174. *A Synagogue Companion*, p. 99.

leads to the belief in Prophecy and in the truth of the Law. In order to firmly establish this creed, God commanded [the Israelites] to make over the ark the form of two angels. The belief in the existence of angels is thus inculcated into the minds of the people, and this belief is in importance next to the belief in God's existence; it leads us to believe in Prophecy and in the Law, and opposes idolatry. If there had only been one figure of a cherub, the people would have been misled and would have mistaken it for God's image which was to be worshipped, in the fashion of the heathen; or they might have assumed that the angel [represented by the figure] was also a deity, and would thus have adopted a Dualism. By making two cherubim and distinctly declaring "the Lord is our God, the Lord is One," Moses dearly proclaimed the theory of the existence of a number of angels; he left no room for the error of considering those figures as deities, since [he declared that] God is one, and that He is the Creator of the angels, who are more than one (*Guide* 3:45).

R. Abraham the son of Maimonides quotes that from their head to shoulders the cherubim had the form of a man, and from their shoulders to the bottom of the body was the form of a bird.

25:22. And there I will meet with you, and I shall speak with you from above the mercy seat, from between the two cherubim that are upon the ark of testimony, of everything that I command you to the children of Israel. — Prophecy came to Moses during the day and he was standing, as God entrusted him, "And there I will meet with you, and I will speak with you..." (*PhM Sanhedrin* 10:1).

FURTHER: Moses heard the voice addressing him "from above the mercy seat, from between the two cherubim" without the medium of the imaginative faculty [that was necessary for other prophets] (*Guide* 2:45; see also on Exod. 33:11).

25:23. And you shall make the table of acacia wood, two cubits in length and one cubit in width, and half a cubit in height. — It is explicit in the Torah that the table is two cubits in length and one cubit in width (Exod. 25:23, 37:10). Rabbi Judah says a "cubit" is five handbreadths. Rabbi Meir says every "cubit" mentioned in the Torah or by the Sages is six handbreadths, except for the golden altar and the horn of the outer altar, and the base [*sovev*] and the pillar [*yesod*], which are five handbreadths, as we will explain in the third chapter of *Middot*. And the law follows Rabbi Meir (*PhM Menaḥot* 11:5).

25:29. And you shall make its *ke'arot* [plates]... — The molds [*defusin*] use to make the showbread are called its *ke'arot* (*Bet ha-Beḥirah* 3:14).

... and its *kappotav* [cups]... — There were two incense bowls [*bazikkin*] in which the frankincense was placed, and that was placed on the table beside the arrangement [of showbread]. And this is called its *kappot* (*Bet ha-Beḥirah* 3:14; see also *PhM Menaḥot* 1:6).

... and its *kesot* [props]... — The table had four sides of gold that were y-shaped at the end that were next to the two arrangements of showbread; two next to each arrangement, and the Torah called its *kesot* (*Bet ha-Beḥirah* 3:13).

... and its *menakiyyot* [rods]... — There were 28 rods of gold; each one was like half a reed. Fourteen were used for each arrangement. And these are called its *menakiyyot*.... Regarding these fourteen rods, one puts the first loaves on the table itself. Three rods were set between the first and second loaves. And similarly, there were three rods between each loaf. And between the sixth and fifth, there were only two rods, since there is not one above the sixth. Thus there are fourteen rods in each arrangement (*Beit ha-Beḥirah* 3:14-15).

FURTHER: There were three molds [*defusin*] of gold for them [the showbread]. In the first, the bread was placed while it was still dough. In the second, it was kneaded. And in the third, it was placed after being removed from the oven so that it would not be damaged (*Temidin u-Musafin* 5:8).

25:30. And you shall set the showbread on the table before Me always. — We are obligated to place the showbread before God always, as He said, "And you shall set the showbread on the table before Me always." And you already know that the Torah means to place hot bread every Sabbath, along with frankincense, and the priests shall eat the bread that was made on the previous Sabbath (*ShM*, Pos. 27; see also *Shoresh* 10).

FURTHER: How does one arrange the bread? Four priests enter [the Sanctuary]. Two are holding two arrangements [of bread; i.e., each priest holds one loaf], and two are holding two [arrangements of] frankincense. And four enter preceding them, two to take away the two arrangements [of bread] and two to take away the frankincense that were on the table. The priests entering stand on the north side with their faces to the south, and those departing stand on the south with the faces to the north. These remove [the previous week's showbread], and these set down [the fresh bread], and they should be within a handbreadth of each other, as it says, before Me always" (*Temidin u-Musafin* 5:4).

Since the Torah says *tamid*, "always," even when the showbreads are exchanged there should be no interruption.

... showbread... — All of the loaves are rectangular, as it says, *leḥem panim*, which means it should have many sides.

The loaves were ten handbreadths in length, five handbreadths in width, and seven fingerbreadths in height (*Temidin u-Musafin* 5:9; also *PhM Menaḥot* 11:4).

... before Me always. — After the festival, on the day after the holiday, they would immerse all of the vessels that were in the Temple, since the commoners had touched them during the festival during the celebration. Therefore they would say, "Take care not to touch the table" when they would show it to the celebrants, so that it would not become impure after the festival by their touching, and would require immersion and waiting until nightfall [to become ritually pure again], and it says, "before Me always" (*Metammei Mishkav u-Moshav* 11:11).

25:31. And you shall make the candelabrum of pure gold, the candelabrum shall be of beaten work, its base and its shaft... — The design of the candelabrum is explicit in the Torah. There were four goblets, two bulbs, and two flowers, on the trunk of the candelabrum, as it says, "and on the candelabrum there shall be four goblets like almond blossoms [*gevi'im meshukkadim*], its bulbs [*kaftoreha*], and its flowers [*u-feraḥeha*]"

(Exod. 25:34). And there was a third flower that was at the base of the candelabrum, as it says, "from its base to its flower" (Num. 8:4). And it had three legs. And there were three additional bulbs on the shaft of the candelabrum, from which six arms extended, three on each side. And each of these arms had had three goblets, one bulb, and one flower. And all [of the ornaments] were decorated as if with almonds. Thus there were twenty-two goblets, nine flowers, and eleven bulbs. The absence of one of these invalidates everything else. Even if one of these 42 ornaments was missing, that invalidated everything (*Bet ha-Beḥirah* 3:1-3).

> In the *halakhot* that follow, Maimonides notes that this only applies if the candelabrum was made from gold, as the verse specifies. However, the candelabrum could also be made of other materials, and in those cases, it did not require this ornamentation. The Chabad website points out that in the times of the Maccabees, the candelabrum was made of iron and coated in tin.

FURTHER: The goblets [*gevi'im*] are like Alexandrian cups with wide mouths and narrow bases. The bulbs [*kaftorim*] are like the apples of Beros which are slightly elongated, like eggs at both ends. The flowers [*peraḥim*] are like the flowers of a column which are like a bowl and whose edges are bent outward. The candelabrum was eighteen handbreadths high:

- Its feet, [base,] and [lowest] flower were three handbreadths high,
- Then two empty handbreadths,
- The next handbreadth had a goblet, a bulb, and a flower,
- Then two empty handbreadths,
- Then a handbreadth with a bulb and two branches stretching outward from it, one to each side, stretching outward and ascending until reaching the full height of the candelabrum,
- An empty handbreadth,

Then a handbreadth with a bulb and two branches stretching outward from it, one to each side, stretching outward and ascending until reaching the full height of the candelabrum,

- Then an empty handbreadth,
- Then a handbreadth with a bulb and two branches stretching outward from it, one to each side, stretching outward and ascending until reaching the full height of the candelabrum,
- [Thus,] three handbreadths remained, with three goblets, a bulb, and a flower (*Bet ha-Beḥirah* 3:9-10; repeated almost verbatim at *PhM Menaḥot* 3:7).

25:33-34. ... *meshukkadim*... — And the explanation of the word in the Torah *meshukkadim* is "made of *shekeidim* [almonds]," which is a craft known to coppersmiths, who beat metal with a mallet until it is made to look like almonds, and this is a well-known craft and does not require explanation (*PhM Menaḥot* 3:7).

Onkelos translates *meshukkadim* as *metzayyerin*, "decorated" (vv. 33-34) and Rashi follows this translation (v. 33). However Maimonides appears to understand it literally: *meshukkadim* comes from *shakeid*, "almond." Most English translations also follow this line of interpretation.

25:37. And you shall make its seven lamps, and raise its lamps, and mount the lamps, to illuminate the space in front of it. — The [absence of one of the] seven branches of the candelabrum invalidate the others, and the [absence of one of the] seven lamps invalidate the others, whether it is made from gold or other metals. And all the lamps were affixed to the branches. The six lamps were affixed to the six branches that extended from the candelabrum, all facing the center lamp that is on the [central] branch of the candelabrum. And the central one faced the holy of holies, and this is called the western lamp (*Bet ha-Beḥirah* 3:7-8; see also *PhM Tamid* 3:1).

מערב

מזרח

25:38-39. And its tongs and its scoops are to be of pure gold. And he shall make it of one talent of pure gold, all of these utensils. — [Maimonides is here addressing a technical point; the Torah states the candelabrum shall be of a 'talent' [*kikkar*] of pure gold. Some of the utensils are all of pure gold. Here, Maimonides is recounting what is counted as being part of the talent of gold, and what is made from a separate supply of gold:] The tongs, scoops, and containers of oil are not included in the talent [of gold]. This is because regarding the candelabrum it says, "pure gold" (Exod. 25:31) and then goes back and says "its tongs and scoops of pure gold" (v. 38) [suggesting the gold for tongs and scoops comes from a different measure of gold]. And the Torah does not say, *"its lamps shall be of pure gold," because the lamps were affixed to the candelabrum and are included in the talent (*Bet ha-Beḥirah* 3:6).

25:40. And see and make in accordance with this pattern [*tavnitam*] which was showed to you on the mountain. — On the meaning of *tavnit*, see *Guide* 1:3, quoted at Exod. 25:9.

Exodus 26

26:1. ... *ma'aseh ḥoshev...* — *Ma'aseh ḥoshev* (Exod. 26:1, 26:31, 28:6, 28:15, 36:8, 36:35, 39:8) means that it should be visible from two sides, front and back (*Klei ha-Mikdash* 8:15; see also v. 36).

26:3. The five curtains shall be coupled together, one to another [*ishah el aḥotah*], and the other five curtains shall be coupled one to another. — The two Hebrew nouns *ish* and *ishah* ["man" and "woman"] were originally employed to designate the "male and female" of human beings, but were afterwards applied to the "male and female" of other species of the animal creation. For instance, we read, "Of every clean beast you shall take to you by sevens, male and female [*ish ve-ishto*]" (Gen. 7:2), in the same sense as *ish ve-ishah* [male and female]. The term *zakhar* and *nekeivah* was afterwards applied to anything designed and prepared for union with another object. Thus we read, "The five curtains shall be coupled together, one to the other [*ishah el aḥotah*]." It will easily be seen that the Hebrew equivalents for "brother and sister" are likewise treated as homonyms, and use, in a figurative sense, like *ish* and *ishah* (*Guide* 1:6).

26:6. You shall make fifty clasps of gold, and join the curtains to one another with the clasps, so that the tabernacle shall be one [*eḥad*]. — Maimonides does not quote this verse directly, but elsewhere Maimonides says that *eḥad*, "one," can sometimes refer to a general category that comprises many individual entities. I have suggested that Maimonides understands *eḥad* in such a sense on this verse, based on his comments at *Yesodei ha-Torah* 1:7. See my "A Shrine of Oneness" (Torah Musings).

26:12. The part that remains of the curtains of the tent, the half-curtain that remains, shall hang over the back of the tabernacle

[*ahorei ha-mishkan*]. — The Hebrew term *ahor* is a homonym. It is a noun, signifying "back," e.g., "over the back [*ahorei*] the tabernacle"; "The spear came out behind him [*ahorav*]..." (2 Sam. 2:23) (*Guide* 1:38; see other meanings of *ahor* there).

26:33. And you shall hang the curtain under the clasps, and you shall bring the ark of testimony within the curtain; and the curtain shall separate for you the holy place and the holy of holies. — In the first Temple, there was a wall one cubit thick that separated between the holy place and the holy of holies. When they built the second Temple, they were uncertain if the thickness of the wall should be included in the measurement of the holy place or the holy of holies. Therefore they made the holy of holies twenty full cubits, and they made the holy place forty full cubits, and they left an additional cubit between the holy place and the holy of holies, and they did not build a wall in the second Temple. Rather they made two curtains, one on the side of the holy of holies, and one on the side of the holy place, and there was a cubit of empty space corresponding to the wall in the first [Temple]. However in the first Temple, there was only a curtain, as it says, "and the curtain shall separate" (*Bet ha-Behirah* 4:2).

FURTHER: It is evident that the object of giving different degrees of sanctity to the different places, to the Temple mount, the place between the two walls, to the hall of women, to the hall, and so on up to the most holy, was to raise the respect and reverence of the Temple in the heart of everyone that approached it (*Guide* 3:45).

425

26:36. ... *ma'aseh rokem* **[a work of embroidery] ...** — Wherever it says in the Torah *ma'aseh rokem* (Exod. 26:36, 27:16, 28:39, 36:37, 38:18, 39:29), it means that the images made on the cloth shall be seen on [only] one side of the fabric (*Klei ha-Mikdash* 8:15).

Exodus 27

27:1. And you shall make an altar of acacia wood, five cubits long and five cubits wide, the altar shall be square, and its height shall be three cubits. — The general dimensions of the altar were not mentioned because the matter was well-known, since it did not change by either adding or diminishing from it. The Sages said that the altar that Moses made was ten cubits, and that which Solomon made was ten cubits, and that which the emigrants [in the Second Temple] made was ten cubits. And when it is written, "its height shall be three cubits," that is from the edge of the *ma'arakhah* [where sacrifices were brought; see *Bet ha-Beḥirah* 2:5] and upward. This clarifies that the altar was ten cubits high: one cubit for the base [*yesod*], five for the middle section [*sovev*], three for the place of arrangement [*ma'arakhah*], and one for the protruding corners [*keranot*], since every corner was one cubit in length, height, and width.

And I will draw it [the altar] and I will write the dimensions in terms of "cubits," as it is described in this Mishnah (*Middot* 3:1), and then I will go back and explain its dimensions and mention how it is

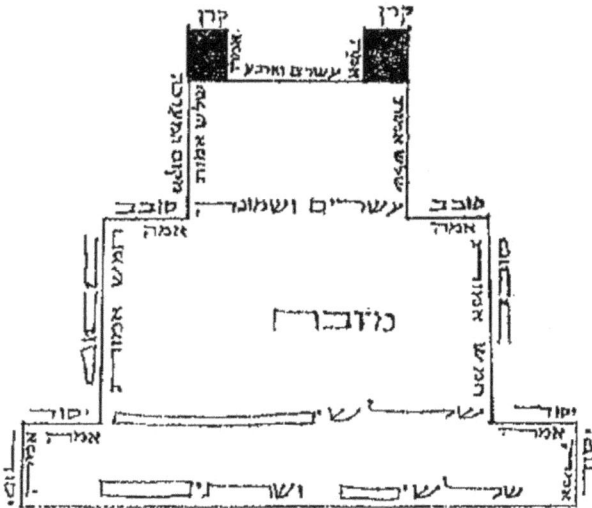

explained in the Talmud tractate *Menaḥot*, for the understanding of
the measurements in the Torah is very difficult, in the place where it
says where they specified the place for the altar, "And David said:
This is the house of the Lord [our] God, and here is the altar of
the burnt-offering for Israel" (1 Chron. 22:1). And this is what the
Sages said: "Rabbi Eliezer said: See the altar is built and Michael
the great minister stands and offers upon it" (*Zevaḥim* 62a). And
the Sages said that three prophets ascended with them from exile:
one testified concerning the altar, one testified concerning the place
of the altar, and one testified about bringing sacrifices even though
there was no Temple. And about what they said 'concerning the
altar' [*al ha-mizbe'aḥ*] is that he testified specifically concerning the
dimensions, and I will explain. And it is imperative to know that
the constructed altar was not hollow like the one that our teacher
Moses, peace be upon him, made; rather it was entirely solid as the
Sages stated concerning its construction (*Zevaḥim* 54a): How do
they build the altar? They bring 32-by-32 bricks for the height of a
cubit and bring different sized—large and small—smooth stones and
they bring plaster, pitch, and [other types of adhesive], and this is the
base [*yesod*]. And they bring 30-by-30 bricks that is five cubits high
and bring smooth stones, etc., and this is the middle section [*sovev*].
And they bring 28-by-28 bricks that are three cubits tall, etc., and
this is the place of arrangement [*ma'arakhah*]. And they bring one
cubit by one cubit and the height of one cubit, and this is the place
of the corners, and do this for each corner. And even though these
matters are known to everyone and it is not necessary to draw them
explicitly, nonetheless I will draw it, as I have set out to do. And here
is the drawing of the altar.

And now I will return to explaining its dimensions. The Sages
already have stated that the *amah* ["cubit"] mentioned in the Mishnah
is a generic cubit [*amah benonit*], which is six handbreadths. And we
have already mentioned in *Menaḥot*, chapter 11, that the cubits of the

golden altar and the corner of the altar and the middle section and the base are with cubits of five handbreadths, and the other cubits of the altar are of six handbreadths; this all comes from the received tradition.

And an allusion of this is from Ezekiel when he said, "These are the dimensions of the altar by cubits, the cubit being one cubit and a handbreadth" (Ezek. 43:13), which means there are two different measurements of the cubit. Perhaps they should all be cubits of five handbreadths? Rather you learn that there is a cubit that is a cubit, and a cubit that is handbreadth longer than the other cubit. It is like saying that there is a "large cubit" and a "small cubit." What emerges from the Talmud after lengthy analysis is that the height of the base is five cubits, as is its entrance, and the height of the *sovev* is thirty handbreadths and its entrance is five, and concerning the entrance of the *sovev* alone do we say that the cubit of the *sovev* is five handbreadths. And the height of the place of arrangement is eighteen handbreadths, and the height of each corner-piece is five handbreadths. However the square of the corner is six by six handbreadths. Therefore the entire height [of the altar] is 58 handbreadths. In the middle, at 29 handbreadths, there is a red stripe six handbreadths from the top of the *sovev*... (*PhM Middot* 3:1; see also *Bet ha-Behirah* 2:5).

27:3. And you shall make its pots [*sirot*]... — The Targum of *sirotav* [its pots] is *pesakhteravateih*, and the singular is *pesakhter* [large pot] (*PhM Eruvin* 10:15).[175]

... to receive its ashes [*le-dasheno*] ... — This is removing the ashes from the altar, and it is called *dishun ha-mizbe'ah*, as in *le-dasheno* (*PhM Yoma* 1:8).[176]

---

175. Jastrow says this word comes from Greek word for wine-cooler. However, Hebrew/Aramaic פסכתר means "large pot." Maimonides also quotes this point at *PhM Tamid* 5:5. Maimonides uses *pesakhter* rather than *sir* when explaining the law (*Temidin u-Musafin* 3:5-6). He says that the *pesakhter* was used for three objectives: to cover coals, to cover a dead animal on the Sabbath, and to remove ashes from the altar.
176. Kapach quotes this comment somewhat differently.

27:8. You shall make it hollow with boards, as was shown to you on the mountain so shall they do. — The Targum of *nevuv luḥot* is *ḥalil luḥin* [a hollow of boards] (*PhM Oholot* 9:3).[177]

---

177. Rashi on the present verse also quotes Onkelos (see also Exod. 38:7).

PARASHAT TETZAVVEH

27:20. And you shall command the children of Israel and they shall bring you pure olive oil beaten for light, to set the lamp to burn always. — [Maimonides includes this in the tenth principle of the *ShM*, where he explains that "it is not appropriate to count introductions which are for some specific purpose":] In this manner, it is not proper to count what it says, "and they shall bring you pure olive oil," but to count instead "to set the lamp to burn always," which is the maintenance of the lamps (*ShM*, Principle 10; see on Exod. 30:7).

Maimonides is saying that the actual commandment is to have the lamp burning. The act of preparing the oil is not counted separately as one one of 613, since it is merely a preparatory act.

... beaten for light... — There are nine types of oil that are all prepared differently. How so?

1. When olives are harvested from the top of branch, they are chosen one by one, then crushed, and placed into a basket. The oil that flows from it is the first type;
2. He goes back and places a beam on it. The oil that flows from it is the second type;
3. If he goes back after he places a beam on it, and crushes it and places a beam on it again, then the oil that flows to it is the third type;
4. Olives are harvested in a mixture and are brought to the roof, and then he goes back and chooses them individually, crushes them, and places them in a basket, the oil that flows from them is the fourth type;
5. If he places a beam on them, then the oil that flows from them is the fifth type;

6. If he places a beam on them a second time, then the oil that flows is the sixth type;

7. Olives that are picked and loaded into a vat until they begin to rot, and then he brings them up [to the roof], dries them, and places them in a basket, then the oil which flows from them is the seventh category;

8. If he goes back and places a beam on them, the oil which flows from them are the eighth type;

9. If he went goes and crushes [with a beam] a second time, the oil which flows is the ninth type.

Even though they are all acceptable for meal offerings, there is none superior to the first type. After that, the second and fourth—and they are equal. And then the third, fifth, and seventh—and the three of them are equal. After that, are the sixth and eighth—and the two of them are equal. And the ninth is the lowest of them all.

Only the first, fourth, and seventh types can be used for the candelabrum, as it says, "beaten *for light*" — it is not acceptable for the candelabrum unless it flows from crushed olives, though for the meal offerings they are all acceptable.

Since all of these are acceptable for meal offerings, why were they counted separately? So that someone would know the type of which there is none higher, those of intermediate, and those of lowest quality. This way, the person who wants to make himself meritorious and conquer his evil inclination and increase his magnanimity should bring his offering from the highest and most praiseworthy type. And about this, the Torah states, "And Abel brought from his choicest flocks and from its fat, and God favored Abel and his offering" (Gen. 4:4). The same is true for anything for the sake of the good Lord, that it should be from the most pleasant and best. If he buys a house of prayer, it should be nicer than his own house. If he feeds the hungry, he should do so from his best and sweetest foods. If he clothes the naked, he should do so from his best clothing. If he consecrates something, he should do so from the best of his possessions, as it says, "All the *heilev*[178] should be for God" (Lev. 3:16) (*Issurei Mizbe'ah* 7:8-11).

... to set the lamp to burn always. — Kindling the lamps overrides the Sabbath and ritual impurity, just like offerings that must be offered at a specific time, as it says, "to set the lamp to burn always" (*Temidin u-Musafin* 3:10).

27:21. In the tent of meeting, outside the curtain which is over [the ark of] testimony, Aaron and his sons shall arrange it [the candelabrum]... — ... the priests are commanded to kindle the lamps always before the Lord, as God, may He be exalted, said, "In the tent of meeting, outside the curtain which is over [the ark of] testimony, Aaron and his sons shall arrange it...." And this is the commandment of *hatavat ha-nerot* (*ShM*, Pos. 25).

... from evening until morning, before the Lord, an eternal statute for all generations for the children of Israel. — How much oil should be placed in each lamp? Half a *log*,[179] as it says, "from evening until morning" — give it a quantity so it can burn from evening until morning. And they may only dedicate the seven lamps of the candelabrum in the afternoon (*Temidin u-Musafin* 3:11; also *PhM Menahot* 4:4 and 9:3).

---

178. The Hebrew word *heilev* usually means "fat," but also has a meaning of the choicest part.
179. A *log* is approximately half a liter.

Exodus 28

28:2. And you shall make holy garments for Aaron your brother for glory and for splendor. — … the priests are commanded to wear garments made for glory and splendor, and then they can serve in the Temple, as God, may He be exalted, said, "And you shall make holy garments for Aaron your brother for glory and for splendor" (Exod. 28:2); "And you shall bring his sons near, and dress them in tunics" (Exod. 29:8). And what are these priestly garments? There are eight garments for a high priest and four for an ordinary priest. And if the priest officiates with fewer than the number of garments specified to him during service, or more garments than that, his service is invalid and he is liable for death at the hands of Heaven. This refers to someone who officiated while lacking [all of his] clothing. And in the tractate *Sanhedrin* (83a), the Sages counted this in the category of those who are liable for death at the hands of Heaven. And the verse does not state this explicitly. Rather, the verse says, "You shall gird them with belts… and the priesthood shall be for them an everlasting statute" (Exod. 29:9), and the explanation is that as long as their garments are upon them, so is the priesthood; but whenever their garments are not upon them, neither is the priesthood, and they are like laymen. And it is explained that a layman who officiates is liable for death (see Neg. 74).

And they said in the *Sifra*: "'And he placed the breastplate upon him' (Lev. 8:8) — This passage teaches a law for the time and a law for future generations, for the daily service and for the service of Yom Kippur. Every day he should officiate with garments of gold, and on Yom Kippur with garments of white."

And they have explained in the *Sifra* that wearing these garments is a positive commandment, as they said, "From where do we know that Aaron should not wear these garments for his own grandeur but because it is a decree of the King? As it says, 'And he did exactly as God commanded Moses' (Lev. 16:34), which refers to these garments. And even though their purpose is beautification, as they are of gold, emeralds, rubies, and other precious stones, he should not have in mind the beauty but only to fulfill the commandment that God commanded Moses—to wear these garments constantly in the Temple (*ShM*, Pos. 33; also *Klei ha-Mikdash* 10:4).

FURTHER: [Maimonides does not quote verses but explains the priestly garments in detail:] There are three categories of priestly garments: garments of an ordinary priest, gold garments, and white garments. The garments of an ordinary priest are four: *kutenet* (tunic), *mikhnesayim* (breeches), *migba'at* (headdress), and *avnet* (sash). These four are made from white linen with sixfold thread, and the sash alone was [also] made with wool.

The high priest has eight garments of gold: the four of a regular priest and additionally *me'il* (robe), ephod (see v. 6), breastplate, and frontplate. The sash of the high priest was embroidered and was not like the sash of the ordinary priest. And the *mitznefet* [mitre] mentioned concerning the high priest is the *migba'at* [hat] mentioned regarding his children. However the high priest wraps it like someone who binds a wound, while his sons wear it like a hat, which is why it is called *migba'at*.[180]

There are four white garments in which the high priest officiates on Yom Kippur: *kutenet, mikhnesayim, avnet,* and *mitznefet.* And these four are white and made from a sixfold thread, and they are only made from linen. And the high priest had two other *kutenets* on Yom Kippur; he wore one for the morning service and one in the afternoon. And the two of them were thirty *maneh* [= 100 silver coins] of Temple funds. And if he wanted to add more from his own funds, he could do so, and then he could make [a more expensive] *kutenet* (*Klei ha-Mikdash* 8:1-3).

---

180. The *Kesef Mishneh* quotes from Nahmanides that *gimel* and *kaf* can interchange, hence it is similar to the root *kav, bet, ayin*, which means "hat."

FURTHER: It is a commandment that the priestly garments be new, attractive, and hang low like garments of men of prestige, as it says, "for glory and for splendor." If they are dirty or torn, too long or too short, raised by the sash, and he performed his service, it is invalid. If they are worn out or too long, and he raised them with the sash so that it is the appropriate length, and he officiated, his service is valid (*Klei ha-Mikdash* 8:4).

> Rashi writes that torn garments violate the provision of "for glory and for splendor" (BT *Zevaḥim* 18b, s.v. *mekora'im*). This appears to be Maimonides' approach as well. However, Nahmanides says it is because of *meḥussar beyudim* (*Hassagot* to *ShM*, Neg. 163).

FURTHER: In order to raise estimation of the Temple, those who ministered therein received great honor, and the priests and Levites were therefore distinguished from the rest. It was commanded that the priests should be clothed properly with beautiful and good garments, "holy garments... for glory and splendor." A priest that had a blemish was not allowed to officiate, and not only those that had a blemish were excluded from service, but also—according to the talmudic interpretation of this precept—those that had an abnormal appearance; for the multitude does not estimate man by his true form, but by the perfection of his bodily limbs and the beauty of his garments, and the Temple was to be held in great reverence by all (*Guide* 3:45).

28:5. And they shall take gold, and blue, and purple, and scarlet, and fine linen. — We may not appoint fewer than two representatives [to oversee] the community's finances [*mamon ha-tzibbur*], and the Sages made a scriptural allusion to what is stated, "And *they* shall take gold," and the minimum plural is two (*PhM Shekalim* 5:2).

Rabbi Abraham Maimonides quotes from his father that the
word "they" refers to Bezalel and Oholiab.

28:6. And they shall make the ephod... — The ephod was as wide
as a man's back from shoulder to shoulder, and its length was from
the elbows [*atzilei ha-yada'im*] to the feet. It had two ends extending
from either side of the weave in either direction, which was tied, and
is called *ḥashav ha-ephod*. All of it is woven in gold, blue, purple,
scarlet, and linen, with twenty-eight threads, as with the breastplate.
One sews shoulder straps on it, so that they should be on the [high]
priest's shoulders (*Klei ha-Mikdash* 9:9).

Rashi says the ephod is "like an apron worn by women who
ride horses" (on Exod. 28:6).

**... of gold, of blue, and of purple, of scarlet, and fine twined linen,
with skilled work.** — The gold of weaving the ephod[181] and the
breastplate [*ḥoshen*] mentioned in the Torah (Exod. 28:15) is made
in the following manner: One takes a thread of pure gold, and places
it with six threads of blue and folds the seven threads together. And
similarly he makes a gold thread with six purple threads, and one
thread with six scarlet and one thread with six of linen. Thus there
are four threads of gold, and there are twenty-eight threads total, as
it says, "And they shall beat the sheets of gold [and cut threads] to
make in the blue, and the purple, and in the scarlet, and in the fine
linen..." (Exod. 39:3), which teaches that a gold thread was woven
into them (*Klei ha-Mikdash* 9:4).

... fine twined linen [*shesh mashzar*]... — Wherever it says in the
Torah *shesh* or *shesh mashzar*, it must be spun with six threads (*Klei
ha-Mikdash* 8:14).

_____

181. I.e., the making of the ephod which is mentioned in the present verse.

28:9. And you shall take two onyx stones, and engrave on them the names of the children of Israel. — He should mount on each shoulder a square onyx stone, set in a mounting of gold. And he engraves the names of the tribes on the two stones: six on each stone in order of their birth. And the name Yosef ["Joseph"] is written Yehosef [יהוסף], so that there are twenty-five letters on each stone. And this is how they are written (see chart).

שמעון	ראובן
יהודה	לוי
זבולן	יששכר
דן	נפתלי
אשר	גד
בנימין	יהוסף

The stone on which Reuben's name is written is placed on his right shoulder, and the stone on which Simeon's name is written is placed on his left shoulder. And on each shoulder one makes two rings: one from at the bottom of the shoulder to above the belt. The two cords of gold are placed in the two rings from above, and they are called chains [*sharsharot*]. And this is the picture of the ephod: (*Klei ha-Mikdash* 9:9).

28:15-16. And you shall make the breastplate of judgment with skilled work, you shall make it like the style of the ephod; of gold, blue, purple, and scarlet thread shall you make it. It shall be square and doubled, its length and width shall be one span.[182] — How is the breastplate made? One weaves a garment with skilled work, from gold, blue, red, and scarlet, with twenty-eight strands, as we have explained. Its length is a cubit, its width is a span, and it is folded in two. Thus it is a span [long] by a span [wide, in the shape of a] square (*Klei ha-Mikdash* 9:6).

---

182. Hebrew, *zeret*, which is half a cubit.

440

28:17. And you shall set in it four rows of stones... — And four rows of stones are attached, as explained in the Torah (Exod. 28:17-20, 39:10-13). Each stone is square and placed in a gold setting that surrounds it from below and four directions (*Klei ha-Mikdash* 9:6).

28:21. And the stones shall have the names of the children of Israel, twelve according to their names, like signets, each engraved with its name, each one engraved with its name, for the twelve tribes. — The names of the tribes are engraved on the stones, in order of their birth, so the name "Reuben" is written on the ruby [*odem*], and "Benjamin" on the jasper [*yashfeh*]. And at first, above "Reuben," [the names] Abraham, Isaac, and Jacob, are written," and underneath it are written "the tribes of God" [*shiftei Y-ah*], so that all the letters are found there (*Klei ha-Mikdash* 9:7).

28:28. And they shall bind the breastplate by its rings to the rings of the ephod with a blue cord to be on the skillfully woven band of the ephod... — Four golden rings are made on the four corners of the breastplate. In the two upper rings from which the breastplate is suspended, two golden cords are placed (see Exod. 28:22-24). They are called "chains" [*sharsharot*] (Exod. 39:15). And in the two lower rings that are opposite the breasts [of the high priests], two cords of blue are placed (*Klei ha-Mikdash* 9:8).

... so that the breastplate shall not come loose from the ephod. — ... we are forbidden from removing the breastplate from the ephod, as God, may He be exalted, said, "so that the breastplate shall not come loose from the ephod." Rather, it [the breastplate] should be connected to it [the ephod]. And at the end of *Makkot* (22a), the Sages included among those liable for lashes someone who loosens the ephod, and from here we know there is a prohibition not to loosen the ephod (*ShM*, Neg. 87).

FURTHER: ... he lowers the chains through the rings on the shoulders of the ephod to the upper rings of the breastplate, so that they touch each other, and so that the breastplate does not come loose from the ephod. And anyone who loosens the breastplate from the ephod or breaks its attachment in a way to destroy it, he is liable to receive lashes (*Klei ha-Mikdash* 9:11).

FURTHER: In order that the form of the ephod and the breastplate should not be spoiled, they were never separated (*Guide* 3:45).

28:30. ... and the Urim and Thummim... — In the second Temple, they made the Urim and Thummim in order to complete the eight garments of the high priest, even though they did not inquire of them. And why would they not inquire of them? Because the holy spirit was not there, and whenever a priest does not speak with the holy spirit and the Divine Presence does not repose there, inquiry is not made.

And how was inquiry made [in the first Temple]? The [high] priest would stand facing the ark, and the person posing the inquiry stood behind him, facing the [high] priest's back. The inquirer would ask, "Should I go [to war] or not?" And he would not ask in a loud voice, nor would he merely consider the matter in his heart. Rather in a low voice, like someone praying to himself. Immediately the holy spirit[183] would envelope the high priest and he would behold the breastplate and see in a vision of prophecy, "Go," or "Do not go" in letters that protruded from the breastplate towards his face. And the [high] priest would answer [the one posing the question], and would say, "Go" or "Do not go."

Two questions should not be asked at the same time, and if he asked [two questions], only the first was answered, and an ordinary priest could not ask. Rather, only a king, or a court, or someone

---

183. According to Maimonides, the "holy spirit" (*ruaḥ ha-kodesh*) is one rung lower than regular prophecy (*Guide* 2:45).

that the community depends on, as it says, "And before Elazar the priest he shall stand…" (Num. 27:21). "He" refers to a kind, "and all the children of Israel" refers to a priest anointed for the sake of war or someone whom the community depends on, "and all the congregation" refers to the high court (*Klei ha-Mikdash* 10:10-12; a similar point is made at *Bet ha-Beḥirah* 4:1).[184]

It is a classic question why Maimonides does not quote a commandment of making the Urim and Thummim. The simplest answer is that Maimonides equated the Urim and Thummim with the stones mentioned at Exod. 28:9 (see there, and his arrangement of the names of the twelve tribes). Maimonides had precedent from *Midrash Lekaḥ Tov* and the Gaonim, Rav Sherira, Rav Hai, and Rav Nissim.[185]

Ra'avad refers to the teaching that five elements were lacking in the Second Temple, two of which were the holy spirit and the Urim and Thummim, yet Maimonides only counts the lack of holy spirit. The possible implication is that, according to Ra'avad, the Urim and Thummim should only be worn when they could be consulted, but in the Second Temple era, they were not (*Bet ha-Beḥirah* 4:1). It appears that according to Maimonides, the Urim and Thummim were part of the eight priestly garments, since he writes (above), "In the second Temple, they made the Urim and Thummim in order to complete the eight garments of the of the high priest, even though they did not inquire of them."

---

184. See further Rabbi Hayyim Angel, "The Theological Significance of the Urim Ve-Tummim." There he writes, "Ramban [Nahmanides] observes that in contrast to the intricate directives pertaining to nearly all other utensils of the Tabernacle, the UT [Urim and Tummim] receive no description whatsoever." (This might explain why Maimonides does not include a description of making the UT in his legal code.) See there, note 2.
185. See Rabbi David Silverberg, "Parashat Tetzaveh: Maimonides on the Urim ve-Tumim'" http://www.mhcny.org/parasha/1020.pdf.

Nahmanides is critical of Maimonides "for not reckoning the use of the oracle as a positive commandment, relegating its status to mere 'counsel'" (Bezalel Naor, trans., *In the Desert a Vision—Rabbi Abraham Isaac Kook on the Torah Portion of the Week*, pp. 155-156, n. 92; see secondary literature there).

In *Guide* 2:45, Maimonides says that the Urim and Thummim are a type of *ruaḥ ha-kodesh*; perhaps this can resolve all the questions: inquiring of the Urim and Thummim cannot be a commandment if its effectiveness had been negated, but wearing the Urim and Thummim is a commandment regardless of its effectiveness, since they bear the names of Israel as described in Exod. 28:9.

28:31. And you shall make the cloak of the ephod entirely of blue. — The cloak is entirely of blue. The strands were twelvefold. Its opening was woven, at the beginning of its weave, and it did not have openings for his arms.[186] Instead, it was divided into two sheets, from the bottom of the throat to the bottom, like all cloaks, and it is only connected just below the throat (*Klei ha-Mikdash* 9:3).

FURTHER: ... it is called "the cloak of the ephod," the cloak that the ephod girds (*Klei ha-Mikdash* 10:3).

28:32. And it shall have an opening for the head in the middle of it, with a woven binding around the opening, the work of a weaver [*ma'aseh oreg*] ... — ... none of the priestly garments were sewn; rather they were woven, as it says, "the work of a weaver" (*Klei ha-Mikdash* 8:19).

... it shall have [an opening] like a coat of armor, it shall not be torn. — ... we are forbidden to tear the opening of the high priest's

---

186. The *Kesef Mishnah* says Nahmanides agrees.

robe. Rather it must be [i.e., remain] woven as a partition, as God, may He be exalted, said. And whoever cuts it with scissors or the like is liable to receive lashes.

FURTHER: Whoever tears the robe is liable to receive lashes, as it says, "it shall not be torn." This applies to all the priestly garments that whoever tears them in a destructive manner is liable to receive lashes (*Klei ha-Mikdash* 9:3).

FURTHER: The garments were also entirely woven and not cut, in order not to spoil the work of the weaving (*Guide* 3:45).

28:33-34. And on its lower hem you shall make pomegranates of blue, purple, and crimson yarns, all around the lower hem, with bells of gold among them, all around. Alternating golden bells and pomegranates, all the way around the lower hem of the robe. — And he brings blue, and purple, and crimson; and strings of each type of thread were spun at times, since the hems are described as "twisted" [*mashzar*]. Thus there were twenty-four threads. And he makes them in the shape of pomegranates whose mouths were not open, and he hands them from the robe [*me'il*]. And he brings seventy-two bells,[187] and seventy-two clappers all of gold, and hangs thirty-six of them on each side [of the robe]. And the bells with the clappers—the two of them—are suspended together and called a "bell" [*pa'amon*]. Alternating bells and pomegranates are around the two hems [of the mantle] (*Klei ha-Mikdash* 9:4).

28:36. And you shall make a forehead plate of pure gold, and engrave upon it, like the engraving of seal: HOLY TO THE LORD. — How was the forehead plate made? He makes a strip of gold that is two fingerbreadths wide and wraps it around from ear to ear and

---

187. Maimonides uses the Hebrew *zuggim*, which means the body of bell, not including the uvula, or clapper.

writes on two lines HOLY TO THE LORD. [The word] HOLY is below and TO THE LORD is above. And if he wrote it on one line, it is valid. And sometimes they wrote it on one line. And the letters protrude on top of it. He would engrave the letters on the back, and it was pressed into wax until it protruded (*Klei ha-Mikdash* 9:1-2).[188]

28:37. And you shall place it on a blue cord, so that it be on the mitre; it shall be on the front of the mitre. — It was pierced at both ends, and a strand of blue wool was below it, threaded through each hole so that it should be tied with a thread at the nape (*Klei ha-Mikdash* 9:1-2).

Maimonides says there were two holes in the forehead band. However, Ra'avad says there was a third hole in the middle. The *Kesef Mishneh* says Ra'avad agrees with Rashi, but that Nahmanides agrees with Maimonides.

28:38. And it shall be on Aaron's forehead, and Aaron shall bear the sin of the holy things that the children of Israel sanctified for all their gifts of holiness, and it shall be on his forehead always, to be appeasement before the Lord. — ... the forehead strip appeases for the impurity of things that are offered, as it says, "And it shall be on Aaron's forehead, and Aaron shall bear the sin of the holy things." However, it does not appease for the impurity of foods nor for the impurity of a person who has become impure from a known impurity unless the impurity is superseded by a communal need, in which case the forehead strip appeases for it. And the forehead plate only appeases when it is on his forehead, as it says, "and it shall be on his forehead always, to be appeasement before the Lord" (*Bi'at ha-Mikdash* 4:7-8).

---

188. This is a debate if it should be written in one line or two.

There is ambiguity in the biblical phrase *ve-hayah al mitzho tamid leratzon lahem lifnei YHVH*. In the Talmud (*Yoma* 7b), it is conceded that the mitre cannot always be on Aaron's forehead, because he can only wear it while officiating. Rabbi Yehudah implies the reading *al mitzho tamid*, "on his forehead always," meaning that whenever the mitre is on Aaron's head, it appeases. It is added that according to Rabbi Yehudah, the high priest should touch the mitre regularly so he is constantly aware of its presence (*shel-lo yasiah da'ato mimmennu*). Rabbi Shimon says *tamid leratzon... lifnei YHVH* means that it always atones, whether or not Aaron is wearing it. Maimonides rules like Rabbi Yehudah that it only appeases when Aaron is wearing it (but he does not include the caveat that the high priest needs to touch the mitre regularly; see Frankel's *Sefer ha-Mafte'ah*). However, Rashi rules like Rabbi Shimon, *afillu eino al mitzho*, "even if it is not on his forehead."

FURTHER: If a handful of a meal offering became impure and then was burned [on the altar], the forehead strip appeases, as it says, "and Aaron [shall bear the sin of the holy things]." If the handful leaves the Temple courtyard, and then is brought back, and burned [on the altar], the strip does not appease, for the strip only appeases for something impure, but not something departed (*Pesulei ha-Mukdashim* 11:19).

FURTHER: [Maimonides comments on the phrase *tumat ha-tehom*, "depth from the deep," a euphemism for dead and buried bodies (M. *Pesahim* 7:7)] — "And impurity of the deep" is impurity of a corpse that is hidden, and is not known about at all, as if it was in the depth. Therefore the mitre appeases, since it is impossible for it to be known about forever, since there is no person in the world who knows that there is a corpse or grave there, to inform us and know that he had become impure so that he could be purified. Therefore, whatever offering he brings when he is impure because of a grave of "the deep" is valid and the mitre appeases for it. The fact that the mitre appeases is explicit in the Torah. God said, "And it shall be on Aaron's forehead, and Aaron shall bear the sin of the holy things that the children of Israel sanctified for all their gifts of holiness, and it shall be on his forehead always, to be appeasement before the Lord" (*PhM Pesaḥim* 7:6).

FURTHER: As it was very necessary that the high priest should *always* be in the sanctuary, in accordance with the Divine command, "and it shall always be on his forehead" (Exod. 28:38), he was not permitted to defile himself by any dead body whatever, even of the above-named relatives (see Lev. 21:10-12) (*Guide* 3:47).

28:39. And you shall embroider the tunic of fine linen... — ... the tunic, whether of a regular priest or a high priest, was embroidered with a boxlike weave, like a bird's jaw, as weavers make durable garments. Its sleeve was woven separately, and it was connected with the body of the tunic by sewing. The length of the tunic was until just above the heel, and the length of the sleeve was until the wrist, and the width was as wide as the hand (*Klei ha-Mikdash* 8:16-17).

Maimonides says this law applies to the high priest and ordinary priests, an opinion with which Nahmanides agrees (on Exod. 39:27). Alternatively, Ibn Ezra (long commentary to 28:39) says it applies only to Aaron, but not his sons.

28:39-40. ... and you shall make the mitre [*mitznefet*] of fine linen of fine linen... hats [*migba'ot*] you shall make for them... — The turban [*mitznefet*] mentioned in the Torah regarding Aaron is the head gear [*migba'ot*] mentioned regarding his sons. Rather the high priest wears it like fabric wrapped around a wound, and his sons wear it like a hat. Therefore it is called a hat [*migba'at*] (*Klei ha-Mikdash* 8:2).

This is also the opinion of Nahmanides (on Exod. 28:31 [end]). However, Rashi seems to assume the *mitznefet* (turban) and *migba'ot* (hats) refer to the same thing: "*Mitznefet*: a rounded hat which is called '*coiffe*' in French, since elsewhere they are called migba'ot" (on Exod. 28:4). Nahmanides rejects Rashi's opinion, because "the *mitznefet* of the high priest is never called *migba'at*" and follows Maimonides.

FURTHER: The turban of the high priest or common [priest] is sixteen cubits long (*Klei ha-Mikdash* 8:19).

Maimonides says the fabric was the same for the high priest and common priest, but the style of wearing was different. Nahmanides also accepts that the cloth was sixteen cubits long.

... and you shall make the girdle of needlework... and you shall make girdles for them... — [Maimonides is commenting on the Mishnaic word *hemyan*:] ... his girdle [*avnet*], which is the belt that he ties around half his body, and the Targum of *avnet* is *hemyan* (*PhM Eruvin* 10:15).

FURTHER: Only the *avnet* [i.e., and no other priestly garment] was embroidered with wool (*Klei ha-Mikdash* 8:1).

FURTHER: The *avnet* of the high priest was a work of embroidery [*ma'aseh rokem*], and it was not like the *avnet* of an ordinary priest (*Klei ha-Mikdash* 8:2).

FURTHER: ... the *avnet* was about three fingerbreadths wide and was thirty-two cubits long. He wraps it around him and repeats it, winding over winding (*Klei ha-Mikdash* 8:19).

28:41. And you shall put them on Aaron your brother, and his sons with him, and you shall anoint them, and inaugurate them, and sanctify them, to minister to Me. — The Sages said: Wherever it says, "to Me," it means lasting [*kayyam*], such as "to minister to Me," which means enduring, and it is not a temporary commandment; rather it is a commandment for all generations (*ShM*, Pos. 176).

FURTHER: He selected priests for the service in the Temple (*Guide* 3:32).

> This passing comment points to the fact that there is a consolidation of holiness, i.e., the holy people (*kohanim*) officiating at the holy place (Temple).

28:42. And you shall make them linen leggings to cover their nakedness; they shall be from their loins to their thighs. — The leggings of the high priest and ordinary priests are from the loins to the thighs, which is above the navel close to the heart until the end of the thigh, which is the knee. And they had straps. And they had no opening for the anus or membrum. Rather, they surrounded him like a sack (*Klei ha-Mikdash* 8:18; see also *Guide* 3:45, quoted at Exod. 20:23).

FURTHER: The mode of worshipping Peor, then very general among the heathen, consisted in uncovering the nakedness. The priests were therefore commanded to make breeches for themselves to cover their nakedness during the service (Exod. 28:42), and, besides, no steps were to lead up to the altar, "so that your nakedness not be revealed on it" (Exod. 20:23) (*Guide* 3:45).

Exodus 29

29:2. ... and wafers of unleavened bread [*rekikei matzot*] anointed with oil... — [Maimonides is commenting on the Mishnah's use of the word *sufganin* (M. *Hallah* 1:4)] The Targum of *rekikei matzot* is *espogin pattirin* (PhM *Hallah* 1:4).

29:5-8. ... and you shall dress Aaron... and his sons you shall bring near and dress them... — What is the order of donning the garments? He puts on the leggings first, and ties the leggings above the navel, above the loins. And then he dons the tunic, and then ties the girdle at the height of his elbows, and he winds it wrap after wrap until he finishes, and then he ties it. And on the *avnet*, it is explained in the tradition, "they shall not gird themselves in anything that causes sweat" (Ezek. 44:18) — in the place they perspire... Jonathan son of Uzziel received this interpretation from the Prophets, and he translates it, "they shall gird themselves on their hearts."

And then he puts on the *mitznefet* like a hat. The high priest, after he puts on the *avnet* he puts on the *me'il*, and over the *me'il*, the ephod, and the breastplate, and ties the belt of the ephod over the *me'il* and under the breastplate. Therefore [the *me'il*] is called the "*me'il* of the ephod" — the *me'il* that is tied closed with the ephod. Then he winds the turban and ties the frontlet [from behind] above the turban. His hair was visible between the frontlet and the turban, and that is where he would place his *tefillin*, between the frontlet and the turban (*Klei ha-Mikdash* 10:1-3).

29:9. ... and the priesthood shall be for them an eternal statute... — When their garments are upon them, their priesthood is upon them, however if they lack anything, they are like commoners [non-priests] (PhM *Sanhedrin* 9:6, quoted also at PhM *Zevahim* 2:1 and 14:10; see also at Exod. 28:2 and PhM *Sanhedrin* 10:1 [beg.]).

29:21. And you shall take some of the blood that is on the altar, and some of the anointing-oil, and you shall sprinkle it on Aaron and his garments and on his sons and his sons' garments with him; and he and his garments shall be hallowed, and his sons and his sons' garments. — Our Law declared the blood as pure, and made it the means of purifying other objects by its touch. "And you shall take some of the blood... and sprinkle it on Aaron and on his garments and on his sons and on his son's garments with him; and he [and his garments] shall be hallowed, and his sons...." Furthermore, the blood was sprinkled upon the altar, and in the whole service it was insisted upon pouring it out, and not upon collecting it, e.g., "And he shall pour out all the blood at the bottom of the altar" (Lev. 4:18)... (*Guide* 3:46).[189]

29:29. ... to install [*le-mashḥah*] them... — for grandeur (*PhM Bekhorot* 4:1).

> The textual problem is that *m-sh-ḥ* literally means "anoint," which it cannot mean in this context (*Mizraḥi*). Rashi writes, "to install [*le-mashḥah*]: to be made great through them [*le-hitgaddel bahem*], since there are some uses of *meshiḥah* that mean authority [*serarah*]." Nahmanides says this might be so, and suggests that since authority is conferred through anointing, perhaps any conferral of authority can take the language *meshiḥah*, even if there is no physical anointing. However, Nahmanides says in this case, the meaning of *le-mashḥah bahem* means to anoint with garments of the high priests over their sons.

29:30. For seven days the son beneath him who is priest shall wear them, who shall enter the tent of meeting to minister in the sanctuary. — How does [the high priest] become anointed with

---

189. See further my *A Theology of Holiness*, p. 67.

clothing?[190] He puts on the eight garments, then removes them, then puts them on again, each day for seven days, as it says, "For seven days the son beneath him who is priest shall wear them" (*Klei ha-Mikdash* 4:13).

29:33. And they shall eat those things by which atonement was made... — ... the priests are commanded to eat the flesh of the holy things [i.e., the sacrifices], meaning the *ḥattat* and the *asham*, which are the most holy offerings, and God, may He be exalted, said, "And they shall eat those things by which atonement was made...." And the language of the *Sifra* is: "How do we know that eating the holy things is an atonement for Israel? As it says, 'and He has given it to you to bear the iniquity of the congregation to make atonement for them before the Lord' (Lev. 10:17). How so? The priests eat and the Israelites are atoned for" (*ShM*, Pos. 89; also *Ma'aseh ha-Korbanot* 10:1).

Malbim points out that Maimonides and Rashi understand this verse differently. According to Rashi, the word *bahem*, lit., "in them," refers to the priests themselves. In other words, the priests eat the offerings to effectuate their own cleansing for any residue of commonness before they were elevated to the status of priests. However, Maimonides understands *bahem* as referring to the Israelites, meaning that when the priests eat the most holy offerings, it causes the Israelites to earn atonement for sin.

... and no foreigner shall eat them, because they are holy. — ... a foreigner [i.e., non-priest] is prohibited from eating the flesh of most holy offerings, as God, may He be exalted, said, "and no foreigner shall eat them, because they areholy." And one is not liable for lashes unless he eats it in the courtyard after the sprinkling of the blood (*ShM*, Neg. 148).

---

190. The high priest can be anointed in two ways: with anointing oil or with clothing.

FURTHER: If a foreigner eats an olive's measure of the flesh of most holy offerings in the courtyard after the blood has been sprinkled, he is liable to receive lashes, as it says, "And they shall eat those things by which atonement was made... and no foreigner shall eat it because it is holy," in a place where the priest eats, and at a time that is appropriate to eat, if a foreigner ate it there, he receives lashes. However, if a foreigner ate the flesh of the most holy offerings outside [the courtyard] he is liable for eating outside, not because he is a foreigner who ate something holy, since priests are not permitted to eat it there. And similarly, if he ate them in the courtyard before the blood was sprinkled he is lashed, but only because he ate before the sprinkling of the blood, not because he is a non-priest (*Ma'aseh ha-Korbanot* 11:18).

29:33-34. And they shall eat those things by which atonement was made, at their ordination to consecrate them, and no foreigner shall eat them, for they are holy. And if any of the flesh of the inauguration or from the bread is left over until morning, then you shall burn the remainder in fire; it shall not be eaten, because it is holy. — We are forbidden from eating *notar*, meaning what is left over of sacred flesh after the time set for eating it. And the Torah does not explicitly forbid eating it, but the punishment of *karet* is explicit for someone who eats *notar*, as God, may He be exalted, said in the portion of *Kedoshim* when speaking of the peace-offering, "And that which remains [*notar*] until the third day shall be burned in the fire, and it is eaten on the third day, it is rejected, and it is not pleasing. And whoever eats it shall bear its iniquity for he has profaned what is sacred to the Lord, and that soul shall be cut off from his people" (Lev. 19:6-8). Therefore it is clear that he is liable for *karet* if he did it intentionally. And if he ate it accidentally, he is obligated to bring a *ḥattat kavua*. And this punishment is written [explicitly], but the prohibition is [derived] from His statement regarding the ordination offering [*millu'im*], "it shall not be eaten for they [*hem*] are holy."[191] And the expression *hem*

---

191. This is either a contraction of vv. 33-34, or a revocalization of יאכל in verse 33 from *yokhal* to *ye'akhel* (for which we would have expected the plural *ye'akhlu*, since it corresponds to *hem*, "they").

454

["they"] includes everything that is invalid among holy offerings that it is not permitted to eat, like *notar*.

And in *Me'ilah* (17b) they said in the Mishnah that *piggul*[192] and *notar*[193] are not combined, since they are two different categories. However, they only said this regarding impurity of hands, which is a rabbinic enactment. However, regarding eating, they are combined, and the *baraita* teaches, "Rabbi Eliezer says 'no one shall eat them, for they are holy' — which adds a prohibition of eating any invalidated holy offering." And *piggul* and *notar* are among the invalidated holy things. Therefore we are forbidden to eat either of them, as He said, "no one shall eat them, for they are holy." And it has already been explained that the punishment for eating *notar* is *karet* (*ShM*, Neg. 131).

FURTHER: ... we are forbidden from eating *piggul*. *Piggul* is an offering that becomes invalid because of an improper thought when it is slaughtered or offered. [This refers to] someone who renders the sacrifice and had in mind that it will be eaten after the proper time, or that the parts which require burning will be burned after the proper time, as we explained in [the commentary to] the second chapter of *Zevaḥim*.

And the source of the prohibition of eating *piggul* is what He said, "no one shall eat them, for they are holy" (Exod. 29:33), as we explained in the previous commandment. And we learn the punishment from the portion *Tzav et Aharon* regarding *piggul*, "And if any of the flesh of your sacrifice of well-being is eaten on the third day, it shall not be accepted, and it shall not be credited to him, it shall be rejected, and the soul who eats of it shall bear its guilt" (Lev. 7:18). And the oral tradition, in explaining this verse, says this verse refers to an offering that became invalid because of [improper] thought at the time it was offered, and

---

192. *Piggul* is the result when a priest brings an offering with the initial intention to eat it beyond the permitted time.
193. *Notar* is when the offering was eaten after the permitted time, but there was no initial intention to delay its consumption.

this is called *piggul* ["refused, rejected, abominable"], as He said, "it is eaten" — to mean that he had in mind for it to be eaten on the third day. And the Sages said, "Incline your ear to hear: this verse refers to someone who intended to have his offering eaten on the third day" (*Zevaḥim* 29a). And it becomes invalid by this thought. And whoever eats it after [having] this thought is punished by *karet*, as he says, "and the soul who eats of it shall bear its guilt," and it says regarding *notar*, "And whoever eats it shall bear its iniquity for he has profaned what is sacred to the Lord, and [that soul] shall be cut off [from his people]" (Lev. 19:8). And in the Talmud in *Kereitot* (5a), the Sages said, "Do not let a *gezeirah shavah*[194] be inconsequential in your eyes, for *piggul* is one of the laws of the Torah, and it was only learned by means of a *gezeirah shavah*, which learns the word *avon, avon* ['sin, sin'] from *notar*. Here is it written, 'and the soul who eats of it shall bear its guilt' (Lev. 7:18), and it is written elsewhere, 'And whoever eats it shall bear its iniquity' (Lev. 19:8) — just as there itx refers to *karet*, so it refers to *karet* here as well." Someone who accidentally eats *piggul* must bring a *ḥattat* offering (*ShM*, Neg. 132).

29:36. And every day you shall bring a bull as a purgation offering for atonement, and you shall cleanse the altar when you atone for it, and you shall anoint it to sanctify it. — [Maimonides quotes a similar verse, "On the day when Moses had finished setting up the tabernacle and had anointed and sanctified it and all its vessels, and the altar and all its vessels, and he anointed them and sanctified them" (Num. 7:1):] All the vessels that Moses sanctified in the wilderness, he only sanctified with oil, as it says, "and he anointed them and sanctified them" (Num. 7:1). And this thing [*davar*] is not practiced in future generations; rather once the vessels are utilized in the Temple in service they are sanctified, as it says, "with which they shall minister in the sanctuary" (Num. 4:12); they become sanctified with their service.

---

194. A hermeneutical principle where, when the same words appears in two contexts, the laws in one case are applied to the laws of the other.

Ibn Ezra says that the anointing (*meshiḥah*) was with blood
and the sanctification was with blood. However, the Talmud
(*Shevuot* 15a), Maimonides, and Nahmanides (on Num. 7:1)
say that anointing and sanctification refer to the same ritual.
(See also *A Theology of Holiness*, pp. 66-67; see also *Guide*
3:45, quoted at Exod. 30:22-23).

29:37. ... whatever touches the altar shall become holy. — ...
when offerings [besides burnt offerings] that had been slaughtered
are raised to the altar, they are flayed and cut up where they are. The
inner organs are lowered [i.e., removed from on top of the altar] and
washed in water, and then raised back up. Then the hide and flesh
are lowered and given to the owners, and the rest is incinerated [on
the altar]. And why should it not all be lowered down but instead
flayed and cut up on top of the altar? Since once something fit to be
burned on top of the altar is raised up, it should not be removed, as
it says, "whatever touches the altar shall becomes holy." Does this
even apply to that which is not fit [to be burned on the altar]? We
learn from "it is a burnt offering on the hearth" (Lev. 6:2). Just as a
burnt offering is fit for the fire, if it is uplifted it should not be taken
down, so too whatever is fit for the fire, if it is raised up, it should
not be taken down (*Pesulei ha-Mukdashim* 3:3; he makes the same
point at *PhM Zevaḥim* 9:7; see also *PhM Zevaḥim* 7:1 and *Pesulei
ha-Mukdashim* 3:14).

**29:40. And a tenth of fine flour mixed with a quarter hin of
beaten oil, and a quarter hin of wine as a drink offering for one
sheep.** — No juices may be offered on top of the altar, only wine and
oil, and this is based on an explicit statement in the Torah regarding
the offerings of oil, and the offerings with wine as a drink offering
(*PhM Terumot* 11:3).

**29:45. And I shall dwell among the children of Israel, and I shall
be for them God.** — Whenever the term [*shakhen*] is applied to
the Almighty, it must be taken consistently within the context in the

sense either as referring to the Presence of His *Shekhinah* (i.e., of His light that was created for the purpose) in a certain place, or of the continuance of His Providence protecting a certain object (*Guide* 1:25; see further at Exod. 24:16).

The *Ephodi* in his commentary on the *Guide* says that *sh-kh-n* on this verse refers to the perpetuity of providence [*hatmadat ha-hasgaḥah*].

Exodus 30

30:7. And Aaron shall burn fragrant incense upon it [the golden altar]; every morning when he tends to the lamps, he shall burn incense upon it. — ... the priests are commanded to place the incense on the golden altar twice each day, as God, may He be exalted, said, "And Aaron shall burn fragrant incense upon it; every morning when he tends to the lamps, he shall burn incense upon it. And when Aaron sets up the lamps in the evening he will burn it" (Exod. 30:7-8) (*ShM*, Pos. 28).

FURTHER: It is a positive commandment to burn incense on the golden altar in the *heikhal* twice each day, in the morning and afternoon, as it says, "And Aaron shall burn fragrant incense upon it...." If he did not burn [incense] in the morning, he should bring it in the afternoon, even if it was intentional. And the golden altar can only be dedicated with the incense offered in the afternoon (*Temudin u-Musafin* 3:1; see also *PhM Yoma* 5:5).

FURTHER: [Maimonides includes this in the tenth principle of the *ShM*, where he explains that "it is not appropriate to count introductions which are for some specific purpose":] In this manner, it is not proper to count what it says, "Take for yourself sweet spices" (Exod. 30:34), but to count burning the incense every day, as it is mentioned in Scripture, "every morning when he tends to the lamps, he shall burn incense upon it. And when Aaron sets up the lamps..." (vv. 7-8). And that is the commandment that should be counted [as part of the 613]. And when it says, "take for yourself sweet spices," it is an introduction to the commandment to explain how this commandment is to be performed and what the incense is made of (*ShM*, Principle 10).

The *Hinnukh* points out that preparing the incense and burning it are mentioned in two separate verses; the preparation is mentioned in Exod. 27:20, and burning the altar is mentioned here (101 [103]). Nonetheless, the *Hinnukh* says that no source counts "preparing the incense" and "burning the incense" as two separate commandments. He adds that Nahmanides counts the burning of the morning incense and burning of the afternoon incense as two separate commandments.

The *Kesef Mishnah* quotes that according to Onkelos, Rashi, and Rashba, the lamps were only burned in the evening, not morning (see next source).

... when he tends to the lamps [*be-hetivo*]... — Lighting the lamps is the *hatavah* (*Temidin u-Musafin* 3:12).[195]

Further: It has already been explained in *Yoma* (32b) that *hatavah*, which refers to cleaning the lamps [*nikkui ha-nerot*] and burning out whatever was left, and changing the wicks, was not done for all seven at one time. Rather he tends to five lamps and then performs another service, and then comes back and tends to the two remaining lamps. And the reason for this is debated. One opinion for why he tends [to five] and then comes back and tends [to the final two] is to experience the entire Temple courtyard [*le-hargish kol ha-azarah*], meaning to expand the amount of time for that service so that it will be recognizable. And the opinion says the reason is because God, may He be exalted, said, *ba-boker ba-boker* ["in the morning, in the morning"], so when he tends to the lamps he should divide it into two mornings (*PhM Tamid* 3:9).

---

195. Maimonides' definition of *hatavah* here may be different than what he quotes in his commentary to the Mishnah; see next source.

The *Kesef Mishnah* points out that the Rashba understands *hatavah* as preparing the wicks (Responsa 79 and 309), and this is Onkelos' opinion as well. Thus for Maimonides, *hatavah* means kindling the lamps, while for Onkelos and Rashba, it refers to preparing the wicks, and the lamps were not burned in the morning, only in the evening. Rashi understands *behetivo* as "cleaning the cups of the candelabrum."

30:9. You shall not offer unholy incense on it, or a burnt-offering, or a grain-offering; and you shall not pour a drink-offering on it.

— … we are forbidden from offering anything on the golden altar in the *heikhal* [except what the Torah says], as God, may He be exalted, said, "You shall not offer unholy incense on it, or a burnt-offering, or a grain-offering; and you shall not pour a drink-offering on it." And anyone who brings an offering or sprinkles blood other than what is legislated is liable to receive lashes (*ShM*, Neg. 82; also *Klei ha-Mikdash* 2:11).

This opinion appears consistent with that of Rashi, who says this verse forbids bringing voluntary incense offerings on the inner, golden altar. However, Nahmanides attacks the opinion of Rashi, because Onkelos translates *ketoret zarah* as *ketoret busmin nukhra'in*, "incense of strange components," which Nahmanides assumes Rashi misunderstood as "strange incense." In other words, according to Onkelos and Nahmanides (and Ibn Ezra), *ketoret zarah* means one cannot offer incense with unauthorized components. However, for Rashi and Maimonides, it means unauthorized incense; in other words, they conclude that voluntary incense cannot be offered on the golden altar.

PARASHAT KI TISSA

30:11-13. The Lord spoke to Moses: When you take a census of the Israelites according to their number when they are counted, each man shall give an atonement for his soul to the Lord, and no plague will come upon them when they are counted. And this is what each man who passes among the counted shall give: half a shekel according to the shekel of the sanctuary (the shekel is twenty gerahs), half a shekel as an offering to the Lord. — ... we are commanded to give a half shekel every year, as God, may He be exalted, said, "each man shall give an atonement for his soul to the Lord" (v. 12), and He said, "And this is what each man who passes among the counted shall give" (v. 13). And it is clear that women are not obligated in this commandment, since Scripture states, "Any *man* who passes among the counted." ... This commandment is only practiced when the Temple is standing (*ShM,* Pos. 171; see also v. 15).[196]

30:15. The rich man should not give more and the poor man should not give less from the half shekel to give the portion of God to atone for your souls. — Even a poor person who is sustained by charity is obligated, and he should ask others or sell the clothes he is wearing, and donate the half shekel of silver, as it says, "The rich man should not give more and the poor man should not give less" (Exod. 30:15). And he should not give a small sum one day and another small sum the next day—rather he should give the entire amount all at one (*Hil. Shekalim* 1:1).[197]

---

196. In his commentary to Exod. 30:13, Nahmanides explores why Hebrew is called *lashon ha-kodesh,* the holy language. First he gives his own answer: "because the words of the Torah, all the Prophecies, and all words of holiness [the "Writings"] were all expressed in that language." He then quotes the opinion of Maimonides: "Do not think that our language is called the Sacred Language just as a matter of our pride, or it be an error on our part, but it is perfectly justified, for this holy language has no special names for the organs of generation in male or female, nor for semen, nor for urination or excretion, excepting in indirect language" (*Guide* 3:8).

197. Elsewhere he writes, "Everyone is obligated to give the half shekel; priests, Levites, and Israelites, converts [*gerim*] and freed slaves. However, women, slaves, and minors are not obligated to give; but if they give, we may accept it" (*Shekalim* 1:7).

Nahmanides entertains the possibility that that this verse should constitute at least one negative commandment, possibly two, but he observes that neither Maimonides or the *Behag* counts this as a commandment.

30:18. You shall make a copper basin and its pedestal [*ve-khanno*] of copper… — The Targum of *kanno* is *besiseih* ["its basis"] (*PhM Kelim* 11:7, 24:6).

30:19-21. And Aaron and his sons shall wash their hands and feet from it. When they enter the tent of meeting they shall wash in water so they not die, or when they approach the altar to minister to burn a fire-offering to God. And they shall wash their hands and feet so they not die, and it shall be an eternal ordinance for him and his generations forever. — … the priests are specifically commanded to wash their hands and feet whenever they need to enter the *heikhal* or to draw near for service. This commandment is known as *kiddush yadayim ve-raglayim* ["sanctification of the hands and feet"], as God, may He be exalted, said, "And Aaron and his sons shall wash their hands and feet from it when they enter the tent of meeting."[198] And if someone violates this positive commandment, he is liable for death at the hands of Heaven, meaning a priest who officiated in the Temple who did not wash his hands and feet is liable for death at the hands of Heaven, as He, may He be exalted, said, "they shall wash in water so they not die" (*PhM*, Pos. 24).

FURTHER: It is a positive commandment for a priest who is officiating to sanctify his hands and feet and then perform service, as it says, "And Aaron and his sons shall wash their hands and feet from it." And a priest who officiates without sanctifying his hands and feet in the morning is liable for death at the hands of Heaven, as it says, "they shall wash in water so they not die." And his service is invalid,

---

198. Maimonides reads vv. 19-20 as a continuous phrase.

whether by a regular priest or the high priest. And how do we know that this service is invalid? As it says, "it is an eternal ordinance for him and his generations forever." And regarding the priestly garments it says, "eternal ordinance." Just as someone who was lacking the proper garments defiles his service as we have explained, so too someone who did not wash his hands and feet defiles his service (*Bi'at ha-Mikdash* 5:1-2; also *PhM Tamid* 1:4).

FURTHER: And He said, "When they enter the tent of meeting they shall wash in water so they not die." The first opinion says that this prohibition only applies to entering the *heikhal* without sanctification of the hands and feet. Rabbi Yosi says this means someone who has not sanctified his hands and feet is also forbidden to enter *bein ha-ulam ve-la-mizbeaḥ* (*PhM Kelim* 1:9).

> The area *bein ha-ulam ve-la-mizbeaḥ* is on a lower level of holiness than the *heikhal*, so Rabbi Yosi is more stringent than the first opinion.

FURTHER: If the high priest did not immerse or did not sanctify his hands and feet, whether between changing clothes or between offerings on Yom Kippur and then performed service, his service is valid. Since those immersions and sanctifications are not equivalent to that of Aaron and his sons, about which it says, "And Aaron and his sons shall wash from it." Only something that applies to everyone is mandatory, and that is the first sanctification (*Bi'at ha-Mikdash* 5:7).

FURTHER: It is a positive commandment to sanctify [one's hands and feet] from the basin, but if he sanctified from one of the other ministerial vessels, it is valid. However, common vessels do not sanctify. If he sanctified in a ministerial vessel outside or in a common vessel inside and then performed service, his service is invalid. And one does not sanctify [by placing his hands or feet] inside the basin or inside a ministerial vessel, as it says, "And Aaron and his sons shall wash their hands and feet *from it*" — and not inside it. And if he sanctified inside it, and performed service, he has not defiled it (*Bi'at ha-Mikdash* 5:10).

> Nahmanides writes, "It is the washing which is the essence of the commandment, but He commanded [the making of] the laver only in order that the water should be ready in it. Thus the absence of the laver does not invalidate the washing, neither is there any duty [to do the washing specifically from the laver]; thus on the Day of Atonement the High Priest washed his hands and feet from a golden jug which they made in his honor. However, what we do learn from the laver [that the Torah mentions], is that the washing [of the hands and feet by the priests] must be performed from a vessel" (on 30:19, trans. Chavel).

FURTHER: How much water much be in the basin? There should not be less water than is necessary for four priests, as it says, "Aaron and his sons" — And Elazar, Ithamar, and Phinehas with him, which is a total of four (*Bi'at ha-Mikdash* 5:13).

30:22-23. The Lord spoke to Moses, saying, "You shall take for yourself the choicest spices...." — It is a positive commandment to make the anointing oil so that it be ready for the things which require anointing with it, as it says, "and you shall make it as the oil of sacred anointing" (Exod. 30:25). And this is how Moses made it in the wilderness: He took some musk, cinnamon, and costus—five hundred shekels of the sanctuary shekel. And 250 shekels of fragrant cane. And when the Torah says, "and sweet cinnamon, half as much, 250 shekels," this means that it was weighed twice, 250 shekels in each weighing. And each one was ground separately, and everything was [then] mixed together and soaked in pure and sweet water until all its potency was absorbed in the water. And a hin of oil was placed on the water; [a hin] is twelve *log*, and each *log* is four *revi'ot*. And everything was cooked on the fire until the water evaporated and only the oil remained, and it was set aside for all generations.

Musk [*mor*] is the blood in a wild animal from India that everyone in every place knows as a fragrance. Cinnamon is a tree that comes from the islands of India whose smell is pleasant and which people use as incense. The *kiddah* is costus. And fragrant cane are the thin reeds that are like red straw that comes from the islands of India, whose smell is pleasant, and they are types of fragrance that the doctors place in balsam (*Klei ha-Mikdash* 1:1-3).

The Ra'avad objects to identifying *mor* with musk, writing, "My mind cannot accept that they would put any animal at all in a sacred act, certainly not the blood of an impure animal. Rather, *mor* is the same as what is mentioned in the Song of Songs, 'I have come to my garden, my sister, my spouse, I have gathered myrrh [*mor*] with my spice' (Cant. 5:1), and this is a type of herb or tree whose fragrance disperses." Ra'avad says *mor* is myrrh. The *Kesef Mishnah* defends Maimonides, saying that it is clear that *mor* is musk (Hebrew מושק). He responds to the Ra'avad's objection by saying, "since its appearance as blood has changed, and become merely like dust, and it is a fragrance that has an exceedingly good smell, why should it be diminished?" See also Ibn Ezra and Nahmanides.

Rabbi Bezalel Naor has pointed me to the comments of Rabbenu Asher to *Berakhot* 6:35. There, the Rosh quotes that Rabbi Zerahiah HaLevi (the *Ba'al ha-Ma'or*) forbade musk, while Rabbenu Yonah permitted it. The Rosh calls into question Rabbenu Yonah's proof for permitting musk. Rabbi Naor continues that this remains an important question in the *kashrut* industry to this day.

FURTHER: The anointing oil (Exod. 30:22-33) served a double purpose: to give the anointed object a good odor, and to produce the impression that it was something great, holy, and distinguished, and better than other objects of the same species; it made no difference whether that object was a human being, a garment, or a vessel. All this aimed at producing due respect towards the Sanctuary, and indirectly fear of God.

When a person enters the Temple, certain emotions are produced in him; and obstinate hearts are softened and humbled. These plans and indirect means were devised by the Law, to soften and humble man's heart at entering the holy place, in order that he might entrust himself to the sure guidance of God's commandments. This is distinctly said in the Law: "And you shall eat before the Lord your God, in the place which He shall choose to place His name there, the tithe of your corn, of your wine, and of your oil, and the firstlings, of your herds and of your flocks: that you may learn to fear the Lord your God always" (Deut. 14:23). The object of all these ceremonies is now clear. The reason why we are not allowed to prepare [for common use] the anointing oil and the incense is obvious; for when the odor [of the oil and incense] is perceived only in the Sanctuary, the desired effect is great; besides [if it were allowed for everyone to prepare the anointing oil], people might anoint themselves therewith and imagine themselves distinguished; much disorder and dissension would then follow (*Guide* 3:45).

30:29. And you shall sanctify them, and they shall be holy of holies; whatever touches them shall become holy. — The inner altar sanctifies things that are invalid, whether they are fit for it or not. However the outer altar only sanctifies things that are fit for it but are invalid, as we have explained. How so? If offerings that became invalid were raised on the outer altar, they should be lowered down. If foreign incense was raised up, it should be taken down, since incense is not appropriate for the outer altar. However, if someone brought a handful of grain offering on the inner altar, whether or not it was valid, it should not be taken down. And similarly in all other situations. Just as the altar sanctifies what is appropriate for it, so too the ramp and the other ministerial vessels sanctify what is appropriate for them, since it says regarding the vessels, "whatever touches them shall become holy." And when someone appropriate reaches the ramp, it should not be taken down, even if it has become invalid. And similarly when anything appropriate enters reaches a vessel, it is sanctified and can never be redeemed, even if it becomes invalid, as we have explained in *Issurei ha-Mizbe'aḥ* (*Pesulei ha-Mukdashin* 3:18).

30:31. And to the children of Israel you shall say: This shall be holy anointing oil to Me for all your generations. — ... we are commanded to have oil made according to exact specifications ready to be used to anoint any high priest when he is anointed, as He said, "The priest who is greater than his brothers upon whose head the anointing oil has been poured" (Lev. 21:10). And similarly some kings were anointed with it, as explained in the details of this commandment. And the tabernacle and all of its vessels have been anointed with it, but anointing the vessels is not a commandment for future generations, as the Sages explained in the *Sifrei* that the act of anointing the tabernacle's vessels sanctified all of the vessels [to be used] in the future. And God, may He be exalted and blessed, said, "This shall be holy anointing oil to Me for all your generations" (*ShM*, Pos. 35).

30:32. And it shall not be poured on human flesh... — ... we are forbidden from anointing [anyone] with the anointing oil that Moses made, with the exception of high priests and kings, as God, may He be exalted, said, "And it shall not be poured on human flesh," and it is clear that whoever anoints intentionally is liable for *karet*. It says, "whoever puts any of it on a stranger shall be cut off [from his people]" (Exod. 30:33). And if he did it accidentally, he must bring a fixed sin offering (*ShM*, Neg. 84).

... nor shall you make anything like it, it is holy, and it shall be holy to you. — [Maimonides is explaining the passage in the Mishnah *ve-ha-mefattem et ha-shemen*, reproducing the Temple's oil, which is a sin punishable by *karet*:] And "remaking the [holy] oil" — This is someone who makes the anointing oil the way that our teacher Moses made it in the wilderness at those exact weights, as God, may He be exalted said, "like it [Hebrew, *kamohu*]." And if he made it to be trained in making it, or to teach others, he is not liable for *karet* unless his intention in making it is to be anointed by it (*PhM Kereitot* 1:1; also *ShM*, Neg. 83).

30:33. Whoever makes a compound like it and places it on a stranger shall be cut off from his people. — [Maimonides is explaining the Mishnah's statement that someone who pours anointing oil on someone unauthorized is liable for *karet*:] Meaning if someone placed the anointing oil that Moses himself made, and this is in accordance with [the Sages'] statement that one is only liable for pouring the anointing oil that Moses himself made, as God said, "and places it on a stranger shall be cut off from his people," which refers to that which Moses made. And know that nothing was made from it and nothing will be made again, except the time that Moses made it, as He, may He be exalted, said, "This shall be [holy anointing oil] to Me" (v. 31). So it is a received tradition that only high priests are anointed, even if he is a [high] priest the son of a [high] priest, he is anointed. It is poured on his head and he is anointed on his eyelids in the shape of a Greek spoon like this.[199] And [all of this is based on what] He said, "And he poured some of the anointing oil on Aaron's head, and he anointed him to sanctify him" (Lev. 8:12).

199. Kapach says that Maimonides originally drew this picture but it was later erased.

And it is specifically permitted to anoint kings from the house of David using the anointing oil. And there is a distinction in this matter, which is that when David, peace be upon him, was anointed with the anointing oil, he merited kingship, as the verses testify (2 Sam. 7:8-12), and also his sons after him were kings, even if they were not anointed with the anointing oil. They said: From where do we know that we do not anoint a king who is the son of a king? Since the verse says, "so that the days of his kingship should be lengthened, him and his children, in the midst of Israel" (Deut. 17:20), which teaches that kingship is an inheritance to children. However, if conflict and strife arose in the stock of David about which person should be anointed king, and then everyone agrees to one of them, or the majority supports one of them, or the Sanhedrin or a prophet or the high priest, or one of them achieved kingship (regardless of how he achieved it), then he is anointed with the anointing oil in order to end the strife and war, and to remove division, and so that the public will know that this person is the anointed of the Lord and they should revere him. And a proof of this is what He said, "in the midst of Israel" — He said it is a time of peace in Israel, meaning that if there is no king son of a king, then it is necessary to have an anointing. However, when there is war, they anoint him. And they said: Why was Solomon anointed? Because of the rebellion of Adonijah. And Joash? Because of the rebellion of Athaliah. And Jehoahaz? Because of Jeohiakim his brother. And just as we are required to anoint a king from the house of David since we said he should be anointed from it like a crown on his forehead, and he should stand at a well of water. They said that kings are only anointed beside a well and they are anointed in the shape of a diadem [*ke-min nezer*]. And if someone adds to the anointing more than these measures, or he anoints not in these places, or not in these times [i.e., under these circumstances] this is close to violating what He, may He be exalted, said, "and places it on a stranger shall be cut off from his people." However, regarding the incense, even if someone took it and burned it, he is

473

not liable for *karet*, but is only liable for *me'ilah* (trespass), since he benefited from Temple property (*PhM Kereitot* 1:1).

FURTHER: If someone anoints with an olive's measure of anointing oil intentionally is liable for *karet*, and accidentally he brings a *hattat kavu'a*, as it says, "whoever puts any of it on a stranger shall be cut off from his people." And he is only liable for anointing with the anointing oil that Moses made, as it says, "of it," and from what it says [about the oil], "This shall be holy anointing oil to Me" (Exod. 30:31). And this oil was never to be made again except for what Moses made. Whether he anoints himself or anoints others, as it says, "and places it on a stranger shall be cut off from his people." (*Klei ha-Mikdash* 1:4-6; see also continuation there).

FURTHER: A person who places the anointing oil on a king or high priest who was already anointed is exempt, as it says, "and places it on a stranger...." And these people are not "strangers" regarding the anointing oil. However, if someone, even a king or high priest, pours it on his flesh, he is liable, as it says, "And it shall not be poured on human flesh" — which implies "any person." And a high priest who took anointing oil from his head and anointed his belly is liable for *karet* if he spread an olive's measure (*Klei ha-Mikdash* 1:10).

30:34. And God said to Moses: Take for yourself sweet spices, balsum, and onycha, and galbanum, spices and pure frankincense, an equal part of each. — The incense was made every year, and making it is a positive commandment, as it says, "Take for yourself... spices." And it is explained in the Torah that there are four spices: balsum, onycha, storax, and frankincense. The rest of the spices were spoken to Moses at Sinai.

And there are eleven spices spoken to Moses at Sinai, and they had an exact weight. Then he would add salt from Sodom, Jordanian branches, and an herb that produces smoke without weighing them. Only certain people knew its identity, which was transmitted individually as a law from one person to another.

And this was the weight of all eleven spices: balsam, onycha, storax and frankincense—70 *maneh* from each one. (A *maneh* is 100 *dinarim*.) And musk, cassia, spikenard, and saffron—16 *maneh*; 12 *maneh* of cosuts; 9 *maneh* of cinnamon; 3 *maneh* of Ceylonese cinnamon. The entire composition was 368 *maneh*.

Everything was ground very fine, and a quarter *kav*[200] of salt of Sodom was added, along with a minimal measure of Jordanian branches and spoke-producing herbs. One *maneh* was burned every day on the golden altar, 365 days a year in accordance with the 365 days of the solar year. The three remaining *maneh* were ground extremely fine [again] on the day before Yom Kippur so that the high priest could take a handful of it to burn on Yom Kippur. The left over is the "remainder of incense" that we mentioned in *[Hilkhot] Shekalim*.[201]

Nataf in the Torah refers to the balsam trees that produce balsam oil. Onycha is unguis odoratus [*tzipporen*],[202] which is used to make incense. Storax is like black honey with a strong smell, and comes from sap of trees that grow in the forests of Greece. These are the names of the species in Arabic: *od balsan, atzpar tiv, mayah, livan, masakh, ketziyah, sanbal alnardin, zefron, kost, od, kesher selikhah,* and *anber* (*Klei ha-Mikdash* 2:1-4; see Nahmanides; see further *ShM*, Principle 10, quoted at Exod. 30:7).

---

200. A *kav* is approx. 1.5 quarts.
201. "And this is what was done with the remaining incense: When the first day of the month of Nisan arrived, they would redeem it [and use it] as payment for the craftsmen's payment, and return the monetary payment to the 'summer altar' [a reference to the burned offerings that were brought on the outer altar], and the craftsmen would take the remaining incense as payment. The [the Temple treasures] would buy the incense back [from the craftsmen, using money] from the new levy [of *shekalim*] in order to offer from the new levy" (*Hilkhot Shekalim* 4:12).
202. See Jastrow, p. 1296.

30:36. And you shall grind [*ve-shaḥakta*] it very fine [*hadek*]… — Regarding the daily incense, God, may He be praised, said, "And you shall grind it very fine…" (Exod. 30:36). Regarding Yom Kippur, it is stated, "two handfuls of finely ground [*dakkah*, from the same root as *hadek*] sweet incense" (Lev. 16:12). This mention of *dakkah* comes to include the act of grinding [*sheḥikah*] (*PhM Yoma* 4:4).

30:37-38. And the incense which you make, you shall not make anything like it for yourselves; it shall be holy to you to the Lord. Whoever makes anything like it to smell it will be cut off from his people. — … we are forbidden to make anything in the form of the incense, meaning from those spices and at those weights, and intending to use it (as incense), as God, may He be exalted, said, "you shall not make anything like it for yourselves." And it is clear to us that whoever violates [this prohibition] and makes something like it and intends to smell its fragrance, he receives *karet* if he did so intentionally, and if he did it accidentally he brings a *ḥattat kavu'a* (*ShM*, Neg. 85).

FURTHER: If someone makes incense from these eleven spices according to their weights in order to smell it, even if he did not actually smell it, then he is liable for *karet* for making it if he made it intentionally. And if he made it accidentally he brings a *ḥattat kavua*. Even if he did not make the entire weight, but only half, or a third, since he made it according to is weight [proportionally], he is liable, as it says, "you shall not make anything like it…. Whoever makes anything like it to smell it will be cut off from his people."

If he made it for training or to transmit to the community, he is exempt. If someone smelled from it but did not make it, then he is not liable for *karet*, but he is like anyone else who benefited from Temple property. And the Torah did not prescribe *karet* except on someone who made it according to its measurements and smelled from it (*Klei ha-Mikdash* 2:9-10).

Exodus 31

31:2-3. Behold I have called by name Bezalel son of Uri son of Hur from the tribe of Judah. And I have filled him [*va-amallei*]... — For the meaning of *malei*, see at Exod. 35:35 and 40:34.

... with the spirit of Godin wisdom [*ḥokhmah*]... — The expression *ḥokhmah* denotes... knowledge of any workmanship (see on Exod. 1:10).

... understanding [*tevunah*], and knowledge [*da'at*]... — [Maimonides does not quote this verse, but his general interpretation of *tevunah* and *da'at* are worth quoting:] The knowledge [*da'at*] that we reach and that we acquire is not really the [true] conception that would be grasped through seeing the abstract form of the concept and grasping it or through comprehending forms [e.g., spiritual entities,] whose very existence is ideal. [With regard to the latter,] their very existence is knowledge, regardless of whether we comprehend them as knowledge. [Our process of] comprehension is referred to as understanding [*tevunah*] and it [leads to] knowledge. Conversely, knowledge [leads] us to understand, making it possible for us to grasp what we comprehend. Thus, it is as if [the *mishnah*] were saying: If we do not comprehend a concept, there is no way we will come to a true knowledge of it. And conversely, if there is no [true] knowledge, there is no way we can comprehend, for our understanding stems from knowledge (*PhM Avot* 3[end]).

31:13. And you shall speak to the children of Israel, saying: You shall surely keep My Sabbaths, for it is a sign between Me and you for all your generations... — Both the Sabbath and idolatry are considered equal to all of the commandments of the Torah. And the Sabbath is a sign between the Holy One, Blessed is He, and between us forever (cf. Exod. 31:13, 17). Therefore, whoever violates one of the other commandments is in the category of the wicked of Israel. However, whoever violates the Sabbath publicly is like an idolator, and the two of them are like a heathen in all respects (*Shabbat* 31:15).

... to know that I am the Lord who sanctifies you. — ... that all the nations shall know that I am the Lord who sanctifies you (*Guide* 3:26).

> The Hebrew *la-da'at* has no antecedent: The Talmud understands that God tells Moses that He wishes to inform Israel about the gift of the Sabbath (*Shabbat* 10b, *Betzah* 16a). Saadiah understands it in the second person, "that you [plural] shall know." Finally, Rashi and Maimonides say that "to know" refers to the other nations of the world, in the third person.

31:14. And you shall keep the Sabbath for it is holy to you... — If a Jew performs forbidden labor on the Sabbath—if he sinned and did it intentionally, it is forbidden for him to benefit from that forbidden labor forever, and other Jews are permitted to benefit from it immediately after the Sabbath, as it says, "And you shall keep the Sabbath for it is holy..." — it is holy but its actions are not holy. How so? If a Jew intentionally cooked on the Sabbath, then other Jews may eat it after the Sabbath, but he may never eat it. And if he cooked accidentally, it may be eaten immediately, either by him or by others, and similarly all other situations (*Shabbat* 6:23; he follows the opinion of Rabbi Yehudah (against the opinion of R. Yohanan ha-Sandlar) in *Bava Kamma* 71a. He also makes reference to this debate at *PhM Terumot* 2:3).

31:15. Six days may work be done, but in the seventh is the Sabbath of rest, holy to the Lord: whoever performs any work on the

Sabbath day shall surely be put to death. — [Capital punishment is] decreed for breaking the Sabbath because the keeping of the Sabbath is a confirmation of our belief in the Creation (*Guide* 3:41).

31:17. Between Me and between the children of Israel it is a sign forever... — See on Exod. 30:13.

... and on the seventh day He rested and was revived [*va-yinnafash*]. — The word *va-yinnafash* is a verb derived from *nefesh*, the homonymity of which we have already explained (see *Guide* 1:41),[203] namely, that it has the signification of intention or will; *va-yinnafash* accordingly means, "that which he desired and accomplished, and what he wished had come into existence" (*Guide* 1:67).

31:18. And He gave it to Moses when He finished speaking with him on Mount Sinai, two tablets of testimony, tablets of stone, written by the finger of God. — On the phrase "finger of God," see *Yesodei ha-Torah* 1:9, quoted at Exod. 9:3.

FURTHER: "And the tablets were the work of God" (Exod. 32:16), that is to say, they were the product of nature, not of art: for all natural things are called the work of the Lord, e.g., "These see the works of the Lord" (Ps. 107:24), and the description of the several things in nature, as plants, animals, winds, rain, etc., is followed by the exclamation, "O Lord, how manifold are Your works!" (Ps. 104:24). Still more striking is the relation between God and His creatures, as expressed in the phrase, "The cedars of Lebanon, which he has planted" (Ps. 104:16); the cedars being the product of nature, and not of art, are described as having been planted by the Lord. Similarly we explain, "And the writing was the writing of God" (Exod. 32:16), the relation in which the writing stood to God has already been

203. "When *nefesh* is used in reference to God, it has the meaning 'will'... (*Guide* 1:41).

defined in the words "written with the finger of God" (Exod. 31:18), and the meaning of this phrase is the same as that of "the work of Your fingers" (Ps. 8:4), this being said of the heavens: of the latter it has been stated distinctly that they were made by a word, e.g., "By the word of the Lord were the heavens made" (Exod. 33:6). Hence you learn that in the Bible, the creation of a thing is figuratively expressed by terms denoting "word" and "speech."

The same thing which according to one passage has been made by the word, is represented in another passage as made by the "finger of God" (Exod. 31:18, Deut. 9:10). The phrase "written by the finger of God" is therefore identical with "written by the word of God," and if the latter phrase had been used, it would have been equal to "written by the will and desire of God." Onkelos adopted in this place a strange explanation, and rendered the words literally "written by the finger of the Lord." He thought that "the finger" was a certain thing ascribed to God; so that "the finger of the Lord" is to be interpreted in the same way as "the mountain of God" (Exod. 3:1), and "the rod of God" (Exod. 4:20), that is, as being an instrument created by Him, which by His will engraved the writing on the tablets.

I cannot see why Onkelos preferred this explanation. It would have been more reasonable to say "written by the word of the Lord," in imitation of the verse "By the word of the Lord the heavens were made." Or was the creation of the writing on the tablets more difficult than the creation of the stars in the spheres? As the latter were made by the direct will of God, not by means of an instrument, the writing may also have been produced by His direct will, not by means of an instrument. You know what the Mishnah says, "Ten things were created on Friday in the twilight of the evening" (*Avot* 5:1), and "the writing" is one of the ten things. This shows how generally it was assumed by our forefathers that the writing of the tablets was produced in the same manner as the rest of the creation, as we have shown in our *Commentary on the Mishnah* (*Guide* 1:66).

Exodus 32

32:4. He took the gold from them, formed it in a mold, and cast an image of a calf; and they said, "This is your god, O Israel, who brought you up out of the land of Egypt!" — … this is the seventh time the Israelites tested God in the wilderness (see Exod. 14:11) and that they would have deserved, as He, may He be exalted, explained about His attributes, saying, "slow to anger and abundant in lovingkindness." The Sages said, "slow to anger with the righteous and the wicked."[204] And the prophet [David] said, describing Him, "The Lord is good to all" (Ps. 145:9) (*PhM Avot* 3:18).

… and cast an image of a calf… — R. Abraham writes, "Evidently that was what they had asked for. I have a tradition from my father and teacher of blessed memory that this was because they still held fast to their astrological beliefs, being convinced that they had left Egypt under the zodiacal sign of the bull and that their destiny was governed by some other superstitious, idolatrous astrological notion" (Quoted by Nehama Leibowitz, *New Studies in Shemot (Exodus)*, p. 553).

32:9. And God said to Moses, "I have seen this nation, and behold it is a stiff-necked nation." — "I have seen this nation" — I have seen their rebellion (*Guide* 1:48).

Maimonides is explaining Onkelos' opinion that when "to see" is applied to God regarding some type of evil, Onkelos renders it metaphorically "it is revealed before Me," and Maimonides says, "In all these examples Onkelos is consistent, following the maxim expressed in the words, 'you cannot look on iniquity' (Habakkuk 1:13)."

---

204. BT *Eruvin* 22a, *Bava Kamma* 50a; this is presented in longer form at BT *Sanhedrin* 111a-b.

32:11. And Moses entreated the Lord his God, and he said, "Why, O Lord, should Your anger burn against Your people that You have taken from the land of Egypt with great power and a mighty hand?" — The passage "And Moses entreated" is read from the Torah during morning and afternoon prayers [of fast days] (*Hil. Ta'anit* 5:5).

FURTHER: At the afternoon service [of Tisha b'Av], "And Moses entreated" is read first, and the second and third readings are from "Chisel for yourself" (Exod. 34:1) to "that I will do with you" (Exod. 34:10) (*Tefillah* 13:18).

32:16. And the tablets were the work of god, and the writing was the writing of God... — See *Guide* 1:66, quoted Exod. 31:18.

... inscribed on the tablets. — The Sages said "'inscribed [*harut*] on the tablets' — 'freedom [*herut*] on the tablets'" (*Eruvin* 54a), which means freedom from temporal obligations and affairs of kings is granted to whoever accepts and does what is inscribed on the tablets (*PhM Avot* 3:5).

32:25. And Moses saw that the nation was revealed [*paru'a*], for Aaron had revealed them [*fera'o*] for those who rise against them. — This *peri'ah* is "revealing" and "denuding" as in "for Aaron had revealed them" (*PhM Kelim* 21:1).

Rashi, R. Saadiah, and Sforno agree that *paru'a* means *megullah*, "revealed." Onkelos, Rashbam, Nahmanides, and Hizkuni say *paru'a* means *batel*, "nullified," i.e., bereft of commandments. Shadal says it means "thoughtless, careless." The *BDB* quotes both meanings.

32:26. And Moses stood at the gate entrance of the camp and said, "Whoever is for the Lord come to me," and all the children of Levi gathered to him. — ... the tribe of Levi never practiced idolatry (*Avodah Zarah* 1:3; Maimonides does not quote the present verse in the passage quoted).

32:29. And Moses said, "Dedicate yourselves today to God, each man by his son or his brother, and to bestow upon you a blessing this day." — Let these persons [who endure persecutions] exult those who suffer dire misfortunes, are deprived of their riches, are forced into exile, and lose their belongings. For the bearing of these hardships is a source of glory and a great achievement in the sight of God. Whoever is visited by these calamities is like a burnt offering upon the altar. It is said to them, "Dedicate yourselves to the Lord this day... that He may bestow a blessing upon you today" (*Epistle to Yemen*, p. 106).

32:31. And Moses returned to God and said, "Alas, this nation has committed a great sin and have made for themselves a god of gold. — Whoever confesses [verbally] and does not resolve in his heart to abandon [the sin] is like someone who immerses [in a *mikveh*] while holding carrion in his hand, for the immersion is not effective until he casts the carrion away, as it says, "... whoever confesses and forsakes [his sin] will be find mercy" (Prov. 28:13). And he must specify his sins, as it says, "Alas, this nation has committed a great sin and have made for themselves a god of gold" (*Teshuvah* 2:3).

32:32-33. "And now if You will bear their sin, but if not, blot me out now from Your book that You have written." And God said to Moses, "Whoever has sinned against Me I shall erase from My book." — ... God, may He be exalted, repays good reward to one who fulfills the commandments of the Torah and punishes those who violate its prohibitions. The greatest reward is the world to come, and the worst punishment is *karet*. And we have already explained this matter sufficiently. And the verse that proves this principle is what it says, "And... if you will bear their sin, but if not, erase me now from this book...." And God, may He be exalted, responded, "Whoever has sinned against Me...." This is a proof that it is known before Him to reward the worshipper [*ha-oved*] and to punish the sinner (*PhM Sanhedrin* 10:1, 11th principle).

> The Mishnah states, "Consider three things and you will not come to sin. Know what is above you: an eye that sees, an ear that hears, and that all of your deeds are written in a book" (*Avot* 2:1). On the phrase "an eye that sees," Maimonides writes, "It is mentioned explicitly in the Torah that our actions are known to Him in the unique manner in which He knows them, as it says, '... blot me out now from Your book that You have written'" (*PhM Avot* 2:1). According to Maimonides reward and punishment is one of the central tenets of Judaism, but it seems that the ability to dispense reward and punishment must be predicated on "an eye that sees," and knows who is meritorious and who is blameworthy.

FURTHER: [Maimonides is commenting on the phrase "Your book":] All these phrases are figurative, and we must not assume that God has a book in which He writes, or from which He blots out, as those generally believe that do not find figurative speech in [this verse] (*Guide* 2:47).

32:34. And now go, lead the people to where I have told you; behold, my angel shall go before you; and on the day that I visit, I will visit their sin upon them. — [Maimonides uses vv. 33-34 to argue the following:] In the Law, there occur instances of the fact that men are governed by God, and that their actions are examined by Him (*Guide* 3:17).

Exodus 33

33:8. And whenever Moses went out of the tent, the nation would arise and gather at the entrance of his tent, and they would look after [*hibbitu*] Moses until he had gone into the tent. — [Maimonides explains that the verb *hibbit* literally means "to see," but can also mean "to view and observe" and "to contemplate":] In this sense the verb is used in passages like the following: "He has not beheld [*hibbit*] the iniquity of Jacob" (Num 23:21), for "iniquity" cannot be seen with the eye. The words "And they would look [*ve-hibbitu*] after Moses" (Exod. 33:8)—in addition to the literal understanding of the phrase—were explained by our Sages in a figurative sense. According to them, these words mean that the Israelites examined and criticized the actions and sayings of Moses (*Guide* 1:4).

33:11. And the Lord spoke to Moses face to face… — What is the difference between the prophecy of Moses and that of other prophets? All of the other prophets [prophesied] in a dream or a vision, but our teacher Moses was standing and awake, as it says, "When Moses came to the tent of meeting to speak to Him, he heard the voice speaking to him" (Num. 7:89). All of the prophets [prophesied] through angels, therefore they saw what they saw through an allegory or parable, but our teacher Moses [did not prophecy] through an angel, as it says, "mouth to mouth I will speak to him" (Num. 12:8), "And the Lord spoke to Moses face to face" (Exod. 33:11), and "he will behold the image of God" (Num. 12:8), which means without allegories; rather he saw the matter clearly, not in riddles and allegories. The Torah testifies [about Moses], "clearly and not in riddles" (Num. 12:8), that he did not prophesy in riddles but clearly, and he saw the matter completely (*Yesodei ha-Torah* 7:7; he references this passage at the end of *Guide* 2:45).

FURTHER: [Maimonides explains that the word *panim* has several meanings: (1) face (e.g., Gen. 40:7, Jer. 30:67), (2) anger (e.g., 1 Sam. 1:18), and in this sense can be applied to God (e.g., Exod. 33:14, Lam 4:16), (3) presence and existence of a person (e.g., Gen. 25:18), (4) an adverb of place, (5) an adverb of time, meaning "before," (6) attention and regard. He applies the third meaning to the current verse:] Another meaning of the word is "the presence and existence of a person," e.g., "He died in the presence [*penei*] [i.e., in the lifetime] of all his brethren" (Gen. 25:18), "And in the presence [*penei*] of all the people I will be glorified" (Lev. 10:3), "He will surely curse you in your very presence [*panekha*]" (Job 1:11). In the same sense the word is used in the following passage, "And the Lord spoke to Moses face to face" (Exod. 33:11), i.e., both being present, without any intervening medium between them, e.g., "Come, let us look one another in the face" (2 Kings 14:8), and also "The Lord talked with you face to face" (Deut. 5:4): instead of which we read more plainly in another place, "You heard the voice of the words, but saw no similitude: you only heard a voice" (Deut. 4:12). The hearing of the voice without seeing any similitude is termed "face to face." Similarly do the words, "And the Lord spoke unto Moses face to face" correspond to "There he heard the voice of one speaking unto him" (Num. 7:89), in the description of God's speaking to Moses. Thus it will be clear to you that the perception of the Divine voice without the intervention of an angel is expressed by "face to face." In the same sense the word *panim* must be understood in "And my face [*panai*] shall not be seen" (Exod. 33:23), i.e., My true existence, as it is, cannot be comprehended (*Guide* 1:37).

... as a man speaks to his friend... — All the other prophets would be terrified, frightened, and trembling, and this was not the case with Moses, as the verse says, "as a man speaks to his friend." Just as a man is not frightened to hear the words of his friend, Moses had the capacity to understand the words of prophecy, and he would stand full stature (*Yesodei ha-Torah* 7:7; also *PhM Sanhedrin* 10:1, seventh principle).

... then he would return to the camp; and his attendant, the *na'ar* Joshua son of Nun would not depart from the tent. — as to the words "For I am a *na'ar*" (Jer. 1:6), it is well known that the pious Joseph, when he was thirty years old, is called by the Hebrew *na'ar*; also Joshua, when he was nearly sixty years old. For the statement, "and the *na'ar* Joshua son of Nun, would minister to him" occurs in the account of the Golden Calf. Moses was then eighty-one years old, he lived one hundred and twenty years; Joshua, who survived him fourteen years, lived one hundred and ten years and must consequently have been at least fifty-seven years old at the time when the Golden Calf was made, and yet he is called *na'ar* (*Guide* 2:32).

> Nahmanides writes, "In my opinion, it is the way of the holy tongue to call any attendant a *na'ar*, for the person of high office is called *ish* [man], and his attendant is called *na'ar*."

33:13. And now if I have found favor in Your eyes, show me now Your ways so that I may know You so that I may find favor in Your eyes, and see that this nation is Your people. — The wisest man, our teacher Moses, asked two things of God, and received a reply respecting both. One thing he asked was that God should let him know His true essence: the other, which in fact he asked first, that God should let him know His attributes. In answer to both these petitions God promised that He would let him know all His attributes, and that these were nothing but His actions. He also told him that His true essence could not be perceived, and pointed out a method by which he could obtain the utmost knowledge of God possible for man to acquire.

The knowledge obtained by Moses has not been possessed by any human being before him or after him. His petition to know the attributes of God is contained in the following words, "show me now Your ways so that I may know You so that I may find favor in Your eyes" (Exod. 33:13). Consider how many excellent ideas found expression in the words "show me now Your ways so that I may know You." We learn from them that God is known by His attributes, for Moses believed that he knew Him, when he was shown the way of God. The words "that I may find favor in Your eyes" imply that he who knows God finds grace in His eyes. Not only is he acceptable and welcome to God who [merely] fasts and prays, but everyone who knows Him. He who has no knowledge of God is the object of His wrath and displeasure. The pleasure and the displeasure of God, the approach to Him and the withdrawal from Him are proportional to the amount of man's knowledge or ignorance concerning the Creator. We have already gone too far away from our subject; let us now return to it.

Moses prayed to God to grant him knowledge of His attributes, and also pardon for His people; when the latter had been granted, he continued to pray for the knowledge of God's essence in the words, "Show me now Your glory" (Exod. 33:18), and then received, respecting his first request, "show me now Your way," the following favorable reply, "I will make all My goodness to pass before you" (Exod. 33:19). As regards the second request, however, he was told, "You cannot see My face" (Exod. 33:20). The words "all my goodness" imply that God promised to show him the whole creation, concerning which it has been stated, "And God saw everything that he had made, and, behold, it was very good" (Gen. 1:31). When I say "to show him the whole creation," I mean to imply that God promised to make him comprehend the nature of all things, their relation to each other, and the way they are governed by God both in reference to the universe as a whole and to each creature in particular. This knowledge is referred to when we are told of Moses, "he is faithful in all My house" (Num. 12:7), that is, "his knowledge of all the creatures in My universe is correct and firmly established," for false opinions are not firmly established. Consequently the knowledge of the works of God is the knowledge of His attributes, by which He can be known.

The fact that God promised Moses to give him a knowledge of His works may be inferred from the circumstance that God taught him such attributes as refer exclusively to His works, namely, "merciful and gracious, long-suffering and abundant in goodness..." (Exod. 34:6). It is therefore clear that the ways which Moses wished to know, and which God taught him, are the actions emanating from God. Our Sages call them *middot* [qualities], and speak of the thirteen *middot* of God (*Rosh Hashanah* 17b): they used the term also in reference to man, e.g., "there are four different *middot* [characters] among those who go to the house of learning"; "There are four different *middot* [characters] among those who give charity" (*Avot* 5:13-14). They do not mean to say that God really possesses *middot* (qualities), but that He performs actions similar to such of our actions as originate in certain qualities, i.e., in certain psychical dispositions, not that God has really such dispositions.

Although Moses was shown "all His goodness," i.e., all His works, only the thirteen *middot* are mentioned, because they include those acts of God which refer to the creation and the government of mankind, and to know these acts was the principal object of the prayer of Moses. This is shown by the conclusion of his prayer, "so that I may know You so that I may find favor in Your eyes, and see that this nation is Your people" (Exod. 33:16), that is to say, the people whom I have to rule by certain acts in the performance of which I must be guided by Your own acts in governing them. We have thus shown that "the ways" [*derakhim*] used in the Bible, and *middot* used in the Mishnah, are identical, denoting the acts emanating from

God in reference to the universe. Whenever any one of His actions is perceived by us, we ascribe to God that emotion which is the source of the act when performed by ourselves, and call Him by an epithet which is formed from the verb expressing that emotion (*Guide* 1:54).

According to Maimonides, Moses made the following two requests:

Moses' Request	God's Response
"show me now Your ways" (Exod. 33:16) = God should let him know His attributes... the ways which Moses wished to know, and which God taught him, are the actions [=*derakhim/middot*] emanating from God.	"I will make all My goodness to pass before thee" (Exod. 33:19).... The words "all my goodness" imply that God promised to show him the whole creation, concerning which it has been stated, "And God saw everything that he had made, and, behold, it was very good" (Gen. 1:31).... God promised to make him comprehend the nature of all things, their relation to each other, and the way they are governed by God both in reference to the universe as a whole and to each creature in particular.
"Show me now Your glory" (Exod. 33:18) = Moses prayed to God to grant him knowledge of His attributes, and also pardon for His people; when the latter had been granted, he continued to pray for the knowledge of God's essence in the words, "Show me now Your glory" (Exod. 33:18)	"You cannot see My face" (Exod. 33:20).

Maimonides understands the phrase "see that this nation is your people" to mean that Moses requested to understand

God's ways so that he might be able to lead the nation. In other words, he was asking for the best way to lead the Jewish people, and the answer was first to receive *kol tuvi* ("all My goodness," v. 19), but the more elaborately recorded answer is the count of the thirteen attributes of God. Maimonides argues based on this that the ideal ruler will lead a nation with these qualities, just as God runs the world with these thirteen attributes. (See also *Maimonides Between Philosophy and Halakhah*, pp. 164-167.)

33:14. And he said, "My Presence [*panai*, lit., "face"] shall go and I will give you rest." — The next meaning of the word [*panim*] is "anger," e.g., "And her anger [*paneha*] was gone" (1 Sam. 1:18). Accordingly, the term is frequently used in reference to God in the sense of anger and wrath, e.g., "The anger [*penei*] of the Lord has divided them (Lam. 4:16); "The anger [*penei*] of the Lord is against them that do evil" (Ps. 34:17); "My Presence [*panai*] shall go and I will give you rest" (Exod. 33:14); "Then will I set My anger [*panai*]" (Lev. 20: 3). There are many other instances (*Guide* 1:37; see further at Exod. 33:11).[205]

33:18. And he said, "Show me now Your glory." — [Moses] asked to know the truth of the existence of the Holy One, blessed is He, as much as could be grasped in his mind [lit., "heart"], as someone knows one particular person whose face he saw from a group of people, and his appearance is impressed upon his mind, so that that person is unique from other people in his mind. Similarly, Moses our teacher requested that the existence of the Holy One, blessed is He, be separate in his mind from other things as it [truly] is (*Yesodei ha-Torah* 1:10, see continuation at Exod. 33:23; see also *Shemonah Perakim* 7 [not quoted]).

---

205. In other words, the word *panim* (and related words like *panai*) literally mean "face," but according to Maimonides is sometimes used to express anger, as in the present verse.

FURTHER: [The use of "show" (*le-har'ot*), causative of "see" (*lir'ot*), refers] to intellectual perception, and by no means to perception with the eye as in its literal meaning: for, on the one hand, the eye can only perceive a corporeal object, and in connection with it certain accidents, as color, shape, etc.; and, on the other hand, God does not perceive by means of a corporeal organ (*Guide* 1:4).

FURTHER: The phrase [glory of God] sometimes signifies "the material light," which God caused to rest on a certain place in order to show the distinction of that place, e.g., "And the glory of God dwelled upon Mount Sinai and the cloud covered it" (Exod. 24:16), "And the glory of the Lord filled the tabernacle" (Exod. 40:35). Sometimes the essence, the reality of God is meant by that expression, as in the words of Moses, "Show me Your glory" (Exod. 33:18), to which the reply was given, "For no man shall see Me and live" (Exod. 33:20). This shows that the glory of the Lord in this instance is the same as He Himself, and that "Your glory" has been substituted for "Yourself," as a tribute of homage... (*Guide* 1:64).

33:19. And He said, "I will make all My goodness pass before you... — See *Guide* 1:54, quoted at Exod. 33:13.

... and I will proclaim the name of the Lord before you... — See at Exod. 34:6

... and I will be gracious to whom I will be gracious, and I will show mercy on whom I will show mercy. — God creates and guides beings who have no claim upon Him to be created and guided by Him; He is therefore called gracious [*ḥannun*] (*Guide* 1:54).

Consistent with this line of thinking, Nahmanides says that *ḥannun* comes from the word *ḥinnam*, "free" (on Exod. 22:26).

492

33:20 And he said, "you cannot see My face, for no one shall see Me and live." — By way of parable, the Sages said regarding the vision of our teacher Moses, peace be upon him, concerning Godly matters that he saw the Creator as much as possible because his intelligence is tied to the hyle, as God, may He be exalted, said, "for no one shall see Me and live," as we have explained in our commentary to *Pirkei Avot*. And the Sages stated (*Yevamot* 49b) that all the prophets had visions in a glass that did not reflect and Moses our teacher had visions in a glass that reflected (*PhM Kelim* 30:2; see also *Guide* 1:54, quoted at Exod. 33:13.).

33:21. And He said, "Behold, there is a place [*makom*] by Me... — we have explained here *makom* in the sentence "Blessed be the glory of the Lord from His place [*mekomo*]" (Ezek. 3:12), but you must understand that the word *makom* has the same signification in the passage "Behold, there is a place [*makom*] by Me," namely, "a certain degree of contemplation and intellectual intuition (not of ocular inspection)," in addition to its literal meaning, "a place," i.e., the mountain which was pointed out to Moses for seclusion and for the attainment of perfection (*Guide* 1:8).

On the theological meaning of the word *makom*, see also Rabbi Joseph Albo's *Ikkarim* 2:17.

... and you shall stand [*ve-nitzavta*]... —The phrase "stood upon it" indicates the permanence and constancy of God, and does not imply the idea of physical position. This is also the sense of the phrase "and you shall stand upon the rock" (*Guide* 1:15, see further at Exod. 2:4).

... upon the rock [*ha-tzur*]." — [Maimonides identifies three meanings of *tzur*: (1) rock, (2) hard stone, (3) the root and origin of all things:] It is in the latter sense that the Almighty is called "rock," He being the origin and the *causa efficiens* of all things besides Himself. Thus we read, "He is the Rock, His work is perfect" (Deut. 32:4), "Of the Rock that begat you, you are unmindful" (Deut. 32:18), "Their Rock had sold them" (Deut. 31:30), "There is no rock like our God" (1 Sam. 2:2), "The Rock of eternity" (Isa. 26:4). Again, "And you shall stand upon the rock" (Exod. 32:21), i.e., be firm and steadfast in the conviction that God is the source of all things, for this will lead you towards the knowledge of the Divine Being (*Guide* 1:16; he also makes passing reference at *Guide* 1:63).

33:22. And when My glory passes by, I will place you in the cleft of a rock... — I can adduce still further support for the opinion of Onkelos from the words "when My glory passes by," which expressly state that the passing object was something ascribed to God, not God Himself, and of this Divine glory it is also said "until I have passed by" (Exod. 33:22), and "And the Lord passed before him" (*Guide* 1:21; see second half of this verse).

> Maimonides' theory, based on Onkelos, is "every expression implying corporality or corporal properties, when referring to God," he explains by assuming an ellipsis of a *nomen regens* before 'God,' thus connecting the expression (of corporality) with another word which is supplied, and which governs the genitive 'God' (*Guide* 1:21, quoted next), and Maimonides' prooftext is the current phrase, since it says "And when My glory passes by," and not "when I [=God] pass by."

FURTHER: The phrase [glory of God] sometimes signifies "the material light," which God caused to rest on a certain place in order to show the distinction of that place, e.g., "And the glory of God dwelled upon Mount Sinai and the cloud covered it" (Exod. 24:16), "And the glory of the Lord filled the tabernacle" (Exod. 40:35). Sometimes the essence, the reality of God is meant by that expression, as in the words of Moses, "Show me Your glory" (Exod. 33:18), to which the reply was given, "For no man shall see Me and live" (Exod. 33:20). This shows that the glory of the Lord in this instance is the same as He Himself, and that "Your glory" has been substituted for "Yourself," as a tribute of homage... (*Guide* 1:64; quoted also at v. 18).

... and I will cover you with My hand until I have passed by. — In asserting that God withheld from Moses (the higher knowledge) [v. 23], I mean to say that this knowledge was unattainable, that by its nature it was inaccessible to Moses; for man, while able to gain perfection by applying his reasoning faculties to the attainment of what is within the reach of his intellect, either weakens his reason of loses it altogether as soon as he ventures to seek a higher degree of knowledge—as I shall elucidate in one of the chapters of this work—unless he be granted a special aid from Heaven, as is described in the words, "and I will cover you with My hand[206] until I have passed by" (Exod. 33:22).

Onkelos, in translating this verse, adopts the same method which he applies to the explanation of similar passages, namely, every expression implying corporality or corporal properties, when referring to God, he explains by assuming an ellipsis of a *nomen regens* before "God," thus connecting the expression (of corporality) with another word which is supplied, and which governs the genitive "God" (*Guide* 1:21)

33:23. And you shall see My back [*aḥorai*]... — [Maimonides counts three meanings of the word *aḥor*: (1) back, (2) after, (3) following a thing and of conforming with the moral principles of some other thing:] In this [third] sense the word occurs in "And you shall see My back [*aḥorai*]" — you shall perceive that which follows Me, is similar to Me, and is the result of My will, i.e., all things created by Me... (*Guide* 1:38).

---

206. For Maimonides' understanding of "hand of God," see *Yesodei ha-Torah* 1:9, quoted at Exod. 9:3.

Isaac Husik, in his notes to Joseph Albo's *Ikkarim*, explains Maimonides' intent as follows: "You shall understand those things which are caused by Me, namely the world of nature" (vol. 2, p. 96, note I).

... but My face [*panai*] shall not be seen. — the perception of the Divine voice without the intervention of an angel is expressed by "face to face." In the same sense the word *panim* must be understood in "And My face [*panai*] shall not be seen" (Exod. 33:23), i.e., My true existence, as it is, cannot be comprehended (*Guide* 1:37; see more fully at Exod. 33:11).

And you shall see My back, but My face shall not be seen. — And God, may He be blessed, responded [to Moses' request in v. 18] that the mortal human mind does not have this capacity, whose body and soul are connected, to understand the truth of this matter fully. Nonetheless He, may He be blessed, revealed matters to him that no man before or after him had known, until he understood the truth of the existence of the Holy One, Blessed is He, in his mind from other entities, just as one person is unique in a group, so that when he sees his back, he recognizes his entire body and clothing in his mind from other human forms, and this is alluded to by the verse, "And you shall see My back, but My face shall not be seen" (*Yesodei ha-Torah* 1:10).

According to Ra'avad, this is a great secret [*sod gadol*], and it is not proper to reveal it to the hoi polloi. (I thank Rabbi Bezalel Naor for reminding me of this reference.)

FURTHER: Moses sought to attain a certain perception which is called "the perception of the Divine face," a term occurring in the phrase, "My face shall not be seen," but God vouchsafed to him a perception of a lower degree, namely, the one called, "the seeing of the back," in the words, "And you shall see My back." We have mentioned this subject in our work *Mishneh Torah*. Accordingly, it is stated in the above-mentioned passage that the Lord withheld from Moses that perception which is called "the seeing of the Divine face," and substituted for it another gift, namely, the knowledge of the acts attributed to God, which, as I shall explain (*Guide* 1:54), are considered to be different and separate attributes of the Supreme (*Guide* 1:21).

Exodus 34

34:3. And no man shall ascend with you, and neither shall anyone be seen anywhere on the mountain; neither shall sheep nor cattle graze before that mountain. — It is not proper to count the commandments that are not practiced for all generations [such as] "neither shall sheep nor cattle graze before that mountain" (*ShM*, Shoresh 3; see there).

34:6. And the Lord caused His face to pass over him [Moses] and called... — [Maimonides applies the fifth meaning of *avar* to this present verse (see at Exod. 12:12 for other meanings)]: [The verb *avar*] is also used figuratively to denote "to abandon one aim, and turn to a different aim and object," e.g., "He shot an arrow, causing it to miss [*le-ha'aviro*] the aim" (1 Sam. 20:36). This is the sense, it appears to me, of this verb in "And the Lord caused His face to pass [*va-ya'avor*] over him" (Exod. 34:6). I take "His face" to mean "the face of God." Our Teachers likewise interpreted "His face" as being identical with "the face of God."[207] And, although this is found in the midst of Aggadic interpretations which would be out of place in this our work, yet it is some support of our view, that the pronoun "His" is employed in this passage as a substitute for "God's"....[208]

Onkelos applies it [i.e., his method of using a *nomen regens*; see at Exod. 33:22] also to "And the Lord caused His face to pass over him" which he paraphrases, "The Lord caused His Presence to pass before his face and called." According to this rendering the thing which passed was unquestionably some physical object, the pronoun "his" refers to "Moses," and the phrase *al panav* is identical with *lefanav*, "before him," as in, "So went the present over before

---

207. Perhaps a reference to *Rosh Hashanah* 17b.
208.   In other words *va-ya'avor* means that God turned away from this matter to another topic, which for Maimonides is "knowledge of the acts attributed to God" (*Guide* 1:21, quoted at Exod. 33:23).

him [*al panav*]" (Gen. 32:22). This is likewise an appropriate and satisfactory explanation....[209]

Should it, however, be considered necessary to assume here an ellipsis, according to the method of Onkelos, who supplies in some instances the term "the Glory," in others "the Word," and in others "the Divine Presence," as the context may require in each particular case, we may also supply here the word "voice," and explain the passage, "And *a voice* from the Lord passed before him and called."

We have already shown that the verb *avar* ["he passed"] can be applied to the voice, as in "And they caused a voice to pass through the camp" (Exod. 36:6).[210] According to this explanation, it was *the voice* which called. No objection can be raised to applying the verb *kara* ["he called"] to *kol* [voice], for a similar phrase occurs in the Bible in reference to God's commands to Moses, "He heard the voice speaking unto him," and, in the same manner as it can be said "the voice spoke," we may also say "the voice called." Indeed, we can even support this application of the verbs "to say" and "to call" to "the voice,' by parallel passages, as "A voice says 'Cry,' and it says, 'What shall I cry?'" (Isa. 40:6).

According to this view, the meaning of the passage under discussion would be, "A voice of God passed before him and called, 'the Lord, the Lord, God, merciful, and gracious'" (The word "the Lord" is repeated; it is in the vocative, for "the Lord" is the one who is called, cf., "Moses, Moses!" (Exod. 3:4), "Abraham, Abraham!" (Gen. 22:11). This, again, is a very appropriate explanation of the text.

You will surely not find it strange that this subject, so profound and difficult, should bear various interpretations; for it will not impair the force of the argument with which we are here concerned. Either explanation may be adopted: you may take that grand scene altogether as a prophetic vision, and the whole occurrence as a mental

---

209. Omitted text quoted at Exod. 33:22.
210. Maimonides' second definition of *avar* is "the passage of sound through air."

operation, and consider that what Moses sought, what was withheld from him, and what he attained, were things perceived by the intellect without the use of the senses (as we have explained above); or you may assume that in addition there was a certain ocular perception of a material object, the sight of which would assist intellectual perception. The latter is the view of Onkelos, unless he assumes that in this instance the ocular perception was likewise a prophetic vision, as was the case with "a smoking furnace and a burning lamp that passed between those pieces" (Gen. 15:17), mentioned in the history of Abraham. You may also assume that in addition there was a perception of sound, and that there was a voice which passed before him, and was undoubtedly something material.

You may choose either of these opinions, for our sole intention and purpose is to guard you against the belief that the phrase "and the Lord passed," is analogous to "pass before the people" (Exod. 17:5), for God, being incorporeal, cannot be said to move, and consequently the verb "to pass" cannot with propriety be applied to Him in its primary signification (*Guide* 1:21).

... the Lord, the Lord... — The word "Lord" is repeated; it is in the vocative, for "the Lord" is the one who is called, cf., "Moses, Moses!" (Exod. 3:4), "Abraham, Abraham!" (Gen. 22:11) (*Guide* 1:21).

> Saadiah understood the verse as, "and the Lord passed before him, and the Lord proclaimed, 'Lord...,'" which is against the traditional reading. According to Dr. Richard Steiner, Saadiah was concerned with the question of one Rabbi Eleazar, who argued to Maimonides, "it is in no way permitted to put them ['Lord' and 'Lord'] together because that condition might lead to false belief" (*Teshuvot ha-Rambam*, quoted in Dr. Richard Steiner, *A Biblical Translation in the Making: The Evolution and Impact of Saadia Gaon's Tafsīr*, p. 151).

Maimonides responded "that he agrees with R. Hai Gaon and all of the other *geonim* that the first 'Lord' is not one of the thirteen attributes," and that he has never heard anyone disagree on that point! His son, Abraham, adopts the same reading.... [In the *Guide* 1:21], however, Maimonides cites the other reading approvingly; his formulation suggests that he had in the interim become aware of Ibn Ezra's critique of Saadia's reading" that the cantillation marks suggest both mentions of "the Lord, the Lord" are to be included in the thirteen attributes (Steiner, p. 151, n. 39).

... merciful and gracious... — ... just as the Holy One, blessed is He, is called merciful, so too you should be merciful; just as the Holy One, blessed is He, is called gracious, so too you should be gracious... (*ShM*, Pos. 8).

Based on *Sifrei*, "Ekev," quoted at *De'ot* 1:6 and *Guide* 1:21 (end). See also Lev. 19:2. However, Maimonides seems to take the opposite approach later: "Whoever says in prayers, 'He who has mercy on the mother bird prohibiting us from taking the mother and the chicks or the One who prohibited us from slaughtering an animal and its young on the same day should have mercy on us,' or anything similar, we silence him, because these commandments are scriptural decrees and not [given out of] mercy. For if they were from mercy, He would not have permitted slaughter at all" (*Tefillah* 9:7; see Rabbenu Manoah there).

... gracious [*ḥannun*] ... — Whenever any one of His actions is perceived by us, we ascribe to God that emotion which is the source of the act when performed by ourselves, and call Him by an epithet which is formed from the verb expressing that emotion. We see, e.g., how well He provides for the life of the embryo of living beings; how He endows with certain faculties both the embryo itself and those who have to rear it after its birth, in order that it may be protected from death and destruction, guarded against all harm, and assisted in the performance of all that is required [for its development]. Similar acts, when performed by us, are due to a certain emotion and tenderness called mercy and pity. God is, therefore, said to be merciful, e.g., "Like as a father is merciful to his children, so the Lord is merciful to those that fear Him" (Ps. 103:13); "And I will spare them, as a man has mercy [*yahamol*, "spares"] his own son that serves him" (Mal. 3:17). Such instances do not imply that God is influenced by a feeling of mercy, but that acts similar to those which a father performs for his son, out of pity, mercy and real affection, emanate from God solely for the benefit of His pious men, and are by no means the result of any impression or change—[produced in God]. When we give something to a person who has no claim upon us, we perform an act of grace; e.g., "Grant them graciously unto us" (Judg. 21:22). [The same term is used in reference to God, e.g.,] "which God has graciously given" (Gen. 33:5); "Because God has dealt graciously with me" (Gen. 33:11). Instances of this kind are numerous. God creates and guides beings who have no claim upon Him to be created and guided by Him; He is therefore called gracious [*hannun*] (*Guide* 1:54).

Dr. Eliezer Berkovits strongly disagrees with Maimonides' "as-if" theology. He writes, "Now this is an opinion that denies the most precious and intimate aspect of God's relationship to the world and to man. The negative attributes will never do. Religion cannot forgo the love and the mercy of God, nor even His justice and anger. Such attributes have to be related to Him in a positive sense or else there is no basis for a living God of religious relevance. / What Maimonides denies God, namely affection and tenderness, are the very essence of the encounter.... God does not act as if He were 'merciful and gracious, long-suffering, and abundant in goodness...'; God is as He is here proclaimed. He is a caring God" (*God, Man, and History*, pp. 55-56).

... slow to anger and abundant in lovingkindness [*ve-rav ḥesed*]... — God judges men with kindness, and not as befits their conduct according to the strict measure, as indicated by [the Sages' interpretation] of His attributes, "slow to anger and abundant in lovingkindness," as meaning "slow to anger for both the righteous and the wicked" (*Eruvin* 22a). And the prophet describes Him, saying, "God is good to all" (Ps. 145:9) (*PhM Avot* 3:15[19]).

FURTHER: In our commentary on *Avot*, we have explained the expression *ḥesed* as denoting an excess [in some moral quality]. It is especially used of extraordinary kindness. Lovingkindness is practiced in two ways: first, we show kindness to those who have no claim whatever upon us; second, we are kind to those to whom it is due, in a greater measure than is due to them.[211] In the inspired writings the term *ḥesed* occurs mostly in the sense of showing kindness to those who have no claim to it whatever. For this reason the term *ḥesed* is employed to express the good bestowed upon us by God: "I will mention the lovingkindness of the Lord" (Isa. 63:7). On this account, the very act of the creation is an act of God's lovingkindness: "I have said, 'The universe is built up in lovingkindness'" (Ps. 89:3),[212] i.e., the building up of the universe is an act of lovingkindness. Also, in the enumeration of God's attributes, Scripture says: "And abundant in lovingkindness" (Exod. 34:6) — *ḥesed* denotes pure charity....

211. Radak explains that *ḥesed* is *yitron ha-tovah yoter al ha-ra'ui*, "additional goodness beyond what is necessary" (Hos. 4:1).
212. Kapach points out that R. Saadiah gives the same explanation in his introduction to the book of Job. Malbim quotes this explanation from Maimonides on Ps. 89:3.

He [God] is called *ḥasid*, "kind," because He created the universe (*Guide* 3:53).[213]

34:7. ... visiting the sins of the fathers on the sons and sons' sons, to the third and fourth generation. — all the thirteen *middot* of God are attributes of mercy with only one exception, namely, "visiting the sins of the fathers on the sons" (Exod. 34:7), for the meaning of the preceding attribute (in the original *ve-nakkeh lo yenakkeh*) is "and He will not utterly destroy" (and not "He will by no means clear the guilty"), e.g., "And she will be utterly destroyed [*ve-nikketah*], she shall sit upon the ground" (Isa. 3:26) (*Guide* 1:54; see further at Exod. 20:5).

> Shadal writes: Maimonides (*Guide* 1:54) says that "visiting the sins of the fathers on the sons" means only that one of God's commandments is that in the case of an *ir ha-niddaḥat* (a city condemned for idolatry), "You shall strike the inhabitants of that city at the edge of the sword" (Deut. 13:16), including the children who have not sinned. You can see, however, how forced and far-fetched this explanation is. Besides, there is no proof for the idea that this principle applies only with respect to idolatry. Even though it is mentioned in connection with idolatry here, we find it also among the Thirteen Divine Attributes (Exod. 34:7), and there it does not refer to idolatry, but is stated in a general way. Who would think that one of the Thirteen Attributes refers only to one particular commandment [i.e., *ir ha-niddaḥat*], and one that rarely—and perhaps never—was put into practice? Besides, if "demanding account of the fathers'

---

213. For more interpretations of the word *ḥesed* see my "Of Loyalty, Duty, and Love: An Exploration of the Meaning of Chesed," available here: http://www.torahmusings.com/2017/05/loyalty-duty-love-exploration-meaning-chesed/

sins" referred to one particular commandment, it would be only fitting for the principle of "exercising benevolence up to the thousandth descendants" (below, v. 6) to refer to a single commandment as well; but just as the one idea is unlikely, so is the other (trans. Klein).

34:13. You shall smash their altars and their pillars you shall destroy, and their sacred trees you shall cut down. — If a tree was planted initially so that it should be worshipped, it is forbidden to derive benefit [from it], and this is the "sacred tree" [*asherah*] mentioned in the Torah (*Avodah Zarah* 8:3).

34:14. For you shall not bow down to a foreign god... — it is stated, "Do not bow down to a foreign god" (Exod. 34:14), to prohibit one who prostrates, even if it is not worshipped in that way (*Avodah Zarah* 3:3; see further *Guide* 3:32, quoted at Exod. 25:8; see also *Shegagot* 14:2).

... for the Lord, whose name is Jealous, is a jealous God. — You must know, that in examining the Law and the books of the Prophets, you will not find the expressions "burning anger," "provocation," or "jealousy" applied to God except in reference to idolatry (*Guide* 1:36; see further at Exod. 20:4).

34:15-16. Lest you make a covenant with the inhabitants of the land, and lust after their gods and sacrifice to their gods, and he invites you, and you will eat from his sacrifice; and you shall take their daughters for your sons, and their daughters shall lust after their gods, and make your sons lust after their gods. — If an idolator makes a party for his son or daughter, it is prohibited to benefit from his feast. It is even forbidden for a Jew to eat or drink what belongs to him there, since he is eating it at a celebration of idolators. And when is it prohibited to eat [at an idolator's meal]? Once he begins to involve and prepare in the needs of the feast, and all the days of the party, and for thirty days after the party. And if he made another feast for the wedding, even after thirty days, it is prohibited until twelve months have passed. And this entire prohibition is because it is idolatry, as it says, "… and he invites you, and you will eat from his sacrifice, and you shall take their daughters for your sons" (*Avodah Zarah* 9:15).

FURTHER: If a gentile slaughters [an animal], even if he slaughtered in the presence of a Jew with a proper knife, even if he is a minor, his act of slaughter is invalid, and someone who partakes of it is liable for lashes, as it says, "and he invites you, and you will eat from his sacrifice." It is forbidden and it is not comparable to a Jew who does not know the laws of ritual slaughter. [The Sages] made a great safeguard regarding this matter, for even a gentile who does not practice idolatry, his act of slaughter is invalid (*Sheḥitah* 4:11-12).

FURTHER: The reason for the prohibition of intermarriage with other nations is stated in the Law, "and you shall take their daughters for your sons, and their daughters shall lust after their gods, and make your sons lust after their gods" (*Guide* 3:49).

34:19. All that opens the womb is Mine, and all of your flocks, and every firstling of your cattle born a male—ox or sheep. — It is a positive commandment to redeem every Jewish man [i.e., every father] to redeem his son who is the firstborn of a Jewish mother, as it says, 'All that opens the womb is Mine" (Exod. 34:19) and "You shall surely redeem a firstborn man" (Num. 18:15) (*Bikkurim* 11:1; see also *ShM*, Pos. 80; see also Exod. 13:1-2).

34:20. The firstborn donkey you shall redeem with a *seh*, and if you do not redeem it you shall break its neck... — See at Exod. 13:13.

... all the firstborn of your sons you shall redeem; and no one shall appear before Me empty-handed. — If [a father] had to redeem his son, and the time arrived to make the pilgrimage to Jerusalem, and he does not have the capacity for both, he should redeem his son and then make the pilgrimage, as it says, "all the firstborn of your sons you shall redeem," and then "and no one shall appear before Me empty-handed" (*Bikkurim* 11:4).

... and no one shall appear before Me empty-handed. — See at Exod. 23:15.

34:21. For six days you shall work, but on the seventh you shall rest; from ploughing and from harvesting you shall desist. — We are commanded to abstain from working the land on the seventh year, as God, may He be exalted, said, "from ploughing and from harvesting you shall desist." And this commandment has been repeated several times, and it says, "it shall be a complete rest [*shabbat shabbaton*] for the land" (Lev. 25:4). We have already mentioned that the Sages said the word "*shabbaton* [cessation]" refers to a positive commandment (see See *ShM*, Pos. 90, from BT *Shabbat* 24b). And He, may He be exalted, also said, "and the land shall observe a Sabbath to the Lord" (Lev. 25:2). The details of this commandment are explained in the tractate *Shevi'it*. And it is only a biblical commandment in the land of Israel (*ShM*, Pos. 135).

FURTHER: It is a positive commandment to abstain from working the land or working with trees on the sabbatical year, as it says, "and the land shall observe a Sabbath to the Lord" (Lev. 25:2), and it is stated "from ploughing and from harvesting you shall desist" (Exod. 34:21). And whoever labors to work the land or the trees on this year nullifies a positive commandment and violates a negative commandment, as it says, "You shall not sow your field and your vineyard you shall not prune" (Lev. 25:4) (*Shemittah ve-Yovel* 1:1; see also *PhM Shevi'it* 1:1, based on JT *Shevi'it* 1:1).

Rashi quotes two interpretations of the phrase "from ploughing and from harvesting you shall desist": (1) it refers to the sabbatical year, (2) it refers to the Sabbath day, but teaches a separate law, namely, that in general ploughing and harvesting are optional activities and therefore forbidden on the Sabbath, but harvesting the *omer* (Lev. 23:9-14) is a commandment, and it overrides the Sabbath.

If this phrase refers to the sabbatical year, then the Talmud asks why this phrase is necessary, because we have other verses to prohibit work on that year (BT *Rosh Hashanah* 9:1). Therefore Rabbi Akiva suggests it refers to work such as ploughing at the end of the sixth year and harvesting at the end of the eight year, and similarly Rabbi Yishmael says it teaches the obligation of "adding from the profane to the sacred." This is the interpretation that Maimonides quotes in *PhM Shevi'it* 1:1.

However, in the *Sefer ha-Mitzvot* and *Mishneh Torah*, Maimonides quotes the present verse to teach the primary prohibition of working on the sabbatical year, and not the derivations of Rabbi Akiva or Rabbi Yishmael. Furthermore, when quoting the prohibition to work at the end of the sixth year, he says it is a *halakhah le-Moshe mi-Sinai*, i.e., a law for which there is no scriptural support.

34:22. You shall make the feast of weeks, with the first fruits of your wheat harvest [*bikkurei ketzir ḥittim*], and the festival of ingathering at the turning of the year. — The two loaves [*shtei ha-leḥem*] are called *bikkurim*, and He clarified them and said *bikkurei ketzir ḥittim*, and surely this is a proof that the *bikkurim* that they brought fifty days prior [on Passover] are *bikkurei ketzir se'orim* [first fruits of the barley harvest] (*PhM Menaḥot* 10:4; also *Temidin u-Musafin* 7:11).

34:23. Three times a year all your males shall appear, before the master, God. — see at Exod. 23:17.

34:24. For I will drive out the nations from before you and I will expand your borders, and no man will covet your land when you ascend to appear before the Lord your God three times a year. — Women and servants are exempt from *re'iyah*, and all males are commanded in *re'iyah*, except for a deaf person, a mute, an imbecile, a minor, a blind man, one who limps, one who is ritually impure, and one who is uncircumcised. And similarly, an elderly man, an invalid, and someone exceedingly tender or delicate who cannot ascend by foot. All of these eleven are exempt, but all other males are obligated in *re'iyah*. A deaf person, even if he has the ability to speak, even if he is only deaf in one ear, he is exempt from *re'iyah*. Similarly, a man who is blind in one eye or limps with one leg, he is exempt. A mute—even if can hear—is exempt. A *tumtum* and an androgynous person are exempt, because they have the doubtful status of a woman. Someone who is half slave and half free is exempt, because in one respect he is still under bondage.

How do we know that all of these are exempt from *re'iyah*? Because it says "all your males shall appear" (Exod. 23:17), which excludes women. And any positive commandment in which women are not obligated, slaves are also not obligated in. Furthermore, it says, "When all Israel come to appear" (Deut. 31:11), which excludes servants.

And it says, "When all Israel come to appear" — just as they come to appear before God, they also come to see the glory of His holiness and the house of His Divine Presence, which excludes a blind man who cannot see, even if he is only blinded in one eye, because his sight is not perfect. And there it also says "so that they will hear" (Deut. 31:12), which excludes someone who does not have perfect hearing; "so that they will learn" (ibid.), which excludes a mute, for whoever is obligated to learn is also obligated to teach. And it says, "when you ascend to appear before the Lord" (Exod. 34:24) — whoever can ascend on his feet, to exclude the lame, invalid, elderly, or tender... (*Ḥagigah* 2:1; see also *PhM Ḥagigah* 1:1, quoted at Exod. 23:17).

34:25. You shall not slaughter the blood of My sacrifice with leaven, and the sacrifice of the feast of the Passover shall not remain until morning. — ... according to tradition, this refers to a little bit past the seventh hour [on 14 Nisan] (*PhM Pesaḥim* 1:4; see also at Exod. 12:15 and 23:18).

The phrase *lo tishḥat al ḥametz dam zivḥi*, "you shall not slaughter the blood of My offering with leaven," seems to be understood as: you shall not offer the blood of My offering when there is leaven, i.e., before noon on 14 Nisan.

34:26. You shall bring the first fruits of your land to the house of the Lord your God; you shall not cook a kid in its mother's milk. — See at Exod. 23:19.

34:28. And he [Moses] was with the Lord forty days and forty nights; he did not eat any bread and did not drink any water, and he wrote on the tablets the words of the covenant, the ten statements. — ... during that holy communion he could ask Him, answer Him, speak to Him, and be addressed by Him, enjoying beatitude in that which he had obtained to such a degree that "he did not eat any bread and did not drink any water"; his intellectual energy was so predominant that all coarser functions of the body, especially those connected with the sense of touch, were in abeyance (*Guide* 3:51).

34:29. And when Moses descended from Mount Sinai the two tablets of testimony were in Moses' hand when he descended from the mountain, and Moses did know that the skin of his face shone when He had spoken with him. — At times the truth shines so brilliantly that we perceive it as clear as day. Our nature and habit then draw a veil over our perception, and we return to a darkness almost as dense as before. We are like those who, though beholding frequent flashes of lightning, still find themselves in the thickest darkness of the night. On some the lightning flashes in rapid succession, and they seem to be in continuous light, and their night is as clear as the day. This was the degree of prophetic excellence attained by [Moses], the greatest of prophets, to whom God said, "But as for you, stand here by Me" (Deut. 5:31), and of whom it is written "the skin of his face shone..." (Exod. 34:29). [Some perceive the prophetic flash at long intervals; this is the degree of most prophets.] By others only once during the whole night is a flash of lightning perceived. This is the case with those of whom we are informed, "They prophesied, and did not prophesy again" (Num. 11:25). There are some to whom the flashes of lightning appear with varying intervals; others are in the condition of men, whose darkness is illumined not by lightning, but by some kind of crystal or similar stone, or other substances that possess the property of shining during the night; and to them even this small amount of light is not continuous, but now it shines and now it vanishes, as if it were "the flame of the rotating sword" (Gen. 3:24) (*Guide*, introduction).

VAYAK'HEL-PEKUDEI

Exodus 35

35:3. You shall not kindle a fire in any of your habitations on the Sabbath day. — ... we are forbidden from punishing sinners and executing punishments on the Sabbath day, as it is said, "You shall not kindle a fire... on the Sabbath day," meaning that you shall not burn someone who is liable for the punishment of burning, and also this applies to other types of execution. And the language of the *Mekhilta* is, "'You shall not kindle a fire' — but fire has already been forbidden. Rather this is singled out to teach that just as burning is one of the forms of judicial execution and does not override the Sabbath, so too other forms of judicial execution do not override the Sabbath." Behold they said that kindling is an exceptional prohibition. But this is not the law. Rather, it is a standard prohibition [but the verse comes to teach something about all prohibitions of the Sabbath (*Shabbat* 70a)], specifically that someone is liable for each and every act of labor independently, as will be explained in its place. The Jerusalem Talmud (JT *Sanhedrin* 4:6) quotes "in any of your habitations" — Rav Ila in the name of Rabbi Yannai says that from here we learn that courts do not render judgment on the Sabbath (*ShM*, Neg. 322; see also *PhM Sanhedrin* 4:1, *ShM* Shoresh 14, and *Shabbat* 24:7).

... in any of your habitations... — meaning, in the courthouse (*ShM*, Shoresh 14).

35:5. Take from yourselves an offering to the Lord, whoever is of a generous heart shall bring it, the offering of the Lord, gold, silver, and bronze. — Regarding vows and pledges, it is not necessary to make a verbal declaration. As long as he resolved in his heart, even if he did not make any verbal declaration, he is obligated. How so? If he resolves in his heart that this animal is a burnt offering or that he will bring a burnt offering, he is obligated to bring it, as it says, "whoever is of a generous heart shall bring it" — by generosity of the heart [alone] he becomes obligated to bring [it]. And so too all sacred vows and pledges (*Ma'aseh ha-Korbanot* 14:12).

35:10. Whoever is wise-hearted of you shall come and make everything that the Lord has commanded. — The expression *ḥokhmah* denotes also knowledge of any workmanship (*Guide* 3:54; for further meanings of *ḥokhmah*, see at Exod. 1:10).

35:13. ... and the showbread... — For Maimonides' discussion of the showbread, see at Exod. 25:30.

35:25. And all the women that were wise-hearted did spin. — Spinning is a task specifically for women, as it says, "And all the women that were wise-hearted did spin" (*Ishut* 21:1; see also *Guide* 3:54).

35:35. He has filled them with wisdom of the heart, to perform all manner of work, of the engraver, and of the artisan, and of the embroider, in blue, and in purple, in scarlet, and in fine linen, and of the weaver, of any work and those that devise skillful works. — The term *malei* is a homonym which denotes that one substance enters another, and fills it, as "And she filled [*va-temallei*] her pitcher" (Gen. 24:16); "An omer-full [*melo*] for each" (Exod. 16:32), and many other instances.

Next, it signifies the expiration or completion of a fixed period of time, as "And when her days to be delivered were fulfilled [*va-yimleu*]" (Gen. 25:24); "And forty days were completed [*va-yimleu*] for him" (Gen. 50:3).

It further denotes attainment of the highest degree of excellency, as "Full [*malei*] with the blessing of the Lord" (Deut. 33:23); "He has filled [*millei*] them with wisdom of the heart" (Exod. 35:35);

"He was filled [*va-yimmalei*] with wisdom, and understanding, and cunning" (1 Kings 6:14). In this sense it is said, "The whole earth is full [*melo*] of his glory" (Isa. 6:3) — All the earth gives evidence of his perfection, i.e., leads to a knowledge of it. Thus also "The glory of the Lord filled [*malei*] the tabernacle" (Exod. 40:34): and, in fact, every application of the word [*malei*] to God must be interpreted in this manner; and not that He has a body occupying space. If, on the other hand, you prefer to think that in this passage by "the glory of the Lord," a certain light created for the purpose is to be understood, that such light is always termed "glory," and that such light "filled the tabernacle," we have no objection (*Guide* 1:19).

Maimonides may contradict himself about how to understand the wisdom ascribed to Bezalel and Oholiab. In *Guide* 3:54, he says, "The expression *hokhmah* denotes also knowledge of any workmanship, e.g., 'Whoever is wisehearted of you shall come and make everything that the Lord has commanded' (Exod. 35:10)...." In other words, the *hokhmah* related to constructing the tabernacle is a technical architectural skill. However, in *Guide* 1:19, he writes that the word *malei* (fill) "... denotes attainment of the highest degree of excellency, as... 'He has filled them with wisdom of the heart' (Exod. 35:35)." Here, the *hokhmah* is a form of greatness, not a technical skill.

Nahmanides writes, "... wisdom is not something that you can fill a vessel with, but instead it denotes perfection, that they [Bezalel and Oholiab] were perfect in wisdom" (on Exod. 25:7).

Exodus 36-38

36:6. And Moses gave a commandment, and they caused the sound to pass [*va-ya'aviru*] in the camp.... — ... [The verb *avar*] is applied to the passage of sound through air, as "And they caused a sound to pass [*va-ya'aviru*] in the camp" (See *Guide* 1:21, quoted in full at Exod. 12:12).

... saying, "No man or woman shall perform any more labor for the offering of the sanctuary," so the people refrained from bringing. — Transferring from one domain to another is one of the primary labors [forbidden on the Sabbath]. And even though this issue, as will all other Torah matters, was given to Moses at Sinai, nonetheless it is stated in the Torah, "'No man or woman shall perform any more labor for the offering of the sanctuary,' and the people refrained from bringing." Therefore you learn that Scripture calls "bringing" [*hava'ah*] a type of labor (*Shabbat* 12:8).

FURTHER: ... transferring from one domain to another is [prohibited] from what God said, "'No man or woman shall perform any more labor for the offering of the sanctuary,' and the people refrained from bringing." We learn that bringing what they were bringing is called labor. They were bringing from the Levite camp, which was a private domain, to a public domain, which is called *hotza'ah* [bringing out] (*PhM Shabbat* 1:1).

36:7. For the stuff they had was sufficient [*dayyam*] for all the work to make it, and more than enough. — [The word *dai* implies sufficiency] e.g., "for the stuff they had was sufficient [*dayyam*]" (*Guide* 1:63, quoted more fully at Exod. 6:3).

37:10. He also made the table of acacia wood, two cubits long, one cubit wide, and a cubit and a half high. — see on Exod. 25:23.

Exodus 39

39:3. And they beat [*vayrakke'u*]... — The Targum of *vayrakke'u* is *ve-radidu*[214] (*PhM Ohalot* 7:2; quoted similarly at *PhM Mikva'ot* 7:7; see also on Exod. 28:6).

... the gold into thin plates [*pahei ha-zahav*]... — The Targum of *pahei ha-zahav* is *tasei de-dahba* (*PhM Kelim* 11:3).

39:22. ... *ma'aseh oreg*... — See at Exod. 28:32.

39:24. ... *mashzar*... — Wherever only the word *mashzar* is used [and not the phrase *shesh mashzar*] it means eightfold (*Klei ha-Mikdash* 8:14).

---

214. Marcus Jastrow defines *r-d-d* as "to beat, stamp, stretch," quoting the Targum of this verse (p. 1451).

Word & Primary Source Indices

Shekalim
1:3, 341
5:2, 438

Yoma
1:8, 429
4:2, 410
4:4, 476
5:5, 459

Betzah
2:3, 375
2:4, 106
2:5, 367

Ḥagigah
1:1, 378, 510
1:2, 99, 374-375

Yevamot
2:2, 268
8:1, 118-119

Ketuvot 3:2, 290

Nedarim 9:4, 52

Sotah
3:6, 270
5:3, 180
5:4, 161
7:2, 214
7:4, 259
8:1, 214

Gittin 5:1, 315

Kiddushin
1:2, 266, 268-269,
      273, 275
1:5, 318
2:1, 88
2:9, 301

Bava Kamma
1:1, 315
1:4, 299, 302, 307,
      309 n.

3:8, 305
3:9, 310
4:8, 94
5:6, 306
7:1, 322
7:2, 310
7:4, 319
8:1, 323

Bava Metzia
3:12, 321
5:12, 341
7:8, 317
7:9, 325
8:1, 327

Sanhedrin
1:1, 323, 353
1:5, 198, 415
3:3, 350
4:1, 352, 515
5:1, 194
7:4, 212, 331
7:6, 371
9:6, 451
10:P5, 226
10:P7, 487
10:P11, 484
10:1, 417, 451

Makkot
3:1, 94
3:3, 95

Shevuot
2:2, 415
4:6, 282
6:5, 322
7:1, 325
8:3, 320

Eduyot
4:3, 366
7:1, 138

Shemonah Perakim
4, 243, 356, 359
5, 234

6, 385
7, 491
8, 53

Avot
2:1, 484
3:2, 259
3:5, 482
3:18, 481, 503
4:4, 174
5:3, 157
5:4, 151
5:18, 255

Intro to *Kodshim*, 398

Zevaḥim
1:1, 115-116
2:1, 451
6:1, 258
7:1, 457
8:12, 347
9:7, 457
14:2, 346
14:4, 397
14:10, 451

Menaḥot
1:6, 421
3:7, 425
4:4, 435
7:6, 130
8:2, 376
8:3, 435
10:4, 509
11:4, 420
11:5, 418

Bekhorot
1:1, 138
1:7, 32
4:1, 452
6:9, 401
8:1, 136
8:8, 305

Arakhin 9:4, 182

Bibliography

Angel, Hayyim. *Through an Opaque Lens*. Revised Second Edition. New York: Kodesh Press, 2013.

———. *A Synagogue Companion: Insights into the Torah, Haftarot, and Shabbat Morning Prayer Services*. New York: Institute for Jewish Ideas and Ideals/Kodesh Press, 2014.

Austin, John L. *How to Do Things with Words*. Cambridge: Harvard University Press, 1975.

Begaj, Pamela. "An Analysis of Historical and Legal Sanctuary and a Cohesive Approach to the Current Movement." *John Marshall Law Review* 42 (2008), pp. 135-163.

Berkovits, Eliezer. *God, Man, and History*. New York: Jonathan David, 1965.

Besdin, Abraham R. *Reflections of the Rav: Lessons in Jewish Thought, Adapted from lectures of Rabbi Joseph B. Soloveitchik*. Jerusalem: The Dept. for Torah Education and Culture in the Diaspora of the World Zionist Organization, 1979.

Bleich, J.D. *Contemporary Halakhic Problems*, vol. 1. New York: KTAV, 1977.

———. *The Philosophical Quest: Of Philosophy, Ethics, Law, and Halakhah*. New Milford, C.T.: Maggid, 2013.

Brown, Francis, et. al. *The Brown-Driver-Briggs Hebrew and English Lexicon*. Peabody Mass.: Hendrickson, 1997.

Cassuto, Umberto. *A Commentary on the Book of Exodus*. Trans. Israel Abrahams. Jerusalem: Magness Press, Hebrew University, 1987.

First, Mitchell. *Roots and Rituals: Insights into Hebrew, Holidays, and History*. New York: Kodesh Press, 2018.

Francus, Yaacov, "Hallel on the Night of Pesach." Virtual Beit Midrash (Internet).

Goldstein, Alec. "Philosophical Implications of Pirsumei Nissa." *Torah Musings* (Internet).

————. "Of Loyalty, Duty, and Love: An Exploration of the Meaning of Chesed." *Torah Musings* (Internet).

————. *A Theology of Holiness: Historical, Exegetical, and Philosophical Perspectives.* New York: Kodesh Press, 2018

————. "A Shrine of Oneness." Torah Musings (Internet).

Gukovitzki, I. *Sefer Targum ha-La'az* (Hebrew). London: I Gukovitzki, 1985.

Halkin, Abraham and David Hartman. *Crisis and Leadership: Epistles of Maimonides.* New York: The Jewish Publication Society of America, 1985.

Herrmann, Frank R. and Brownlow M. Speer. "Facing the Accuser: Ancient and Medieval Precursors of the Confrontation Clause." 1:34 (1994), 481-552.

Husik, Isaac. *A History of Medieval Jewish Philosophy.* New York, Harper & Row, 1966.

Kahn, Ari. "Amalek: A Question of Race (Updated 2014)." (Internet.)

Kaplan, Lawrence J. *Maimonides Between Philosophy and Halakhah: Rabbi Joseph B. Soloveitchik's Lectures on the Guide of the Perplexed.* Brooklyn: KTAV, 2016.

Kellner, Menachem. "Maimonides, Crescas, and Abravanel on Exod. 20:2: A Medieval Jewish Exegetical Dispute." *Jewish Quarterly Review* 69:3 (Jan. 1979), pp. 129-157.

Kook, Abraham Isaac. *Orot.* Introduction, Trasnaltion and Notes by Bezalel Naor. Jerusalem: Maggid/Orot, 2015.

Leibowitz, Nehama. *New Studies in Shemot (Exodus).* 2 vols. Jerusalem: Maor Wallach Press, 1996.

Milgrom, Jacob. *Numbers.* Philadelphia: The Jewish Publication of Society Press, 1990.

————. *Leviticus 1-16.* New York: Doubleday, 1991.

Murphy, Todd. *Pocket Dictionary for the Study of Biblical Hebrew.* Downers Grove, IL. InterVarsity Press, 2003.

Naor, Bezalel. *In the Desert—A Vision: Rabbi Abraham Isaac Kook on the Torah Portion of the Week.* Spring Valley, NY: Orot Inc., 2000.

————. *Shod Melakhim: Iyyunim ba-Sefer Mishneh Torah* [Hebrew]. Spring Valley, NY: Orot, 2017

Rubin, Eliezer. *Amram NItztavveh be-Mitzvot Yeteirot* [Hebrew] (Internet).

Silverberg, David. "Parashat Tetzaveh: Maimonides on the Urim ve-Tumim." Maimonides Heritage Center (Internet.)

Soloveitchik, Joseph B. *Fate & Destiny: From the Holocaust to the State of Israel.* Hoboken: KTAV, 2002.

————. *Worship of the Heart: Essays on Jewish Prayer.* Hobken: KTAV, 2003.

————. *Kol Dodi Dofek: Listen—My Beloved Knocks.* New York: Yeshiva University Press, 2006.

Steiner, Richard C. *A Biblical Translation in the Making: The Evolution and Impact of Saadia Gaon's Tafsir.* Cambridge: Harvard University Press, 2010.

Student, Gil. "The Heresy of the Ten Commandments." *Torah Musings* (Internet.)

————."What Is the Shekhinah?" *Torah Musings* (Internet.)

Tawil, Hayim. *Lexical Studies in the Bible and Ancient Near Eastern Inscriptions.* Eds. Abraham Jacob Berkovitz,, Stuart W. Halpern and Alec Goldstein. New York: Yeshiva University Press, 2012,

Twersky, Isadore. *Introduction to the Code of Maimonides (Mishneh Torah).*New Haven: Yale University Press, 1980.

Wiederblank, Netanel. *Illuminating Jewish Thought.* vol. 2. New Milford, CT: Maggid Books/Yeshiva University Press, 2018.

WIgmore, John H. "The History of the Hearsay Rule." *Harvard Law Review* 17:7 (May 1904), pp. 437-458.

Ziegler, Aharon. *Halakhic Positions of Rabbi Joseph B. Soloveitchik.* Northvale, NJ: Jason Aronson Press, 1998.